Louis XIV's Assault on Privilege

Changing Perspectives on Early Modern Europe

James B. Collins, Professor of History, Georgetown University
Mack P. Holt, Professor of History, George Mason University

(ISSN 1542–3905)

Changing Perspectives on Early Modern Europe brings forward the latest research on Europe during the transformation from the medieval to the modern world. The series publishes innovative scholarship on the full range of topical and geographic fields and includes works on cultural, economic, intellectual, political, religious, and social history.

Private Ambition and Political Alliances: The Phélypeaux de Pontchartrain Family and Louis XIV's Government, 1650–1715
Sara E. Chapman

The Politics of Piety: Franciscan Preachers During the Wars of Religion, 1560–1600
Megan C. Armstrong

"By My Absolute Royal Authority": Justice and the Castilian Commonwealth at the Beginning of the First Global Age
J. B. Owens

Meat Matters: Butchers, Politics, and Market Culture in Eighteenth-Century Paris
Sydney Watts

Civic Christianity in Renaissance Italy: The Hospital of Treviso, 1400–1530
David Michael D'Andrea

Law, City, and King: Legal Culture, Municipal Politics, and State Formation in Early Modern Dijon
Michael P. Breen

Transforming the Republic of Letters: Pierre-Daniel Huet and European Intellectual Life, 1650–1720
April G. Shelford

Reformation and the German Territorial State: Upper Franconia, 1300–1630
William Bradford Smith

Jenatsch's Axe: Social Boundaries, Identity, and Myth in the Era of the Thirty Years' War
Randolph C. Head

Enlightened Feudalism: Seigneurial Justice and Village Society in Eighteenth-Century Northern Burgundy
Jeremy Hayhoe

The King's Bench: Bailiwick Magistrates and Local Governance in Normandy, 1670–1740
Zoë A. Schneider

The Scourge of Demons: Possession, Lust, and Witchcraft in a Seventeenth-Century Italian Convent
Jeffrey R. Watt

Expansion and Crisis in Louis XIV's France: Franche-Comté and Absolute Monarchy, 1674–1715
Darryl Dee

Noble Strategies in an Early Modern Small State: The Mahuet of Lorraine
Charles T. Lipp

Louis XIV's Assault on Privilege: Nicolas Desmaretz and the Tax on Wealth
Gary B. McCollim

Louis XIV's Assault on Privilege

Nicolas Desmaretz and the Tax on Wealth

Gary B. McCollim

University of Rochester Press

First published 2012

University of Rochester Press
668 Mt. Hope Avenue, Rochester, NY 14620, USA
www.urpress.com
and Boydell & Brewer Limited
PO Box 9, Woodbridge, Suffolk IP12 3DF, UK
www.boydellandbrewer.com

ISBN-13: 978-1-58046-414-7
ISSN: 1542-3905

Library of Congress Cataloging-in-Publication Data

McCollim, Gary B.
Louis XIV's assault on privilege : Nicolas Desmaretz and the tax on wealth / Gary B. McCollim.
p. cm.—(Changing perspectives on early modern Europe ; v. 15)
Includes bibliographical references and index.
ISBN 978-1-58046-414-7 (hbk.)
1. Desmarets, Nicolas, 1648–1721. 2. Fiscal policy—France—History—17th century. 3. Taxation—France—History—17th century. 4. Income tax—France—History—17th century. 5. France—History—Louis XIV, 1643–1715. I. Title.
HJ2646.M33 2011
336.240944'09032—dc23

2012003541

A catalogue record for this title is available from the British Library.

This publication is printed on acid-free paper.
Printed in the United States of America.

To Annie

Le coeur a ses raisons que la raison ne connaît point.

Contents

Illustrations

Figures

Tables

Preface

The study of fiscal-policy formation in the age of Louis XIV cannot be undertaken lightly or briefly, unfortunately for the reader. There are too many subjects that require explanation, such as royal finances, the King's Council, the royal court, the relationship between the royal government and its critics, etc. Wherever possible, I have tried to eliminate topics that seemed extraneous or that threatened to lead to discussions with only a tangential relationship to the theme of this book. It is for this reason that I have neglected any discussion of "mercantilism," an anachronistic term that appeared in the late eighteenth century and has prevented any objective discussion of the financial system and policies of the Old Regime in France. The control of commerce was more an evolving set of policies inherited from the medieval past than a conscious macroeconomic policy of the royal government. Kings inherited trade barriers and duties. They did not invent them. If anything, the royal government sought to suppress these barriers but the circumstances of foreign policy and provincial reluctance to go along with the crown prevented anything but the most inconsistent pursuit of this aim.

A second reason for avoiding this debate is that this book focuses on finances rather than commerce. The latter is considered only insofar as it involves the problem of increasing government revenues. For all practical purposes, commerce is not a part of this study.

There is the matter of the spelling of proper names of the many characters involved in royal finances under Louis XIV. The seventeenth century did not have any standard rules for spelling. Many historians have chosen to modernize the spelling of seventeenth-century names. In each case I have adopted the practice of employing the orthography used by the person himself so that researchers who examine original documents from the period will be able to determine the identity of an author by looking at the spelling of his name. For instance, many historians call Louis XIV's last finance minister Desmarets while the man himself spelled his name Desmaretz. Contemporary spelling varied from Desmarest to Desmarais to Des Marets, but I have chosen to spell his name as he spelled it. I follow the same practice with Delacroix and Dubuisson, who were often referred to by contemporaries as de la Croix and du Buisson. I have used the shorter Boisguilbert rather than Boisguillebert, although the owner of that name spelled it both ways. Desmaretz's predecessor spelled his name Chamillard, while historians have adopted Chamillart. The famous *surintendant des finances* whose fall in September 1661 inaugurated Louis XIV's personal rule spelled his name Foucquet, while his enemy, Colbert, spelled it Fouquet. I am not choosing sides in that rivalry, however, by spelling the name the way its owner spelled it.

I have added a glossary of terms at the end of this book. Some terms will be explained in the text as well as defined in the glossary.

I would like to acknowledge the assistance, either spiritual or material, that many people and organizations gave me as I labored in the archives and arcana to produce this work. Many friends, who are too numerous to name, listened to my ideas and contributed much to my understanding of this confusing period of history. John C. Rule, my advisor, first suggested this topic and has since offered advice, encouragement, and enthusiasm to my efforts. Joan Kozar helped with translating several difficult passages and made the translation more felicitous than I could ever have hoped. Mathieu Dusart was kind enough to lend me a copy of his master's thesis on Nicolas Desmaretz's wealth. Jim Collins has been wonderful in offering suggestions and advice for this work. The staff at the University of Rochester Press, from Suzanne Guiod, Ryan Peterson, and Tracey Engel, along with a host of others, has been very helpful and much appreciated. I would especially like to acknowledge the encouragement I received from my friend the late Sharon Kettering, who, during the last three decades, urged me to get this published. It is my fault that it was not published until after her death. It was not for want of trying that it has taken so long. Over the course of the three decades since I began my research, two separate computers destroyed copies of this book as I was preparing it for publication. And finally, I would like to thank my wife, Ana, who has provided love and support along with editorial comments and advice. These people helped me to realize whatever success this work has achieved. Its failures and omissions are my own.

Abbreviations

A.A.E.	Archives du Ministère des Affaires Étrangères
A.N.	Archives Nationales
Arsenal	Bibliothèque de l'Arsenal
Assemblée Nationale	Bibliothèque de l'Assemblée Nationale
B.N.	Bibliothèque Nationale
Guerre	Archives du Ministère de la Guerre
Mém. et Doc.	Mémoires et Documents
mss. fr.	manuscrits français
n.a.f.	nouvelles acquisitions françaises

Introduction

In 1710 the government of Louis XIV implemented a tax on income called the *dixième* (tenth) that required each property owner to declare the income that he received from any property that he owned. This tax violated one of the principles of French society at the time because it disregarded the social status of the property owner and only evaluated the tax owed on the basis of the income produced by the property. In effect, the new law disregarded the privileges that Louis XIV's government had worked so hard to preserve or create in fashioning an ordered society. Previously, French social thinking had allowed certain social groups to remain exempt from direct taxation because they contributed to the state in other ways, that is, by serving in the military or in various courts, enforcing the king's justice. In addition, the royal government had worked to grant privileges to certain corporate entities, such as towns and provinces with representative assemblies, and to sell privileges to anyone who could afford to buy them.[1] The dixième would appear to wipe away all of those distinctions and to reduce the measure of one's place in society to how much wealth one's property earned. All property owners were equal and measured their contributions to the French state by how much money they earned. (The law did exempt church property from paying this tax because the Church could not be seen as paying for war, the principal reason for taxation.)

The traditional history of the Old Regime has repeated the argument for many years that the privileged orders did not pay direct taxes. In fact, recent historical research has described Louis XIV's fiscal system as an alliance between the crown and the privileged orders to milk money from the lower orders and distribute it in the form of pensions, interest payments, offices, and gifts to the privileged orders. The privileges that the royal government created were then used to force the privilege holders to borrow money for the state; in return, the government would pay the interest on the loan from revenues derived from taxing the nonprivileged.[2]

Nevertheless, the creation of the *capitation* in 1695 punctured that alliance by requiring all people to pay a tax based on either their social status or the status of the offices they held. The capitation recognized the existence of the various social orders in French society by levying a different amount of tax on each of twenty-two social levels as designated by the royal government. While it was the first direct tax under the Old Regime that required everyone to pay, the royal government's financial desperation led to the exemption of certain groups, beginning with the Church but soon extending to other privileged groups in return for payments of as much as six times what they owed for one year's capitation. The capitation would be abolished in 1698 and recreated in 1701 to last for the remainder of the Old Regime.[3]

The dixième went even further by taxing the amount of income earned from property ownership and ignoring the social status of the owner. The dixième of 1710 was not, strictly speaking, an income tax because it did not tax the income earned from labor. By taxing the income derived from property ownership, the dixième was aimed squarely at the wealthy. The oft-quoted aphorism of Marshal Vauban that only one-tenth of French society could be considered wealthy and the rest were either starving or simply surviving illustrates the problems faced by a government in a society where wealth was so unevenly distributed. At least four out of five French subjects were involved in agriculture and the production of food. The majority of peasants owned little if any property and either rented or worked as day laborers on other people's land to survive.[4] Thus, while subject to the capitation, these peasants would be exempt from paying the dixième. Those peasants who rented land would be required to report the amount of rent they paid and to whom. The nonagricultural population included workers who were not property owners either. The people subject to the tax on property were mostly the wealthy and the better off, not the overwhelming majority of the population, who were poor peasants or workers.

The dixième continued to exist for seven years until 1717, two years after the death of Louis XIV. Despite its suppression in 1717, the idea survived that every property owner, regardless of his social status, could be asked to contribute to the state during a time of emergency. The dixième was revived briefly during the War of the Polish Succession from 1733 to 1737 and again during the War of the Austrian Succession from 1740 to 1749. It was revamped in 1749 as the *vingtième* (twentieth) and would remain in effect until the French Revolution. We might ask today how the government of Louis XIV violated the social norms that the regime itself had done so much to uphold.

France was at war for twenty-two of the last thirty years of Louis XIV's reign. During this period France endured bad weather, including two terrible winters (1693–94 and 1709), as well as various subsistence crises caused by poor crop yields that not only killed off livestock but also caused subsequent starvation and epidemics of disease that eliminated large numbers of the French population. While the winter of 1693–94 has been shown to have killed more people than the 1709 Siberian winter, the memory of the 1709 winter haunted the French throughout the eighteenth century. Both winters produced horrible famines that reduced the population to eating anything, and created public disturbances that forced France's wartime government to devote attention and manpower to internal affairs as well.[5]

During these trying times, the government often revalued its coinage in order to stimulate commerce and increase tax revenues. Old Regime France used the *livre* (l.) as its unit of account. The livre was divisible into 20 *sous* (s.), which were in turn divisible into 12 *deniers* (d.). With 240 deniers in every livre, a single livre could be divided by two, three, four, five, six, eight, ten, and twelve, a flexibility that the modern decimal system does not have. Yet, there was no coin called the livre, nor one worth a single livre. The exact value of a livre is difficult to determine because it was never stable in relation to gold or silver, or to staples that were needed to survive. The gold *louis* and the silver *écu* varied in value throughout the reign. Silver coinage was more prevalent than gold in France, but even in cases where the amount of silver contained in a coin and its value in livres are known for a specific date, a government declaration could change the value of that coin within a month's time. In 1641 there were 26 livres, 10 sous to a marc of silver. By 1709 the proportion had changed to 35 livres, 9 sous, 1$^{1}/_{11}$ deniers per marc of silver.[6] The government had adopted a policy of reducing the amount of precious metal in its coinage in order to increase the amount of coins and encourage their circulation within France. Nevertheless, the amount of silver in circulation declined from 18,518,000 marcs in 1683 to 13,544,177 in 1715.[7]

Over the course of sixty-eight years the price of silver had increased by one-third, or, in other words, the livre had been devalued in relation to silver by one-third. Unless one is interested in buying silver, however, such alterations in the relationship of metal to monetary values is of little help in determining the impact of a rising tax burden on the taxpaying classes. Pierre Goubert described a serge-weaving family of five in Beauvais who earned 108 sous per week. They ate 70 pounds of bread each week, each pound costing ½ sous. When the harvest was abundant, they were relatively secure. In the aftermath of the miserable winter of 1693, however, the price of bread soared to more than 2 sous per pound. Before the price returned to normal, two members of this family had perished.[8]

The shortage of money was a major reason for revaluing the coinage by reducing the quantity of precious metals in order to increase the amount of currency in circulation. Seventeenth-century France did not have banking and credit institutions that would have allowed the government to extend the money supply. It did have an unofficial network of moneylenders who were willing to extend credit to local consumers. In fact, local commerce depended on the extension of credit to survive. Very few large retail purchases involved the exchange of money. Instead, local merchants extended credit to their regular customers until the customers were able to collect the coinage to pay their bills. This method of operation extended to the upper layers of society and included the government itself, which relied on credit from the so-called financiers who were able to attract large-scale loans to back government operations. As government expenses increased during the reign of Louis XIV, the government pressed the financiers for more loans and pressured the various, privileged corporations to extend their credit to the crown's war effort.[9]

The major royal expense was the military. During the peaceful years of the 1660s, when Louis XIV began his personal rule, the crown rarely needed 100 million livres to pay its bills. The last thirty years of the reign, however, were marked by two major wars that pitted France against most of Europe. The War of the League of Augsburg, also called the Nine Years' War, ran from 1688 to 1697 and saw France fighting against all the major powers of Western Europe: Spain, the Netherlands, England, Austria, the Holy Roman Empire, Savoy, and Portugal. Spain and Bavaria became France's allies during the War of the Spanish Succession from 1701 until 1714, but France's enemies soon occupied Bavaria, and Spain was the scene of a horrible civil war that pitted the forces allied with France against forces allied with its enemies. During these wars France's army increased in size from 250,000 during the Dutch War of the 1670s to 340,000 during the 1690s, but the strain of war and the demographic disaster of 1693–94 reduced France's ability to raise troops during the War of the Spanish Succession, when the army only amounted to 255,000 troops. The increasing expenses forced France to reduce support for its navy, which had been the third most powerful in Europe in the 1670s. By 1715 France's navy was half the size of England's and was no longer able to confront France's enemies on an equal basis.[10]

The cost of government rose almost steadily during the reign of Louis XIV. When we consider that average annual expenditures during Colbert's first decade in power—a decade of peace (1662–71)—were less than seventy million, the royal government would spend more than three times that amount every year after 1704. The rise in government expenses exceeded anything that can be blamed on inflation or monetary manipulation. During the last twenty-five years of the reign of Louis XIV, the finance minister, whose official title was controller general of finances (regardless of his other responsibilities, which will be discussed later), was forced to focus his efforts on supplying money to meet the ever-increasing financial demands of the Sun King's government.[11]

Professional historians have largely ignored, or left unexplored, the later part of the reign of Louis XIV, that is, until the last thirty years. At a 1999 meeting of the Society for French Historical Studies at Georgetown University, the title of one session acknowledged that historical scholarship has largely ignored the period—"Between the Sun King and the Age of Light: Rethinking the 'Black Hole' in Old Regime French Historiography, 1690–1730." John C. Rule has been in the forefront of the efforts to redefine the end of Louis XIV's reign. His articles on Louis XIV's last foreign minister, Jean-Baptiste Colbert de Torcy, and his efforts to reform the foreign ministry are part of Rule's endeavor to instill a historical interest in the neglected period.[12] In a major call for more research, first published in 1973, he defined what remained to be done.[13] This book is an effort to uncover some elements of an ignored or misunderstood history.

James B. Collins has described the period at the end of the reign of Louis XIV as one of the most fertile and imaginative in the history of Old Regime political development. It was during these years, when France was almost constantly at war, that France produced what Collins calls a mature monarchical state, wherein the institutions of the monarchy began to function in ways that resemble a modern state government rather than the personalized and inconstant ways of medieval and Renaissance governments. The state became an actor separate from the monarch in accord with Louis XIV's dying words: "I am dying, but the state remains."[14]

There was a concerted effort by the government of Louis XIV, especially during the last years of his reign, to seek out new ideas and to listen to complaints about the fiscal and financial system that paid for the French state. Historians, however, have treated the end of the reign of Louis XIV as a time of crisis and chaos that resulted in bankruptcy because the government had exhausted its credit and burdened the state with tremendous debts that were only eliminated by the turmoil of the rise and collapse of John Law's bank during the Regency following the reign of Louis XIV.[15] Much of modern scholarship has either mentioned the men who ran the government, especially its finances, simply as part of the government, or has ignored them entirely.[16] Given the lack of information about the actions of the king's late ministers, some prominent surveys have either denounced them for missing the opportunity to reform France's finances,[17] or have simply praised them for saving France from disaster during the War of the Spanish Succession.[18]

Louis XIV's last controller general of finances, the man who instituted the dixième, was Nicolas Desmaretz, who served from February 20, 1708, until his dismissal on September 15, 1715, two weeks after Louis XIV's death. He had been trained by his uncle Jean-Baptiste Colbert, who had been in charge of French finances from 1661 until 1683 and for whom he had worked for nineteen years, rising to become his principal assistant. After his uncle's death in 1683, Desmaretz was dismissed from the government in disgrace when he was accused of corruption. During the following twenty years when he was out of government service, Desmaretz served as a secret adviser to Colbert's successors and participated in the intellectual discussion over how taxation could either hurt or encourage France's social and economic development. When he returned to government in 1703 he dealt personally with those men and women who advocated new government policies and ideas that might have taken France down a different road in the eighteenth century.

Desmaretz presented a defense of his ministry entitled *Compte rendu de M. Desmaretz au Régent.*[19] It was published under the title *Mémoire sur l'administration des finances depuis le 20 février 1708 jusqu'au 1er septembre 1715* and circulated throughout Europe.[20] Desmaretz was defending his actions as minister because he was being investigated, along with all the financiers, for activities going back to 1688.[21] He was also offering himself as the best man to run French finances in the aftermath of Louis XIV's death. He was seconded in his efforts by his former *commis* or assistant, Jean-Roland Malet, who provided him with information taken from the government's records for the years of his ministry and later wrote his own defense of Desmaretz, although it was not published until 1789.[22]

While Desmaretz had had a reputation throughout the eighteenth century as a strong-minded minister who worked to encourage French economic growth while defending the state from its foreign enemies,[23] that reputation disappeared in the aftermath of the French Revolution and Desmaretz himself was forgotten, along with all the other ministers from the latter half of Louis XIV's reign. Nineteenth-century historians, with their admiration for firm financial principles that required a balanced budget and well-ordered bookkeeping, tended to exalt the reputation of Colbert at the expense of the men who either preceded or followed him. In fact, one book's title from the late nineteenth century actually sums up the general opinion of this historical period until very recently: *Le désordre des finances et les excès de la spéculation à la fin du règne de Louis XIV et au début du règne de Louis XV.*[24] In light of recent research, we would argue that the "disorder" masked a vibrant debate about the role of the state and the proper measure of a subject as a taxpayer.

The first scholarly treatment of Desmaretz was a law thesis by René Dumas published in 1927.[25] Dumas relied heavily on the materials published by Arthur-Michel de Boislisle in the late nineteenth century taken from an archive created by Desmaretz under the supervision of his secretary, Gilbert Clautrier, that now form the basis of the G^7 series of documents in the Archives Nationales. Like his uncle Colbert, Desmaretz believed that the crown should have an archive of its finances and a knowledge of past decisions for future reference. He collected papers and correspondence from his predecessors, going back to his uncle's ministry. Clautrier remained in the ministry after Desmaretz's departure. Indeed, his descendants were still working on royal finances in 1789.[26]

Joël Félix wrote a brief biography and study of Desmaretz's ministry as part of a biographical dictionary of France's finance ministers that was published in 2000. He focused on Desmaretz's struggles to restore monetary solvency amid France's recurring debts, thus reducing the dixième to one of the measures that helped France get through the war until peace was achieved.[27] This book expands on Desmaretz's accomplishments, especially the dixième, and sets them in the context of the events of their time and ideas about fiscal and financial policy that existed at the time.

We will look at the evolution of ideas about taxation and finance within the government of Louis XIV during the last thirty years of the reign. Any proper discussion of such a topic requires an examination of the fiscal system as it was, before discussing any changes that some people wanted. The many and varied taxes that the king inherited in 1661 when he began his personal rule evolved from the medieval past and were administered by private financiers who lent their credit to the state.

Very few governments in history have been able to maintain a balanced budget while fighting a war. Louis XIV's France was no different. In order to pay for the wars of the last years of the reign, the royal government had to borrow larger sums of money than ever before. Credit is the lifeblood of any modern state but the French monarchy had never enjoyed the confidence of its investors because it was above the law and had evaded its debts on several occasions over the course of its long existence. The crown, therefore, had to rely on indirect methods for raising large sums of money in a hurry. Investors had more confidence in private financiers and local institutions that were subject to royal justice. Any finance minister would have to learn to juggle these private individuals and institutions to appeal to those with money to lend.

The rising level of expenditure as the reign progressed forced the government to turn to methods for raising money that were called extraordinary because they appeared at times when money was desperately needed. They were hardly unusual because they had been employed during earlier crises, such as the Wars of Religion or the Thirty Years' War. They had helped to provoke the Fronde in 1648 and would cause a certain amount of unrest after 1688. They were limited in that they could only raise certain amounts of money and they had a detrimental effect on what was called ordinary revenues.

Although historians have generally said that the economy of France was stagnant throughout the reign of Louis XIV, some research has questioned this kind of generalization.[28] Nonetheless, the men in government worked diligently to extract greater quantities of money from the economy. Colbert created a relatively effective system for extracting money and credit that worked well during peacetime. The strain of war after 1688 seriously debilitated Colbert's system, as his successors were forced to resort to open borrowing and hidden loans at ever-increasing rates of interest.

In 1695 a new, temporary tax called the capitation was added to the older, direct taxes because the government could not borrow any more money. The capitation taxed social status rather than income. A person's tax depended on his status or the status of any office he held rather than on his wealth. Even though the capitation was suppressed in 1698 with the return of peace, it had provoked such outcries about its fairness that the government granted more leeway to local tax administrators in the collection of the capitation when it was restored again in slightly different form in 1701.[29]

The capitation proved to be an inadequate resource once war resumed in 1701. The string of defeats suffered by French arms beginning in 1704 caused serious disruptions in France's state credit machinery. A 10 percent surtax was added to the capitation in 1705 and was extended to all other taxes before the year was over. The royal government survived the disasters of 1706 and 1707 through frantic borrowing by whatever means were available. By 1710 France was forced to adopt the dixième, a tax on the income of property owners.

Desmaretz would have to adapt his policies to the institutions at hand. We will look at these institutions and the men who occupied key positions in the political and financial administration of the realm. Policy passed from the minister through the King's Council because the king in council had to approve all laws. In reality, the supposedly unified council was a collection of separate subcommittees or special groups that acted as the council for certain specific purposes, one group for one purpose and another for a different reason. The king himself attended the groups that decided new policies. Those the king did not attend merely adapted established policies to new circumstances. They all functioned under the rubric of the King's Council, but only the Royal Council of Finances could formally approve any new taxes, like the dixième. By the end of the reign, however, the Royal Council of Finances had become a fiction behind which the controller general dominated policy discussions and issued decisions in the council's name.

At the nadir of the reign, Louis XIV turned to Colbert's nephew, Nicolas Desmaretz, a man who had been chased from the government on suspicion of fraud following his uncle's death in 1683. Even the king is supposed to have called him a crook (*fripon*) when Controller General Chamillard mentioned his name in 1699. Yet, many people at court and in Paris regarded him as the only man who could save France's finances.

Between the death of Colbert in 1683 and Desmaretz's appointment as controller general of finances, three men occupied that position: Claude Le Peletier from 1683 until he resigned in September 1689, Louis de Phélypeaux de Pontchartrain from 1689 until he resigned to become chancellor in September 1699, and Michel Chamillard from 1699 until the king accepted his resignation in February 1708. Of the men who succeeded Colbert as finance minister, only Le Peletier came from outside the finance ministry. Pontchartrain had been an intendant of finances for more than two years before becoming controller general; Chamillard had been an intendant of finances for nine years before ascending to the controllership general, and Desmaretz had a long history with the finance ministry under both his uncle and Chamillard. When his uncle died, Desmaretz was the only intendant of finances, but he was already suspected of accepting kickbacks and other financial misdeeds. Colbert had been ill for more than a month before he died on September 6, 1683. Thus, Louis XIV had time to think about whom he was going to select as his new finance minister.

Claude Le Peletier was the Le Tellier clan's choice to succeed Colbert on September 6, 1683. In the early part of Louis XIV's personal rule (1661–1715), the men who worked as ministers were members of one of two clans that appeared to be in competition for royal favor. In 1683 Colbert and his allies controlled finance, Paris, the navy, and the foreign ministry, while the Le Telliers controlled the Chancellery, the war ministry and its dependencies, and the post office. Colbert's death presented an opportunity for the Le Telliers to control the finance ministry and shift the balance of power in their direction. Le Peletier was related by blood and loyalty to the Le Tellier clan. He was able to reinforce his family's position by putting his brother, Michel Le Peletier de Souzy, in a position of importance and nominating his own successor as controller general of finances.

Much has been made of the Colbert–Le Tellier rivalry, and the conflict between the families has often seemed more acute because the personalities of the finance minister, Colbert, and the war minister, François-Michel Le Tellier, marquis de Louvois, were brusque to the point of brutality. Both men competed for royal favor. The general tenor of ministerial activity under Louis XIV, however, was one of cooperation and coordination. After the disappearance of the Le Tellier clan, the Le Peletiers and their allies, the Phélypeaux de Pontchartrain, might even been seen as a new faction in competition with the Colberts within the government, a faction that would persist for the remainder of the Old Regime. None of these later ministers was as rude or abrupt as Colbert or Louvois, with the possible exception of Desmaretz himself.[30]

Louis XIV disliked dealing with the quarrels between Colbert, his finance minister, and Louvois, his war minister. His decision to appoint an ally of the Le Tellier clan, Le Peletier, would be the first of a series of failed efforts to prevent the clash of interests between the two ministries from disrupting his council. After Louvois was succeeded in 1691 by his twenty-three-year-old son, Louis-François-Marie Le Tellier, marquis de Barbezieux, Louis XIV reduced the war minister to being responsible for military supplies, while the king concentrated on military strategy. Nevertheless, the king had to endure the sharp-tongued criticism of his finance minister, Louis de Phélypeaux de Pontchartrain, Le Peletier's successor. When Louvois' son died unexpectedly in 1701, Louis XIV appointed his friend Michel Chamillard, the controller general of finances, to be war minister and finance minister at the same time, thinking this would prevent any quarrels for the king to settle. This experiment failed, however, because the burden of both offices exceded one man's abilities and health.[31]

Although the son of a treasurer of France in the Paris Bureau of Finances, Le Peletier nevertheless studied law and rose to be a president in the Parlement of Paris in 1660 and provost of merchants in Paris (1668–76), where he worked with Colbert, the secretary of state in charge of Paris. He became a semester (half-year) councilor of state in 1673 and an ordinary (full-year) councilor of state in 1678 while serving as honorary dean of the faculty of law in Paris during the years 1677–81. His mild temperament supposedly won over the king, who said that he did not want a finance minister who was too harsh on his people, perhaps a backhanded slap at Colbert. Le Peletier continued to serve as a *president à mortier* (one of eight judges besides the first president) in the Paris Parlement during 1686–89 while he was controller general. He spoke freely and frankly with the king, who was reluctant to let him resign in September 1689. Louis XIV persuaded Le Peletier to stay on as a minister of state and to sit on government councils that advised the king. Le Peletier took over supervising the post office after Louvois' death in July 1691 until he left the court permanently in September 1697, although he did return for an annual visit every year until his death in 1711. He was affable, a conciliator, and scrupulous in his dealings with others, a trait that caused some at court to ridicule him as "Ministre Claude" for being a man who refused to use his influence for personal gain.[32]

Le Peletier's resignation from the post of controller general of finances in September 1689, just as France was preparing for a pan-European war, is difficult to understand. He sought to relinquish the finance ministry as war was beginning in Germany in 1688. He may have disapproved of the war that began with the devastation of the Rhineland by French forces seeking to deprive France's enemies of support and supplies from the region. His resignation can be seen as a recognition on his part of his failure to prevent the war. Le Peletier may not have looked forward to having to quarrel with Louvois over military expenses during a war. He may also have been uncomfortable dealing with financiers and accountings. Just before he turned over the controller general's function to his handpicked successor in September 1689, Le Peletier wrote to his friend Nicolas de Lamoignon de Basville, the provincial intendant in Languedoc: "All the men and officers involved in the management of money are of a strange nature. My heart has much difficulty in getting accustomed to them."[33]

Le Peletier's successor was Louis de Phélypeaux, comte de Pontchartrain, the son of a judge at the trial (1661–64) of the former superintendant of finances Nicolas Foucquet. Pontchartrain began his career in law as a counselor on the Parlement of Paris in 1661 at age eighteen. The king chose him, in 1677, to be first president of the Parlement of Rennes, a sensitive post where a revolt had recently been suppressed. Although he was small in stature, Ponchartrain's diplomatic abilities earned him praise at court, where he was recalled in April 1687 to become the third intendant of finances. (Colbert had operated with just two intendants of finances.) He became controller general on September 20, 1689, with Le Peletier's recommendation. He took on additional responsibilities as secretary of state for the navy and the Maison du Roi in November 1690, following the sudden death of Colbert's son, Seignelay. He entered the Conseil d'en haut (Council of Ministers) in November 1690, where he would sit until July 1714 as one of the king's closest advisors. In September 1699 he resigned as finance minister and secretary of state to become chancellor of France, the king's chief legal advisor.

During his tenure as a minister from 1689 until 1714 Pontchartrain would be a major reforming element at court. He created the capitation in 1695. Pontchartrain, however, is also the minister who relied heavily on the policy of selling offices or privileges to pay for the war. According to the memorialist Saint-Simon, who liked him, he was lively and witty, but other opinions indicate that he was an impatient man with a sharp tongue who tended to select the course of least resistance. In any case, both the king and his influential, secret second wife, Madame de Maintenon, began by admiring Pontchartrain's abilities and relying on his judgment, but the king may have tired of his impatience and sharp tongue. When Ponchartrain was named chancellor in September 1699, he told Saint-Simon that it was the happiest day of his life, not because he had become chancellor but because he had given up finances. According to Henri-François Daguesseau, a future chancellor himself, Louis XIV was more concerned about getting rid of Pontchartrain as controller general than he was in naming him chancellor. Pontchartrain had clashed with the king too often and had lost the support of Madame de Maintenon. The king was looking forward to having a more agreeable personality to work on his finances. Pontchartrain remained a minister with considerable influence inside the government but his influence on financial policy declined as chancellor. He retired from court and resigned as chancellor when peace was restored in July 1714.[34]

Michel Chamillard (as he signed his name) began a career intended for the clergy but the 1675 death of his father, who had been one of the prosecutors in the trial of Nicolas Foucquet, forced him into public life as a counselor to the Parlement of Paris in 1676. His billiard-playing brought him to the attention of the king, who enjoyed the game and appreciated Chamillard's skill. Of all of Louis XIV's ministers, Saint-Simon said that Chamillard was the one the king liked best. Like Pontchartrain before him, he was a friend of Le Peletier and supported by Madame de Maintenon. Chamillard was named master of requests in 1686 and participated in several investigations of the tax farms as well as the situation in Touraine,

Poitou, Guyenne, and Normandy. In 1689 he was named provincial intendant in Rouen although the Marquis de Sourches says he would have preferred to remain at court. In 1690, with the king's help, he bought one of the offices of intendant of finances that were created that year. He managed Madame de Maintenon's personal affairs and was appointed in 1695 to manage the affairs of the school at Saint-Cyr that the king's wife had founded for young, orphaned noblewomen.

Chamillard was well liked at court, where he was anxious to be of service to everyone. Scrupulously honest, even severe at times, Chamillard was patient and hard working, but was by all accounts a man of limited abilities. He became controller general of finances on September 5, 1699, and, to his surprise, on January 7, 1701, he added the responsibilities of being secretary of state for war when Louvois' son died unexpectedly. He is supposed to have said to Louis XIV, "You want me to be Colbert and Louvois at the same time." Clearly, the king wanted his friend to be the wheel horse of the government as it fought the War of the Spanish Succession. Louis promised to help Chamillard but the minister's health declined as France's armies were defeated and the problems in finance increased. Finally, after securing for his son the right to inherit the office of secretary of state for war in January 1707, Chamillard persuaded his friend the king to let him resign as finance minister in favor of Chamillard's friend and ally Desmaretz on February 20, 1708. Chamillard told Desmaretz, "Sir, you give me life, and I give you death."[35]

The dixième arose from the climate of ideas in France and within Desmaretz's coterie. The government of Louis XIV did not exist in a vacuum. The government had official and unofficial methods for receiving complaints, grievances, appeals, and even advice. The crown relied on advice-givers (*donneurs d'avis*) at court who lobbied in favor of new policies from which they hoped to profit if they were adopted. Also, the ministers were aware of various reform ideas circulating in France. The government relied on a network of officials, especially the provincial intendants who, as masters of requests, had ties to the King's Council, to investigate the originators of these ideas, advise the government on the impact of any new policies, and report any reactions from the local populace. The interplay between the concerns and ideas of the minister and the suggestions and complaints from the kingdom led to the emergence of the dixième as well as the other policies Desmaretz adopted.

Desmaretz and his assistants were personally in contact with some of the people who are today regarded as the foremost reform thinkers of their time: Vauban, Boisguilbert, John Law, and the Abbé de Saint-Pierre, among others. The minister and his assistants also corresponded with many less prominent people who offered ideas about reforming or altering the financial machinery of the French state. However impractical or unrealistic some of this advice might have seemed, it was not ignored.

We will examine the events and circumstances that forced the French government to adopt financial and fiscal policies that were contingent on the events of the battlefield or the negotiating table. Recently, Thierry Sarmant called for a study of the daily practice and reality of political power during what he calls the "great moments" (*grandes heures*) of French history. He stated that we have learned much about the public and private lives of France's monarchs, the political ideas and institutions that supported the monarchy, the organization of the ministries, and the biographies of the significant actors, but we know very little about how these men, ideas, and institutions came together to produce and carry out policies.[36] The adoption of policy involved the interaction of circumstance, necessity, and the perception of what was possible. This book represents an attempt to provide a study of how institutions, men, and ideas came together at a moment in time to act in the face of events.

Desmaretz pursued policies that enabled France to survive the worst years of the War of the Spanish Succession and to emerge with some semblance of dignity, with a Bourbon still on the Spanish throne and the end of Habsburg control of all the lands surrounding France, a problem that had faced every French king since François I in the early sixteenth century. The end of the war left France in worse financial condition than any time since the Fronde. The government of Louis XIV turned from making war to liberating itself from the debts incurred from two wars. The ideas and programs undertaken by Desmaretz prior to Louis XIV's death on September 1, 1715, indicate how he intended to liquidate France's debts. Unfortunately for those policies, Louis' death led to Desmaretz's second expulsion from government. His policies had antagonized too many powerful forces. The post-louisquatorzian Regency would resort to several contradictory and inconsistent measures to resolve the debt problem.

Chapter 1

The Fiscal System under Louis XIV

The Royal Tax Farms

Governments depend on credit to survive. One kind of credit is the short-term loan that modern governments make to themselves. In other words, the government spends money in a steady, regular way that has nothing to do with the pace of revenue collection to pay those bills. Old Regime France could not lend money to itself. Instead, it borrowed money from financiers who were employed either as contractors or officeholders to collect taxes and send the revenues to the state. All of these revenue collectors employed similar methods for paying the state while collecting its revenues.

One way of understanding French royal finances is to know how a revenue farm operated.[1] In France, revenue farming appeared at a time when property ownership meant exercising civil authority. When kings were living off their domains, they did not exactly administer the properties. They leased their property to a third party, who promised to pay them a set lease price in monthly, quarterly, or annual installments for a given period of time.

In the Middle Ages, property meant either land or certain rights, or both. For instance, a landholder might also hold the right of justice over the residents of his land. He might also have a toll bridge or a watermill or some other revenue-producing rights on the same piece of land. If he was a great, landed lord, he might have several estates with adjoined rights. Finding them too troublesome to administer directly, he might have leased them, separately or together, to the highest bidder, who promised to pay the lease price regularly. The lord was only concerned with his revenue from this "farm" and took little interest in its daily operation. The farmer who administered the property replaced the lord and enjoyed all the privileges of the actual lord in his absence. The farmer was gambling on profiting from the property by squeezing each and every right for every sol he could get, and by hoping for a good harvest. The proprietor was relieved of the everyday worries of running his property in return for a steady income. All of this, of course, appeared at the stage of Europe's economic development when these rights and dues could be traded for money. Revenue farming was a common practice among the great lay and ecclesiastical landlords of the thirteenth and fourteenth centuries.

The principles of revenue farming were applied to taxes as a source of public revenue when the French monarchy began to assume the attributes of sovereignty. The feudal king derived his income from his landed wealth and the rights or fees of his position as a feudal lord. He created revenue farms for these sources of income. When the right to levy taxes on people outside the royal domain became a permanent feature of the French monarchy in the fourteenth century, the king committed the privilege of collecting these taxes to royal tax farms. Legally and technically, the Old Regime recognized no difference between the proprietorship of a feudal king over his personal income and the rights of a sovereign king to tax the public.

The need for new sources of revenue preceded the development of government institutions to administer these funds. Originally, these tax farms were set up to collect specific fees in specific places. The tax farmer relieved the monarchy of the burden of creating a professional group of tax administrators. The equipment, records, and employees belonged to the tax farmer. By the sixteenth century the king had reimbursed the tax farmer by a variety of means and took possession of the bureaucracy and equipment of the farms. Thereafter, the tax farmer promised to maintain the equipment and pay the salaries of the employees when leasing the farm.

By the seventeenth century, leases on these farms usually lasted six years, though the bureaucracy administering them was permanent, and the rules and regulations of taxation were fixed. The lessee therefore assumed all the risks. In good years he hoped to make a profit; if times were bad, however, he would take a loss. During those six years, the royal government surrendered the hope of any increased revenue in return for a guaranteed foreseeable income derived from the lease.

The tax farm was an instrument of the government. It disbursed funds at the local level to pay its employees. After 1522, when the government instituted *rentes*, bonds on the Hôtel de Ville of Paris that were to be paid from the revenues of the *aides* or *gabelles*, the tax farmers of the aides or gabelles disbursed this money directly to the payers of the rentes at the Hôtel de Ville without passing through the Royal Treasury. The purchaser of a rente was lending money to the crown in return for payments in interest from the income of the king's tax farms. Such disbursements were listed and deducted as charges against the lease payments. By the time of Louis XIV, the royal government was using the tax farms for the purpose of transferring funds within France and saving the cost of transporting money from the local level to the Royal Treasury and back. The whole process became a simple bookkeeping procedure.

The tax farms became credit institutions for the government as well. The government could issue *assignations* as recognition of a debt by promising to pay the principal and interests from the receipts of a tax farm. On presentation of the assignation by the bearer, a tax farmer, on the orders of the controller general, could pay the amount of the assignation in full when it was due, or at a discount if it was cashed early.

The farmer could also borrow money from the investing public by issuing short-term notes called *billets des fermes.* Although they began as a measure for helping tax farmers to overcome temporary cash-flow problems, billets des fermes became a method of granting the government advances on lease payments. Farmers resorted to billets to satisfy royal requests for advance payments by borrowing from the public at interest. The payment of both assignations and billets des fermes was deducted from the lease payments as charges.

The scattered tax farms were gradually consolidated into one large company known as the General Farms or *fermes unies.* The consolidation process was long and required more than a century to complete. The monarchy was trying to reduce the costs of duplicate services and charges against separate leases for essentially the same purpose.

In the Old Regime taxes were divided into two basic groups: *impositions* and *perceptions.*[2] The General Farms and other tax farms administered the collection of a large number of revenue sources known as perceptions. Today, we use the term indirect taxes to describe these sources of revenue. Impositions were collected by another group of financiers known as receivers general of finances (*receveurs généraux des finances*), who were venal officials rather than tax farmers. They owned the right to receive the funds collected and to transfer money to the Royal Treasury.

Perceptions involved all sorts of indirect taxes levied on a variety of goods and services. Outside the General Farms, there were other tax farms in France, such as those granting monopolies to manage the postal service, the sale of tobacco, the control of gold and silver products, and other items that were never part of the General Farms. The General Farms administered the collection of the largest variety of perceptions, which were broken down into four major categories.

The first category where revenue farming began encompassed the rents, dues, and income derived from the royal domain, the property of the king in his capacity as a feudal and land lord. The king's domain varied in size and rights throughout France. It expanded as the realm expanded, delaying the process of consolidating the General Farms. The farms of the royal domain were the oldest but were also the last to be united to the General Farms. The second group of perceptions administered by the General Farms was called the aides. These were sales or excise taxes on a variety of goods, mostly beer and wine. The third category was somewhat similar and was called the *traites*, tariffs collected on goods as they crossed certain provincial or foreign borders or as they entered certain towns. The traites had been partially consolidated in the late sixteenth century, creating a large area of northern France known as the Five Great Farms. Trade between the Five Great Farms and the rest of France was restricted by the traites, heavy import-export duties. There were also traites among several provinces that were reputedly called foreign provinces because of their relatively recent acquisition by France.

The last group of perceptions was the infamous gabelles or salt taxes. Salt was a necessity not just for seasoning food, but for preserving it in the absence of refrigeration. The sale of salt was a royal monopoly. The price of salt varied from province to province. North central France was the *pays des grandes gabelles*, where the tax was high. Each geographic area known as a parish—called a "fiscal parish," a tax designation that was not necessarily similar to the church parish—was forced to buy a fixed amount of salt annually. Southeastern France was the *pays des petites gabelles*, where the price of salt was lower. Other areas of France paid even lower prices and were not forced to buy fixed amounts of salt annually.

In 1681 Colbert welded these four separate sets of tax farms together into a single lease called the Lease Fauconnet. A lease of any tax farm took the name of the frontman, known as the *adjudicataire-général*, who was simply the person who lent his name to the company rather than a major investor in the lease. French law made no provision for corporations or limited-liability stock companies. Someone had to sign the lease as the lessee, but this person was usually not a major investor. The last important financier to sign a lease was François Legendre in 1668, for all of what would become the General Farms, except for the farm of the domain. Thereafter, frontmen were known as *hommes de paille*, or straw men. They gave the lease standing in law and were backed by forty wealthy financiers known as the General Farmers, who promised to help each frontman carry out the terms of his lease.

The General Farms were royal property that included the tax rights and the machinery to collect those rights. They had a permanent staff, a set of rules, and the physical hardware to perform their task. The Lease Fauconnet was to collect 137 separate taxes. The bureaucracy of the General Farms existed separately from the lease and continued to function as a *régie*, or government-run administration, when the government could not persuade any financiers to lease the farms.

The company of the General Farmers was a syndicate of financiers who performed two services for the state. They administered the General Farms, hiring and paying the staff, buying supplies of salt, and maintaining the buildings and equipment. Their most important function, however, was to provide the government with money on the basis of their personal credit. They provided the government with money in advance of the collection of taxes. At the signing of a lease they advanced a deposit to show their good faith. The deposit was deducted with interest from the last year's lease payment. The deposit was thus a loan. In 1681 they advanced 8 million livres, and required each farmer to contribute 200,000 livres.[3] The same advance was made in 1726 when the General Farms were leased again. The 1726 lease was the first since 1709 to complete its six-year term successfully. Leases signed in 1715 and 1717 were broken as the government stumbled through John Law's banking experiment and the clean-up that followed the bankruptcy of Law's bank.

During the intervening period there is evidence that the individual contribution of each farmer may have been higher. Several *arrêts* (decisions on a point of law or fact) issued by the Royal Council of Finances during Desmaretz's ministry admitted members to the company of General Farmers to replace members who had died. These new members were required to pay 450,000 livres to the receiver general of the farms, who was to use this money to reimburse the estate of the dead General Farmer.[4] One member of the General Farms estimated in 1700 that the profit from one farmer's investment could be as much as 14 percent, if he invested his own money, and 9 or 10 percent, if he borrowed his funds.[5] It would appear that Colbert's experiment, since its beginning in 1681, had achieved a certain recognized level of profitability. The disasters at the end of Louis XIV's reign and the financial instability of the Regency apparently reduced that prestige to the same level it had occupied in 1681.

The General Farmers could be called upon to lend money to the government during the course of the lease in the form of advances on the next year's lease payment. Membership in the company of General Farmers and the deposit made at the beginning of each lease proved that a financier had good credit standing and that the government could rely upon him to lend his credit to the king. Consistently skirting bankruptcy, the royal government needed third parties to borrow money from a public that was reluctant to lend to the crown. When the farms went into régie in 1709 and again in 1719, the government lost this vital source of credit.

Colbert had built that source of credit through relentless administrative effort. He canceled leases with the various farms signed during Nicolas Foucquet's tenure as surintendant des finances. Colbert's close supervision over the activities of the farms reduced the amount of charges and graft taken by the farmers. The renegotiated leases raised revenues coming into the Royal Treasury. Colbert ordered the farmers to keep weekly accounts, which his staff supervised. His stated purpose was to reduce the impositions on the population as a whole and to make the tax farms the most important part of the government's finances. During the 1660s, while working to consolidate the farms, he reduced France's direct taxation, called the *taille.* He also avoided seeking advances from the farms until the necessities of the Dutch War in the 1670s forced him to do so. This war delayed the consolidation of the General Farms until 1681. The Dutch War also upset the financial house of cards he had built in the 1660s, but he hoped to rectify the difficulties. Unfortunately, he died before he could complete this work.[6]

Table 1.1 illustrates the resources all the various tax farms, not just the General Farms, provided to the monarchy from 1662 until 1707, during the reign of Louis XIV. There are no reliable figures for the years 1708 to 1715. The charges were funds deducted from the lease price to pay for farm expenses or local expenditures, or to pay the interest for the rentes.

Table 1.1. Revenue from tax farms, 1662–1707.

Year	Lease Price	Charges	Royal Treasury
1662	48,599,764	23,949,131	25,941,653
1663	45,876,026	19,638,821	20,461,771
1664	53,964,509	20,767,121	29,630,614
1665	43,908,160	14,482,890	30,229,516
1666	44,395,201	15,514,763	25,908,232
1667	44,668,745	14,473,540	29,674,253
1668	45,779,954	14,415,840	30,407,775
1669	47,883,584	13,953,283	34,980,300
1670	50,077,890	14,380,079	37,032,809
1671	51,652,334	12,148,566	36,753,865
1672	51,707,834	13,168,088	31,502,025
1673	52,591,334	13,749,601	37,074,431
1674	54,069,385	13,995,757	37,711,892
1675	58,285,500	14,168,040	38,177,687
1676	57,991,750	15,544,684	33,402,725
1677	60,547,666	15,897,870	33,983,953
1678	59,254,332	17,190,472	34,070,926
1679	59,283,565	17,341,009	30,679,220
1680	60,661,057	16,239,910	29,463,552
1681	62,528,783	16,862,500	37,805,053
1682	65,210,750	6,044,582	49,699,723
1683	65,892,000	13,652,012	42,575,456

(continued)

Table 1.1. *(concluded)*

Year	Lease Price	Charges	Royal Treasury
1684	65,652,000	13,239,700	41,965,359
1685	66,273,529	17,071,814	42,057,709
1686	65,743,000	17,122,100	43,265,254
1687	65,829,584	17,582,270	45,424,120
1688	64,847,500	16,807,691	42,789,809
1689	66,106,666	17,410,955	36,002,725
1690	69,916,207	18,615,106	35,992,943
1691	68,142,034	20,183,082	32,934,159
1692	63,065,495	20,830,098	33,139,408
1693	63,794,500	22,980,891	24,826,220
1694	64,558,000	24,333,813	19,973,842
1695	65,547,440	24,812,481	16,795,334
1696			
1697	61,221,706	29,451,454	11,076,574
1698			
1699	65,971,750	35,079,376	21,688,861
1700	66,526,750	39,394,845	27,131,905
1701	66,456,750	36,684,118	29,772,632
1702	64,739,849	38,344,754	26,395,095
1703	54,465,000	40,904,133	13,560,867
1704			
1705	55,680,000	41,846,000	13,134,000
1706	59,520,000	43,607,000	15,913,000
1707	60,937,000	47,251,304	13,685,696

Note: The figures for the Royal Treasury include all funds received in one year rather than just the funds for that year's lease payment.

Source: This table was constructed from information found in A.N. KK 355 for the years 1662–99. There is no data given for the years 1696 and 1698. Information for the years 1700–1707 comes from Boislisle, *Correspondance des contrôleurs généraux*, 2:583–99. There is no information given for the year 1704. Boislisle's data is based on estimates within the controller general's office. The book KK 355 cites pages in the account books of those same bureaus where each item can be found.

Colbert had begun trading on the credit of the farms in 1671 via advances. In 1680 he created a lending institution backed by the credit of the gabelles called the *Caisse des emprunts* that provided short-term credit to depositors who left their money in the *caisse* in return for a promissory note for repayment of the deposit, with interest, at a set date. His financial system rested on the credit of the tax farms that provided the government with 49 percent of its total revenues in 1683, the year of his death. Colbert had increased royal revenues from the General Farms by more than three-quarters from what they were in 1661. With the help of his nephew, Desmaretz, Colbert codified laws on the gabelles and aides in two *ordonnances* in 1680 and 1681. He did not succeed in codifying the laws on the royal domain or for the traites although the results of his work on the latter were released in 1687 as a summation of the legal practices involved in their collection.[7]

Colbert's successor, Claude Le Peletier, was quick to dismantle the Caisse des emprunts immediately and the General Farms when the lease expired in 1687. He replaced the single lease with two leases: the Lease Domerque for the gabelles and traites and the Lease Charrier for the aides and domain. The combined lease price was lowered from 64,123,000 livres annually during the last year of the Lease Fauconnet to 63 million livres for the two new leases.[8] Le Peletier's reasoning is difficult to understand. An account of the last year of the Lease Fauconnet shows that the total product of the aides, gabelles, and traites for 1687 was more than 65 million livres. The account gives no figures for the domain.[9] On the surface it would appear that Le Peletier gave away what could have been a substantial profit from the crown. The War of the League of Augsburg started in 1688, however, and would have wiped out any profit. Le Peletier resigned as controller general of finances in September 1689.

The War of the League of Augsburg pitted France against all the major powers of Western and Central Europe. Alone and without allies, France would have to rely on its own financial resources. Colbert's system depended upon indirect taxes, the first to suffer in wartime. Le Peletier's successor, Louis de Pontchartrain, embarked on a policy of alienating rentes against the farms and selling offices. The result can be seen in the increase in the amount of charges against the revenues of the farms. Colbert's credit instrument was being sapped for every sol it could deliver. The level of payments from the farms began a descent that would never reverse for the remainder of the reign.

In 1691, as a gesture of defiance to France's enemies, the government broke the two leases on the General Farms and recombined the General Farms under the Lease Pointeau, but at a total price of only 61 million livres annually. While less than the combined two leases, it was above any realistic estimate of the profit to be derived from the General Farms. The General Farms finished the six-year lease in 1697 with a total indebtedness of 50,683,497 livres. The annual charges against all the royal tax farms was almost 30 million livres, higher than anything Colbert had permitted. The General Farms were granted a large indemnity to repay the losses to the farmers and to return the farms to solvency. The new lease of 1697 set the annual price at 58,750,000 livres annually. The high payments line for the year 1699 is largely a bookkeeping phenomenon representing the so-called indemnity of 18 million livres and a loan against 1700 and 1701 of 20 million.[10]

Slipping profitability reduced the price to 41.7 million livres in 1703, when the lease was renewed for only three years during the War of the Spanish Succession. In order to shore up the falling profitability of the General Farms, a royal declaration on March 3, 1705, increased the price or tax on all items covered in the domain, aides, and gabelles by two sous per livre, or 10 percent.[11]

The General Farms were declining in profitability, owing to a host of causes. War slowed economic activity. Rentes against the revenues of the aides and gabelles, as well as the creation of new offices with certain regulatory or monopoly rights in commerce, increased charges against the farms. These offices artificially raised prices and reduced the amount of commercial activity. In addition, officers received a salary called *gages,* paid from the revenue of the General Farms, while the fees for their services reduced commercial activity. The rising amount of contraband goods escaping the General Farms' tax collectors also increased the costs of enforcing the rights of the General Farms.

In 1708, when Desmaretz became controller general of finances, the farms were producing no revenue for the Royal Treasury. In fact, they were unable to pay their own debts. Rentes had fallen behind. Billets des fermes and assignations went unredeemed. In 1706 the lease on the General Farms had been renewed for another three years for only 40 million livres annually. Yet, an account for the last year of this farm revealed an average return of slightly more than 37 million livres per year for the three years of the lease. In addition, the king recognized a debt of 18 million livres owed to the previous lease, on which he promised to pay 5 percent interest.[12]

Desmaretz was unable to persuade the company of General Farmers to renew the lease in 1709. The king recognized an additional debt of 13,416,415 livres, to be repaid at 5 percent interest. The General Farms were put into régie, meaning that the General Farmers would administer the farms in return for a fee of 6 deniers for every livre (2.5 percent) of all the farms' revenues. The General Farms would remain in régie for five years, depriving the government of a valuable source of credit during the most desperate years of Louis XIV's reign.[13]

The General Farms were finally leased again on September 15, 1714, in the name of Louis François Nerville. The lease ran retroactively from 1710 until 1715 at a price of 36.6 million livres for 1710 and 1711, and 44 million livres for the last four years.[14] A new lease to run from 1716 to 1721 was signed shortly before Louis XIV's death in the name of Edmé de Bonne. The lease was to pay 46.3 million livres the first year, 46.8 million livres the second year, and 47.3 million livres for the last four years.[15] The government needed 45 million livres just to pay the rentes against the farms. After Louis XIV's death, this lease was revoked. A new lease in the name of Paul Manis replaced it with a slightly higher price of 48.5 million livres annually.[16]

Colbert had created a successful credit mechanism for the state during peacetime. Peace, however, was not a normal state of affairs for early modern France. Colbert's successors were forced to tap the farms to pay the ever-increasing costs of war after 1688. The last leases signed during Fouquet's time on what would become the General Farms paid 36.9 million livres annually to the crown.[17] By the end of the reign the crown needed more than that just to pay the interest on the rentes. By 1708 the General Farms existed simply to pay those debts and the other charges against the farms. They were useless as a source of credit.

One account for the year 1712 reports that the farms outside the General Farms paid almost 18 million livres to the crown. There were also rentes paid from the revenue of these farms but there is no indication as to how much of this fund was used to pay rentes against these farms.[18] In any case, 18 million livres was not enough to pay one-tenth of the annual expenses of the government in 1712. War and the flood of offices and unredeemed paper debts had destroyed commerce. The perceptions were no longer a viable source of revenue. The government was forced to turn to other sources.

The Other Ordinary Revenues

The main source of revenue remaining to the government was the impositions, mainly the taille. The taille was not a direct tax as we would describe it today. The Church and the nobility were exempt from the taille. It was a tax on the heads of households who were subject to the taille, called the *taillables,* but each taillable paid a different amount. The government levied the taille along with its supplements on the fiscal parish. A committee of two to seven collectors, who were themselves taillables living in the parish, would assess the wealth and ability to pay of every taillable in the parish. One taillable might pay one amount because it was the judgment of the collectors that he could afford it, while another taillable paid a different amount for the same reason.

Over the years since the taille was imposed during the reign of Charles VII (1422–61) to pay for a standing army, a host of supplements had been added. The amount of the taille granted to Charles VII was 1.2 million livres. By the time of Cardinal Mazarin's ministry (1643–61) it amounted to between 40 and 43 million livres, when all of the supplements to the taille were added.[19] These supplements included the *taillon* for certain military units, the *ustencile* to help pay for the army's winter quarters, and the *vivres* and *étapes* that were a burden to the towns and villages along the army's fixed routes as it moved to the front. During the wars at the end of the reign those towns and villages along the routes to the frontiers with Flanders, Germany, Italy, and Spain were most repeatedly taxed to pay these expenses, meaning that they paid more than villages that were remote from the frontier or any major roadways. In addition, the troops, particularly the cavalry, foraged for supplies to feed their animals. These additions, in those provinces near the military fronts, could amount to as much as the taille itself. Although these additions were not part of the funds recorded by the Royal Treasury, they influenced tax collection locally.[20]

The nobility and the Church were not the only groups exempt from the taille. In the course of time, various social and corporate bodies were granted exemptions from the taille as rewards for services rendered to the monarchy. All servants of the crown—that is, public servants, those people who served on a royal law court or were employed in the royal tax farms—were exempt from paying this tax because of their service. Most venal offices carried the exemption from the taille as one of the perquisites of the office. The king also sold letters of exemption in return for large sums of money, usually some multiple of the amount the payer was assessed for the taille.

The taille taxed rural areas more heavily than urban areas or towns. Certain towns, such as Paris, Lyon, and Marseille, were completely exempt from contributing anything to the taille. In addition, the inhabitants of France's larger towns did not pay the taille for either their urban or rural properties. Towns near royal chateaux or scenes of prominent royal ceremonies, such as St. Denis and Reims, were also exempt. Some other towns, such as Toulouse and Poitiers, were allowed to "subscribe" (*abonner*) to the taille for a fixed annual sum, to be raised either by taxing wealth directly or by levying certain sales taxes, called *octrois*, on goods entering the towns. With royal approval the revenues from these taxes would go to pay the town's subscription, or *abonnement*. Even where cities did contribute to the taille, urban property was assessed at a lower rate than property in rural areas. For example, the city of Beauvais paid only 8 percent of the taille owed for the entire Beauvaisis, while the city of Meaux only paid 4.5 percent of what its election owed.[21]

The royal government did not have the authority to levy the taille in the *pays d'états* (provinces with provincial legislatures or estates), where the provincial estates controlled taxation. The crown only had the authority to impose the taille on the generalities of the *pays d'élections* (provinces with offices called elections), of which there were nineteen during the reign of Louis XIV.[22] Most of these were part of the *pays de taille personnelle,* where the status of the head of the household determined whether or not he paid the taille. In other words, the taille was levied on people who were neither privileged nor had bought any exemptions.

The kingdom of France was divided into two distinct sections according to how the taille was paid. All provinces that still maintained provincial estates, as well as the generalities of Montauban and Grenoble and the elections of Condom and Agen in the generality of Bordeaux, were part of what was called the *pays de taille réelle.* The taille in these areas was based on real property rather than personal status. Certain property was termed noble and was exempt from being assessed to pay the taille, regardless of the status of the owner. Other property was termed common (*roturier*) and the owner had to pay the taille, regardless of his status. The levying of the taille was based on land rolls known as *cadastres* that were notoriously out of date, despite periodic efforts to update them. Also, city property was greatly undervalued in relation to rural property.

While assessing the taille for each taxpayer was less subject to the abuses found in the *pays de taille personnelle,* collecting the taille and its supplements in the *pays de taille réelle* was difficult because noblemen and other privilege-holders who owned common property resisted any efforts to force them to pay their taxes. The use of legal proceedings was complicated by the support that royal judges gave to these kinds of tax evaders, with whom they often shared ties of kinship or clientage.

The royal government decided on the amount of taille each generality would pay the spring before it was to be paid. A notice, called a *brevet* of the taille, was sent to the provincial intendant in that generality. Since Richelieu's ministry, the intendant had been responsible for apportioning the taille and its supplements, and deciding the amounts that each of the subdivisions in the generality, called elections, and each parish within the various elections had to pay. A second brevet of the taille paid for any local expenses, such as fees for the officers handling the funds, the maintenance of bridges and highways in the generalities, repairing the harbors or churches in the generalities, funds to pay to exempt the generalities from other fees and duties owed to newly created offices, and the salary and upkeep of local officials.

Upon receiving the two brevets the intendant would consult with local officials, called the *élus,* in each election. Officially, these men determined whether an election could bear its assigned burden, and reported back to the central government. In reality, local lords and notables pressured the intendant and the élus to reduce the taille for their estates. In any case, the intendant and the élus would take into account the opinions of the local elites before recommending the amounts each election and parish could bear. The central government would respond in the autumn with two documents called the *commission* of the taille and the *mandements.* The former levied the amount of money owed by each election and the latter apportioned that money to each parish within the election.[23]

The royal provincial intendant was a symbol of the growing intrusion of the royal government into local life. In the sixteenth century the officers of the Bureau of Finances had apportioned the taille and its supplements. They were local notables whose loyalty was more local than royal. The king's power was distant and felt only rarely. The Bureau of Finances, as a special law court, heard local cases involving taxes, including all complaints about the assessments, as a court of first resort. Its officials were the local administrators everyone knew or heard about.

The appearance of the royal provincial intendant as a supposedly itinerant representative from the king posed no permanent threat to the position of local officials. When the provincial intendant became a permanent fixture during Richelieu's ministry, however, the people more readily felt, and resented, the royal will. This new presence was one of the reasons for the rebellions of the 1630s and the Fronde (1648–53). By the 1660s the intendant had usurped the administrative functions of the Bureau of Finances in each generality and presided over meetings of the élus for the apportioning of royal taxes. The intendant was usually an outsider with very few local roots. He was usually a master of requests of the hotel of the royal palace (*maître des requêtes de l'hôtel du palais*) whose career revolved around obtaining and keeping royal favor.[24]

The mandement, commission, and brevet apportioned impositions to the parish, election, and generality. Despite the presence of the intendant to remind provincials of a distant royal government, that government did not tax individuals. It taxed corporate entities like the parish (or the quarter or hundredth in towns).[25] Residents of the parish subject to the taille took turns acting as tax collectors. Each parish had two to seven collectors, depending on its size. The collectors apportioned the parish's taxes among its taillables by estimating their ability to pay. The change in collectors from year to year placed the burden of this task on the shoulders of local men who might be illiterate, incompetent, or insolvent. Because nobles and officeholders were exempt from both the taille and the *collecte,* many educated and wealthy men were removed from the list of possible collectors who were legally responsible for the payment of the parish's taxes. The alternation of this responsibility made the tax arbitrary and unpredictable.[26] Collectors might vary the amount of taxes to be paid from year to year as favors to friends or relatives, out of vindictiveness toward enemies, or simply because of ignorance of people's ability to pay. The élus tried to obviate these potential problems by supervising the list through their power to sign and approve the taille roll. The intendants also drew up a separate roll, called the *taxe d'office*, for each election in order to apportion tax among the major personages of an election, such as the taillables living elsewhere, employees of the tax farms, holders of offices that had been suppressed, and victims of disasters. These so-called *coqs du village* might inhibit the collectors from properly assessing their wealth. Widows and disaster victims were on the list to benefit from royal grace with reduced or no taxes.[27]

The collectors were responsible for remitting the taxes they collected to the taille receivers in the election on fixed dates. A contract between the collectors and the receivers set the terms for these payments. The collectors received a small fee for their services, but they were also subject to legal proceedings if they failed to remit their funds on the due dates. If the collectors were poor, the taille receiver had very little to seize and posed no threat to them. As temporary representatives of the parish, collectors could be incompetent in the apportionment of taxes, and dilatory in their collection. If they had very little property, they had no reason to be expeditious in performing their duties. They might also be rewarded in future years when someone who had benefited from their behavior became a collector. In any case, the wealthiest members of the parish feared the collecte more than the taille itself because the burden of paying the parish's taxes would most likely fall on them. Thus, they were motivated to try to obtain exemptions from the taille by either purchasing offices or obtaining letters of exemption.

The taille receiver was a financier and a venal officer who owned the right to receive tax moneys. He, in turn, had promised, via contract, to remit funds at fixed dates to the receiver general of finances for the specified generality. Unlike the tax farmers, who were gambling on making a profit, the taille receiver was limited to withholding only specific portions of the funds he handled, and the receiver general could only withhold a slightly larger portion. They did have their office expenses paid out of the taille receipts as well.

The receiver general of finances, another financier who owned his office, signed a contract called *résultat du conseil* with the Royal Council of Finances to remit funds for that year at fixed dates in fifteen to eighteen monthly payments for one year's taille to the Keepers of the Royal Treasury, another category of venal officers. At each level, these officers owned the right to handle tax funds during a specific year. For example, there were usually two taille receivers in each election, one for the even-numbered years and one for the odd-numbered years. The receivers general of finances and the Keepers of the Royal Treasury might, however, serve every third year. Unlike tax farmers collecting perceptions, these men owned the right to receive money by virtue of owning their offices. They were private financiers with other business interests who had purchased the right to receive government funds in return for a promise to lend their credit to the king by supplying him with a fixed sum of money on fixed dates, thus guaranteeing him a regular income. Like the tax farmers, the receivers general and receivers particular (as the taille receivers were sometimes called) served as local bankers, transferring royal money through a bookkeeping procedure and thus saving the cost of transporting money to and fro. The cost of this service, however, was deducted as charges against the impositions collected.[28]

To illustrate this process, we can examine a résultat for a receiver generalship for 1709 made between the Crown and the receiver general of finances for Lyon, Paulin Prondre,[29] who, because of a dispute over his rights to his office, had ceded his year of exercise to Noel Rousseau,[30] a receiver and payer of rentes at the Hotel de Ville. The total tax imposed on the Lyon generality for 1709 was 1,380,510 livres after an arrêt of the Council dated September 1, 1708, granted a reduction of 100,000 livres. From this total, 679,491 livres was to be deducted to pay for a variety of local expenses, or to be paid to several special treasurers. The three largest deductions, totaling 413,928 livres, were to pay the office expenses of the elections and the receiver general's office, including the salaries of the Lyon Cour des Monnaies. Another 57,521 livres was granted to the receiver general for his fees at the rate of 10 deniers per livre (slightly better than 4 percent), for the total of 1,380,510 livres he was to receive. The Keeper of the Royal Treasury was to receive 701,019 livres in fifteen monthly installments of 46,734 livres, 12 sous, beginning on January 1, 1709. The résultat was delayed because of bargaining and was not dated until January 15, 1709.[31]

The receiver general thus contracted to pay a debt to the king over a fixed interval in return for handling the receipts from the impositions in his generality. He then made his contracts with the receivers particular, who were making their agreements with the parish collectors. No individual subject owed a debt directly to the crown. Parishioners owed the collectors, who owed the receiver particular, who owed the receiver general, who owed the government. Each of these intermediaries could approach the government to request the use of constraints—such as the seizure of property, the lodging of archers and *huissiers* (the closest English equivalent is "bailiffs") in someone's house, or the lodging of troops—to coerce a debtor to pay his debts. Receivers general of finances acted as credit institutions in much the same way as the tax farmers. The central government would issue assignations as an acknowledgment of a debt to be paid with interest from the revenues of a receiver general. After honoring the assignation, the receiver general would receive a quittance from the Keeper of the Royal Treasury recognizing that he had paid the designated sum. Also, like the tax farmer, the receiver general would be asked to advance a sum of money to the government that would be deducted from any payments owed to the Keeper of the Royal Treasury, along with the interest due on the loan. The receivers general would borrow from the public at interest by issuing *billets des receveurs généraux.*[32]

The revenue from impositions declined under Colbert as he concentrated on increasing the profitability of the tax farms (see table 1.2). It was only during the years 1676–78 that he increased the level of impositions. His constant policy was to rely on perceptions that were paid by everyone without exemption. He also surveyed the accounts of the receivers general and particular to reduce unnecessary costs. His successors also avoided relying on impositions as a source of increased revenues. They turned to other sources of income after 1687. Pontchartrain and his successor, Michel Chamillard, sold a host of venal offices and rights granting exemptions from the taille. The taille increasingly became a burden for those who could not afford to raise money to buy an office or a monopoly right. It also became more difficult to collect. By selling exemptions, the government depended more and more on collecting impositions from the poorest elements of society. Nevertheless, in 1705 Chamillard increased the taille by two sous per livre, or 10 percent, a surtax that would remain in effect throughout the eighteenth century until the Revolution.[33] Chamillard also asked the receivers general and the general farmers for a significant advance on future revenue that still had not been repaid by 1708.[34]

Table 1.2. Revenue from the taille, 1662–1707.

Year	Taxes	Charges	Royal Treasury
1662	40,969,949	13,500,009	24,340,137
1663	37,991,651	13,674,891	16,403,355
1664	36,233,029	13,714,769	22,115,592
1665	35,295,219	10,975,549	22,919,078
1666	36,084,610	13,945,234	19,262,764
1667	36,699,050	11,645,051	23,146,500
1668	36,033,894	11,042,210	23,331,448
1669	33,832,240	7,908,211	25,184,369
1670	34,019,709	6,825,538	26,527,277
1671	33,845,397	6,796,921	30,543,413
1672	34,798,663	7,032,394	26,444,458
1673	36,645,510	6,951,457	29,009,463
1674	37,181,692	11,785,721	29,855,463
1675	38,122,830	7,016,136	24,715,312
1676	40,270,451	7,625,126	31,141,957

(continued)

Table 1.2. *(concluded)*

Year	Taxes	Charges	Royal Treasury
1677	40,421,347	7,292,999	28,676,957
1678	40,480,256	7,059,372	29,996,460
1679	34,939,753	6,718,101	26,789,369
1680	32,904,828	6,667,676	23,894,660
1681	33,915,452	6,482,090	23,118,549
1682	35,023,336	6,521,159	26,378,482
1683	37,907,943	6,554,534	27,536,082
1684	37,698,011	6,538,316	25,019,197
1685	35,464,225	6,593,956	22,307,819
1686	33,875,295	6,698,997	25,486,604
1687	33,738,290	6,651,498	25,016,817
1688	33,856,390	6,689,101	25,944,201
1689	34,065,201	6,800,485	25,768,751
1690	36,989,939	7,613,868	26,756,933
1691	36,992,084	7,572,728	28,532,421
1692	36,840,125	7,982,985	25,886,463
1693	36,640,757	8,433,664	28,415,824
1694	36,437,023	8,817,500	25,540,911
1695	34,590,145	8,759,638	22,840,550
1696			
1697	32,017,866	9,898,076	18,695,040
1698			
1699	30,726,934	9,884,660	12,214,176
1700	30,727,147	9,566,455	21,160,692
1701	34,716,261	8,494,753	26,221,508
1702	34,213,484	9,004,309	25,209,175
1703	34,455,685	9,347,152	25,108,533
1704			
1705	38,315,548	11,798,823	26,516,725
1706	36,543,000	11,580,000	15,867,000
1707	38,566,310	12,820,895	25,745,415

Note: This table represents a history of the impositions in the nineteen generalities of the pays d'élections from 1661 to 1707, with information taken from A.N. KK 355 and Boislisle and Brotonne, *Correspondance des contrôleurs généraux*, 2:583–604. There is no data for the years 1696, 1698, and 1704. The amounts of charges and taxes do not equal the amounts received by the Royal Treasury because some taxes were not collected in the year they were assessed.

Receipts from the pays d'*états* were recorded separately in the accounts of the controller general of finances. In fact, it is incorrect to assume that the taille was levied in each and every province with its own provincial estates or assembly. Many pays d'*états* simply paid a *don gratuit* (free gift) in lieu of acknowledging that they owed the crown any impositions. The assembly might have replaced the taille with an indirect tax on trade. In any case, all taxes in the pays d'*états* were paid to financiers called treasurers or receivers of the bourse of the estates, who then paid the Royal Treasury after deducting their fees for handling the money, along with local charges for road maintenance and other matters. During the reign of Louis XIV the crown's receipts from the pays d'*états* remained relatively unchanged except for funds coming from territories added to France. The pays d'*états* and the newly added territories, such as Flanders, Roussillon, Franche Comté, and Alsace, paid no more than 4.5 million livres in impositions, from which 1–2 million were deducted as charges.

The clergy of France also provided a free gift that was voted on every five years at their general assembly. While the clergy's contribution was never fixed, the crown came to rely on the wealth of the French Church during times of necessity to provide either a free gift or a special subsidy in return for being exempted from new taxes. During the War of the League of Augsburg (1688–97) the clergy offered the crown gifts totaling more than 30 million livres, as well as almost 5 million in taxes on offices governing ecclesiastical property and rights. Most of this money was voted after 1695 when the rest of France was paying the capitation. During the last three years of the war the clergy paid an annual subsidy of 4 million livres instead of submitting to the capitation. When the capitation was renewed in 1701 at the beginning of the War of the Spanish Succession, the clergy renewed its subsidy. The money for the subsidy was taken from clerical funds or loans against certain clerical revenue sources. Between 1690 and 1707 the clergy paid 61.5 million livres to the royal government. The government also received 5.5 million livres by taxing a variety of offices governing Church rights and property. In addition, the government hoped to raise 32.5 million livres from the sale of offices collecting the right of *amortissements* (damages due from the *gens de mainmorte* from property in their hands). Excluding this last contract, the clergy paid the king an average of more than 3.7 million livres annually during the period.[35] In the accounting of the controller general, these funds would have been split between the free gifts and the casual revenues.

Casual revenues came from taxes paid by all venal officeholders, the famous *paulette* created by Sully in 1604. The tax was supposed to equal one-sixtieth of the value of the office. Casual revenues also included revenue from offices that were sold directly by the crown rather than through an intermediary financier called a *traitant*. These offices were usually at court or on the royal council.

The last source of ordinary revenue was the royal domain, specifically the forest. Lumber was a major building material and source of heat. Most feudal lords sold their farmland during the sixteenth century but kept their woodlands, which required little upkeep and produced good profits. The royal woods never produced more than 2 million livres annually. Altogether, the woods and casual revenues amounted to no more than 6 percent of the ordinary revenues.[36]

After 1687 ordinary revenues were incapable of supporting the state of Louis XIV's France and the wars of the last years of the reign. The crown was forced to turn to extraordinary measures to raise money.

The Extraordinary Affairs of Finances

In the accounting procedure of the Old Regime, extraordinary sources of revenue were divided into several categories. One such category was merely a bookkeeping operation called *les deniers revenants bons,* or money that had been set aside for specific purposes but was left unspent. It then returned to the Royal Treasury.

Another category was the *débets des comptables. Comptables* (accountables) were any officials who handled royal money, such as the receivers general. They were supposed to have their annual accounts checked by the King's Council within three years of the exercise of their offices. The accountables then paid to the Royal Treasury any money found to be owed to the king. Conversely, the crown had to pay any money it owed to the accountables. This process was referred to as purification (*épuration*) of the accounts. Colbert and Le Peletier performed this task regularly, but the disorder of the wars at the end of the reign caused the government to neglect these duties in order not to cast suspicions on the creditworthiness of the accountables. By 1714 the accounts for the years 1700 and after had not yet been checked. The government had granted suspensions because of slow tax collections and its own inability to pay its debts. The crown had to pay any debts owed to the accountables if their accounts were purified. The crown needed the credit of these officials more than it needed their accounts checked.[37]

The government also derived profits from minting money recorded as an extraordinary source of income. Philip the Fair had used this seigniorial right as a source of revenue. It later became an attribute of sovereignty and a monopoly of the crown, which could declare that money had changed in value, thus requiring alterations to the amount of gold or silver in each coin. Most French money was silver. In the case of a change in value, the king would order all old money to be brought to the mints and "reformed." The crown charged a fee for performing this "service." Several

French kings found this process to be a valuable source of revenue during a crisis, and Louis XIV was no exception. Colbert had tried to rationalize minting operations but he, too, relied on the mints for income. After Colbert, major remintings were ordered in 1686, 1689, 1693, 1701, 1704, and 1709. The profits derived from this system varied. Some documents reveal a declining amount of specie coming to the government's mints with each "reform."[38] The gold and silver had either left France or was hidden by its owners in the hopes of better days. The constant reminting made money a commodity for speculation.

A second reason for ordering reminting or changing the accounting value of coins was to encourage the circulation of money as everyone tried to get rid of coins before their value changed. It was hoped that this increased circulation of coins would lead to the collection of higher amounts of money via perceptions or impositions through the increased sale of agricultural products. A constant refrain in the controller general's correspondence is the loss of commerce because people were hiding their money.

In 1701 the "reform" occurred so rapidly that the royal mints had to issue *billets de monnaie*, mint bills that promised to repay their holders for coinage brought to the mint, with interest. The government recognized a debt on the part of the mints and promised repayment in specie at a set date that was always postponed. By 1704 the ratio of mint bills to specie available ceased to have any meaning. The government was simply issuing the bills and not repaying them. It did pay the interest until 1707. Mint bills joined various other papers issued by the tax farmers, receivers general, and other royal accountables as subjects of speculation and indeterminate value. By 1708, together with unpaid assignations, bills of the treasurers of the Extraordinary of War and the Navy, and promises of the recreated Caisse des emprunts, the amount of paper "money" in circulation had a face value of almost 400 million livres in government indebtedness.[39]

The government had borrowed money in ever-increasing amounts by selling rentes—government bonds that promised their purchasers annual dividends, to be paid by the rente-payers attached to the Hotel de Ville of Paris, the *postes*, the royal lotteries, or the clergy—against various revenue sources. The legal interest rate was one-eighteenth of the purchase price, or denier 18 (5.5 percent) in the parlance of the day. Most rentes were perpetual because the government did not plan to reimburse the investor for the principal. The government was creating a perpetual income source that the investor could pass on to his heirs. Some rentes had lifetime (*viagère*) limitations, because they would be reimbursed at the death of the purchaser. They carried a higher interest rate to facilitate the reimbursement. The interest rate depended on the age of the purchaser.[40]

In times of emergency the government borrowed money at interest rates higher than the law permitted. During the War of the League of Augsburg, it borrowed money at denier 16 (7.1 percent) or denier 12 (8.3 percent).[41] In 1698 the loans were reimbursed by means of new rentes at or below the legal limit (denier 18).[42] With the beginning of the War of the Spanish Succession, however, interest rates rose again.

Another form of obtaining loans was to pressure officeholders by offering a salary increase in return for a one-time contribution. Owners of venal offices either purchased the office or inherited it as a kind of property from a relative. The original purchase price set the salary (*gages*) for the office. By purchasing the office, or simply owning it, the officeholder had property against which he could borrow money. The office usually exempted the owner from paying impositions or from collecting them. It also paid a salary and allowed the collection of fees attached to the performance of certain duties reserved for that office. Officeholders were a select group of people whom the government could force to borrow more money. By owning or purchasing an office, the officeholder had revealed that he had credit and could borrow a large sum of money. An augmentation of the salary was a forced loan the government demanded of its officeholders. From the death of Colbert in 1683 until the end of 1714, various officeholders were called upon to pay over 205 million livres to the king in return for more than 11.5 million livres in augmented gages.[43] Like rentes, gages were not always paid regularly. They were a risky investment.

New offices were created and sold as a source of revenue. François I (1515–47) was the first king to sell offices simply to raise money.[44] Originally, the crown sold off parts of its judicial machinery, such as judgeships or positions in the law enforcement system, but after 1688 the crown began selling the rights to sell or perform certain commercial functions as a monopoly. The pressure of war turned the sale of offices into a game for speculators. The sale of offices was another royal financial endeavor undertaken by private financiers. The government, often in collusion with a syndicate of private financial speculators, created offices to perform certain functions in the belief that there was a market for them.[45] Pontchartrain supposedly said, "Every time Your Majesty creates an office, God creates a fool to buy it." Unlike taxes, office-purchasing was a voluntary act, or so the government and its financier friends could pretend.

In theory, the king was selling off activities and rights that he controlled by creating special offices (monopolies) to perform them. Offices that had already been sold were often redefined to create second offices for even-numbered years, or third or fourth offices for every third or fourth year. Offices created held monopoly rights to sell certain products or perform certain services. If offices sold well, new offices were created to assist them. For example, after the creation and sale of offices of keepers of the records of baptisms, marriages, and burials, the government created the offices of controllers of those same records. The creation of a new office was not necessarily intended to create a new office. The crown would accept offers from the owner of an older office to buy a new office in order to prevent the value of the old office from declining. If the corporate leadership of a town, province, or generality could raise money to pay for the offices, the crown was willing to suppress the offices in those locations, meaning that the monopoly right did not exist where the offices had been suppressed.[46] The government merely wanted to raise money by attracting "voluntary" contributions from existing privileged persons or corporate entities that could raise the money.

The government did not administer the sale of most offices (or rentes or augmented gages) directly; instead, private financiers offered to perform this service for the crown. In fact, these financiers were often the very people who proposed the creation of the offices. They, or sometimes disinterested parties, submitted ideas to the government, which then judged each idea in terms of its workability, desirability, and attractiveness to potential buyers. Ideas that were rejected at one time might seem more attractive at a later date as government finances became more desperate. Offices that were unsellable in one form might be reworked to make them more attractive to potential buyers.

Once the functions, perquisites, gages, and other details defining a new office were settled, the government determined the value of the office and granted the right to sell it to a group of financiers with sufficient financial power to undertake the operation. A résultat or traité was then signed in council, granting the right to sell these offices to a company headed by a "straw man" who, as in the operation of a tax farm, was not a major investor but simply the person necessary to give this group standing in law. The financiers, called traitants, signed the traité promising to help the "straw man" fulfill the obligations of the contract.

A typical traité would contain certain provisions:[47]

1. The king would grant the right to sell the offices (rentes or augmented gages) to the straw man and his *cautions* (backers). (All cautions were not necessarily financiers themselves, but were sometimes *prête-noms*, straw men, behind whom were people who did not want their names on these documents.)[48]
2. The total price for the offices, called the *forfait*, was established.
3. The backers (traitants) of the traité were granted a rebate or discount called a *remise en dedans* that was usually the equivalent of one-sixth or less of the forfait. The keeper of the Royal Treasury recognized the payment of the remise by issuing an *ordonnance comptant* stating that the funds were accounted for by the Royal Treasury. The traitants were also granted a bonus called a *remise en dehors* that was usually equal to one-tenth (two sous per livre), to be received from

the purchaser at the time of the sale. In other words, the purchaser of an office (or rentes or augmented gages) that cost 10,000 livres would have to pay as much as 11,000 livres for the office, but the company of traitants would only have to account to the Royal Treasury for 8,333 livres, 4 sous.

4. The Royal Treasury could be paid the balance of the forfait in a variety of ways. There was usually a down payment to be made shortly after the signing of the traité, to be followed by monthly, bimonthly, or quarterly payments until the balance was received. As with the farms and impositions, the crown was receiving money independent of the rate at which the company received their funds. In effect, the financiers were lending the crown money in return for both the discount and the bonus as interest on that loan.
5. The traitants were usually given the rights to exercise the functions of the offices and to receive the salary and fees until the offices were sold.
6. The traitants were instructed to issue receipts to the purchasers of the offices. The receiver general of the casual revenues would then issue a *quittance* to anyone who brought him a receipt. The government's receipt recognized that the funds for the purchase of the office had been received when, in fact, the crown had received no funds from the purchaser.
7. The traitants were to account for the collection of the principal of their loan to the Royal Council of Finances alone. They did not have to account for the discounts or bonuses.

In effect, the financiers were lending the government five-sixths or more of the forfait in return for the power to sell the offices and to enjoy both remises, along with all the privileges of the offices until they were sold. Enjoyment of the rights and privileges of the offices was supposed to make the offices more attractive to potential buyers. If an office produced a profit along with exemption from taxation, it might attract a previously unexempted person with funds. People holding older offices of a similar type might also buy the new offices to have them attached to their old offices, or to have the new offices suppressed.

Great companies of traitants existed with the ability to borrow money to finance these loans and the employees to carry out the sale of the offices. They could pay higher interest rates than the government offered on its loans (rentes) because the profits to the investors in the traités usually ran anywhere from 20 to 32 percent of the amount invested.[49] Their borrowing, however, caused problems when they were unable to sell the offices and repay the loans they undertook. Some traités were created to suppress older ones by offering a means of repaying loans undertaken by the earlier traité. The Royal Council sometimes had to issue arrêts granting cease-and-desist orders to all creditors of companies that backed certain traités. Such arrêts suspended legal pursuits for a set period of time and ordered the traitants to pay the interest on their promissory notes.[50]

In other words, the government's insatiable need for money prompted the creation of a whole other category of promissory notes in addition to the mint bills and the notes of the tax farmers and receivers general, etc. Some traités were never successful, and traitants sometimes could not meet their obligations to the government. The controller general calculated receiving funds from these companies and issued assignations promising payment from the receipt of revenues from different traités, thus adding more paper to the swirling debts of the royal government.

During Pontchartrain's tenure as controller general (1689–99), the total amount of forfaits was valued at 351,497,991 livres, out of which the traitants kept 82,713,277 livres (23.5 percent) in discounts and bonuses. During Chamillard's tenure (1700–1707), the total amount was 259,055,645 livres, out of which the financiers kept 60,107,543 livres (23.2 percent). Under Desmaretz, during 1708, the total amount of forfaits was extremely high, at 63,209,209 livres, but it declined very rapidly during the following years. By the end of his ministry the total amount for the years 1708 to 1715 was 147,571,849 livres, with the traitants keeping only 30,957,290 livres (21.0 percent).[51] The average annual amount on the forfaits for Pontchartrain's ministry was 31,954,362 livres. For Chamillard's ministry it was 32,381,955 livres. For Desmaretz's it was 18,446,481 livres, but for the period from 1709 to 1715 it was only 12,051,805 livres per annum.

Desmaretz said, in his defense of his ministry, that he wanted to turn away from reliance on traitants. There is evidence, however, that many offices were simply not selling. Desmaretz may have been forced to turn away from traités whether he wanted to or not.[52] Traditional sources of revenue were no longer capable of producing any significant income. The farms could barely pay the interest on loans against them. The sale of offices had removed vast numbers of France's wealthier citizens from the tax rolls. Desmaretz had to find some new method of raising revenue.

The Capitation

The creation of the capitation, in 1695, had already initiated one new source of revenue. All of the previously discussed methods for raising money were put to the test during the War of the League of Augsburg (1688–97), when France stood without allies against the major powers of Western Europe: England, the Netherlands, Spain, Austria, Bavaria, and various German principalities. Eventually, even Portugal and Savoy joined France's enemies. The weather problems of 1693–94 that led to crop failures, reduced economic activity, and a sharp decline in revenues, worsened matters.

Throughout the reign of Louis XIV, the government tried to obtain information about how other sovereign powers raised the money to pay for war. The idea of a capitation, or head tax, emerged when the Holy Roman Emperor Leopold I introduced just such a tax on every inhabitant of his hereditary lands, including the clergy, in 1690. Within France the growing debate over taxation did not include discussion of whether this kind of tax should exclude any category of persons. In other words, the discussion assumed that all people, without exception, should be subject to whatever new tax was implemented.

Instead, the debate began over whether status or wealth should be the basis of the head tax. Basing this tax on wealth would require some method of discovering the wealth of every Frenchman. A *mémoire* that Desmaretz wrote to his uncle, Charles Colbert de Croissy, secretary of state for foreign affairs, in July 1693 (now in the archives of the Foreign Affairs Ministry), discusses a series of financial measures under consideration, including a new tax called a general capitation.[53] Desmaretz opposed any new tax on the taillables, who were already paying 55 million livres. He also doubted that those who were exempt from the taille could be forced to pay a new tax, and wondered what basis could be used to determine what such people would pay. He favored a tax on the owners of houses in Paris and other large towns at the rate of one-fifteenth or one-twelfth of a year's rent. Desmaretz's opinion prevailed during 1693. A tax on houses was adopted in August 1693 but the échevins (town councilors) of Paris protested against it and instead proposed to pay some sort of head tax that divided Parisian society into six groups, with each group paying a different rate.[54]

Pontchartrain, during his tenure as controller general of finances, gave his own opinion on what form the new tax should take in a letter dated October 27, 1693, addressed to his cousin, Gilles de Maupeou d'Ableiges, the intendant in the Auvergne (Riom). Ponchartrain rejected a tax based on the ability to pay because he felt it would be too dangerous, subject to abuses, and the cause of perpetual complaints. He favored a tax on the rents received by building owners or a head tax with rates based on a division of society into three or four groups, because these taxes, he said, would be easier to collect and would cause less delay in their establishment.[55] After the final adoption of the capitation in 1695, Pontchartrain would tell his associates that the tax had taken on several different forms until it was finally adopted.[56]

Alain Guéry makes the claim that taxation on the basis of wealth as we understand it in the twentieth century was beyond the traditional mental makeup of the seventeenth century.[57] Yet, many people did believe that all people should contribute to the good of the state in proportion to their individual abilities to pay. Saint-Simon, in condemning the man blamed for this tax, Nicolas de Lamoignon de Basville,[58] also presented Pontchartrain as being opposed to taxes that were not fixed and unchangeable. (Pontchartrain was a friend of Saint-Simon's and one of his major sources of information.) If Pontchartrain told the Duke of Saint-Simon that he opposed taxes based on a proportion of one's wealth and the duke confused his argument with an argument against the capitation, what Pontchartrain told his cousin, Maupeou d'Ableiges, in October 1693 was in keeping with the duke's distorted memory of events. Saint-Simon merely transferred that argument from an opposition to a tax, under whatever name, on wealth to an opposition to any new tax that was not easy to collect. Pontchartrain was apparently arguing against the tax on wealth that many other people seemed to favor.

Jules-Louis Bolé, marquis de Chamlay, a military advisor to the king and to his war minister, participated in these discussions. From 1675 until 1715 Chamlay served as a chief of staff for the French armies, even though he did not actually hold the rank. He was an advisor to Louvois until the latter's death in July 1691 and then to the king himself, who is said to have offered him the post of secretary of state for war, but the modest Chamlay declined to replace the son of his mentor, Louvois. In any case, Chamlay had regular access to the king and was an almost constant guest at Marly, Louis XIV's private chateau, to which courtiers avidly sought invitations. He was a fervid believer in taxes that were proportionate to a person's ability to pay.[59] Chamlay and Pontchartrain exchanged letters discussing the form that a new tax should take. Chamlay opposed the idea of a head tax because, in his opinion, it taxed ephemeral qualities. He also opposed creating a new perception (because it would threaten the already tenuous income of the General Farms), a voluntary tax (because it would be futile), or a tax based on apportioning taxes among all people (because it would be subject to the same abuses as the taille). Chamlay instead favored collecting taxes on the basis of one-twentieth of each person's wealth.[60]

Among Chamlay's extant papers is a letter dated December 22, 1693, that calls for a tax on all non-taillables. This proposed tax would also be based on a person's ability to pay, estimated in a manner similar to the taille.[61] Chamlay's papers contain several undated memoranda on the capitation as well as other tax proposals, indicating that Chamlay was consulted about many financial measures.

Michel Le Peletier de Souzy was also looking for a solution to France's financial dilemma. An intendant of finances since January 1684 and, after the death of Louvois in July 1691, the director general of fortifications, a position that gave him regular access to the king, Souzy was one of six intendants of finances under Pontchartrain. He was also an official in the war ministry and would have been in contact with Chamlay. Chamlay told

Pontchartrain that Souzy was considering an undisclosed plan to raise 50 million livres.[62] Whatever this plan may have been, Souzy would be the intendant of finances who administered the collection of the capitation when it was adopted.

Chamlay and Souzy worked regularly with Sebastien Le Prestre de Vauban, the great engineer of fortifications and sieges. Vauban wrote a mémoire on the capitation in late 1694 that recommended a new tax of one-fifteenth of each person's wealth. He also made estimates as to the wealth of various elements of French society, such as the church. His proposal required that other taxes be reduced or eliminated when his capitation was collected. Vauban also would permit taxpayers to pay their taxes in kind rather than in money alone as the royal government required. Vauban presented his memorandum to Louis XIV in February 1695 after the capitation had already been declared, although he had clearly been working on his project before the establishment of the capitation. His project was probably discussed among high-level government officials, if not with the king himself. Despite the adoption of the capitation in 1695, Vauban would continue to write and discuss ways of reforming France's tax system.[63]

The terrible winter and harvest of 1693–94 reduced the population of France by more than a million souls (out of an estimated population of 21 million people). The War of the League of Augsburg dragged on with inconclusive fighting and peace negotiations that went nowhere. The government realized that a new source of funds was needed if it was to survive the 1695 campaign. After considering these different choices Pontchartrain sent a letter to each provincial intendant on October 31, 1694, revealing the government's intention to levy a new general tax called the capitation for all royal subjects to pay. He asked the intendants to examine Pontchartrain's general description of such a tax, with rates running from 1,000 livres to 10 sous (a half-livre). Only the clergy and the indigent poor would be exempt. The intendants were to report on the condition of their provinces and to draw up a census (*dénombrement*) of each parish and its ability to pay such a tax.[64]

The discussion within the Royal Council took place while the provincial intendants were conducting their own research in their provinces. On December 10, 1694, the Estates of Languedoc proposed that the king establish a war subsidy or capitation on all French subjects, based on their ability to pay. The proposal from Languedoc seems to have weighed heavily in the Royal Council's discussions, because Cardinal Pierre de Bonsy, archbishop of Narbonne and president of the Estates of Languedoc, received the king's expression of gratitude when the capitation was finally adopted.[65] Both Mitard and Guéry speculate that Saint-Simon blamed Basville for inventing the capitation because of this expression of royal gratitude to the Estates of Languedoc where Basville was intendant.

The letter to the intendants preceded by two weeks the opening of discussions within the Royal Council of Finances on November 13, 1694. Pontchartrain knew that a new tax was about to be adopted but he could not be too detailed in his description of its forms, except to say that it would be based on status rather than wealth. Louis XIV called for further discussion of the capitation in the Royal Council on November 16 and 23 before the government chose to adopt a head tax instead of a tax on wealth.[66] Apparently, the controller general's opinion had prevailed. From November 23, 1694, until January 15, 1695, the Royal Council worked to establish the exact level of taxation by dividing society into twenty-two classes with taxes ranging from two thousand livres to one livre. The tax was to be called a capitation rather than a subvention as had been proposed. The major problem delaying its final adoption was the question of whether or not to tax the clergy.[67] The clergy was entirely exempt from paying the capitation, but they did pay 4 million livres annually as a subsidy during every year the capitation existed (from 1695 until April 1698).[68] It never raised more than 30 million livres in one year and only produced 59 million livres during its entire existence.[69]

The declaration[70] that established the capitation is an apologetic document that explains the causes of the war, along with the history of financial measures undertaken by the government to finance the war up until that point, and measures that the government used to avoid burdening the people, such as creating offices or selling rentes. It goes on to explain that the new tax, the capitation, would not require financiers, would not pay any remises (expenses to the financiers), and would expire three months after the declaration of peace. After the intendants, with the assistance of local officials, drew up rolls of the capitation, each person was required to pay the capitation in two installments, half on March 1 and the other half on June 1 of every year. Attached to the end of the declaration is the list of people who would pay the capitation, beginning with the first class (which would pay two thousand livres) and proceeding through each of the twenty-two classes by title to the last class, which paid only one livre. The declaration concludes with a statement that recognizes the fact that the capitation seemed to be an attack on the privileged orders, and states that the crown did not see this law as an attack on the privileges of the orders, which the crown would always recognize and support.

While the capitation, by recognizing different categories of taxpayers, would seem to have reinforced the ideas people had about societal organization, it failed to collect the expected 50 million livres per annum because many taxpayers either would not pay or could not afford the tax that they were asked to pay. The government confessed, when it renewed the capitation in March 1701, on the eve of the War of the Spanish Succession, that the capitation had not produced the revenues expected from each individual as levied in the classes that had been established in 1695.

The capitation as renewed in March 1701 was a different kind of tax, one that apportioned taxes in a manner similar to the taille.[71] Under the new system, taillables paid a capitation that was related to the amount they contributed to the taille. Non-taillables were to pay amounts based on estimates of their wealth made by the provincial intendant in conjunction with other members of the group to be taxed. In effect, the capitation had become a tax on estimated wealth. One person from the nobility in each election was to assist the intendant, and the various corporations of officers were to apportion among themselves the amount each member was to pay. The intendant and the leaders of the corporate bodies negotiated the total to be paid by the corporate body. Noblemen paid their capitation directly to the receiver particular, while taillables paid the collectors. Officers in the various corporations paid their capitation to the officer charged with paying their gages, and he transferred the funds to the Royal Treasury. In effect, the government had retreated from taxing individuals directly to taxing corporate entities, which would then apportion the amount to be paid by individual members.

After beginning as a prominent effort to circumvent the traditional methods by which the French monarchy raised revenues, the capitation became an adjunct to the taille in 1701. Its apportionment was based, for most Frenchmen, on the amount of one's share of the taille. Nonetheless, the capitation did require that those Frenchmen not subject to the taille contribute something. Unfortunately, the privileged orders were reluctant taxpayers who made tax collection difficult. Officers refused to pay the capitation if their gages had not been paid, a situation that became more common as the War of the Spanish Succession dragged on. The government had to grant frequent discharges to avoid embarrassing great families who claimed to be unable to pay. For example, Desmaretz granted a request from the Duke of Mortemart, his cousin by marriage, for a reduction in the amount of his capitation from that of a duke to that of a first gentleman of the King's Chamber, because the duke pleaded poverty on account of the expenses he had undertaken to serve in the army.[72]

The government's desperate need for money led to a declaration in 1705 that augmented everyone's capitation by 10 percent, or 2 sous per livre.[73] Similar increases had already been legislated for the farms and the taille. The government depended on the capitation and the 10 percent increase to raise 32 million livres.[74]

The royal government, by 1708, had borrowed money beyond any reasonable hope of repayment. The mints, farms, receivers general of finances,

Table 1.3. Debts owed in February 1708.

For the new mint bills reformed in 1707	72,000,000
Bills of the General Farmers and receivers general	54,435,825
Unreformed mint bills held by various treasurers	9,570,248
Bills of the subfarmers of the *aides*	7,200,000
Promises of the gabelles	60,453,760
Bills of the Treasurers of the Extraordinary of War and his adjuncts for 1706 and 1707	61,705,827
Interest owed on all of the above	27,991,665
Unacquitted ordonnances owed by various treasurers	102,366,833
Revenue for 1708 consumed in advance	54,833,833
Revenue for 1709, 1710, 1711, and 1712 consumed in advance	14,286,670
Loan from Genoa	2,000,000
Debt owed to Bernard for loans made to maintain the army	11,000,000
Debt owed to the Hogguer brothers for loans made in 1706 to maintain the army in Italy	5,000,000
Total debts	482,844,661
Estimated funds needed for 1708	202,788,354
Total needed	685,633,015

Source: Desmaretz, *Compte rendu,* in Boislisle and Brotonne, *Correspondance des contrôleurs généraux,* 3:673.

treasurers of the navy and the extraordinary of war, the clergy, and a vast number of private individuals had extended their credit for the government. When Nicolas Desmaretz became controller general of finances in February of that year, he discovered a practically bankrupt government. Table 1.3 shows the exact condition of France's finances and reveals a long list of debts.

The only assured revenue available from the various sources was 20,388,338 livres. Desmaretz was faced with an apparently impossible task. Louis XIV told Desmaretz when he appointed him controller general that he did not expect the impossible. He would not blame Desmaretz if the situation worsened, and would be grateful if it improved.[75] What he did not say is that he had turned to a man he had once dismissed from his government on suspicion of taking graft because he was well connected to the financial establishment of France and because everyone in that establishment had confidence in his abilities to revive France's finances.

The Financiers

The fisco-financial system as described required men with the financial means to support the various contracts to collect the government's revenues. These men would have to have the means to pay the crown regularly every month or quarter, regardless of the pace of revenue collection. These men were servants of the crown whose reward was profit rather than honor and promotion. While much has been made of the difference between the *noblesse d'épée* and the *noblesse de robe*—the hereditary nobility who claimed descent from France's ancient warrior class, as opposed to the royal servants who gained nobility via service in the royal judiciary or bureaucracy—these financiers represented another kind of nobility in the service of the crown. This nobility served the crown by providing money to support the government.

The financiers, despite their ill repute in society, ranked fairly high in terms of legal status, as the capitation of 1695 reveals. Within the hierarchy of nobility of service the table of ranks for the capitation drawn up by the Royal Council of Finances at all levels placed the financiers below the noblesse d'epée, noblesse de plume, and noblesse de robe (in that order), but above the commoners. For example, in the first class that paid 2,000 livres—including the Dauphin and other princes of the blood, the chancellor, the head of the Royal Council of Finances, the secretaries of state, and the controller general of finances—the last four groups mentioned are the keepers of the Royal Treasury, the treasurers of the Extraordinary of War, the treasurers of the navy, and the general farmers. While the twentieth class started with a variety of junior officers, guards, and archers, followed by seigneurial judges and lawyers, it then listed the treasurer collectors of Languedoc, keepers of the taille rolls, fiscal procurers, and clerks in the presidial courts, controllers of the farms, and others. In a rank-conscious society the financiers had a rank beneath the warriors and judges but above the common workers.[76]

While the term "financier" can imply anyone who lends money, we are concerned here only with those moneylenders who were important enough to lend money to the crown. These men could be receivers general of finances, general farmers, or traitants. They had proven their ability to raise funds for the crown and were able to insinuate themselves into the government because they were useful. Another group of financiers consisted of those officials whose duty it was to pay out royal money, such as the treasurers of the Extraordinary of War or other royal treasurers. While the latter were not sources for revenue, some were important enough to lend significant credit to the crown, such as the treasurers of the Extraordinary of War, whose loans in 1706 and 1707 amounted to more than 60 million livres. These royal financiers signed leases or résultats with the King's Council. Daniel Dessert has estimated that between 1653 and 1720 there were only 3,000 such people in all of France, including 201 receivers general of finances, 264 general farmers, and 693 traitants. These categories, however, were not mutually exclusive. A financier might hold the position of receiver general of finances while he was also investing in government contracts to supply munitions or to sell offices; financial endeavors were not limited to one field. By combining receivers general, general farmers, and only those traitants who signed at least 10 résultats for extraordinary affairs, Dessert reduced the total to 534 men whom he calls the principal financiers. He based his evidence, however, on the chambres de justice of 1661–65 and 1716–17. The former investigated the period before 1661, and the latter the years 1688–1715. Dessert admits, therefore, that the period between 1661 and 1688 is only partially known.[77]

A chambre de justice was an extraordinary court established to investigate the activities of financiers and officeholders during a preceding war or time of difficulty. It usually resulted in the abolishment of offices judged to be illegal or unnecessary, a reduction in interest rates on loans, and the pursuit of financiers for excess profits. In addition to shaking down the financial community, a chambre de justice was both a political instrument to distract public attention by blaming economic difficulties on the men under investigation, and a subterfuge for declaring bankruptcy by reneging on debts. Henri IV used chambres de justice several times (1597, 1601–2, 1605, and 1607). The Estates General of 1614 had asked that these kinds of courts be set up every ten years, but the government of Louis XIII did not follow this recommendation. Once France entered the Thirty Years' War as an active combatant, however, chambres de justice were held in 1635, 1643, 1648, and 1656. Colbert launched a grand inquisition from 1661 until 1665 into the financiers who had supported the royal government from 1635 until 1661, including Foucquet's supporters, but his nephew Desmaretz later wrote that the chambre de justice aroused such suspicions and fears among the financiers that his uncle needed several years to persuade them to cease worrying about any investigations into their activities ever again. The chambre de justice that existed during 1716–17 following the death of Louis XIV was the last court of its kind in the Old Regime. It was too crude an instrument to be used in a society that was increasingly dependent on credit.[78]

Contemporaries saw the financiers as a sort of deviant group, somewhat immoral if not to say unchristian (i.e., Protestant or Jewish), or possibly foreign, who had become wealthy through nefarious means. The stereotypical financier who had begun his working life as a lackey or a peasant formed such an important part of the popular cultural beliefs of the time that Alain-René Lesage described the financier Turcaret in his play of the same name as having begun his career as a lackey, while in *Les Agioteurs*

Florent Carton Dancourt's financier, Trapolin, begins as a peasant.[79] Aristocrats like Saint-Simon and social reformers like Vauban found financiers distasteful, upsetting the social balance and interfering in their plans for reforming society.

Dessert, however, has stated categorically that, in his research on the financiers during the reign of Louis XIV, he has not found a single man who fits the stereotype.[80] Of the 534 principal financiers, 495 began their careers holding some sort of charge, either a commission or an office. Out of that group, 422 claimed some title of nobility, including 30 who claimed descent from the nobility of the sword. Out of 275 families, 272 were French. Out of every 20 families, 19 were Catholic. Most came from those provinces where either war or government was important—Paris, Champagne, Burgundy, Loire, the Midi, or Lyon. In any case, they all began their careers by performing some sort of financial service for the nobility or the crown. They did not concentrate on one area of investment, although François Berthelot monopolized the supply of gunpowder to the army, and Pierre Reich de Pennautier concentrated his activities in Languedoc and southern France. They would often manage the estates of some important person at court, where they mixed their own personal fortunes with that of the owner to make both sides wealthy. The most successful financiers eventually bought offices such as those of receiver general of finances, treasurer, secretary on the King's Council, clerk on the royal council, or possibly even judges on a superior court of some kind. In short, they were not outsiders but products of the society in which they lived.

An example of a typical financier who will be discussed at length later is Paul Poisson de Bourvalais, a Breton whose father and grandfather had been notaries in Laval. Bourvalais began working in finances as a commis to Jean Thévenin the elder, who became acquainted with Pontchartrain when the latter was first president of the Parlement of Brittany. Bourvalais struck out on his own in 1687 and married a chamberwoman named Suzanne Guihou in the household of the Marquis de Sourches; her brothers and nephews would make their fortunes supporting Bourvalais. His real rise in royal finances began when Pontchartrain became controller general of finances in late 1689. Between 1690 and 1709 Bourvalais signed 161 traités, more than anyone else, making him the *chef de file*, or most important, of the traitants. In 1697 he was the sole caution for a traité to sell the officers of controllers of the marriage bans, with a forfait of 3.6 million livres. He also invested in royal tax farms and contracted to supply the army and navy. He became a secrétaire du roi in 1695 and secretary on the Conseil des finances and keeper of the archives of the council in 1710. In 1716 the chambre de justice taxed him 4.4 million livres, a sum that he was able to reduce by negotiations, after which he was allowed to keep 450,000 livres.[81]

The financiers generally worked together in groups, with their names often appearing on the same contracts as cautions supporting a similar prête-nom. Their finances were often interconnected, as they lent each other money to purchase land or offices, to provide dowries for daughters, or for other, undescribed purposes. Dessert writes that searching these contracts to uncover information about the financiers' sources of wealth would be a fruitless enterprise, not only because the purpose behind such loans was often left unstated, but also because go-betweens were frequently used to protect the "better" elements of society from being named as financiers' business partners.[82]

Above all, financiers believed in secrecy. While they lived ostentatiously in order to persuade society that they were rich and well connected, they did not prove to be as wealthy when pressed by the royal courts as they appeared. The financiers did not reveal where their money came from, but, if the accountings for the chambre de justice of 1716–17 can be believed, it is clear that they were not as rich as others assumed. Two-thirds of the 164 financiers taxed by the chambre de justice who provided information on their fortunes were worth somewhere between 400,000 and 1 million livres. But being a financier, in itself, was not a guarantee of wealth: almost one-fifth of those listed by the chambre de justice died either poor or in difficult circumstances. Many went bankrupt or left vacant legacies that no one would claim because of the debts assigned them.[83]

Some financiers went bankrupt before the royal courts investigated them. For example, one of the two treasurers of the Extraordinary of War, Charles Renouard de la Touanne, died of a stroke (apoplexy, as it was called at the time) in June 1701 at his chateau at Champs-sur-Marne on the day it was announced that he and his business partner, Jean de Sauvion, were going to be arrested and put in the Bastille. Renouard de la Touanne had begun his career as a commis to Colbert before he succeeded his father as a secrétaire du roi in 1670. That same year he became a receiver general of finances for Orléans, a position he gave up in 1685 when he became treasurer general of the Extraordinary of War. He was involved in some financial affairs and invested in overseas trade as well as the General Farms. The War of the League of Augsburg bankrupted him, forcing the government to arrest him and seize his property in an effort to settle his debts. He owed a total of 10.2 million livres—400,000 to the crown and the rest to private lenders. He and his partner only had 6 million livres' worth of assets to back these loans. His death on the eve of the War of the Spanish Succession was not a good omen for French finances.[84]

The absence of great fortunes in the hands of the financiers led Dessert to postulate that these men were simply go-betweens or *arbitrageurs*, to use a modern term. Like modern stockbrokers, financiers used their connections to really wealthy families in France to enhance their personal importance as intermediaries between the members of France's social and political elite and the financial market, where the bargaining took place and the deals were made. Dessert's speculation is more than a guess. His work on Mazarin's fortune and Foucquet's story, when added to a host of other recent scholarship,[85] has pointed to the fact that the fisco-financial system that supported the monarchy and its policies was actually a mass of interlocking financial interests where the elite were able to invest in the crown's business and amass huge fortunes. Mazarin's fortune at his death was the largest private fortune in Europe. Colbert and the other ministers who ran the government in the aftermath of Mazarin's death were not as shameless in their pursuit of personal aggrandizement as Mazarin had been. Yet, Colbert was able to establish his family's fortune because he controlled access to many different kinds of government contracting.

The appearance of paper money in the form of promissory notes, assignations, and unpaid quittances led to the involvement of bankers in royal finances. Bankers made their living by transferring money from one place to another in the form of *lettres de change.* They enjoyed their greatest involvement in royal finances during the War of the Spanish Succession, at least until the near collapse of Samuel Bernard in 1709.[86]

Bernard was reputedly the wealthiest man in Europe during the last thirty years of the reign of Louis XIV. The sources of his fortune have always been believed to be his connections to the Protestant refugees after the revocation of the Edict of Nantes, as well as to the Protestant banking community in Europe. At the time of his marriage in 1681 he was a simple Protestant merchant in Paris, with very few important witnesses in attendance at his wedding. He converted to Catholicism in December 1685, two months after the revocation of the Edict of Nantes. Under the protection of Pontchartrain, he engaged in finance, signing fourteen traités during the War of the League of Augsburg as well as supplying grain during the aftermath of the terrible winter of 1693–94. As a banker, Bernard was engaged in supplying specie for France's armies outside of France, as well as supplying funds for France's embassies and secret expenses. He abandoned finance to concentrate on banking in 1700. He was a deputy to the Council of Commerce, a founder (along with Antoine Crozat)[87] of the French Compagnie des Indes and the South Seas Company, and sold slaves in the French and Spanish colonies under the asiento after 1701. Bernard emerged relatively unscathed from the War of the Spanish Succession, during which he continued to supply grain to France and specie for the French military and embassies abroad, although Desmaretz heavily protected him when he nearly foundered in 1709.[88]

Financiers, including bankers, carried the weight of and collected the profits derived from Louis XIV's foreign and domestic policies. They built the canals, improved the roads, supplied money for Vauban's fortifications and Pontchartrains's navy as well as his colonial enterprises, and provided the supplies for France's armies during the wars that scarred the end of Louis XIV's reign. The policymakers who negotiated with them, above all the controller general of finances, knew of their troubles and weaknesses at the end of the reign. With bankruptcy either imminent or concealed for many of France's financial institutions and supporters, the government needed new sources of revenue and sought new ideas about where to find them.

Chapter 2

The Rise of the Administrative Monarchy

The King's Council

Louis XIV's reign marked the emergence of a new system of conciliar government that would endure with some small changes for the rest of the Old Regime until the French Revolution. Under the legal traditions of the Old Regime the king governed France by making law and policy in council. While the king was the source of the law, he could only make law, including tax law, in council. The King's Council was a legal fiction that included a variety of committees and subcommittees. Louis XIV rearranged the King's Council to suit himself so that policymaking only took place on those bodies of the King's Council that he himself attended. This so-called Louisquatorzian Revolution took place in three stages, although only the second would have a direct bearing on the financial administration of the crown.

The first stage took place abruptly on March 9, 1661, upon Cardinal Mazarin's death, which removed the king's mentor from the scene and allowed the king to emerge as his own principal minister. Louis XIV wanted to remove any weaknesses or any persons who might seek to obstruct his ability to govern France himself. He doubted the rigor of affairs handled by Chancellor Pierre Séguier, who was seventy-two years old and had served as chancellor since 1633. Louis saw disorder in the council over which Séguier presided. Ultimately, Séguier would be the last chancellor to share the task of governing royal finances together with the surintendant des finances simply by virtue of his presence on all branches of the King's Council. Even while Séguier was chancellor, Surintendant des Finances Nicolas Foucquet could order expenditures on his signature alone. Mazarin's household intendant, Jean-Baptiste Colbert, had warned the king as early as 1659 that Foucquet was running royal finances for his personal profit. Shortly before his death, Mazarin had elevated Colbert to be one of Foucquet's two intendants of finances in order to keep track of Foucquet's administration.[1]

In his *Mémoires* Louis XIV wrote an evaluation of the men around him at that time. He referred to an informal group of three of them as his Council of Ministers, which he called the *Conseil d'en haut.* These men included

Foucquet; Michel Le Tellier, who had been secretary of state of war for almost twenty years; and Hugues de Lionne, who was de facto foreign minister, although Henri-Auguste Loménie de Brienne held the title of secretary of state of foreign affairs.[2] Significantly, Chancellor Séguier was excluded from this group. Louis also excluded his mother, Anne of Austria, much to her surprise. She had sat on this council since May 1643, when she became regent, and thereafter while Mazarin lived. He also excluded other members of his family, in addition to great noblemen and ecclesiastics. The Council of Ministers would meet thereafter two or three times a week, its members summoned by simple royal invitations.

And although Chancellor Séguier did not belong to this group, other chancellors would later sit on the Conseil d'en haut during the next fifty-four and a half years of Louis XIV's reign. Le Tellier would become chancellor in 1677, Pontchartrain in 1699, and Daniel-François Voysin upon Pontchartrain's resignation in 1714. All three of these men, however, had already been members of the Council of Ministers when they were elevated to the chancellorship. While their appointment to the chancellorship confirmed their knowledge of state procedures, their membership on the Conseil d'en haut was in recognition of Louis' opinion of their wisdom. Besides Séguier, two other chancellors during Louis XIV's reign would never sit on the Council of Ministers: Étienne d'Aligre, who became keeper of the seals in 1672, following Séguier's death, and chancellor in 1674; and Louis Boucherat, who succeeded Le Tellier in 1685. (After Séguier's death there were rumors that Louis XIV was going to abolish the office of chancellor as he had the offices of constable and admiral.)[3]

The second stage of Louis XIV's reordering of the government took place only six months after the first, in September 1661. Since this measure was the most important of the three, however, we will return to it after a brief discussion of the third stage in Louis' program, the regulation of January 3, 1673, which restricted membership on the Council of State (*Conseil d'État*) to twenty-one ordinary councilors of state. Of these councilors, only three would be from the sword nobility (*conseillers d'état d'épée*) and three would be clergy (*conseillers d'état d'église*). The king selected all the councilors of state, including twelve "semester councilors," who served for only half the year. Other officials having *entrée* into the King's Council of State were the chancellor, the controller general of finances, the intendants of finances, four secretaries of state, and the head (*chef*) of the Royal Council of Finances. Also, the dean (i.e., senior) master of requests had the right to sit on the council for the whole year, while the other masters of requests sat only during the quarter-year they were on duty, unless granted entrée by the chancellor. Except for minor changes after 1760, this regulation fixed the membership on the Council of State until the French Revolution.[4]

The regulation of January 3, 1673, following Séguier's death, reduced the Council of State to hearing legal cases on appeal from other royal courts. The chancellor could preside over this council, defined as the *Conseil des parties* or *Conseil d'État privé.* Every person with the title of secretary of state, controller general of finances, director or intendant of finances, councilor of state, or master of requests had the right to sit on the Council of State with the chancellor. It met twice a week in the *Salle du Conseil* in the royal palace. By this regulation Louis XIV sought to end the disordered way in which council business was conducted while Séguier was alive.[5]

The Council of State also met twice a week as the *Conseil d'État et des Finances,* the latest evolution of the Conseil des Finances that had appeared in the sixteenth century. During these meetings the council considered cases involving disputes between individuals and communities about taxation and royal money, in an attempt to regularize policies that had already been adopted elsewhere.[6]

Prior to Louis XIV's personal rule, a subcommittee of the Council of State called the *Grande Direction des Finances* was responsible for making financial policy. It prepared matters for discussion in the full council. It was a restricted group dominated by either the chancellor or the surintendant des finances. All of the other financial officers of the council, including the controllers general, the directors and intendants of finances, the four officers known as secretaries of finances, and the keepers of the Royal Treasury (or the Royal *Épargne,* as it was known before Colbert's ministry), belonged to it. Special letters granted a select number of councilors of state and masters of requests permission to attend meetings of this body. Prior to 1661, the Grande Direction had met twice a week without the king in attendance, to survey all receipts and expenses, set tax levels, grant leases on farms or set terms for other royal contracts, grant permission to local corporations to levy local taxes, and hear all legal cases appealed or evoked to the King's Council involving finances and the crown's interests. In 1661 the creation of the Royal Council of Finances took away most of these responsibilities.[7]

Prior to the regulation of January 3, 1673, Louis XIV implemented the second and most important of his alterations to the royal government: the creation of a council body to advise him on the control of royal finances. After Mazarin's death, Colbert understood the young king better than Foucquet, who still thought he had a chance of succeeding Mazarin as principal minister. Colbert instructed the king on his finances and subtly undermined Foucquet's position. Louis XIV had an innate fear of an all-powerful minister and, on September 5, 1661 (the king's birthday), he had Foucquet arrested. Ten days later, the king suppressed the office of Surintendant des Finances and assumed the powers of the office himself.[8] Although previous kings had suppressed the office of Surintendant des Finances only to have a successor recreate the office, Louis XIV's suppression turned out to be permanent.

The regulation of September 15, 1661, created a new council called the Royal Council of Finances (*Conseil royal des finances*) to advise the king on financial matters. It was to consist of an official called the *chef* (head) and three councilors of state, one of whom was to be an intendant of finances. The chancellor could attend meetings of the Royal Council, as it was called, but only if invited by the king.[9] The intendant of finances who sat on the Royal Council in September 1661 was Colbert. Four years later, on December 12, 1665, Colbert was commissioned as controller general of finances, and thereafter attended in that capacity, as did his successors.[10]

The seventeen articles of the regulation of September 15, 1661, also describe the organization and duties of the Royal Council, which was established to be the chief policymaking body in interior affairs involving the royal domain, taxes, tax farms, commerce, and all revenue sources. The Conseil d'en haut was thus relieved of these duties. Under Louis XIV the Royal Council met twice a week, except when the king was away. In the last part of the reign, when Louis was at his private residence at Marly, the Royal Council only met on Tuesdays. By meeting eighty or so times a year, the Royal Council became relatively equal to the Conseil d'en haut, which met two or three times weekly, and superior to the Council of Dispatches, which languished as the reign progressed.[11]

The king reserved for himself the power to sign all financial ordonnances concerning expenses made by the accountables, as well as all documents concerning remises, interest on loans, and other expenses. The intendant of finances (later the controller general) was to assist him in administering the Royal Treasury and keeping registers of receipts and expenses. The intendant would report on all accounts of the farms, *bois* (woodlands), domains, and other receipts. The king would then give him orders to transmit to the proper officials. He was not to communicate the information contained in the royal registers to anyone without the king's express orders. He was also to cosign all ordonnances with the king before communicating them to the proper financial officers.

Colbert and his successors were supposed to report all accounts of the farms, receivers general of finances, bois, domains, and extraordinary affairs, as well as other receipts, to the Royal Council of Finances to be confirmed (*arrêtés*) and signed by the king and the members of the Royal Council. The one, specific duty assigned to Colbert as sole reporter was to begin each meeting by introducing for discussion a report on one account from the farms, receivers general, etc., for examination by the Royal Council, which would then determine any obstacles to achieving maximum efficiency in the receipt of revenues, as well as ways to increase those revenues. Any requests for employment in new offices were also to be reported and resolved in the Royal Council.

The chancellor attended this council's meetings to help decide matters requiring his signature, such as brevets of the taille, any arrêt imposing taxes, any sign to be posted listing the terms of leases on the farms determined by the Royal Council and granted by the Grande Direction, traités on extraordinary affairs, arrêts accepting loans, rolls of the Royal Treasury and other accountables (the accountables could attend these sessions as well), and any diminution granted to the farms or royal taxes. All arrêts and expeditions of the Royal Council were to be signed by all of its members.

The head (*chef*) of the Royal Council also had specific duties. He sat on all branches of the King's Council, in the place formerly occupied by the Surintendant des Finances. His chief duty was to chair meetings of a subcommittee of the King's Council called the *Petite Direction des Finances*, which included all members of the Royal Council as well as all intendants of finances and the controller general of finances. The chancellor was specifically excluded from this group. The Petite Direction examined ways to increase the king's ordinary revenues and to enforce the receipt of these funds more efficiently at the Royal Treasury. All decisions of the Petite Direction were reported to the Grande Direction for final approval.[12] During the reign of Louis XIV the heads of the Royal Council were dukes and peers: Nicolas de Neufville, maréchal-duc de Villeroy (1661–85); Paul de Saint-Aignan, duc de Beauvillier (1685–1714); and François de Neufville, maréchal-duc de Villeroy (1714–30).

The creation of the Royal Council of Finances in September 1661 further reduced the chancellor's authority. Excluded from the Conseil d'en haut in March, he now served as a member of the Royal Council only when invited to attend. The administration of ordinary revenues was in the hands of the Petite Direction (from which the chancellor was excluded), and only subject to review by the Grande Direction. The chancellor served as chairman of this committee, where his influence was reduced to approving or rejecting recommendations of the Petite Direction. As it turned out, the restriction of the chancellor's authority was limited to Séguier alone, because all of his successors sat on the Royal Council of Finances, including Le Tellier and Voysin, neither of whom had been a member of this body before appointment to the chancellorship.

After 1665 the controller general of finances became the prime mover in the details of financial and commercial administration. He sat on all council bodies and could remove matters from discussion if he felt they were too important to be discussed outside the Royal Council of Finances.[13] He thus directed the discussion of policy. The chancellor lost the power to name masters of requests to report important financial matters, because the controller general had to report all such matters to the Royal Council.[14]

A set of subcommittees or bureaus of the King's Council was created to prepare legal matters before the entire council heard them. Some of these bureaus were concerned with finances. After Séguier's death in 1672 a series of arrêts issued in the Royal Council created special bureaus to handle

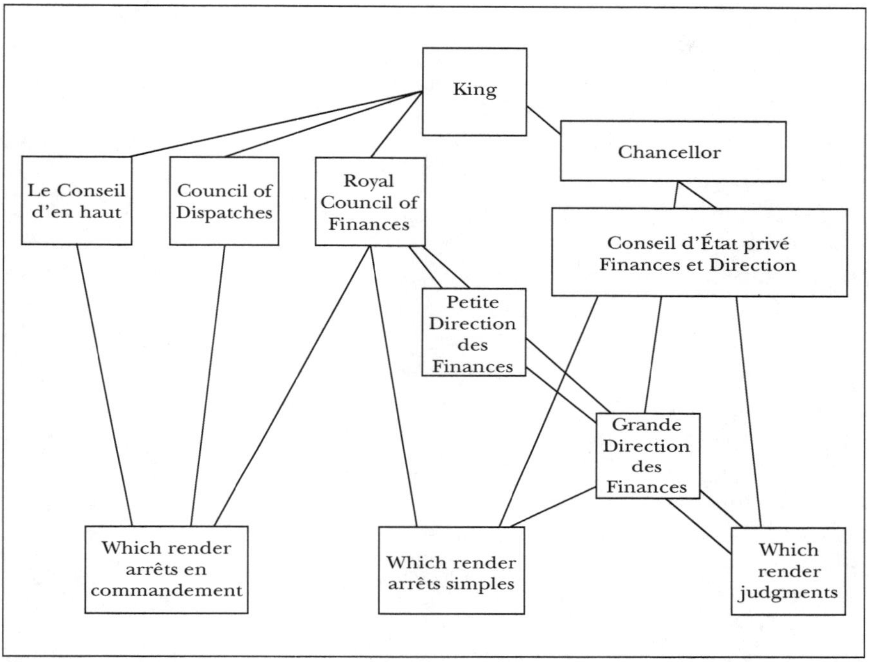

Figure 2.1. The King's Council. As reorganized by Louis XIV, the council would remain unchanged except for the disappearance of the Conseil d'État privé Finances et Direction sometime in the latter part of the seventeenth century.

legal cases on a variety of affairs, such as the control of *francfiefs* (a tax owed by commoners who acquired noble land) and *amortissements* (amortization of debts), the farms, rentes, domain, aides, traites, and debts owed by the towns and communities of the realm.[15] Colbert was attempting to impose order on the way in which the council handled royal finances. He had a prominent role in selecting members for these bureaus.

Most of these committees gradually came under the chairmanship of Colbert's uncle, Henri Pussort, who also had become a member of the Royal Council of Finances when d'Aligre became keeper of the seals in April 1672.[16] Pussort was a stern lawyer who had assisted Colbert's efforts in the 1660s to squeeze the profiteers upon whom Foucquet had relied. Pussort gradually rose to head all of these bureaus and was the dean (i.e., senior) member of the council of state when he died on February 18, 1697.[17] No other councilor of state ever held as much authority over finances as Pussort.

Pussort's death led to a series of efforts to reform the council's handling of finances, in much the same way that Séguier's death had done in 1672. Suggestions for reform were circulated among members of the Royal Council.[18] The result was a consolidation of all of the bureaus into two: one to hear all cases involving the domain, and the other to hear cases involving the gabelles, traites, and aides.[19] Five years later, another reorganization replaced the newly created bureaus with two new ones: one heard cases involving the aides and the domain, while the other heard cases involving the gabelles, traites, taille, and other financial affairs. The bureaus of financial affairs would remain essentially unchanged from that moment until 1787.[20]

Councilors of state and masters of requests permanently staffed these two bureaus and were by chosen by the controller general of finances, who could also serve on the bureaus, along with selected intendants of finances and the two councilors of state on the Royal Council. Members of these bureaus received an extra salary for their work. Whenever members of these bureaus died or became unable to perform their duties because of health problems or absence in the provinces, the controller general was literally besieged by requests to fill the vacant seats.[21]

Other bureaus of the council handled matters that were tangentially related to finances, such as the bureau of the *postes* and *messageries*, the bureau that researched titles of nobility, and the bureau for the sale or repurchase of the domain. Their staffs were also permanent but much smaller than those of the committees that heard financial cases.[22]

Alongside the more or less permanent bureaus of the council existed extraordinary commissions, which the council created to perform specific functions. Once their assigned tasks were complete, the extraordinary commissions ceased to exist. Because contemporaries often used the term "bureau" to refer to both commissions and bureaus, there is some confusion about the difference between them.[23] Every bureau or commission of the King's Council submitted its decisions to the entire council for final approval. The bureaus that judged financial affairs, however, submitted their judgments to the Grande Direction, but even this decision required final approval by the Royal Council of Finances.[24]

Despite this mass of confusing organizations, some of which sprung up unexpectedly like weeds on the palace lawn, they all existed under the legal umbrella of the theoretical unity of the King's Council. Matters of policy during the reign of Louis XIV, however, were decided on only in those council bodies attended by the king himself. Two councils, the Conseil d'en haut and the Royal Council of Finances, remained vital to policy formation. The Council of Dispatches, a relatively new organization that appeared before the personal rule of Louis XIV, lapsed into near oblivion before being revived shortly before Louis' death. During the reign of Louis XV, it handled the rising problems with the provinces and parlements that confronted the king in the eighteenth century.[25] Under Louis XIV, however, quiescent superior courts and the difficulties of perpetual war raised foreign policy and government funding to preeminence; thus, the Council of Ministers and the Royal Council of Finances became the most important bodies on the King's Council.

The Secret of the King's Council

All council deliberations were conducted in secrecy. At the opening of the first meeting of the Royal Council of Finances in 1661, Louis XIV asked members to take a separate oath and to swear not to divulge the secret of the council:

> The first thing that I desire of you is secrecy; and as I esteem it important and necessary for the good conduct of my affairs, I am very content to tell you that if I learn that someone has said something about what will take place here, I will follow my first instinct in order to oust from my council him who would be capable of such weakness.
>
> And the second is that I want each of us to be charged with the good or bad success of whatever affair, after I have made a decision and given orders, and that everything be executed and supported with firmness, sincerity, and secrecy.[26]

As formulated in the mind of Louis XIV, the doctrine of unity of the council seems to have been a sort of early modern example of democratic centralism. Council members were not to reveal the different opinions expressed within the council; once made, decisions were to be supported. Although Louis XIV was not the first king to espouse this kind of idea, he was no more successful in seeing it implemented than any of his predecessors.

The doctrine of secrecy nonetheless did obscure much that took place in council. The duc de Saint-Simon called the Royal Council of Finances a *paperasserie* (a mountain of administrative papers) in which most of the business consisted of signing and initialing a host of documents. He even reported that the members of the council were often surprised to hear of actions they had supposedly taken.[27] To determine the validity of Saint-Simon's criticism, we must try to peer behind the veil of secrecy surrounding conciliar activities.

In Old Regime legal theory, royal law took several forms as it emerged from the King's Council. The king was sovereign and made law with the advice of his council. A legal ordonnance, not to be confused with a financial ordonnance, was a permanent law covering several subjects. An edict, by contrast, was a permanent law on a single subject, and a declaration was a temporary law or an interpretation of an edict or ordonnance.[28] Such laws had to be decided in the king's presence. In finances, these laws could only be decided in the Royal Council and, thus, were reported by the controller general of finances.

Another kind of decision made in the King's Council appeared publicly as an *arrêt du conseil*, a decision by the king in council that was both sovereign and definitive on a question of law or fact. Arrêts took two forms. An *arrêt en commandement* contained the words "Le Roi Étant en Son Conseil," indicating that the decision was made in the king's presence. A secretary of state signed decisions of this kind and kept the originals in his archives.[29] Louis XIV insisted that no arrêt en commandement could be signed and made public without his explicit order.[30] All arrêts en commandement on financial matters must have been issued from the Royal Council of Finances on the report of the controller general of finances, because Louis XIV did not attend meetings of the Conseil d'État et des Finances or the Grande or Petite Directions.

The other form of arrêt was an *arrêt simple en finance*, which employed the words "Le Roi en Son Conseil" in its formulary. The king did not have to be present at sessions that decided on this kind of arrêt. Therefore, any council body that had jurisdiction over finances could issue an arrêt simple in finances. The secretaries of finances, venal officers who served quarterly, kept the original copies of these decisions, as well as register books that listed the arrêts and the names of the persons who reported them.[31]

The originals of the arrêts simples in finances and the register books can be found in the E series of documents conserved the Archives Nationales in Paris. Table 2.1 compares the number of arrêts simples in finances reported by the controller general to the total number of arrêts reported each year, from 1661 to 1715. If we remember that the controller general was the only official allowed to report matters to the Royal Council and that he did not report matters elsewhere, the significance of the figures shown in this table will be evident. The register books for the years 1661 to 1670 only survive for a quarter of those years, but I have included the count to show how much things changed, beginning in 1672.

The year 1672 is important for two reasons. Chancellor Séguier died in January. His successor, d'Aligre, was more favorable to Colbert and one of the original members of the Royal Council of Finances. The Dutch War, the first major war of Louis XIV's personal rule, also began in this year. The pressure of war finance and the absence of Séguier might explain both the increase in the amount of arrêts during the war (always more than 2,750 annually) and the rising percentage reported by the controller general (from a third to more than half). The Royal Council's role in finances appears to have increased significantly as the demands for money increased.

The Dutch War ended in 1678. Le Tellier was chancellor and apparently attended the Royal Council as if the chancellor had always done so. D'Aligre had been a member of the Royal Council since 1661 and was allowed to retain the right to enter the Royal Council despite his elevation to keeper of the seals and, later, chancellor. Louis XIV trusted Le Tellier and would not have denied him the right to sit on the Royal Council when he became chancellor in 1677. By 1684 his attendance on that body was taken for granted.[32]

Table 2.1. Arrêts simples in finances by reporter, 1661–1715.

Year	Controller General	Percent	Directors	Percent	Masters of Requests	Percent	Total
1661	203	38.96%	0		318	61.04%	521
1662	213	28.36%	0		538	71.64%	751
1663	255	37.78%	0		420	62.22%	675
1664	192	20.71%	0		735	79.29%	927
1665	158	30.21%	0		365	69.79%	523
1670	325	30.69%	0		734	69.31%	1059
1672	935	33.46%	0		1859	66.54%	2794
1673	1145	33.63%	0		2260	66.37%	3405
1674	1487	43.88%	0		1902	56.12%	3389
1675	1842	53.11%	0		1626	46.89%	3468
1676	1581	50.95%	0		1522	49.05%	3103
1677	1088	45.48%	0		1304	54.52%	2392
1678	990	52.94%	0		880	47.06%	1870
1679	1153	57.88%	0		839	42.12%	1992
1680	1093	59.27%	0		751	40.73%	1844
1681	1625	72.84%	0		606	27.16%	2231
1682	1543	73.93%	0		544	26.07%	2087
1683	1144	67.10%	0		561	32.90%	1705
1684	1121	61.22%	0		710	38.78%	1831
1685	1009	61.79%	0		624	38.21%	1633
1686	1078	64.17%	0		602	35.83%	1680
1687	1140	69.77%	0		494	30.23%	1634
1688	1280	68.52%	0		588	31.48%	1868
1689	1164	68.88%	0		526	31.12%	1690
1690	1491	78.06%	0		419	21.94%	1910
1691	1687	82.70%	0		353	17.30%	2040
1692	2419	87.64%	0		341	12.36%	2760
1693	3269	92.95%	0		248	7.05%	3517
1694	2924	91.89%	0		258	8.11%	3182
1695	2633	91.74%	0		237	8.26%	2870
1696	2804	90.98%	0		278	9.02%	3082
1697	2803	93.25%	0		203	6.75%	3006

(continued)

Table 2.1. *(concluded)*

Year	Controller General	Percent	Directors	Percent	Masters of Requests	Percent	Total
1698	3438	94.71%	0		192	5.29%	3630
1699	2839	92.84%	0		219	7.16%	3058
1700	3020	93.38%	0		214	6.62%	3234
1701	1966	63.93%	897	29.17%	212	6.89%	3075
1702	863	27.86%	2070	66.82%	165	5.33%	3098
1703	982	30.08%	2126	65.11%	157	4.81%	3265
1704	1385	38.67%	2070	57.79%	127	3.55%	3582
1705	1447	42.42%	1849	54.21%	115	3.37%	3411
1706	1350	41.72%	1777	54.91%	109	3.37%	3236
1707	1312	48.15%	1331	48.84%	82	3.01%	2725
1708	2458	88.93%	155	5.61%	151	5.46%	2764
1709	2602	95.73%	0		116	4.27%	2718
1710	2793	97.01%	0		86	2.99%	2879
1711	2833	97.82%	0		63	2.18%	2896
1712	2536	97.31%	0		70	2.69%	2606
1713	2467	98.33%	0		42	1.67%	2509
1714	2542	98.00%	0		52	2.00%	2594
1715	1860	97.03%	0		57	2.97%	1917

Note: See A.N. E 1683^{29-187} for the register books, and E 348^{B}–879 for the originals of the arrêts simples for Louis XIV's reign, from September 1661 to September 1715. Some cross-checking was necessary to ensure accuracy. There are lacunae in the registry books. For the Colbert era the register books for the last quarters of the years 1661 through 1665 and 1670 survive. The series really begins in 1673. The first quarter of each year is missing until 1687. There are gaps for the second quarter of 1689, the first half of 1694, the first quarter of 1708, and the last quarter of 1712. I filled these gaps by counting the originals of the arrêts.

There are several possible reasons for the increased percentage of arrêts in finances reported by the controller general and the consequent decrease in those reported by masters of requests. With the chancellor attending the meetings of all the council bodies that governed royal finances except the Petite Direction and the various bureaus, we can wonder how jealously he conserved his authority to assign matters to the masters of requests for reporting. Colbert, a former assistant to Le Tellier and now a power in his own right, would not cede his authority over financial matters to his former master. The Conseil d'État et des Finances, where the masters of requests reported all matters for discussion, began meeting less regularly after the creation of the Royal Council.[33]

After the Dutch War the number of arrêts in finances remained relatively low (around 2,000 annually), but the controller general's share increased to almost three-quarters by Colbert's death in September 1683. Le Peletier's ministry was characterized by fewer arrêts (around 1,750 annually) and a slight decline (to less than 70 percent) in the controller general's share of the total. During this period, Chancellor Le Tellier died in 1685 and was replaced by another member of the Royal Council, Louis Boucherat. Boucherat may have regarded the other council groups that had jurisdiction in financial matters as less important. He was also described as a man of mediocre ability.[34]

The Conseil d'État et des Finances ceased meeting altogether sometime between 1687 and 1697–99, while Boucherat was Chancellor. A regulation of the council dated June 17, 1687, mentions it. The renewal of war in 1688 could explain the increasing number of arrêts in finances (to as much as 3,500 annually and never fewer than 2,900), as well as the increasing share of the controller general (to more than 90 percent) in reporting them. Pussort's death in 1697 removed an important personality from the Royal Council, and Colbert's last influence on finances. The mémoires on how to manage finances that circulated within government circles after Pussort's demise do not even mention the Conseil d'État et des Finances. Neither does *L'État de France,* which began appearing annually in 1698, nor *L'Almanach royal,* which first appeared in 1699.[35] By then the Council of State and Finances had ceased meeting at all. The sharp increase in both the number of arrêts in finances and the percentage reported by the controller general between 1688 and 1693 seems to point to 1693 as the year the Conseil d'État et des Finances finally disappeared.[36] The bureaus and the Petite and Grande Directions had become subordinate to the Royal Council, which now approved all their measures, accounting for the small percentage of arrêts reported by someone other than the controller general.

One other possible explanation for the disappearance of this council body was the increased role in the government undertaken by the king himself. After the death of Louvois in July 1691 and the appointment of his twenty-three-year-old son, Barbezieux, as his successor, Louis XIV assumed larger responsibilities within his government. Barbezieux was reduced to being in charge of military supplies, while Louis XIV, with the support of Chamlay, guided tactics and strategy from Versailles. By splitting Louvois' functions as director general of fortifications with Souzy and his duties as surintendant des bâtiments with Édouard Colbert de Villacerf (and his successors), the king now met with three separate officials rather than discussing matters with one man, as had been the case while Louvois lived.

Jean-Christian Petitfils says that Louis XIV really took personal control of his government after the death of Louvois in 1691. He describes the period from 1661 to 1691 as a time when the king allowed powerful ministers like Colbert and Louvois to manage the government directly while he oversaw them. After 1691 Louis XIV directly managed his government, reading dispatches, and dictating responses to a greater degree than he had previously done.[37]

The king worked as much as eight or nine hours a day administering France, and might have decided that he did not need an extraneous body like the Conseil d'État et des Finances. Instead, he might have allowed his finance minister to assume almost total responsibility for managing the crown's finances as well as any disputes that might have arisen over taxes and spending. He might have been in agreement with his controller general (probably Pontchartrain) to reduce the number of unnecessary meetings because of the pressures of war and finances.

The years 1701 to 1708 saw the brief resurrection of two offices of director of finances. Both directors entered the Royal Council to report matters as administrative assistants to the controller general. Michel Chamillard became controller general of finances in September 1699. When Louvois' son Barbezieux died in January 1701, Louis XIV named Chamillard secretary of state for war. In order to assist the beleaguered minister, the king had the offices of directors of finances created in June 1701.[38] Desmaretz later suppressed these offices when he became controller general in February 1708.[39] When the share of arrêts reported by the directors of finances during this period are added to those reported by the controller general, the share of arrêts reported by all three men rose to more than 95 percent.

During Desmaretz's ministry the number of arrêts simples in finances hovered between 2,500 and 2,900 annually. Nonetheless, the controller general's share of the amount reported climbed to more than 98 percent. The controller general of finances then dominated the communication of financial matters to the council. He reported more than 98 percent of all arrêts simples, in addition to all arrêts en commandement, declarations, edicts, and ordonnances. By virtue of his duty to bring all accounts to the Royal Council, he controlled the information that served as the basis for all the council's decisions. He corresponded with provincial intendants, governors, and local officials on a wide variety of subjects. His ministry was the central axis of the monarchy in finances. He superseded the chancellor in financial matters.

There is a single register in the Archives Nationales that records all matters discussed before the Royal Council of Finances during the year 1736.[40] It records 151 separate matters that resulted in 129 arrêts—24 arrêts en commandement and 105 arrêts simples.[41] Michel Antoine has discovered that 545 arrêts en commandement were issued on the report of the controller general that year, and 2,093 arrêts simples.[42] The ratio of arrêts issued to those discussed is better than twenty to one. Antoine believes that in 1736 the arrêt had ceased to represent the result of decisions made in council, and instead had become a decision made within the bureaucracy of the controller general's offices. These decisions were given dates to coincide with meetings of the Royal Council. This phenomenon had actually developed during the ministries of Pontchartrain, Chamillard, and Desmaretz in last half of the personal government of Louis XIV.

Criticism of the controller general's dominance of finances as well as the reduced role of the Royal Council appeared in an anonymous letter written by the duc de Saint-Simon some time between the death of the Duke of Burgundy in February 1712 and the registration of Louis XIV's will in July 1714. Saint-Simon refers to the Royal Council as a vain phantom of its intended purpose. Its members, he says, only learned of decisions they had supposedly made when these decisions were made public.[43]

The abbé de Saint-Pierre, in a description of the King's Council written on July 3, 1702, says that, since the creation of the offices of directors of finances a year earlier, Controller General Chamillard reported very little to the Royal Council.[44] Yet, the register books and arrêts simples in finances in the Archives Nationales for the year 1702 show no fewer than 843 arrêts simples (27.8 percent of the total for the year) as being reported by the controller general.[45] Obviously, decisions were being made in the name of the Royal Council under the signature of both the chancellor and the head of the Royal Council that were not appearing for discussions. (The two councilors of state on the Royal Council who had signed arrêts since the creation of the Royal Council of Finances had ceased doing so in the 1690s.)

The capitation came into existence after months of discussion, among officials and others, as to what form the new tax should take. When the controller general finally brought the issue before the Royal Council for discussion in the presence of the king, the issue was not yet settled. The Royal Council in the mid-1690s was still a viable forum for debating government policy. The pressure of events and the passage of time would blur the memories of contemporaries. Saint-Simon would later say that the capitation was adopted without discussion, and Vauban wrote that it was adopted hastily.[46]

The adoption of the dixième in September–October 1710 was much more rapid and with less input from the Royal Council. In fact, the council barely debated the matter. Desmaretz presented a completed edict on September 30, 1710. It was issued as a royal declaration on October 14 of that same year.[47] The Royal Council was transformed into a formality rather than a forum for discussing policy options sometime between 1695 and 1710. The controller general decided whom to consult and under what conditions. His special access to the king made the Royal Council simply a place to discuss the technicalities of whether the new tax law should be an edict or a declaration but not whether such a tax should be adopted.

Chamillard wrote to Louis XIV on September 17, 1707, describing the deplorable conditions of French finances. He requested that, if Louis XIV insisted that he remain at the controllership general, "that Your Majesty agree to rely on me and to approve everything that I propose, either in discussions with You, or in Your Royal Council, that will have any relation to finances."[48] Although Louis XIV probably chose to ignore the presumptuousness of Chamillard's proposal, the access to the king by the controller general outside the Royal Council gave the minister a special position from which to persuade the king to adopt the minister's point of view.

The concept of the King's Council was deliberately kept undefined in law. The king made law on the advice of his council, but he could call any consultation with a member of his council, or anyone else, a council.[49] Louis XIV was a prudent man who did not make decisions hastily or without consultation. His fear of being dominated by one minister or favorite pushed him to consult a wide variety of people before deciding anything. In addition to his thrice weekly meetings with his Conseil d'en haut, once or twice weekly meetings with his Royal Council of Finances, and once or twice monthly meetings with the Council of Dispatches, he had separate working sessions with individual ministers and officials. He worked twice a week with his secretary of state for war, once a week with the secretary of state for the navy and the Maison du Roi, several times a week with the secretary of state for foreign affairs, twice a week with the controller general of finances, once a week with Souzy as director general of fortifications, once a week with either the superintendent or director of bâtiments, and once a week with his confessor to discuss church matters.[50] He also consulted with generals and military men like Chamlay at irregular but frequent intervals.[51] In addition, Saint-Simon refers to the duc de Chevreuse as a secret minister of state. Chevreuse never attended a council meeting but he had access to state papers and was often seen in private conversations with the king.[52] If the king chose to do so, he could call any of these meetings receiving advice from his council. Yet, all laws were usually dated according to official meetings of the actual council.

Louis XIV controlled access to his person by outsiders on a regular basis. The king of France was supposed to be open and available to receive requests or appeals from any of his subjects. Louis, however, established a rigid routine of meetings with groups of councilors whom he appointed. In addition, he selected who would sit on policymaking bodies such as the Royal Council or the Conseil d'en haut. While he granted audiences to outsiders if appeals were made through someone who could vouch for them at court, the king controlled his agenda and resisted any change in his routine.

Secretary of State for Foreign Affairs Jean-Baptiste Colbert, marquis de Torcy, who was also Desmaretz's cousin, wrote a journal of his activities during the crucial years 1709–11.[53] Torcy had been foreign minister since 1696 and, like Desmaretz, was Colbert's nephew. He did not sit on the Royal Council of Finances. From November 1709 until May 1711, however, he did record discussions and debates among the members of the Conseil d'en haut, which at that time included the king, his son the Dauphin, and his grandson the Duke of Burgundy, as well as Torcy, Desmaretz, the war minister Voysin, Chancellor Pontchartrain, and the head of the Royal Council of Finances, the Duke of Beauvillier. Except for Torcy and Voysin, all of these men also belonged to the Royal Council of Finances.

Torcy probably kept this journal because he recognized the seriousness of the situation for France. Enemies were occupying French soil. Royal finances were in disarray. French armies were demoralized after years of defeat and retreat. Desperate negotiations with the enemy began in 1709 and were renewed in 1710 in a vain attempt to make peace. The Allies (as they were called) demanded that Louis' grandson Felipe V leave the Spanish throne and, if necessary, be chased from it by French armies. Louis XIV agreed to a host of territorial concessions and offered to pay a subsidy to the Allies, but he would not budge on their demands that he use his own troops to remove his grandson from Spain in order to restore the Habsburgs.[54] Torcy does not mention finances except to say that they were in a desperate condition. He kept his journal only to defend his activities in case he was accused of surrendering too much.

During foreign policy discussions Desmaretz promised that money would be available for certain subsidies that might alleviate pressure from the Allies.[55] When two Spanish vessels landed on French soil carrying silver from the New World, Spain insisted that France pay them a 6 percent tax called the *indult.* Desmaretz proposed issuing an arrêt in finances granting France the 6 percent to defray the costs of the three French vessels that had escorted the Spanish ships.[56] Here the Conseil d'en haut, instead of the Royal Council, seemed to be issuing financial decisions. In reality, the minister was proposing a solution without discussion.

One time in November 1710 Louis XIV permitted the Conseil d'en haut to engage in policy discussion concerning foreign trade but Controller General Desmaretz provided the report, not Torcy. In this case, Desmaretz was expressing advice from the Council of Commerce, an advisory body consisting of merchants and town representatives that had been established in 1700. The Council of Commerce usually advised the Royal Council of Finances. Desmaretz read two mémoires from the advisory group, both for and against the cessation of trade with the Dutch.[57]

If the Royal Council of Finances declined in significance during the latter part of Louis XIV's reign, we must determine how the king restrained his finance minister. Financial matters and their administration, as Louis XIV himself said, were considered beneath the dignity of royalty, but he believed that it was his duty to keep track of them. He kept a book in which he recorded all the ordonnances signed by his hand for all the expenses he authorized, as well as a record of all funds received.[58]

One indication of what Louis XIV thought was important would be the restrictions he placed on the King's Council in financial affairs during his absences whenever he departed to lead his armies in the field. A regulation of April 18, 1674, ordered that, while he was away, the Conseil d'État et des Finances and the Grande Direction were to meet as usual under the chairmanship of the chancellor, and the Petite Direction under the chairmanship of the head of the Royal Council of Finances. The chancellor was to convene the Royal Council in his apartment, where they could discuss all extraordinary affairs and traités. They could also certify and sign all accounts of receipts and rolls granting the execution of extraordinary affairs, as well as rolls imposing taxes on officeholders. They were to observe the laws recognizing the sale of new offices. They were also to examine any requests to lower the lease price owed on any new tax farm. The king reserved for himself the right to approve all rolls and accounts of the Royal Treasury, as well as monthly accounts of receipts and expenses. Colbert was to bring those to Louis, along with a report of what took place in the meetings of the Royal Council each week. The king signed this arrêt personally, with Colbert signing as secretary of state for the Maison du Roi and the navy.[59]

The king revealed what he thought was important in financial affairs and what was not. He allowed the council to approve details while he kept track of the flow of funds. He would survey all of their decisions in order to see that they observed the practices he had established. Indeed, the regulation of April 1674 enjoined the council to maintain the good order he had established, and not to depart from it.

Louis XIV, however, did not travel outside his circle of chateaux in the Paris region during the last twenty-two years of his reign. Further evidence of his role in financial matters is meager. Colbert reportedly kept a book of projected expenditures and funds for presentation to the king. These were cursory and designed to spare the king from hearing many of the details,[60] but Colbert kept for himself a comprehensive projection for expenditures and receipts that he worked to realize. His nephew Desmaretz renewed the practice of keeping a detailed register for reference purposes. Apparently, the ministers between Colbert and Desmaretz did not maintain this practice; nor did Desmaretz's successors.[61]

Throughout his reign, Louis XIV's personal intervention in financial matters is difficult to discover. Every minister sent letters that mentioned in some way that they were writing on the king's orders. Louis XIV did personally sign leases for the farms.[62] There are instances of his correcting the wording on ordonnances comptant ordering the payment of funds to Monsieur le Grand, who was in charge of the king's stud farms and stables, because the original wording gave le Grand the quality of a peer of the realm, something he was not.[63]

The king did hear all proposals to increase revenue. The controller general kept lists of proposals for revenue-increasing schemes and was constantly besieged by people who had ideas for increasing the government's income. For example, on a proposal to reestablish a hundred offices of *veneurs conservateurs* for the king's woods, Desmaretz wrote: "Rpté. Le Roy a refusé cette proposition."[64] Sometimes the proposals had the backing of important people at court, such as the royal cousin the Duke of Vendôme, who offered to have twenty million livres' worth of unreformed mint bills brought to the crown to be reissued as new bills. Vendôme undoubtedly hoped that this plan, which allowed the king to keep one-quarter of the total amount raised, would earn him some financial gratification. On April 29, 1710, Desmaretz reported the offer to the king, who rejected it.[65] Sometimes the king merely asked that a proposal be put off until another time, like the one made in September 1711 by Gérard du Challart to administer the king's rights in Luxembourg.[66]

Desmaretz often presented matters to the king or the Royal Council that he himself did not like or support. When de la Garde, Desmaretz's commis, asked him to look over a proposal sponsored by the Duchess of Noailles for creating offices of conservators of the property and foundations of the Church, Desmaretz wrote that the people making this proposal did not understand the problem. De la Garde responded that his records for similar proposals that had been rejected in the past were in Paris. (The court usually spent one or two months at Fontainebleau during the late summer and fall while Versailles was repaired and cleaned.) After Desmaretz looked over the proposal again, along with comments by others in the government, de la Garde wrote, "Refusé a Font^au le 12 juillet 1708," indicating that, despite Desmaretz's doubts, he presented the proposal to the king or council and it was rejected.[67]

In July 1715, when the traitants proposed a new traité to pay off debts they had acquired in carrying out older traités, Desmaretz himself, who was developing his own ideas for paying France's war debts, reported the proposition. The Royal Council of Finances rejected it. Desmaretz noted that the time was not right for extraordinary affairs, meaning another traité on top of those to which the crown already owed money.[68]

Louis XIV was more than a passive player in governing the royal finances. He sometimes passed along warnings to his minister about potential conflicts between policies and reality. After the disastrous winter of 1709 the government issued a regulation on the collection of the taille that called upon the mayors and officials of each town, bourg, or parish to assemble to discuss the ability of their locality to pay its tax. They were to divide the taillables into four groups on the basis of wealth. The first group comprised the wealthiest, including anyone who had purchased an office for 10,000 livres or less since January 1, 1689. For people in these kinds of offices, the crown had canceled all exemptions to the taille and its collection. The wealthiest taillables were required to pay their tax in two payments in July and October. They could also be named as collectors and be required to pay the whole parish's share or suffer legal constraints, including the seizure of grain, as ordered by the taille receivers. The other three groups in the locality had their payments deferred until later dates and divided into three or four payments.[69]

The king presented Desmaretz a memorandum on July 16, 1709,[70] which pointed out that the new regulation on taille collection conflicted with another measure that had forbidden the seizure of grain in order to avoid depriving people of seed for replanting.[71] The king asked for a reconsideration of these policies in order to avoid disaster. He was relying on the credit of the wealthiest people in each locality to make loans for replanting. If they were required to pay the taille in July and October when money was needed to purchase supplies for replanting, the locality might not be able to seed the ground for the next spring. The king was thinking about the long-term consequences of unplanted land and the legal persecution of the people on whom he was depending to help save France from starvation.

In his *Mémoires*, after deploring princes who rely wholly on others to do their work, the young Louis XIV wrote to his son about the proper role of the finance minister:

> For those private individuals, approaching their position with no greater care than to preserve their own liberty to dispose of everything as they see fit, often put much more of their skill into obscuring this matter [i.e., finances] than to clarifying it, whereas a king, who is its legitimate lord, puts as much order and precision as he can into everything; aside from the fact that I was personally often relieved of this work by Colbert, whom I entrusted with examining things that required too much discussion and into which I would not have had the time to go.[72]

Determining what role a septuagenarian king played in policymaking is different than listening to the boasts of a young king to his son. While recent historical investigation has said that the aged Louis XIV's health was not as strong as previously believed, he was able to continue his unchanging round of activities until a week before his death in 1715.[73] His knowledge of the details of his finances remains a mystery, however. We do have

Desmaretz's testimony to Saint-Simon on the morning after his appointment to the controller generalship. He told the duke that the king said he was well aware of how bad the situation was and that he would be grateful if Desmaretz could find a remedy. The king said, however, that he would not blame him if the situation went from bad to worse. Desmaretz told Saint-Simon that he was surprised at how much the king knew about his finances. He had assumed that much of the details had been hidden from the king.[74]

The Controller General of Finances

From the time of Henri II to the personal rule of Louis XIV, the administration of finances fluctuated between a collegial or conciliar system and the preeminence of a single minister. Louis XIV's resolution of the vacillation in the monarchy's practices proved to be permanent. He suppressed the office of surintendant des finances and limited the powers of the chancellor. These two offices had vied for control of royal finances for over a century, but they both lost the struggle and were replaced by the mere appearance of a conciliar system. Indeed, the Royal Council of Finances was a front behind which the controller general of finances dominated the administration of finances.

The position of controller general of finances first appeared in 1554 when Henri II suppressed the offices of controllers of the treasury, casual revenues, and extraordinary affairs, along with the keepers of their registers. He united all these functions into one office called the controller general of finances. In the course of the following century, as the monarchy experimented with a variety of ways to administer its finances according to the personality of the king and his ministers, the position of controller general was suppressed, recreated, and divided among two, four, or eight men. Some controllers general dominated finances and eventually became surintendants des finances themselves, like Pierre Jeannin in 1616 and Michel Particelli d'Émery in 1647.[75]

When the office of surintendant des finances was suppressed for the last time in September 1661, there were two controllers general of finances, Barthelémy Hervart and Louis le Tonnelier de Breteuil, both of whom served alternately on a quarterly basis. On December 12, 1665, Louis XIV suppressed their offices and commissioned Colbert as controller general. Louis believed that he could not be dominated by a minister who had independent power, because he had reduced the finance minister to a revocable commission without the ability to order major expenditures.[76] Despite the king's belief, he never dismissed any of his controllers general, nor did he limit their powers in any way.

The original function of the controller general was to oversee all royal receipts and expenditures. In the Old Regime, control meant keeping a duplicate set of books indicating the receipts and expenditures made at the Royal Treasury and the casual revenues. The controller general was not a comptable; he did not handle royal funds, and royal money did not pass through his hands. He was an ordonnateur, an official who ordered the receipt and expenditure of money, and gave orders to the comptables. He was an officer of the Chambre des Comptes (Chamber of Accounts), that is, an accountant. He kept track of the value of each venal office and its tax (*paulette*), kept records of all purchases of such offices, and sent out the brevets that granted offices to their purchasers.[77]

The controllership general carried with it the position of councilor of state, with the right to sit on all branches of the Conseil d'État and the right to express an opinion there. After 1665 all controllers general received letters granting them admission to the Royal Council of Finances. Admission to the Conseil d'en haut, however, was not immediately forthcoming.[78] Colbert and his successor, Le Peletier, sat on the Conseil d'en haut from the date of their arrival in power, in 1661 and 1683 respectively. Pontchartrain had to wait fourteen months, from September 1689 until November 1690, when he became secretary of state for the navy and the Maison du Roi, before he entered the Conseil d'en haut. Chamillard also had to wait fourteen months, from September 1699 until after the acceptance of the Spanish crown on behalf of Louis XIV's grandson (November 1700), before he sat on the Council of Ministers. Desmaretz waited nine months, from February until November 1708, before he joined the Conseil d'en haut.[79]

The controller general of finances usually dressed differently from the *gens de robe*, a term that covered secretaries as well as councilors of state. When Colbert was both controller general of finances and secretary of state for the Maison du Roi and the navy (1669–83), when Pontchartrain held both posts (1690–99), and when Chamillard was both controller general and secretary of state for war, they dressed as the *gens de robe courte*, in a *manteau* (coat) of modest colors, with no red or blue especially. Chamillard wore a gray suit but he only adopted gold buttons when he became secretary of state. Desmaretz wore a gray suit with gold buttons and a gold cravat or tie.[80]

After 1667 the controller general of finances kept two books recording the financial transactions at the Royal Treasury. One, called the *Journal*, recorded ordonnances for expenditures made in the Royal Council of Finances, along with a monthly record of receipts made at the Royal Treasury. The second book, called the *Registre des fonds*, recorded the receipts and expenditures by category. Receipts were recorded from the farms, the receivers general, the bois, etc. Expenditures were recorded according to their type, such as those for the *Maisons royales* or the *Marine*.[81]

The secretaries of state and the controller general of finances expedited ordonnances for expenditures, even though the king and his Council decided measures of this kind. The secretary of state for the Maison du Roi and the navy issued all ordonnances for the maisons royales, *bâtiments*, navy and galleys, buildings and fortifications near seaports, pensions and gratifications for officials in those departments, and payment for all couriers he dispatched and received, along with the extraordinary expenses of the provinces under his administration. In 1709 this secretary of state administered the generalities of Paris, Soissons, Orléans, Poitou, and La Marche, as well as correspondence with the Parlement of Paris.

The secretary of state for war did the same for expenses in the extraordinary of war, the artillery, *pain de munition* and *étapes* (supplies to the army), fortifications on land and at the frontiers, pensions and gratifications to the troops, and the general accounts of the ordinary of war (royal musketeers, *gendarmes*, light horse, bodyguards, and the French and Swiss guards). He also expedited ordonnances for the payment of the appointments of all governors and lieutenants general in the provinces and other places in the realm, as well as their couriers and provinces. His own provinces included the Lyonnais, Metz, Toul and Verdun, Franche Comté, Lorraine, Alsace and Strasbourg, Flanders, and the *pays conquis*, which included Artois, Roussillon, Conflans, and Cerdaigne. He was also in charge of the superior courts found in these provinces.

The secretary of state for foreign affairs expedited ordonnances for expenses involving France's diplomats, foreign subsidies, and the so-called *Affaires secrettes* (a whole series of clandestine expenses that subsidized France's allies abroad). He also paid for his couriers and provinces, which included Brittany, Provence, Dauphiné, Sedan, Berri, Champagne and Brie, Limousin, Angoumois, Xaintonge, Navarre and Béarn, and the pays of Bigorre and the Nebouzan, along with the superior courts in those provinces.

The secretary of state for the *Religion Prétendue Réformée* had very few government responsibilities after the revocation of the Edict of Nantes in 1685. He signed all orders to pay the pensions and gratifications of the new converts, and the extraordinary expenses of his many provinces—Guyenne, Perigord, Rouergue, Languedoc, Foix, Maine, Perche, Laval, Normandy, Touraine, Anjou, Bourbonnais, Nivernais, Auvergne, Burgundy, Bresse, Bugey, Gex, Valromey, La Rochelle, Aunis, Brouage, Picardy, Boullonnais, and the Îles de Ré and Oleron, along with the superior courts to be found in them.

The controller general of finances expedited ordonnances under the king's orders for all appointments, pensions, gratifications, and gages of the Council of State, the chancellor, the head and councilors of state on the Royal Council of Finances, ministers and secretaries of state, all officials of the various council bodies, the intendants of finances, the first president and other officers of the superior courts, the provincial intendants, and the marshals of France. He also expedited general payment orders for the expenses of the Swiss Leagues as well as reimbursement of all offices, rentes, domains, and augmented gages. He handled any ordonnances granting remises to traitants and the interest due on any loans made to the king. He had no provinces directly under his control. The inability of the controller general or any other royal official to oversee all royal expenditures was a major weakness of the royal government that was never corrected until the French Revolution.[82]

The peculiarities of Old Regime's administrative divisions, as revealed above, would make it appear that the controller general's influence was restricted to those areas listed, and that his control over a large part of government expenses was nonexistent. His control, however, extended beyond these restrictions through a variety of channels. First, the matter of issuing various ordonnances did not guarantee their payment. No official at the Royal Treasury, or any treasury, could pay money to anyone bearing ordonnances unless he had received an order to do so from the controller general of finances. For expenses of 1,000 livres or more the controller general signed and sent an expense list called an *état de distribution* to the keeper of the Royal Treasury. For voyages and expenses under 1,000 livres the controller general sent an *ordonnance du petit comptant.* Until one or the other of these documents was received, the holder of an *ordonnance comptant* could not receive any money.

Even before anyone received an ordonnance comptant, the controller general of finances had to have the ordonnance presented to him. He would arrange the funding for all such ordonnances. Those larger than 300 livres had to be presented to the Royal Council for Louis XIV's signature. After the Royal Council, the controller general would send all ordonnances to the premier commis in the *contrôle général des finances* in charge of the Journal and the Registre des fonds, where all ordonnances were registered. The page number of the entry in the Journal was recorded in the Register. At the end of each month, Louis would look at the Register while his controller general read from the Journal. The king kept a running total of each month's receipts and expenses that he recorded in the Journal. A total annual calculation of the same was made for each category of receipt and expenditure.[83]

The king regulated expenditures with each secretary of state and left it to the controller general to find the funds to pay them. While some might think that there was no budgetary control, men like Colbert and Desmaretz made great efforts to restrict expenses. Even the secretaries of state had some discretion. And all ordonnances had to be sent to the controller general for registration before being issued to their recipients.

The payment of these funds came from a variety of treasurers. The controller general of finances supervised these venal officers because they were all comptables.[84] At the end of the reign of Louis XIV there were twenty-six different treasuries—ranging from the Maison du Roi to the Extraordinary of War and including the Royal Treasury and the Receiver of the Casual Revenues—each with two or more treasurers.[85] These officials received payments from the Royal Treasury and paid funds to the holders of ordonnances in the various departments under their jurisdiction. These men were private individuals who had bought the right to manage these funds. They were allowed to keep a certain amount of the money, called *taxations,* that passed through their hands. In times of delay they could borrow money to sustain funding until the Royal Treasury paid them. Of course, such loans were not interest free; the interest was added to their payments from the Royal Treasury.[86]

The treasurer who handled the largest sums of money outside the Royal Treasury was the treasurer of the Extraordinary of War, who was responsible for paying the troops as well as for seeing to the provision of their food and ammunition. He paid for the supply of guns, uniforms, and shoes. He also handled all extraordinary expenditures for the governors and lieutenants general in the provinces and places of the realm and paid for the *commissaires de guerre.* While the ordonnances for the payment of these expenses came from the secretary of state for war, the treasurer of the Extraordinary of War discussed his expected payments with the controller general.[87] In 1706 and 1707 these treasurers (there were three of them serving in alternate years) issued promissory notes worth more than 60 million livres to maintain their payments. In other words, they borrowed the money and were subsequently unable to repay the debts, leaving yet another set of unpaid royal paper in circulation, where speculators could buy or sell at the going market price.[88]

Desmaretz and Daniel-François Voysin, who became secretary of state for war in June 1709, frequently consulted each other during 1709–10 because of the growing financial problems caused by the Great Winter of 1709 as well as the administrative mess left behind by Voysin's predecessor, Chamillard, who obligated funds without informing the controller general. The king served as a mediator between the two ministers. Desmaretz believed that military expenses had to be reduced to a level lower than Voysin wished. The king persuaded Voysin to retrench the army's expenses. Desmaretz went so far as to ask for all the information regarding the expenses of every type of military unit.[89] The two ministers had to work together to force the treasurers of the Extraordinary of War to fulfill their duties. They also had to deal with the problems of transferring funds at the local level for winter quarters or for the *étapes.*[90]

Besides restricting the secretaries of state by funding, providing for the expenses, and governing the accounts of the comptables, the controller general of finances also influenced the kinds of arrangements that the secretaries of state could make with private financiers. For example, military supply was contracted to private companies. These companies bid against each other for the right to supply food to the troops on various fronts. The secretary of state for war negotiated directly with these munitioners, but the controller general decided the kind of funding he could promise them. Because the government relied heavily on borrowing from future revenues, the controller general decided which revenues and for what year the assignations would be granted. These types of decisions influenced the terms of the contracts that the secretary of state could obtain.[91]

The description of the powers of the secretaries of state is deceptive. Many matters, including arrêts en commandement and letters to the officials in various provinces, were drawn up in the bureaus of the contrôle général des finances. Secretaries of state were instructed merely to sign them and send them to the proper people. The chancellor received similar orders.[92]

One possible explanation for the confusion over the difference between the controller general and the secretaries of state is that Colbert, Pontchartrain, and Chamillard each served as both controller general and secretary of state simultaneously: Colbert from 1669 until his death in September 1683, Pontchartrain from November 1690 until he became chancellor in September 1699, and Chamillard from January 1701 until February 1708, when he resigned as controller general. During the remainder of the Old Regime after 1708, no one would be both controller general and a secretary of state. The controller general's direct relationship with the king made it difficult for a secretary of state to resist his orders, unless he himself had a closer relationship with the king. And while the controller general need only persuade the king to adopt his measures, the secretaries of state merely carried out policies that had already been decided. If anything, the secretaries of state slowed the execution of the controller general's orders. Later in the eighteenth century, in order to overcome this problem, some people recommended turning the controller general into a fifth secretary of state.[93]

The controller general of finances oversaw the operations of the royal tax farms. He also surveyed the activities of the revenues and expenses of the receivers general of finances. He often worked with the General Farmers and receivers general in groups or individually to reduce waste and increase the revenues coming into the Royal Treasury. His concern over the revenues that came from taxation led to a growing correspondence with the provincial intendants, who were supposed to prod the local administrators of the farms and involve themselves in the fair apportionment and efficient collection of the impositions.

As sole reporter to the Royal Council, the controller general was the official charged with exposing ideas on financial and fiscal expedients.[94] He brought all rentes, short-term loans, new taxes, and extraordinary affairs before the Royal Council after a preliminary examination by his bureaus and by the appropriate officials. Once the council accepted a proposed affair, the controller general or his assistants negotiated with financiers to set the terms of the traité and decided which financiers they would admit to the company of backers called cautions.[95] The controller general also controlled the rolls by which the Royal Council acknowledged the sale of offices.

The controller general had a prominent role in the selection of provincial intendants, even though the secretaries of state were supposed to handle correspondence with the provincial authorities. The controller general's opinion of a master of request's performance of his council duties could determine his selection for a provincial post. Once named by the king, the instructions of the provincial intendants were written in the contrôle général des finances. The secrétaires du roi disputed this loss of some of the emoluments of their offices. Chancellor Pontchartrain tried to reclaim the right to draw up these instructions for the Grand Chancellery, but Desmaretz informed him that the practice of sending letters from the controller general's bureaus was traditional, going back beyond the time when Pontchartrain had been controller general. Despite Pontchartrain's insistence and the king's desire that the two men resolve their dispute, the controller general did not lose any authority in regard to the provincial intendants.[96] Any *commissaire départi en province*, and any master of requests hoping for such an appointment, knew that his career might very well depend on the favor of the controller general of finances.

The personal ties that characterized early modern governments and the relationship between the center and the provinces[97] were also part of the financial world. While institutions like the General Farms or the receivers general of finances were important, the men who occupied these positions and their relationships to the controller general of finances and his assistants often determined what the government did or was able to do. A finance minister whom the financiers knew and trusted was more likely to attract loans than one who was indecisive, hesitant, or too legalistic because of a lack of familiarity with finances.

In the 1690s, with the first great wave of the sale of offices, the election of local officials ceased. Thereafter, all such offices were venal. The controller general's influence grew in proportion to his control over the sale of offices and over the paulette. Tocqueville recognized the controller general as the primary figure in the Old Regime's governmental machinery. He saw the controller general as not only the minister of finances but also as the minister of the interior, minister of public works, and minister of commerce.[98] A brief list of the activities that the controller general supervised, directly or indirectly, reveals his authority outside the realm of finances: the mints, the postes as a tax farm, all interior commerce and any exterior overland commerce, weights and measures, royal trading monopolies, industry, mining, agriculture, grain commerce, forests, bridges and highways, canals, river traffic, royal buildings, and the policing of all these activities. In addition, all police officials in provincial cities, other than the lieutenant general of police for Paris, were venal officeholders subject to the approval of the controller general. The controller general was also responsible for royal charity, including the general hospitals and the Hotels Dieu. His concern for public order led to policing vagabonds and controlling the price of grain.[99]

All these responsibilities entailed large pecuniary remunerations. Table 2.2 shows the controller general's appointments for the year 1708. The controller general of finances was the highest paid official in the royal government. Desmaretz's personal income increased from the figure shown above to 134,000 livres, according to his projected expenses for the year 1711. The primary reason for the raise was that, upon joining the Conseil d'en haut, Desmaretz became a minister of state, for which he received 20,000 livres. By 1711 his direct payments from the Royal Treasury exceeded any other minister's revenues, including those of the chancellor, who received only 110,000 livres, and the secretary of state for war, who was paid 121,150 livres.[100]

Table 2.2. Appointments of the controller general for 1708.

For his appointments as councilor to the Royal Council of Finances	7,500
For three-quarters gages du Conseil	1,500
For three-quarters pension	4,500
For his quartier retranché	4,500
For the extraordinary appointments of the controller general	14,000
For his appointments because of the Royal Treasury	10,000
For the expenses of the *cahier* (notebook) of the said department	6,000
For the expenses of the notebooks of the finances	8,000
Because of the work in finances	26,000
For the acquit patent	3,000
For the extraordinary gratifications	20,000
For the servants	1,000
Total	106,000

(continued)

Table 2.2. *(concluded)*

For his commis:	
For the department of the bois and the acquit patent	6,100
For the commis in dispatches and the acquit patent	5,500
For the commis in the department of bridges and highways and *acquit patent*	5,500
For two commis and their acquit patent	10,167
For the appointments of Le Rebours holding the register of finances for 1708	10,000
For the extraordinary appointments	6,000
For three-quarters gages du Conseil	1,500
For the acquit patent	3,000
For the acquit patent of Sr. Quenet	3,000
For the acquit patent of Sr. Gestard	3,000
For the appointments of Bercy, who was charged with examining the états *au vray* from April 15 to December 31, 1708	8,500
For the appointments of Le Rebours, working on the domain for 1708	4,000
Total for commis	66,267

Note: These figures are a consolidation of Chamillard's and Desmaretz's appointments for the year 1708.

Source: Boislisle and Brotonne, *Correspondance des contrôleurs généraux*, 3:664–65.

The controller general of finances had other sources of income that are more difficult to ascertain. The Estates of Brittany paid him 3,000 livres and 1,000 livres for one of his commis every two years. Languedoc paid him 3,000 livres annually, while Burgundy paid 12,000 livres every three years. He received nothing from the Estates of Provence and Artois.[101] At the signing of the lease on the General Farms the controller general received a large gift. Desmaretz received 350,000 livres in 1715 when the lease was finally renewed.[102] While no other source of income can be known for certain, it would have been uncharacteristic of the Old Regime if Desmaretz had not received other gratifications as well. Surely, he received gifts from those seeking favors or positions, or to do business with the royal government.

Louis XIV also made a habit of presenting a gift of 200,000 livres to the children of his ministers when they married. Desmaretz refused to accept such a gift for his daughter in 1708 because of the financial condition of the royal government. After some bargaining with the king, it was decided to give her an annual pension of 10,000 livres instead.[103]

The Intendants of Finances

The controller general had a group of official assistants called the intendants of finances.[104] The name intendant is confusing because the intendant of finances, unlike similarly named officials in the provinces or the army, was a member of the King's Council by right, and was thus close to the monarch. Like other financial offices and institutions, the intendants of finances endured a host of transformations after the position first appeared in 1518. In the years leading up to Louis XIV's personal rule, the number of these officials was reduced from twelve to six in 1657, and then to four in 1658.[105] The remaining four positions were venal offices until 1660, when Louis XIV suppressed all of them and created two new commissions of intendants of finances.[106] Colbert held one of the commissions and Denis Marin, the husband of one of Colbert's cousins, held the other.[107]

The post of intendant of finances was so lucrative that, in the ranking of society in the capitation of 1695, it was ranked in the second class, which paid 1,500 livres, together with dukes and peers, marshals of France, crown officers, and the first president of the Parlement of Paris. In salary, Colbert and Marin each received 12,000 livres from the Royal Treasury. By 1690 the salary had risen to 40,000 livres, and it doubled again before the suppression of the intendancy after the death of Louis XIV.[108]

The intendants of finances kept their own offices and archives separate from that of the finance minister. Françoise Mosser has researched the private archives of the Lefèvre d'Ormesson family, whose ancestors were intendants of finances from 1722 until 1777. Desmaretz's archive, which survives as the G^7 series in the Archives Nationales, is only part of the financial records of the time. When he was controller general he had seven intendants of finances. Therefore, we can only surmise what the intendants were doing from the records kept by Desmaretz and his clerks.

The intendants of finances represented the quintessence of the evolution of the Conseil du Roi from a court of law to an administrative entity, because they maintained the attributes of councilors of state while performing the duties of bureaucrats. After 1665 the intendants of finances served as assistants to the controller general of finances, with separate administrative responsibilities under his supervision. The intendants sat by right on the Conseil d'État et des Finances and on the Grande and Petite Directions, and divided labor among the various bureaus and extraordinary commissions of the council that had jurisdiction over financial affairs. Each of the intendants worked individually with the controller general on matters over which they had administrative responsibilities that were to be discussed in the Royal Council of Finances, where the controller general would introduce the material.

When Colbert became controller general of finances in 1665, his commission as intendant of finances was given to Vincent Hotman, another relative by marriage.[109] Colbert, despite his responsibilities as surintendant des bâtiments and secretary of state for the navy and the Maison du Roi, operated with only two intendants of finances throughout his ministry.[110] When Marin died in 1678, Desmaretz replaced him and thereby inherited responsibility for direct taxation and the crown's credit system. Hotman, however, died in March 1683 and his commission remained vacant during the last six months of Colbert's lifetime.[111]

Desmaretz's dismissal in December 1683 allowed Le Peletier to name both intendants of finances. Le Peletier's brother, Michel Le Peletier de Souzy, filled Hotman's commission, while François Le Tonnelier de Breteuil replaced Desmaretz.[112] Breteuil's commission would eventually be suppressed in 1701. He would be paid 150,000 livres, the same amount of money that his father had received in 1665 when he had been forced to resign as controller general of finances in order to pave the way for Colbert's ascension to that newly fortified position.[113] In April 1687 a third commission of intendant of finances was created for Louis II de Phélypeaux de Pontchartrain.[114] The division of administrative responsibilities among what were then three intendants of finances is not known.

Le Peletier de Souzy was the brother of Controller General of Finances Claude Le Peletier, with whom he often quarreled. Saint-Simon believed him to be the smarter of the two brothers. He had been a master of requests and a provincial intendant in Franche Comté in 1668 for the brief period it was under French control, and then in Flanders during 1668–83, where his work with Vauban in helping to fortify Lille attracted the king's attention. He became a semester councilor of state in 1683 before accepting a commission as intendant of finances. When Louvois died in 1691, Louis XIV separated the responsibilities for French fortifications from the war ministry and gave them to Souzy. As director general of fortifications until the end of the reign, Souzy would have a weekly face-to-face meeting with the king, making him what Saint-Simon called a semiminister of state, a *tiercelet de ministre.* He became an ordinary councilor of state in 1693. When it appeared that war over the Spanish succession was likely, he passed his intendancy of finances to his son, Michel Robert Le Peletier des Forts, on December 27, 1700, in order to free himself to focus on fortifications. Nevertheless, he entered the Royal Council of Finances on October 8, 1702, as one of the two councilors of state who sat on that body. Souzy remained a strong personality at court throughout the period and was more responsible than his brother for implanting the Le Peletiers at the highest levels of robe nobility. He died as dean (i.e., senior) councilor of state in 1725.[115]

Pontchartrain's commission as intendant of finances was allowed to lapse when he became controller general of finances in September 1689.[116] In February 1690 an edict created four offices of intendants of finances in addition to the two existing commissions.[117] These offices were bought, in order of seniority, by Nicolas Heudebert Dubuisson, Louis-Urbain Lefèvre de Caumartin, Michel Chamillard, and Joseph-Jean-Baptiste Fleuriau d'Armenonville. All of these men were masters of requests at the time they bought the offices of intendants of finances, although Armenonville had not quite completed the necessary formalities for becoming a master of requests when he purchased his intendancy.

Dubuisson was an expert accountant and money manager who had already served the crown for thirty-five years when he became intendant of finances. Unlike most of the intendants mentioned here, he apparently had no blood ties to anyone else in the government. A Norman, he became a secrétaire du roi in 1655, a master in the Chamber of Accounts in 1664, and master of requests in 1679. He kept all three of these charges long enough to receive letters of veterance and, hence, nobility. He served briefly as intendant at Limoges in 1684 before becoming procurer general in the 1685 Chambre de l'Arsenal that was investigating false claims of nobility. Dubuisson had a reputation for being clever in finances and one of the strongest members of the King's Council in those areas in which he was expert. He would serve as intendant of finances from February 1690 until he was forced to retire in July 1714 because he had become too old to carry out his duties. He died extremely wealthy and left behind 175,000 livres in rentes, with a total capital of more than 3 million livres.[118]

Caumartin was Pontchartrain's cousin and soon became his right-hand man in the finance ministry. Descended from a well-established robe family, he rose to extreme popularity in court circles during the 1690s when his chateau at Saint-Ange in the region of Fontainebleau where the court summered was the scene of much social life. Although many people regarded Caumartin as a witty man, Saint-Simon accused him of being overbearing and arrogant, leading to his fall from favor at court. Caumartin was the focus of two different scandals in the late 1690s that, according to Saint-Simon, ruined his chances of being named either chancellor or controller general. One issue involved accusations of grain hoarding during the famine or shortage of 1698–99. Caumartin claimed that his estate manager, Claude Miotte, and the local taille receiver had amassed the grain discovered on a property he was leasing. Pontchartrain was able to protect his cousin while forcing Miotte and his partner to pay fines of 1,000 livres each, as well as confiscating the grain in question. Caumartin remained an intendant of finances until the suppression of the offices in 1716.[119]

While an intendant of finances was automatically a member of the King's Council, he lost both positions when he gave up his intendancy. The king, however, could appoint an intendant of finances to one of the existing positions of councilor of state as a reward for his services. Breteuil and Souzy were both already councilors of state when they became intendants of finances in 1684. None of the four new intendants of finances created in 1690 had previously been a councilor of state. When Caumartin was named semester councilor of state in 1697 and appeared in council wearing the robe of a councilor of state, he provoked a nasty quarrel over seniority. (Intendants of finances wore manteaus rather than robes on the council.) Louis XIV settled the quarrel by a regulation of the council that determined that seniority on the Council of State would date from the first day that anyone sat on the council, regardless of any later changes in his position, as long as his career on the council was uninterrupted.[120]

Armenonville was the brother-in-law of former Controller General Le Peletier, whose wife was Armenonville's much older half-sister. He had served as a premier commis in Le Peletier's bureaus, where he was regarded as a possible future minister. Armenonville would become one of the two directors of finances in 1701 and a semester councilor of state in 1705 before losing his position within finances when Desmaretz was named controller general and suppressed the offices of the directors of finances. Saint-Simon says that there was no love lost between the two men. Armenonville returned to power during the Regency to become secretary of state for war in 1716 and keeper of the seals in 1722.[121]

When Pontchartrain tripled the number of intendants of finances, he established, or probably reestablished, a new subcommittee on the Council of State known as the Assembly of the Intendants of Finances. It included all the intendants of finances, as well as all members of the Royal Council of Finances except the king and the chancellor, thus making it a duplicate of the Petite Direction. The Assembly of the Intendants of Finances was a clearinghouse for handling matters that were too important for the controller general and the intendant to decide alone but not significant enough for the king's attention. The appearance of the Assembly of the Intendants of Finances probably correlated to the disappearance of the Conseil d'État et des Finances during the 1690s. The exact nature of the work of the Assembly of the Intendants of Finances is somewhat murky. It does not appear in any list of the administrative units of the King's Council that was published in *L'Almanach royal*.[122]

The nomination of Chamillard as controller general[123] led to changes in the administration of finances. He sold his intendancy of finances to a nephew of Pontchartrain's, Armand-Roland Bignon de Blanzy, who was also a master of requests.[124] With acceptance of the will of Carlos II of Spain, it was clear that France might be on the verge of a new European war. Thus, Le Peletier de Souzy would be forced to focus on his responsibilities as director general of fortifications. In December 1700 Souzy had his commission as intendant of finances turned into an office with the right of inheritance going to his son, Michel-Robert Le Peletier des Forts, in whose favor he immediately resigned.[125]

After the death of Secretary of State for War Barbezieux on January 5, 1701, Chamillard was named to replace him. In order to help the minister with his increased responsibilities, two officers of directors of finances were created. Thereafter, the controller general would concern himself with the general overall policy, while the two directors would manage the day-to-day operation of the finance ministry. The creation of two directorships of finances in June 1701 led to the suppression of two of the positions of intendant of finances—the commission held by Breteuil, and the office that belonged to Armenonville, who bought one of the two new directorships. Armenonville's elevation was a blow to the ambitions of both Caumartin and Dubuisson, who had to stand by and watch a much younger man with less seniority promoted over their heads. It was particularly difficult for Caumartin who, according to Saint-Simon, had once had ambitions of becoming chancellor or controller general.[126]

The other director of finances was an outsider, Hilaire Rouillé du Coudray, the son of a provincial intendant, who had served as premier commis to Simon Arnauld de Pomponne when the latter was secretary of state for foreign affairs in the 1670s. He was never a master of requests but he was a councilor in the Grand Conseil, a reporter in the chancellery, and procurer general in the Chambre des Comptes before becoming director of finances in June 1701. He sold this office to Desmaretz in October 1703.[127]

Two new offices of intendant of finances were created in August 1704 for relatives of Chamillard's. His cousin, Alexandre Le Rebours, bought one office and his brother's father-in-law, François Guyet, bought the other. Guyet had been a master of requests since 1689 and served as intendant at Pau during 1699–1701 and at Lyon during 1701–4. Saint-Simon disliked both men, calling them impertinent fools, but he particularly detested Le Rebours, who had begun a normal robe career as a councilor in the Grand Conseil and grand reporter in the chancellery before he resigned them with the coming of war in 1689 to pursue a military career. Chamillard called him back to the contrôle général to serve eventually as the premier commis des finances in 1703 before he became an intendant of finances as well. Prior to Le Rebours' appointment to the intendancy, all of his predecessors since Desmaretz's appointment had been master of requests. Le Rebours' accession to the post of intendant of finances caused some heated discussions among the masters of requests.[128]

Chamillard's last act as controller general really disturbed the finely honed legal niceties at court. With Desmaretz's appointment as controller general of finances in February 1708, the two offices of directors of finances were abolished, reducing Armenonville to being a simple councilor of state. To help reimburse the holders of these offices, a seventh office of intendant of finances was created at a price of 800,000 livres, more than twice the price of the other intendancies. It was created especially for Chamillard's friend and ally Jacques Poulletier, a financier who was rumored to have helped Chamillard purchase his own office of intendant of finances in 1690. Poulletier had begun his career as a war supplier and had graduated to becoming one of the receivers general of finances in Lyon in 1685, where he stayed until 1704. He also bought an office of secrétaire du roi in 1690 and kept it until 1711, earning nobility for himself and his family. In 1704 he sold his receivership general of finances to buy an office of keeper of the Royal Treasury. During his career he had been the backer of twenty-four traités, a General Farmer for three years, and a munitioner for both the army and the navy. By allowing him to purchase a seat on the King's Council, Chamillard was admitting a former comptable to the court that judged the accounts of other comptables. Although Poulletier's son was a master of requests, he himself had never been one and thus came almost entirely from outside the circle of robe families who dominated the council. And, to complete the scandal, he was to be the intendant of finances who oversaw all payments for war: the extraordinary of war, *pain de munition, vivres et étapes,* and the artillery. Although he was technically one of the *garçons du contrôleur general,* his responsibilities would put him in daily contact with the war minister, Chamillard.[129]

In all, Desmaretz inherited seven intendants of finances, each with his own ties to other men in the government. Caumartin and Bignon de Blanzy were related to and allied with Pontchartrain. Des Forts was the son of Souzy, one of the two councilors of state who sat on the Royal Council of Finances. Le Rebours and Guyet were relatives of the war minister, while Poulletier was clearly an ally of long standing. Dubuisson's connections are unknown. Desmaretz was only able to change this team when opportunity presented itself.

In August 1709 reasons of health forced Chancellor Pontchartrain's brother to resign as intendant for Paris. Bignon de Blanzy was related to the chancellor and his son, Jérôme de Phélypeaux de Pontchartrain, the secretary of state who had the generality of Paris under his department. Desmaretz and Jérôme agreed to have Bignon de Blanzy, a master of requests, appointed intendant of Paris. Desmaretz was able to have his own son-in-law, Charles Henri Malon de Bercy, buy the office of intendant of finances from Blanzy. A master of requests, Bercy had begun working in the contrôle général des finances during the ministry of his uncle Pontchartrain.[130]

The king promised his first physician, Guy Fagon, that his son, Louis Fagon, who had become a master of requests in 1709, would fill the next vacancy among the intendants of finances. When Poulletier died in April 1711, however, his son Pierre, a master of requests, received permission to take over his father's office.[131] Louis Fagon would have to wait until Dubuisson's forced resignation as intendant of finances in July 1714 to buy his intendancy.[132]

The intendants of finances divided their responsibilities along lines that remained relatively unchanged after 1690, despite some shuffling of portfolios as positions for intendants disappeared in 1701, reappeared in 1704, and were expanded in 1708. Generally speaking, a change in the person holding an office of intendant of finances did not entail a change in the responsibilities of that office. In other words, the responsibilities that Chamillard held from 1690 until he resigned in 1699 were passed on to Bignon de Blanzy, who passed them on to Bercy in 1709. The government published official lists of the responsibilities of the controller general and his intendants of finances in *L'Almanach royal.*

Table 2.3 reveals that the controller general supervised each of the men who dealt with these matters in greater detail. For example, Desmaretz would work with Dubuisson on the bois and the Swiss Leagues, and with Caumartin on the gabelles and the accounts of Burgundy and Languedoc. Of all the intendants of finances, however, Le Rebours was the most important because he controlled the accounts of the Royal Treasury, as well as those of other treasuries, the farms, and the rentes.

Table 2.3. The responsibilities of the controller general and his intendants of finances in 1708.

Desmaretz, controller general of finances, rue Vivienne:

- The Royal Treasury and the casual revenues
- The general direction of all the king's farms
- The clergy
- Commerce and the marine du Levant et Ponant
- The extraordinary of war and artillery
- Pain de munition, vivres and étapes
- Bâtiments and maisons royales
- Rentes
- Pays d'états
- The mints
- The Parlements and superior courts of the realm
- Bridges and highways, dikes along the Loire River, waterways and streets of Paris
- Manufactures
- Octrois des villes and debts of the communities
- The Swiss Leagues

Dubuisson, rue d'Orléans au Marais:

- The detail of the waters and forests
- *États* (accounts) au bois

(continued)

Table 2.3. *(concluded)*

Dubuisson, rue d'Orléans au Marais—*(continued)*

Chambres des Comptes
Débets revenant bons au Roi
The Swiss Leagues

Bignon de Blanzy, rue Neuve St. Augustin:

The generalities of the pays d'élections and their accounts
The taillon (a subsidiary tax to the taille)
The Grand Conseil
The accounts of Navarre and Béarn
The farm of the control of notarial acts
Bridges and highways

Des Forts, rue Couture Sainte Catherine:

The detail of the accounts of the domain
The accounts of the finances of Artois, Provence, Brittany, and the generality of Metz
The impositions in Flanders, Franche Comté, and Alsace
The farm of the greffes

Guyet, rue Sainte Anne:

The detail of the aides and stamped paper
Octrois des villes and debts of the communities

Le Rebours, rue Neuve St. Merry:

The detail of the Five Great Farms and the tobacco farm
Domaine d'Occident
The detail of the rentes
The detail of the saltpeter and powder farms
The detail of the Royal Treasury and others (meaning other treasuries)

Caumartin, rue Sainte Avoye:

The detail of the gabelles and their accounts
The accounts of the finances for the generalities of Dijon, Toulouse, and Montpelier

Poulletier, rue Couture Sainte Catherine:

The Extraordinary of War
Pain de munitions, vivres and étapes
The Parlements and the superior courts
The bureaus of finances

Source: L'Almanach royal (1709), 51–53. This list was taken from lists that were printed and distributed by the *huissiers* of the council. Examples can be found in A.N. G^7 1850.

The list of the intendants' responsibilities is incomplete because other areas of administration were divided among the intendants of finances as well. Lists not meant for public eyes were kept in the contrôle général des finances, with an indication of which intendant administered the traité for which extraordinary affair.[133] The intendant of finances negotiated directly with traitants on the terms of a traité and then asked the controller general to approve the results as well as the membership in the company of traitants who would be accepted as cautions to provide the necessary advances to the crown.[134] The intendants of finances were thus in contact with men who were making propositions to create new offices, rentes, or whatever else would increase the revenues of the crown. Their knowledge of finances and financiers gave them an important role in establishing any new policies that required money to be carried out. They were in constant contact with the controller general over their official and unofficial responsibilities, even to the point of preparing the arrêts that he would report to the Royal Council of Finances.[135]

The position of intendant of finances gave these officials a certain amount of independence from the controller general. They were subordinate to him, but as members of the King's Council, relatives of other royal officials, and owners of their offices, they were certainly more important than any ordinary commis. They kept their own offices and records and received a salary from the Royal Treasury to maintain their own commis and clerks.

J. F. Bosher has described the administration of finances between the controller general and the intendants of finances as a collegial system with an approximate equality among these men.[136] The records for Desmaretz's ministry reveal too much deference from the intendants of finances for that conclusion to be true. Saint-Simon referred to the intendants of finances as *les garçons* of the controller general.[137] Yet, Dubuisson and Caumartin kept their offices during three separate ministries, raising the question of whom they were dependent on. Both Pontchartrain and Chamillard had to divide their time between finances and their secretaryships of state, which probably allowed the intendants of finances to have more discretion over their administrative responsibilities than under Desmaretz, who instituted more regular face-to-face meetings and stringent reporting requirements.[138]

The personalities of the intendants of finances contributed to their influence with the controller general. No controller general after Le Peletier would ever name his entire corps of intendants, although Pontchartrain did triple the number of these officials. Desmaretz inherited six holdovers and had a seventh thrust upon him almost immediately. He was able to replace these men only by the accidents of nature, and then only by negotiating with the king and other powers at court. In any case, he had probably established a working relationship with these men while he was director of finances. Generally speaking, he entrusted the younger men, like Bercy, Fagon, Poulletier fils, and des Forts, with great responsibilities on the various bureaus and extraordinary commissions of the council. Problems involving naval finances were always referred to Caumartin.[139] Dubuisson was the eldest of these men, and apparently had no blood ties at court. He was not a confidant of Desmaretz's, nor was he ever given any extraordinary affairs to administer, unlike the other intendants. Desmaretz also placed very few affairs in Guyet's hands.[140]

Desmaretz's closest confidants among his corps of intendant of finances were his son-in-law Bercy, who still headed the office administering the *états au vray*, and Le Rebours, who, in addition to being an intendant of finances, was also the *premier commis des finances.* Both of these men were appointed to almost every important extraordinary commission of the council that was created while Desmaretz was controller general. Des Forts was also relatively close to Desmaretz and received many similar appointments. He also administered the collection of the capitation, however. The overwhelming importance of military spending increased the influence of Poulletier père and fils as well.

In 1708 Desmaretz became the focal point of any effort to increase the crown's revenues or reform the royal finances. His workload was extremely heavy, when one considers that he met once or twice a week with the Royal Council of Finances, three times a week with the council of ministers or Conseil d'en haut, and at least once a week personally with the king. The Council of Dispatches, the Grande and Petite Directions, and the Assembly of the Intendants of Finances met once every two weeks. Desmaretz also had individual working sessions with his intendants of finances and intendants of commerce, commis like de la Garde and Le Cousturier, and trusted allies like Vaubourg, Bouville, and Nointel. He also conferred with the tax farmers, the receivers general of finances, prominent financial officers in the pays d'états and the clergy, and with financiers like Bernard, the Hogguer brothers, Crozat, and others. As the principal dispenser of royal patronage, he was besieged by office-seekers and their advocates, who were usually important courtiers with whom he had to meet personally as a matter of protocol because they were too exalted to be left to one of his commis. He gave public audiences in Paris and met with individuals who wished to discuss matters with him that they claimed were important. His health gave way at three separate occasions under the strain. As his ministry grew, he began to employ intermediaries to see these people and advise him of what took place.

Any proposal to create a new tax or to increase revenues by any other means would have to be approved by the policymaking apparatus that Louis XIV had created to govern France. The Sun King had adapted France's existing policymaking organizations to suit his style, but simultaneously the conciliar form of government that emerged from the Middle Ages was giving way to the administrative monarchy, where the power to decide resided with the ministers who used the councils as a cover for their decisions.

Chapter 3

Nicolas Desmaretz and Company

His Biography

Nicolas Desmaretz, the second son of Jean Desmaretz and Marie Colbert, was born in Soissons on September 10, 1648.[1] He studied rhetoric and philosophy at a Jesuit school in Reims but did not complete his studies. His uncle Jean-Baptiste Colbert called him, at the age of fifteen, to the contrôle général des finances, where his parents corresponded with Colbert about his activities.[2]

In the eighteenth century the Desmaretz family claimed four generations of magistrates prior to Nicolas. We do know that Nicolas's grandfather was a *procureur du roi* in the bailliage of Vermandois and substitute *procureur general* in Laon at his death in 1611 at age thirty-five. These facts stand in sharp contrast to Saint-Simon's claim that Desmaretz's grandfather had begun life as a *manant gros laboureur* (wealthy landowning peasant) who enriched himself as the steward of the estates of the abbey at Ourscamp near Noyon.[3]

Saint-Simon also said that Colbert raised the Desmaretz family from obscurity. Jean Desmaretz, who was born in 1608 and was thus three years old when his father died, bought an office of treasurer of France in the Soissons Bureau of Finances in 1634, after having been a receiver of the taillon for the generality. He held the office of treasurer of France when he married Marie Colbert on June 25, 1646, when Jean-Baptiste Colbert was merely a commissaire des guerres and secretary to Michel Le Tellier. The Colbert family borrowed heavily to provide a dowry of 40,000 livres for Marie, thus indicating an equal match between an upwardly mobile family of secondary magistrates from Soissons and a family of drapers-turned-royal servants from Reims. As a result of the heavy sacrifices made to get this match, Marie Colbert was the only one of Colbert's sisters who married; four other sisters became nuns. If anything, the Desmaretz clan was superior to the Colbert clan, except that Colbert's ties to the court foreshadowed a possibly bright future.[4]

After 1661 Jean Desmaretz's career was tied to Colbert's rise in the government. As a member of the Bureau of Finances of Soissons, Jean assisted the provincial intendant on tax matters and often performed the duties of the provincial intendant during the latter's absences from 1664 until his own death in 1682.[5]

In a memorandum written for his cousin, Colbert's son Seignelay, Nicolas Desmaretz described his activities as Colbert's assistant. In April 1664 he was charged with expediting the accounts of the Maison du Roi and all royal households, as well as handling the mémoires and placets for Colbert. During the War of Devolution (1667–68) he worked almost alone with his uncle because the other commis were either absent or ill. When the Lease Legendre of 1668 changed the royal tax farms, Desmaretz was in charge of their administration. Reports from the tax farmers who were required to tour the provinces were used to help draw up the reforms undertaken by Colbert, with Desmaretz playing a fundamental role in the regulation of the farms.[6]

In 1669 all accounts of expenditures (*états au vray*) by comptables had to be presented to the Royal Council of Finances before being sent to the Chambre des Comptes. Colbert established a special section in the contrôle général des finances to verify these accounts. He put Desmaretz in charge and gave him the duty of reporting the accounts to the Royal Council.[7]

The Dutch War (1672–78) increased Desmaretz's activities and responsibilities, especially in the field of credit and borrowing. He was in charge of many extraordinary affairs designed to raise money without traités, such as taxes on the treasurers of France and the Paris police. He also directed efforts to lower interest rates on loans by repurchasing rentes. His activities included investigations into debts owed by past traités and negotiations with the clergy for loans or enhanced gifts.

Desmaretz's importance to his uncle is evident in the number of important offices or commissions he received. He became a counselor in the Parlement of Paris in 1671,[8] a supernumerary councilor of state (with the right to enter the council without legally being a member) in 1672, and a master of requests in 1674, despite his youth. That same year he was dispensed from obeying the regulations of the council established on January 3, 1673, when his right to enter the council and express an opinion was maintained.[9] His right to sit and voice an opinion on the Royal Council of Finances was necessary if he was to report on the accounts of the comptables as head of the section Colbert had created in the contrôle général des finances. On July 25, 1678, he became an intendant of finances, one of two official assistants to Colbert, and by law a councilor of state.[10] He sat with his great uncle Henri Pussort and the future controller general Le Peletier on the bureaus of the council that heard cases involving the aides and the domain.[11]

After the war, when he was intendant of finances, Desmaretz checked the accounts of the receivers general of finances and the traitants. He also edited the codification of 1680–81 of the laws on the General Farms.[12] Desmaretz had become an expert on all aspects of royal finances, from expenditures to tax collection, from loans to accounts. After the other intendant of finances, Vincent Hotman, died on March 14, 1683, he was not replaced prior to Colbert's death on September 6 of that year. Thus, Desmaretz was the only intendant of finances and should have been indispensable to Colbert's successor, Le Peletier. Nevertheless, Desmaretz was dismissed on December 23, 1683, forced to resign all his offices and commissions, and exiled to his estate at Maillebois because of his involvement in a contract to mint money.

A dearth of coinage was endemic to France's economy in the seventeenth century. The monetary system of France relied on coins in general commerce. War led to the export of precious metal and caused the monarchy to devote valuable amounts of its resources to obtaining gold and, more commonly, silver for import into France for the manufacture of coins to keep the wheels of commerce turning. There were several instances in the seventeenth century when the crown resorted to contracting for the manufacture of coins of small denominations. Each of these instances resulted in a serious outbreak of counterfeiting, coin shaving, and other problems.[13]

During the Dutch War, at the instigation of Louis Béchameil, a secretary to the council of finances and a major financier who was related to Colbert and whose daughter Madeleine married Desmaretz in 1673,[14] Colbert agreed to lease the right to mint coins in small denominations of two, three, and four sous to a company of financiers from Lyon under the name of Jean-Baptiste Lucot, who was called a bourgeois of Lyon but was actually a simple prête-nom or frontman, probably a commis or assistant to one of the investors. The principal backers of this traité were André Clautrier (a gold thread manufacturer),[15] Gaspard Hindret de Beaulieu (a Lyon refiner with ties to the Colbert clan), Abraham de Can, Jean-François de La Live, and Jean Solu. The lease ran for three years, from October 1674 until October 1677, and paid 1.89 million livres to the Royal Treasury. The new pieces were underweight in the proportion of silver to the legal value of the coins; in other words, the king was issuing money with a legal value that did not correspond to the intrinsic value of the silver in the coins. What was worse, the manufacturers did not control the quality of their product, with the result that the coins did not all contain the same quantity of precious metal. In one royal inspection of seven coins, two were found to contain less silver than the other five.

The amount of coins to be minted was not stated in the traité, only the places where the work was to be done and the amount of time to be spent on the work each day. The minting had to be done in Paris and Lyon, and only during daylight hours, described as thirteen hours during winter and sixteen hours during summer. The crown supplied the equipment for the work. When the company complained about the small size of the Lyon mint, they received permission to move the work to the bourg of Neufville, four leagues upstream. Neufville was a marquisate belonging to the Villeroy family, whose leader was also head of the Royal Council of Finances at the time. Most of the money was minted in Neufville rather than Paris. The profits from the traité were so excessive that, on November 14, 1676, Colbert persuaded the Royal Council to require the company to pay an additional 500,000 livres to the crown.

The underweight four sous pieces were produced in such great quantities that they became the principal money for the average French subject. The uneven quality of the coins attracted counterfeiters both within and outside of France. The minting of these coins ceased with the expiration of the lease, and minting reverted to being an administered function under the control of Christophe de La Live, brother to Jean-François and brother-in-law to Abraham de Can.[16] After the expiration of the lease Desmaretz, as his uncle's principal advisor on monetary affairs, worked to end the flood of counterfeit coins in France. The four sous pieces were finally devalued to 3½ sous in March 1679.

Despite rumors of excessive profits and bribes to prominent people in high places, nothing further was done to pursue these matters while Colbert lived. The rumors mentioned Desmaretz foremost because he was undertaking expensive renovations at Maillebois, the estate he had purchased in 1676.[17]

The death of Colbert deprived Desmaretz of his principal benefactor and protector. Colbert's office of secretary of state for the Maison du Roi and the navy went to his son, Jean-Baptiste Colbert de Seignelay. Another son, Jules-Armand Colbert d'Ormoy and de Blainville, had the right to inherit the office of surintendant des bâtiments, but he had military rather than administrative ambitions. He was easily persuaded to sell the office to François-Michel Le Tellier de Louvois, the secretary of state for war and son of Chancellor Le Tellier.

The controllership general of finances was not an office but a commission granted by the king's will. Louis XIV announced his choice for Colbert's successor the day after Colbert's death, but the matter had been under consideration for some time because Colbert had been seriously ill since August 18.[18] The king apparently considered many candidates, according to various stories.[19]

The choice of Le Peletier, who immediately entered the Conseil d'en haut, swung the balance of power in the struggle for influence with the king to the Le Telliers. They now held the chancellorship, with its legal powers; the position of secretary of state for war, with its administrative power in the generality of Lyon; and the controllership general of finances, for which Desmaretz worked. Together with their control over the fortifications, bâtiments, and postes, they had a formidable power base. The Colberts had only one minister in place, although an important one, in Croissy, the secretary of state for foreign affairs. Seignelay would not enter the Conseil d'en haut until September 1689. Immediately after Colbert's death, these two had to contend with Le Tellier, Louvois, and Le Peletier, who worked almost every day with Louis XIV.

The Le Telliers almost immediately launched an investigation into what was called the "affair of the four sous pieces," referring to the Lucot contract to mint coins and the suspected graft and corruption surrounding that contract. Reports came from a new intendant at Lyon of contraventions of the terms of the original lease. An earlier report written while Colbert lived had given the mint at Lyon a clean bill of health. After further correspondence the Royal Council of Finances launched an official investigation following an arrêt reported by Le Peletier himself on December 4, 1683.[20]

Clautrier was the first to fall into the government's hands. His statements were taken during December and January. This information led to the arrest on December 21, 1683, of François Bellinzani, who had served under Colbert as inspector general of manufacturing and commerce, and director general of the domaine d'Occident and of the royal trading companies. Two days later, Desmaretz's cousin Seignelay told him to go to Maillebois. He would later be asked to resign his office of master of requests.[21]

The Le Telliers and their underlings pressed Bellinzani for evidence against Colbert's nephew and Colbert's administration as far back as 1661. This was the ultimate revenge of Nicolas Foucquet's allies, who had been hounded by Colbert and his allies in the 1660s. (Foucquet had died in 1680.) Unfortunately for their plans, Bellinzani died in prison in April 1684. The persecution of Colbert's financial supporters continued to the detriment of the state's credit. The government pursued Bellinzani's heirs for money that it claimed he owed for his involvement in finances. Among the statements that he made before his death, Bellinzani claimed that the financiers behind the four sous-piece lease paid him 120,000 livres, five-eighths of which (75,000 livres) he paid to Desmaretz. He made this payment after the lease was settled, and it was not unlike other gratifications paid to royal servants at the time.

In April 1684 a special court called the Chambre de l'Arsenal took over the investigation into this affair, along with others derived from Bellinzani's testimony.[22] The financiers behind the contract to mint four sous pieces were fined over 1.5 million livres, but they never paid this entire sum. In addition to their share of the fine, the Bellinzani family was asked to pay 200,000 livres as well as to account for 110,700 livres that Bellinzani supposedly owed to the royal government. Forced to give up the receivership general of finances in Lyon that he had acquired in 1679, Clautrier along with his partner, Hindret de Beaulieu, were each fined 3,000 livres and exiled from Paris and Lyon for three years. The whole affair ended in 1687.[23] The Chambre de l'Arsenal was a miniature Chambre de justice like that which Colbert had initiated in 1661 to pursue Foucquet's people. It investigated all sorts of financial affairs in order to keep the public eye on past matters as a means of convincing them that the new administration was more diligent in handling royal finances than Colbert had been. Chamillard would begin a similar process in 1700.

Saint-Simon, who was not an eyewitness to any of these events, repeats many false stories about Desmaretz's fall, saying that Colbert himself, shortly before his death, had uncovered Desmaretz's criminal acts, and that Le Peletier dismissed Desmaretz in front of an audience of onlookers. Several eighteenth-century histories repeat these stories. There is no evidence in any of Colbert's papers that he had turned against his nephew. During his last three weeks of life, Colbert was unable to sign anything.[24] Desmaretz's own account of his dismissal describes his cousin Seignelay as telling him in private to go to his estate at Maillebois until he received further orders. Desmaretz wrote that he was not asked to resign his position as master of requests until six months later, and that Seignelay held on to his resignation for several months until the king instructed him to turn it over to the treasurer of the casual parties, where it could be sold to someone else.

Desmaretz never admitted to having done anything wrong. At the instigation of his uncle Croissy, he wrote one mémoire to defend himself in which he laid the blame on the Le Tellier clan for besmirching his reputation. According to Desmaretz, Chancellor Le Tellier quickly realized that he had misjudged Le Peletier, whom he discovered to be not very diligent, of limited intelligence, and lacking the necessary knowledge to be a good finance minister. Thus, the chancellor had to destroy Desmaretz's reputation as the Colbert clan's candidate for that position. Desmaretz criticized the investigation because witnesses were persuaded to say what the investigators wanted to hear. They had hoped that Bellinzani would provide them with evidence tying Desmaretz to all sorts of chicanery. After Bellinzani's death the Le Telliers resorted to spreading rumors by telling the king that they kept uncovering new evidence against Desmaretz that linked him to suspicion of wrongdoing under Colbert.[25]

One historian has described Desmaretz as having "already had a reputation for being unable to distinguish his private purse from that of the king."[26] The controller general and his assistants, the intendants of finances, did not handle the king's funds and, thus, could not mix their purse with that of the king. Desmaretz was accused of accepting money from those who did business with the crown in return for contracts or profits that were beyond those legally allowed or described in their contracts. The charge was never proven when it was first made against Desmaretz when he worked for his uncle, or later when he was controller general, but anyone who worked for the government and accepted money from people doing business with the government was automatically suspected of being influenced by that money. There is no doubt that Desmaretz received money from government contractors, office-seekers, and others. In fact, every senior government official did the same thing. Like all royal ministers, Desmaretz became wealthier because he served the king. It cannot be proven that he was more or less corrupt than his colleagues or that his ministry was more or less efficient because of the monetary nexus that connected him to the financiers.

During Desmaretz's lifetime the people who made these kinds of charges verbally were either unable or unwilling to prove them after his dismissal from the government, either in the 1680s following his uncle's death or after 1715 following Louis XIV's death. If his enemies were unable to prove these charges and therefore did not press them, there is nothing that can be added to the record. If his enemies were unwilling to press these charges, their motives for making them can be questioned. Perhaps they did not want to expose the entire corrupt network that supported the magnificence of Louis XIV and his society.[27] Or perhaps these charges were simply politically motivated to remove Desmaretz from office. Or, they wanted to remove Desmaretz from power and were reluctant to go further out of fear of exposing their own corruption. In any case, the charges haunted Desmaretz for the rest of his life, and even after his death.

Recent scholarship has shown that the men who worked at the highest levels of the French government made fortunes that cannot be explained by the money they earned as ministers or from their properties. Joseph Bergin has exposed how Cardinal Richelieu enriched himself so greatly in the service of France that he left a fortune worth more than 22 million livres at his death. Cardinal Mazarin, who died in 1661 and left an estate worth 37 million livres, has been called the wealthiest private individual in Europe. He made his fortune through government contracting and outright fraud, with the help of good business managers like Colbert and Foucquet. Colbert's fortune at his death was less than 5 million livres but it was still more than could be made from his salary and personal income. The same can be said of Louvois, who left a fortune of more than 8 million livres. The unfortunate Foucquet left behind a fortune that has been estimated as worth either 15 million or 18 million livres at the time of his arrest, but he had debts equal to his worth. His arrest prevented him from repaying his debts.[28]

Claude Le Peletier, by contrast, who had a reputation for being honest, left behind a fortune worth almost 1.5 million livres. Michel Chamillard, another man with a reputation for honesty, left a legacy worth slightly more than half a million livres. Both men did not die in office, however, but left the government several years before their deaths, although they both continued to receive 20,000 livres annually as ministers of state until their decease.[29]

According to the marriage contract with the family of Madeleine Béchameil, Desmaretz had a personal worth of 50,000 livres at the time of his marriage in 1673. Madeleine's dowry added 100,000 livres to the community property. At the time of the marriage, Desmaretz held various commissions but no offices. Whether he had acquired any property is unknown. His major property acquisitions occurred during 1678–80, when he acquired Maillebois and lands in the Thymerais. He also rearranged local communities, moving villages from one place to another and angering the local populations, whose protests the Le Telliers probably picked up in their efforts to collect evidence on Desmaretz's possible involvement in corruption. During his twenty years out of power, Desmaretz acquired small parcels of land in the Maillebois area. He also inherited some land in Picardy from his mother in 1703. His second period of property acquisition took place after he became minister in 1708, when he bought land in Paris and Versailles, along with some property in Picardy and in Champagne. At the time of his death in 1721, his wealth, including landed property, liquidity, personal effects, books, and wine, amounted to approximately 1.35 million livres, with a total of 400,000 livres in debt. He earned 36,400 livres in income from his properties.[30] Interestingly, Desmaretz's personal fortune at his death was less than that of Claude Le Peletier, a reputedly honest man who had accused Desmaretz of corruption.

By the standards of the Western world in the twenty-first century, the men who worked for the government of Louis XIV were all corrupt. Their corruption left them open to being accused of some sort of malfeasance, as happened to Foucquet and Desmaretz. Many parts of the world, however, do not regard it as corrupt if someone in authority accepts gifts from someone else for whom they have performed some government service, such as granting a contract, pension, or gratification. Refusing to accept those gifts would be regarded as insulting because it would imply that there was something wrong, that the gifts were inadequate, or, worse, that the offer of a gift implied that the action was immoral. The refusal of a gift would also make the giver beholden to the person who had done him a favor. The person who offered the gift would thus try to achieve a material balance by doing something for the person who had done him a favor. The moral indebtedness, however, would remain and would be acknowledged by word and deed.[31]

No legal investigation or court decision ever determined whether Desmaretz's involvement in the four sous-piece affair was illegal and subject to criminal prosecution. Nevertheless, his reputation suffered permanent damage. The Le Telliers were glad to rid themselves of Colbert's handpicked successor by tarnishing his name, especially in the king's mind.

Despite the effort to destroy Desmaretz, Le Peletier corresponded with him and even adopted his advice in policy matters. Desmaretz's uncle Croissy tried to get him appointments in the foreign service but the slanders of the Le Telliers blocked him at every turn. Desmaretz was not allowed to leave Maillebois until March 1686,[32] after the death of Chancellor Le Tellier, when Paul de Saint-Aignan, duc de Beauvillier and Colbert's son-in-law, was head of the Royal Council of Finances, thus adding another Colbert to the balance of forces in the government.

The anti-Colbert faction usually referred to as the "Le Tellier faction" did not disappear with the death of Chancellor Le Tellier in 1685 or his son Louvois in 1691. Colbert's successor, Claude Le Peletier, was a defender of the Le Telliers. As we have seen, he appointed his brother Michel Le Peletier de Souzy as an intendant of finances and later added Louis de Phélypeaux de Pontchartrain to his coterie of assistants. While Le Peletier tried withdrawing from the government in 1689, and finally did withdraw in September 1697, his brother would remain in major positions in the government until his death in 1722. Pontchartrain would also be a major player in the government for the rest of the reign until his resignation in July 1714. These men and their supporters would be the survivors of the Le Tellier faction at court and would continue to have a role in the royal government into the reign of Louis XV.

When Desmaretz did return to power in 1703 he would use his position to help those friends who had suffered during the purge of 1683–87. Bellinzani's heirs were protected and finally discharged from the debts Bellinzani owed by an arrêt reported by Desmaretz himself in 1714.[33] The maréchal-duc de Villeroy, who had been connected to the affair of the four sous pieces, remained a close personal friend of Desmaretz's and would succeed Beauvillier as head of the Royal Council of Finances in September 1714. The de la Lives and Paulin Prondre, who was rumored to have been a silent partner in the affair, would serve as receivers general of finances and advisors to the future controller general of finances.[34] Clautrier's son Gilbert would serve as Desmaretz's secretary from 1703 until the latter left government.

During the 1680s Desmaretz was a secret financial advisor for both his family and Le Peletier, whom he counseled on the regulations of the farms of the traites that were released in 1687.[35] He wrote that he conferred on several occasions with Pontchartrain when the latter was controller general of finances. He also claimed that he had submitted proposals to Beauvillier that the Royal Council adopted, earning the crown 60 million livres during the years 1689–91.[36] His activities from 1693 until 1699 are wrapped in mystery. He must have been in regular contact with his family because he appeared at so many family functions during the period where he signed legal documents but neither he nor anyone else has described his activity.[37]

The ascension of Michel Chamillard to the controllership general of finances in September 1699 inaugurated Desmaretz's reappearance on the political stage as a behind-the-scenes advisor. Chamillard's mémoire to Louis XIV in November 1699 describing the state of royal finances when he assumed the controllership concludes with a paragraph mentioning the attachment of a mémoire by M. Desmaretz that would clarify the necessity of increasing revenues to meet expenses.[38] Although the attached mémoire has not survived, Chamillard's open acknowledgment of Desmaretz's assistance was an advancement over the silence about Desmaretz that Le Peletier and Pontchartrain had practiced with the king. We also know that Desmaretz played an important role in Chamillard's aborted attempt to recover debts from the financiers in 1700 before the War of the Spanish Succession began, but, again, Chamillard could not employ Desmaretz openly.[39]

Desmaretz's political position was ameliorated possibly because, with Torcy as foreign minister and Beauvillier on the Royal Council of Finances, and both men on the Council of Ministers, the Colbert clan seemed to be on the rise. Beauvillier tried but failed to have Desmaretz named as a financial advisor to Louis XIV's grandson, Felipe V of Spain, in 1701. Chamillard opposed this posting because he did not want to give up his best advisor.[40]

Chamillard's appointment to assume Barbezieux's office as secretary of state for war while keeping the controllership general of finances overwhelmed the man. Because he directed so much patronage from these two positions, Chamillard increasingly worked with Madame de Maintenon's advice on finding people for government positions. Maintenon had recommended Desmaretz to Chamillard in 1699 and probably supported the minister's efforts to persuade Louis to recognize Desmaretz's services more openly.[41] Together, Maintenon, Chamillard, and the Colbert clan, with the possible support of Chancellor Pontchartrain, persuaded the king to acknowledge in a public audience on September 19, 1703, that Desmaretz had his confidence. Less than a month later Desmaretz would replace one of the directors of finance, Hilaire Rouillé du Coudray, to become one of the two principal assistants to the controller general.[42] After twenty years of political oblivion, Desmaretz had returned to the very place he had been—as one of the two principal administrative assistants to the finance minister—when his uncle died.

During the next four and a half years Desmaretz assumed a larger and more involved role in managing the royal finances. On paper he was responsible for the gabelles, the Five Great Farms, the tobacco farm, water and forests, the Chambre des Comptes, the postes and messageries, powder and saltpeter, the domaine d'Occident, the Grande Conseil, the accounts of Navarre, Béarn, Alsace, Flanders, Franche Comté, Metz, and, notably, the mints.[43] Desmaretz was also involved in settling affairs after a few serious bankruptcies among the financiers in 1704–5 threatened the crown's access to foreign credit.[44]

Alongside Desmaretz, the other director of finances was Joseph-Jean-Baptiste Fleuriau d'Armenonville, whose half-sister was married to Claude Le Peletier, representative of what remained of the Le Tellier clan at court. Armenonville was thirteen years Desmaretz's junior. According to a letter from Chamillard, Desmaretz wanted to eliminate Armenonville because he did not want any equals in his position in the finance ministry. Both directors of finances reported matters to the Royal Council of Finances and thus had influence over policy. When the directorship was abolished after Desmaretz became controller general, Armenonville was reduced to serving as a councilor of state on the King's Council but not on any of the subcommittees with which Desmaretz worked.[45]

By 1704 Chamillard began pleading periodically with the king to allow him to resign as controller general. When his eighteen-year-old son, the marquis de Cany, was given the right to inherit the position of secretary of state for war in January 1707, the minister's grumbling increased in proportion to his family's apparent security. In January 1708 Cany married Colbert's granddaughter, the daughter of the duc de Mortemart and niece to both Beauvillier and Chevreuse.[46] The precarious health of the overburdened minister broke down in early February.[47] Finally, after securing a tenuous family alliance with the Colberts, perhaps in order to ingratiate himself with them further, Chamillard was able to persuade Louis XIV to accept his resignation as controller general of finances and to appoint Desmaretz as his successor.[48]

Desmaretz himself appears to have been taken unawares by this turn of events. His role in finances had increased in January when he assumed responsibility for the extraordinary of war and other details.[49] Many people in France took this news as the announcement of his appointment as controller general and sent their congratulations. His staff was busy sending out denials when the real appointment was announced.[50]

Desmaretz served as controller general for the rest of Louis XIV's reign, but he did suffer from health problems that at times prevented him from carrying out his duties. On February 21, 1713, at Marly, Desmaretz attended the usual Tuesday meeting of the Royal Council of Finances in some pain from his gout. He only attended the following day's meeting of the Conseil d'en haut because he was carried there on a special chair with a back and arms that could be removed during the meeting and then reattached so that he could be carried out.[51] Desmaretz later had a more serious attack of gout that led to cancellation of meetings of the Royal Council of Finances on March 23, 26, and 30, 1715, because only he, as controller general, could report to the Royal Council.[52]

Desmaretz had been living on the rue Vivienne in Paris, where he was his cousin Torcy's neighbor. When he became minister he bought a chateau at La Marche near Versailles that had belonged to Chamillard. He would use La Marche as his residence when he was expected to be at Versailles on a daily basis and the rue Vivienne as his residence in Paris. In 1710 he built a beautiful new hotel on the rue Richelieu with an entrance on the rue Saint-Marc, and removed himself from the rue Vivienne, where he had lived when he was in Paris since the 1680s.[53]

Desmaretz's relationship with the duc de Saint-Simon contained the seeds for much of the antipathy that the duke would relate in his memoires. Maillebois, the estate to which Desmaretz was exiled in 1683, is only about 20 kilometers from La Ferté Vidame, the seat of the Saint-Simons. The memorialist was only eight years old when Colbert's nephew was asked to leave Versailles. Saint-Simon says that his father introduced Desmaretz to local society and let the locals know that the exile was not to be treated as a pariah. Desmaretz recognized this debt to the elder Saint-Simons and visited them whenever he was at Maillebois after his exile ended. The younger Saint-Simon felt that Desmaretz owed him a debt as well because of what his father had done for him. Later, when Desmaretz as finance minister failed to show enough gratitude or to treat Saint-Simon with enough warmth, the duke swore to bring him down.

Saint-Simon's memoirs contain several, possibly repetitive, descriptions of Desmaretz's character:

> He was a big, good looking man, with a pleasant face and an appearance that indicated wisdom and gentleness, which however were the two qualities that it lacked the most. . . . He was a man with a sharp mind, slow and lazy, but ambition and the love of wealth spurred him onward.[54]
>
> He was a man who had more sense than wit, and who sounded more sensible than he actually was, somewhat heavy and slow, who spoke well and with some charm, yet [was] harsh, hot tempered, and dominated by an uncontrollable bad temper. Desmaretz was only a friend out of self-interest.[55]
>
> He had enough wit and sense that nothing should have been lacking in that area that might affect his behavior, and yet he lacked everything.[56]
>
> [Desmaretz had] a temperament that he did not master, and which made even women fear him, and . . . a laziness that slowed everything he did. His conduct was so depraved that no one would give good odds for his future.[57]
>
> Desmaretz was a boar who was so totally buried in his wallow that he ignored almost everything that was happening around him.[58]

Saint-Simon's story of the cause of his final break with Desmaretz says more about the duke's narrow view of his position in society and his duty toward the state than the writer realized. He sets the scene in 1711, one year before the death of the duc de Chevreuse, after explaining how Desmaretz had been seduced by his new friends at court and had allowed relations with his old friends, like Saint-Simon, to go cold. The duke deferred speaking to the finance minister about certain unpaid appointments until his wife pressed him to do so. He waited until after dinner, when he knew the minister would be in his office at Versailles. Upon seeing him, the finance minister approached him very excitedly and began talking before the duke could speak. He was complaining about how he was being criticized or accused of all manner of misdeeds while everyone was constantly after him for something. While the minister's complaints were vague and unfocused, he was clearly speaking to a friend about his troubles. The duke, however, had business on his mind and tried to interrupt the minister several times. Upon spying the papers in Saint-Simon's hands, Desmaretz took them, saying that he would see what could be done. While the minister continued talking, the duke made his escape. He told his wife and friends about this contretemps and swore from that moment to put the minister outside of any situation where he could brutalize anyone again. One of Desmaretz's commis informed Saint-Simon expressly the next day that his appointments had been paid.[59]

Despite the personal animosity and vitriol in Saint-Simon's descriptions, Desmaretz was apparently a hard man to like, for he seems to have had some of his uncle Colbert's personality. Colbert had been known as *le Nord*, the North Wind, because of his cold, abrupt nature. Desmaretz was that and more so, and had an occasional fit of temper that frightened people given to more courtly behavior so much that women at court disliked dealing with him. Given his extensive workload, Desmaretz was probably short-tempered and impatient at times. Hence, Madame de Saint-Simon sent her husband to request payments of what were probably her appointments. Desmaretz nonetheless had loyal friends like the maréchal-duc de Villeroy, whose friendship was not just based on financial interests. As to Saint-Simon's estimates of Desmaretz's lack of intelligence or wit, we must remember that the memorialist branded everyone he disliked, including Louis XIV, as being slow-witted, unintelligent, and poorly educated. Saint-Simon was very much like an eighteenth-century version of a blogger writing his memoirs in secret without having to worry about the reaction of his audience to his excesses.

We have another description of Desmaretz in a letter written in early 1709 by the duc de Chevreuse to François de Salignac de la Mothe-Fénelon, archbishop of Cambrai, preceptor to the Duke of Burgundy (the king's grandson and presumptive heir to the throne), and the ostensible intellectual leader of the group of reformers who had gathered around Burgundy. This group included Chevreuse and Beauvillier as well as Saint-Simon. Chevreuse's letter describes all the members of the council of ministers to Fénelon, who was living in his archdiocese in accordance with the king's command. (Louis XIV had ordered him to reside in his archdiocese following the Quietist controversy in the late 1690s.) Chevreuse praised Torcy and Beauvillier while dismissing Chamillard and Chancellor Pontchartrain as *inutile* (useless) in the great affairs of state. In a separate paragraph, he wrote:

> I forgot to speak to you about M. Desmarets [*sic*]; the more we see him at work, the more [he shows] good sense, just judgment, [and is] full of vigilance for that which concerns the part of state business committed to his care, and the more learned in fundamentals than anyone in everything that is useful or necessary for the realm, with a firm will to procure it.

Desmaretz's weakness, according to Chevreuse, was in matters of war and foreign affairs, in which he had little experience, but that would come with time.[60]

Another source within the government, the foreign minister Torcy, who was also Desmaretz's cousin, wrote that discussions in the Conseil d'en haut were more substantial after Desmaretz joined, and especially after Voysin had replaced Chamillard. Torcy came to rely on his cousin in struggling to build a coalition among the ministers to forge a successful peace.[61]

Desmaretz was a hard worker and, like many courtiers who emulated the king, he enjoyed hunting and what the French call the joys of the table. Desmaretz's personal interests are not indicated by the titles of some of the manuscripts sold after his death. He did enjoy studying the exotic culture of the Orient, not an unusual trait for a man of means in this era.[62] Although his library contained 3,029 books at his death, only 1,322 were identified in the inventory made after his death. Only 719 (or 54.4 percent) were in French, while 538 (or 40.7 percent) were in Latin and 11 (or 0.8 percent) were in both Latin and French. There were 2 Hebrew Bibles (along with 65 French Bibles, 16 in Latin, and 6 listed as polyglot), 35 books in Italian, and 7 in Spanish. History was the largest category (364 books, or 27.5 percent), jurisprudence next (313 books, or 23.7 percent), and finally literature (269 books, or 20.3 percent). His contemporary literary reading materials included books by La Fontaine and Perrault. He had a dictionary by Pierre Bayle, along with the *Dictionnaire de Trévoux*. We cannot say whether he read any of these books or simply collected them. He did have some valuable books, but the total value of his books in relation to his personal fortune, when compared to that of other wealthy Parisians, was less than the average of 5 to 10 percent of the total. His library only equaled 4.6 percent of his total wealth.[63] Such is the fragmentary nature of the evidence concerning his personality. Fortunately, we know more about his professional activities.

Figure 3.1. Nicolas Desmaretz, minister of state and controller general of finances. Engraving by Vallet. Reproduced with permission from Bibliothèque Nationale de France.

Saint-Simon had a favorable opinion of Desmaretz's wife, Madeleine, whose manners and upbringing were graceful and elegant, in sharp contrast to what the duke regarded as the bourgeois avidity for attention of Madame Voysin, the war minister's wife. Madeleine Desmaretz was raised by her father in a house of elegance and art where she became accustomed to royal attention and socializing with France's elite. The king must have been charmed by Madame Desmaretz, because she received one of the few royal guided tours of the gardens of Marly on April 18, 1709. She entertained the king's granddaughter-in-law and favorite, the Duchess of Burgundy, at a party on January 30, 1711. She supported a school attached to the church of St. Eustache in Paris that trained poor children to work. Despite her charming nature, Madame Desmaretz was apparently high-strung and given to bouts of illness that culminated in her final sickness.[64]

She had ten children, of which nine (four boys and five girls) attained adulthood; their fortunes reflected the fortune of their father.[65] One son and two daughters went into the church. Three sons became soldiers and gentlemen. The fact that three daughters and the eldest son married reveals Desmaretz's social importance at the time of these marriages.

One of Desmaretz's daughters, Marie-Madeleine, married Louis-Vincent, marquis de Goësbriand, on February 14, 1695, at a time when her father was out of government and out of royal favor. Goësbriand was a soldier and a royal equerry. He was eleven years younger than his father-in-law, and fifteen years older than his bride. He had already risen to the rank of brigadier by the time he married Marie-Madeleine. During the Nine Years' War he spent his military career in Italy, where he returned during the Spanish Succession and rose to lieutenant general before being wounded at the siege of Turin in 1706. He commanded the center in the attack on the Allies at Toulon in 1707. His heroic defense of Aire from September until November of 1710 further enhanced his reputation as a soldier. In 1711 he was admitted to the Order of the Holy Spirit, France's highest order of knighthood. He was also made governor of Verdun. Saint-Simon refers to him as Desmaretz's *fort riche* son-in-law whose wealth led to the marriage of his son to a member of the marquis de Châtillon's family.[66]

Charlotte-Angélique Desmaretz married a very wealthy master of requests, Charles Henri de Malon, seigneur de Bercy, on September 22, 1705, after her father had returned to government as a director of finances. At the time of his marriage, Bercy was the commis in charge of the bureau of the états au vray but he would soon assume a very important position in financial administration, where he worked with his father-in-law. Bercy was the son of a master of requests, Anne-Louis-Jules de Malon, seigneur de Bercy. The elder Bercy became a master of requests at the same time as Desmaretz in 1674. The two men knew each other and had worked together in the royal administration while Colbert was alive. The elder Bercy died in 1706 and left his fortune to his son.[67] Desmaretz was now able to marry his family into the administrative nobility, the noblesse de plume, but even greater marriages ensued after he became minister.

Louise Desmaretz married Louis-Pierre-Maximilien, marquis de Béthune, a member of the Sully clan, on January 9, 1709. Her father had been named minister of state in November 1708 in acknowledgment of his position as one of the king's closest advisers and collaborators. Béthune would eventually inherit the title duc de Sully in 1730, thus making Louise Desmaretz a duchess. This marriage placed the Desmaretz clan among the highest social levels in France, the dukes and peers. The king wanted to honor Desmaretz by providing a gift of 200,000 livres to the bride, but, given the sorry state of royal finances, the minister would not have it. According to both Dangeau and Saint-Simon, Desmaretz and the king haggled over how much of a pension to grant Louise Desmaretz before they agreed to a royal pension of 10,000 livres.[68]

Like the male descendants of the Colberts, Desmaretz's male children either entered the Church or served in the military. The eldest, Jean-Baptiste-François Desmaretz, marquis de Maillebois, enlisted in the military at age twenty-one and rose to the rank of brigadier just before the siege of Lille that began in August 1708. By the time the citadel surrendered on December 8, 1708, his father was serving as minister of state. The Allies insisted on keeping Maillebois as a hostage, in lieu of debts they insisted the French owed, because he was the son of the French finance minister. Maillebois escaped in March 1711, when the Allies threatened to imprison the hostages in order to press the French to repay the debts. His escape made him a national hero. His reward came the next year on the death of his cousin Seignelay (Colbert's grandson) in February 1712, when Maillebois was given the charge of master of the king's wardrobe, even though the charge was supposed to cost 500,000 livres The king gave him 200,000 livres outright, and the rest in a royal guarantee called a *brevet d'assurance.* On January 26, 1713, Maillebois married Marie-Emmanuelle d'Alègre, daughter of another military man, the marquis d'Alègre. The couple received a royal gift of 200,000 livres and Maillebois was named lieutenant general of Languedoc, with an income of 20,000 livres. Desmaretz's family was clearly ensconced in the highest levels of the nobility, with close proximity to the king. In fact, Saint-Simon says that by 1712–13 Desmaretz had become one of the king's favorites, as symbolized by the advancement of his son Maillebois.[69]

Two of Desmaretz's daughters became nuns. Marie Thérèse became abbess of Hières in the Paris diocese, and Elisabeth-Julie was a nun in the priory of Villarceaux in the Rouen diocese where her aunt Charlotte-Thérèse was prioress. After defending his thesis at the University of Paris in

1705, Pierre Desmaretz later became abbé of Saint-Bénigne in Dijon in July 1710 and abbé of Saint-Nicolas-aux-Bois in the diocese of Laon in January 1715.[70] These children, especially Pierre, benefited from their father's position as well. In fact, Nicolas Desmaretz's financial acumen established the entire Desmaretz clan in a prominent position throughout the eighteenth century.

Nicolas Desmaretz had two younger brothers in the clergy who rose to prominence, despite his own eclipse during 1683–1703. Jacques Desmaretz rose to be agent general of the clergy during 1678–85, after which he was named bishop of Riez. After Nicolas had returned to power, Jacques was given a richer bishopric at Auch in 1713. He died in 1725. Vincent François Desmaretz began his career in the navy, rose to the rank of ship's captain, and bought a company of French guards in 1680. He quit the service by 1687 to study canon law and entered a seminary in 1692. He became agent general of the clergy in 1698 and then bishop of Saint Malo from 1702 until his death in 1739.[71]

In February 1708 Colbert's nephew, the recipient of all the great minister's financial and fiscal training, as well as his principles for commerce, finally received his appointment to the position for which he had trained. As a former intendant of finances who had a prominent role in Colbert's tax farm reforms, Desmaretz should have been a true believer in the state's control of commerce for political purposes, a *dirigiste* par excellence, and the emblem of Colbertism.

His Ideas

Nicolas Desmaretz never wrote any lengthy treatises explaining his financial theories, but he did supply his relatives with proposals during the first ten years of his exile from power. These proposals permit us to understand how he approached finances and commerce during his years in exile before he returned to a position of responsibility.[72] During his own ministry, Desmaretz wrote memoranda for the king, Madame de Maintenon, and his cousin Torcy.[73] Finally, short pieces written by Desmaretz after the death of Louis XIV also contain financial proposals for dealing with the postwar situation.[74]

Desmaretz had great admiration for his uncle Colbert, whose ministry he saw as a golden age, something to which France should strive to return. Several of Desmaretz's writings compare the situation in 1661, when Colbert came to power, to that of 1683, when Colbert died. He then explains why the situation deteriorated since his uncle's death.[75] Desmaretz was particularly critical of the damage that Le Peletier's actions had done to royal credit. The foundations of the state's credit, according to Desmaretz, rested on the ability of the king's finance minister to deal with the men who lent their money to the state.

Desmaretz was extremely critical of the purge of the financiers and lending institutions undertaken after Colbert's death. The Caisse des emprunts, which had allowed the king to borrow large sums of money for short periods of time by issuing interest-bearing promissory notes backed by the revenue from the gabelles, was dismantled within one year after Colbert died. To repay these debts on such short notice required increasing interest rates on perpetual rentes from denier 20 (5 percent) to denier 18 (5.5 percent) in order to sell 3.4 million livres' worth of rentes and a million livres in augmented gages. Even rentes sold during Colbert's ministry at denier 20 had to be recalled and sold at denier 18, a process that actually cost the king money. Instead of paying out 2 million livres for every twenty invested, the crown was forced to pay 3 or 4 million livres. Le Peletier also rejected an offer in 1687 to maintain the unified General Farms that would have increased the lease price by a million livres annually. Instead, he accepted a combined bid that divided the General Farms for 1.5 million livres less than another bid. Desmaretz could only marvel at such decisions.[76]

While most of his writing is filled with references to money, credit, and taxation, and includes a large measure of statistics and figures that can confuse or mystify someone who is not familiar with the details, Desmaretz did write two major memoranda that reveal his ideas about the role of the king's finance minister, the wealth of nations, taxation, and government spending, without referring to statistics. Discussing the years immediately after his exile from the government, Desmaretz says that his cousin Seignelay called him to Sceaux, the residence of the senior Colberts, in the spring of 1689. Here Seignelay asked him to write a series of memoranda on finances that would be acceptable for the king to read. Desmaretz described one such memorandum that discussed how royal credit could be reestablished after the damage caused by Le Peletier's purge of the financiers who had supported Colbert. A copy of this memoir, dated May 29, 1689, exists in the Archives Nationales.[77] It mentions neither Colbert nor Le Peletier by name, but it does compare their actions as finance ministers. Perhaps Desmaretz intended this nineteen-page paper to support the Colbert family's efforts to have one of their own replace Le Peletier, who had been asking to be relieved of his duties for some time.

According to Desmaretz, Colbert had established credit so thoroughly that people could hardly wait to invest in royal affairs. Colbert assiduously courted the financial community after taking power in 1661, when credit had been exhausted. His constant vigilance, skill, and acquaintance with various business circles were necessary to attract private money to royal coffers. In addition to having the qualities of a good finance minister, Colbert understood one great truth—that amassing great quantities of useless treasure was less important to the crown than setting the tax rate at a point where taxes were easiest to collect with as little constraint as possible.

The fundamental principle of Colbert's ministry was that royal credit depended on the credit of the *gens d'affaires*—the tax farmers, receivers general of finances, and financiers—who would be asked to borrow money from the public in order to advance money to the crown in times of need. In Desmaretz's mind, a good finance minister would have to manage (*ménager*) these men by honoring them with graces and marks of favor that would attract investors who wished to profit from those who benefited from royal favor. Any financiers who worked less than satisfactorily to attract loans should be set out from the others, and replaced when necessary. At the same time, the minister should insure prompt and exact repayment of royal loans to these men so as to encourage investors to place their money at the king's disposal.

By 1672 Colbert had so completely gained the confidence of the financial community that, with only two weeks' notice, he was able to raise 8 million livres in coin to accompany the king during the opening campaign of the Dutch War. Royal credit was so well established that Colbert had little trouble borrowing money to support eight years of the greatest war France had ever fought. (Desmaretz was writing in 1689 before the Nine Years' War, or the War of the Spanish Succession.) Colbert saw to it that men who were efficient and exact, and had good credit, occupied the ranks of the tax farmers, receivers general of finances, secretaries of the council, and other profitable offices. By extending the rights and privileges of these offices, Colbert avoided the creation of new offices when he needed money.

In 1661 Colbert found that direct borrowing from the public through the sale of rentes revealed that royal credit had sunk so low that rentes were selling for interest rates as high as denier 5 (20 percent), denier 4 (25 percent), and even denier 2 (50 percent), like the 1.2 million livres in rentes created by Foucquet in 1661. Colbert's efforts lowered interest rates so much that, by 1674, he could sell rentes at denier 14 (7.1 percent), and then proceed to lower the interest rate to denier 20 (5 percent) while simultaneously paying for a war. The public had such confidence in Colbert that rentes sold with ease. Colbert paid close attention to guaranteeing the prompt payment of rentes by overseeing the activities of the payers of the rentes. He also made the sale of government bonds so profitable for notaries that they found purchasers for him rather than forcing him to resort to traitants with high fees. By reducing the delay between the creation and the sale of rentes, Colbert sustained the government's supply of money in order to reinforce its good credit.

The Caisse des emprunts, backed by the profits of two tax farmers, completed Colbert's efforts to reinforce royal credit. Colbert was able to borrow as much as 36 million livres by issuing short-term promissory notes.

Le Peletier distrusted this innovation and dismantled it after accusing its administration of corruption. A good finance minster, said Desmaretz, would have corrected the abuses rather than destroying the institution.

According to Desmaretz, Le Peletier's administration lost the confidence of the business community by being dilatory or indecisive when businessmen submitted suggestions to the government. The purge of certain businessmen by the Chambre de l'Arsenal persuaded the rest of them to refrain from involving themselves too closely in government affairs for fear of later condemnations. Le Peletier was forced to turn to lesser-known men to fill positions in the tax farms and receiverships general of finances, and thus did not succeed in attracting investor confidence. The final characteristic of Le Peletier's administration that cost him business confidence was government hesitation about adopting new policies. The government circulated memoranda about policy changes but rarely decided anything until its indecision dissuaded the business community from supporting the proposed policies.

Desmaretz's main argument is that a royal finance minister should maintain the credit of the richest and most trusted financiers. If any action is necessary to correct administrative abuses, this action should tend to increase the efficiency of managing royal credit, not destroy the credit of the accountables and gens d'affaires: "The rule in these kinds of occasions is to make them fearful and to take from them, in this fear, their best effects; then it is certain that you will be able to demand more surely one million from a businessman while maintaining his credit than taking one hundred thousand while holding him in prison."[78] The king's minister, Desmaretz believed, must cleverly encourage these kinds of people to maintain their possessions in the open so as to better sustain their credit and retain their loyalty, rather than frighten them into hiding their belongings to avoid prosecution. Close supervision of their activities would inhibit excessive profiteering to some extent. Once the time of need passed, the government could then prosecute any flagrantly abusive practices.

Desmaretz regarded the controller general as the proper person to manage a great number of financiers upon whom the credit of the state rested. (Some historians take a contrary view in describing Louis XIV's state as totally dependent on the financiers.)[79] Desmaretz insisted that a good minister must keep close watch over his flock of financiers, checking their accounts and discussing the details of their business. He claimed that Le Peletier had a practice of simply granting audiences that produced no decisions. Once the king's minister gained the financiers' trust, he could encourage them to borrow larger sums of money, and thus make them more dependent on royal funds for maintaining their credit. They became loyal servants of the crown because their welfare was tied to the welfare of the state. By keeping a close watch on their affairs, the minister prevented excessive profiteering and would be able to seize their goods during calmer times if he discovered corruption in the way they handled the king's business. Desmaretz saw a symbiotic relationship between the state and the financiers, between two dependent parasites living off each other, instead of a dependency that was only beneficial to the financiers.

In order to maintain this credit machinery, the government required revenue from taxation and fees. France's tax system depended upon commerce and the existence of monetary exchange. The largest source of income for the crown was the royal tax farms that received money from perceptions and trading monopolies, both of which relied on commercial exchange to be successful. Therefore, the impositions or direct taxes were levied only in coin, thus requiring the taxpayers either to produce goods for sale or to be paid a wage for their labor. Tax collections passed through the hands of the very men who extended their credit to the government while deducting the principal and interest of their loans from their payments to the government. They also dispensed money locally on the orders of the government, thus helping to maintain the money supply in the provinces in order to sustain a certain level of commerce.

Desmaretz worried about the circulation of money within the French economy because any decline in the circulation of money would reduce tax revenues or make the collection of taxes more difficult. He believed that there was a proper balance to be maintained between the level of taxation and the amount of government expenditures. In a paper that he wrote to Le Peletier himself, Desmaretz criticized the high level of taxation that the government had maintained since the end of the Dutch War.[80] This high level of taxation took the form of higher taxes on salt, stamped paper, tobacco, gold, silver, tin, beverages, and certain monopolies, such as the right to sell freshwater fish in Paris. Such taxes led to a shortage of specie in the provinces and caused a decrease in the amount of commerce that further reduced revenue. The decrease in revenue caused certain people in the government (whom Desmaretz does not name) to advocate higher levels of taxation to make up for the shortfall. Instead of increasing revenue, however, the new, higher taxes accelerated the decrease in revenues. The decline in the amount of specie in the French economy was accentuated by the huge amounts of money sent to the frontiers and beyond to maintain an excessively large royal army. Desmaretz's arguments seem in some ways to be similar to the present-day debate over the rate of taxation and its impact on the economy.

In order to restore the circulation of money, Desmaretz recommended that the controller general have an exact knowledge of the conditions within each province and the kinds of business conducted there. Industries such as weaving and stocking-making would help to alleviate poverty by providing the poor with work and money. The government should also maintain a public works program of road- and canal-building to encourage the development of trade in the provinces, Desmaretz wrote. And while he did not recommend any major effort to start new industries, he felt that existing industries should receive help through subsidies, tax exemptions, and especially proper monetary policies that would end the money shortage. The employment of the poor would increase commerce and give them the wherewithal to purchase livestock and increase their stakes in society. In keeping with this argument, Desmaretz criticized a policy that prevailed in the department of bâtiments under Louvois that failed to pay workers an adequate wage for the heavy labor involved in making the Eure River navigable. Higher pay would have attracted more workers and increased their ability to pay their taxes, as well as to feed and clothe their families, thus stimulating commerce: "It's by these channels that money is spread, taxes are paid, and the State subsists, like the human body by the circulation of blood in the little arteries that are spread throughout all the parts that compose it."[81]

Desmaretz had the same ideas in 1687 that Boisguilbert would publish in 1695. Desmaretz, like Boisguilbert, saw wealth as the product of the industry of the French people, not as something defined by useless treasure or the amount of gold or silver circulating in the economy. Colbert's policies, by contrast, have sometimes been described as "bullionist," in that they measured wealth in terms of the amount of gold and silver within France.[82] This is a false reading of mercantilist thinking, however. It conveniently encourages the idea that men like Boisguilbert and Vauban were tremendous innovators years ahead of their time. Desmaretz wanted France to have a favorable balance of trade internationally in order to keep a large stock of specie within France that would provide the stimulus for greater trade and industry, and thus increase the taxable wealth of France. The crown would see increased wealth from the industry of the French people that had been encouraged by protectionist trade measures to facilitate the accumulation of capital to finance the expansion of the economy.[83]

Desmaretz's note to Le Peletier was probably generated by the government's quest for more information about what to do in the face of serious economic difficulties. A commission of masters of requests and councilors of state, which included Chamillard and Daguesseau among others, had been created in 1687 to look into the problems of rural poverty by examining the situation in the generalities of Orléans and Tours. They issued a memorandum detailing these problems and how to remedy them.[84] It was at this time that La Bruyère wrote his famous description in *Les caractères* of the French peasantry as wild animals that turn over the ground and subsist on black bread, water, and roots.[85] Desmaretz was clearly a man of his times who, from his place of exile at Maillebois, was able to see the evidence of poverty around him. The fact that his nemesis and persecutor consulted him was remarkable, but what he said was less so.

Desmaretz concluded his memorandum to Le Peletier with a condemnation of the excessive number of privileged people who were exempt from the taille.[86] He was writing in 1687, prior to the great expansion of the number of offices granting exemption from the taille that occurred in the 1690s. These exemptions made the taille a real burden to the poor. Desmaretz would repeat this criticism when he was a minister. He would go so far as to attempt to end these exemptions temporarily in 1709 and permanently in 1715.[87]

The most revealing comment by Desmaretz came in reaction to the proposed capitation that was under discussion as early as 1693. His uncle Croissy, the foreign minister, furnished him with information on matters under discussion by the government. After criticizing one proposal to augment the value of coinage, another to send gold and silverware to the mints in order to increase the money supply, and another to lower interest rates on rentes, Desmaretz disparaged the idea of creating a new tax called the capitation. He doubted that those people who were already paying the taille and its supplements to the tune of 55 million livres annually could support another tax. And he wondered how such a tax could be imposed on those who were exempt from the taille, particularly how would it be proportioned and what constraints would be used for its collection. He favored taxing the rents paid on houses in Paris and France's other cities by more than one-twentieth, maybe as much as one-twelfth or one-fifteenth, because this kind of tax was much more reasonable and easier to collect.[88]

Desmaretz's discussion of taxing property in the year 1693 is significant because the royal government had just established a new law requiring the control of notarial acts by edict in March of that year. The edict required that transfers of property by sale, testament, or judicial inventory in cases of unpaid debt or vacant succession be registered (including the payment of a fee) with the controller of notarial acts, a new set of officers created to finance the war effort. (Notaries in France kept property records but their archives were secret. The establishment of the control of notarial acts was an attempt to make these records public.) By instituting this new tax along with the registration of legal documents, the government was beginning to create an archive of property and property ownership. In December 1703, shortly after Desmaretz became director of finances, the government instituted a new tax called the *centième denier* (one-hundredth denier, or 1 percent) on any exchange of property, thereby giving the government greater incentive to oversee the controllers of notarial acts. According to this new tax, anyone selling property, which of course required registration with the controllers of notarial acts, would pay a tax on 1 percent of the sale value of that property.[89]

The creation of the control of notarial acts and the subsequent tax on any exchange of property increased the amount of information available to the government on property ownership, making it easier to decide to tax wealth produced by property. The proposals Desmaretz was making were premature in the sense that the government did not yet have the knowledge base to implement a tax on wealth. At the same time, the government was implementing policies that could provide the basis for this kind of tax. Desmaretz was clearly looking down the road to see the possibilities that such information could create.

Desmaretz's 1693 mémoire contains the nucleus of his later policies, particularly the development of a tax on wealth. In the debate over taxation and the best way to raise money to pay for the ongoing wars that entangled France during the last years of Louis XIV's reign, Desmaretz came down on the side of those who wanted wealth to be taxed, as opposed to the taxation of status, increased taxes on trade, or burdening the propertyless classes with even more taxes. Desmaretz was saying that, if France was going to find the resources to continue to fight the war, it would have to look for money among the wealthy.

Desmaretz believed that the controller general of finances had to be a man who could inspire confidence in the business community while at the same time keeping track of the activities of all comptables and tax farmers. He favored the existing system of taxation that relied on the attraction of profitability to lure financiers into serving the government, as opposed to a bureaucratic system in which the state controlled the machinery of credit and tax collection, such John Law would later propose.[90] The controller general, Desmaretz theorized, should instead fill key positions in finance with men who had a good credit rating and were trusted by the investing public. He should be aware of all their business arrangements in order to be better able both to tap those who could best supply large sums when necessary, and to punish excessive profit-taking after the crisis had passed. Although we lack any evidence for Desmaretz's political theories between 1693 and his return to the government in 1703, we know enough to understand his development and to see how experience changed him and persuaded him to rethink some policy recommendations.

His Commis and Associates

Historians have often asked how large the government bureaucracy was under Louis XIV. For example, it was once famously said that, at the beginning of Louis XIV's reign, all of the foreign ministry personnel could fit in one carriage, but not so by the end of the reign. Michel Antoine, in his book on the King's Council, presents a table based upon material printed in *L'almanach royal* in which he counts the number of commis and premier commis working under the controller general and his subordinates during

1762–75. The controller general had anywhere from four to eight premier commis and one or two secretaries, while each intendant of finances had between one and seven premier commis and possibly one secretary. There was also an official position within the contrôle général des finances called the premier commis des finances who was not necessarily the controller general's premier commis. The premier commis des finances oversaw the detail of the Royal Treasury and could have had as many as six premier commis of his own. *L'almanach royal* did not begin relating the names of these people until 1762.[91]

Antoine believes that the number of these underlings had been increasing throughout the eighteenth century, thus implying that there had been a steady growth in the number of bureaucratic assistants working for the controller general and his intendants since the eighteenth century began, or, more accurately, since the decimation of the royal administration that took place immediately after the death of Louis XIV. During the Sun King's reign, the number of intendants of finances increased between the years 1660 and 1708. After Louis' death, the offices of intendant of finances were suppressed entirely during 1715–22. Indeed, the whole period from 1715 until 1740, a period of peace for France, might well have seen a smaller number of commis and secretaries in the finance ministry than either the years before 1715 or the years after 1740. Desmaretz was controller general of finances at the pinnacle of bureaucratic expansion during the reign of Louis XIV. The post-louisquatorzian purge of financial offices and financiers reduced the number of bureaucrats administering royal finances for the next generation until financial necessity spurred the demand for more people to assist the finance minister.

Desmaretz worked with seven intendants of finances as well as six intendants of commerce. The latter were created in May 1708 as replacements for the directors of finance to handle matters under discussion before the Council of Commerce. They were under the supervision of both the controller general and the secretary of state for the navy because both ministers had responsibility for administering commerce: the controller general for overland and internal trade, and the secretary of the navy and colonies for overseas trade. In any case, the thirteen different intendants working with the controller general each had their own commis and assistants. The intendants of commerce were simply masters of requests with direct responsibility for commercial issues; they were not financial officers or councilors of state like the intendants of finances. The Council of Commerce was more of an advisory panel for the government than a governing council.[92]

The controller general clearly had the largest headquarters staff of any of the ministers. Excluding the administration of the Royal Treasury, the casual parties, the General Farms, and the receivers general of finances, the contrôle général des finances had about 80 staff members in 1691 and between 100 and 120 in 1714. At the same time, the War Ministry had about 40 staff members in 1691 and between 50 and 60 in 1714. The secretary of state for the Maison du Roi and the navy had about 25 staff members in 1691 and approximately 50 in 1714. The foreign ministry had between 15 and 20 at the same time, and the secretary of state for the so-called reformed religion had a constant staff of 10 throughout this period.[93]

Antoine[94] has tried, on different occasions, to count the number of commis working in the controller general's office. He has been able to get some measure of the different kinds of officers who worked under the controller general. Besides the premier commis des finances, there was a bureau for dispatches, a bureau for the bois, another for the waters and forests, another for the bridges and roadways (*ponts et chaussées*), another for the registers of the controller general of finances, and another to verify the accounts (*états au vray*) of each comptable. While we can determine the names of some of these officials, and how much money they were given to pay their staffs, we cannot know how many people worked for them.

The office of the premier commis des finances was responsible for drawing up forecasts of expected revenue and expenses, assigning funds to pay for those expenses, and instructing the comptables responsible for paying those expenses. He was also responsible for drawing up the king's accounts (called the *états au vray*) for presentation to the Royal Council of Finances before the proper Chambre des Comptes heard them for final verification. Under Colbert, the premier commis was Antoine Hercule Picon, until Le Peletier transferred the responsibility to Guillaume de Bie in November 1684. At de Bie's death in January 1696, the responsibility passed to Olivier de Vallée, until Chamillard transferred it to his cousin, Alexandre Le Rebours, on February 5, 1703. Le Rebours would buy an office of intendant of finances in August 1704 while keeping his position as the premier commis des finances.[95]

In 1669 Colbert established an office under the premier commis des finances charged with checking the accounts of all comptables before presentation before the Royal Council of Finances; he put his nephew Desmaretz in charge of it. It was called the *bureau des états au vray*, the *états au vray* being what the accounts were called once they had been verified. Le Peletier selected his cousin François de Paris de Coutes to replace Desmaretz to head this office under Guillaume de Bie. At de Bie's death, however, Pontchartrain put it under his nephew, Desmaretz's future son-in-law, Charles Henri de Malon de Bercy, who would keep this responsibility until the end of the reign, even after he became an intendant of finances in 1709.[96]

In February 1689 two offices of gardes-commis of the registers of the controller general's office were created and bought by Pierre Soubeyran and Philippe Joseph Perrotin de Barmond. The commis in charge of these registers had to keep track of all expenses and receipts of revenue on an annual basis, and made one copy of the registers for the controller general of finances and another for the secretary of state for the Maison du Roi. Perrotin and Soubeyran would keep their offices for the remainder of Louis XIV's reign.[97] The policy of creating offices to help pay for the war began early with the creation of these offices in finance, in contravention to Colbert's opposition to having venal offices, offices that were bought and sold, within the controller general's offices. He wanted to keep control over the financial administration within the orbit of the controller general of finances. Venal officers had an independence that prevented their dismissal at the minister's discretion.

Most of the men working under Desmaretz and his commis—Turlin, Tuffereau, Bessat, Quesnet, Rasmus, Lespineau, and others—had undefined responsibilities, despite Boislisle's admirable essay on their activities.[98] Some received payments from the Royal Treasury or the General Farms, or as a result of specific commissions by arrêts of the council.[99] While they were neither policymakers nor administrators, they oversaw the activities of others and supplied policymakers with the information and support needed to carry out policy. They executed the necessary paperwork for securing the payment of funds to the Royal Treasury. There were no central personnel records for the contrôle général des finances. In addition, each intendant of finances hired his own staff, including premier commis, and each premier commis hired and fired his own staff.

The most famous of Desmaretz's commis was Jean-Roland Malet, who wrote the first history French royal finances using statistics derived from the actual records. Although written approximately in 1720, probably as part of an effort to return Desmaretz to managing royal finances during John Law's experiment, it was not published until 1789, as a contribution to the debate surrounding the calling of the Estates General. The son of a royal carpenter, Malet began life in a relatively modest position as a financier before he assumed, in 1704, a position as premier commis to Alexandre Le Rebours, the premier commis des finances who controlled the books for the Royal Treasury. While Malet may have officially been Le Rebours' commis, his position under Desmaretz improved to the point that the controller general relied on him to provide data on royal finances and to attend important meetings at the minister's side. In 1707 Malet acquired an office of secrétaire du roi (with a purchase price of 80,000 livres), an office that he kept for the requisite twenty years in order to acquire hereditary nobility. He sold the office in 1728. He also acquired significant seigneuries in 1709 and 1713, the latter with the help of the Colberts. By the time of his death in 1736, Malet had acquired many titles: écuyer (squire), seigneur de l'Amirault, knight of the Order of St. Michel, and former ordinary gentleman in the king's chamber. He also acquired a bit of infamy when he was elected to the Académie française in 1714 solely on the basis of a poem he wrote in praise of the success of French armies the year before.[100]

Malet was clearly an important figure under Desmaretz, but in certain ways he was less important than some of the minister's other commis. Malet may have had access to all information pertinent to receipts and expenses at the Royal Treasury, which may explain why he was named in several arrêts as the person responsible for supervising the granting of the visa (signature) on all assignations against the Royal Farms in 1709 and the Royal Treasury in 1709 and 1710.[101] Notes in the margins of papers and correspondence in Desmaretz's office indicate, however, that the minister rarely referred matters to Malet. He referred matters to Clautrier, de la Garde, the intendants of finances, and even other prominent financial officials, but he referred very few matters to Malet. It is possible that Malet had access to everything the minister saw, or that the papers referred to him are missing from the record. There is a set of books in the G^7 series of the Archives Nationales in which Clautrier kept a monthly record of where or to whom he referred letters or placets.[102] A look at these registers indicates that, while most of the matters were referred to intendants of finances, certain commis, particularly Le Cousturier and de la Garde, stand as their equals, insofar as the amount of material referred to them goes. Malet rarely received more than one referral a month. It is difficult to reconcile the importance Richard Bonney has assigned to Malet with the fact that other commis seemed to control administrative responsibilities that gave them an importance above that of a simple accountant or historian.[103] Malet was probably the equivalent of a modern plans or resources management officer, who kept the books, wrote reports, and had access to all the information that crossed the minister's desk, although he himself did not have an administrative fiefdom of his own. He was at least Clautrier's equal, but his importance to historians should not exaggerate his influence among his contemporaries.

The most important of Desmaretz's commis was Jean-François Charmolüe de la Garde, who had been a loyal servant to Desmaretz since the 1670s. His father and brother were both treasurers of France in Soissons, where they probably worked with Desmaretz's father. De la Garde acquired an office of secrétaire du roi in 1706, although he claimed that his family had been noble since 1591. De la Garde lived in Desmaretz's hotel on the rue Vivienne until 1708, when the importance of both men forced de la Garde to move to new quarters on the Place des Victoires. He was clearly a personal commis whose loyalty was to Desmaretz rather than to whatever offices he held. Desmaretz entrusted him with many sensitive matters, such as keeping lists of requests for employment, preparing various rolls of offices for the king to sign at each meeting of the Royal Council of Finances, and keeping track of the various proposals for increasing royal revenues in order to make summaries of them for the minister to report to the council. Between 1708 and 1713 de la Garde was responsible for certain extraordinary affairs with a total forfait of 4,984,000 livres. His administrative responsibilities made him the equal to several intendants of finances, at least in regard to the matters Clautrier referred to him and his contacts with many financiers.[104]

Gilbert Clautrier, son of the André Clautrier of the four sous-piece affair, came to Desmaretz's employ in October 1703, when the latter became director of finances. Clautrier had been a premier commis to Charles Renouard de la Touanne, treasurer general of the Extraordinary of War until June 1701. Clautrier then took a position as a provincial treasurer of war in Arras, where he handled local troop finances. He apparently disliked this work because the abbé Jérôme Gourreau de la Proustière, who ran Chamillard's household, heard his requests for a new position court. Proustière managed to bring Clautrier's plight to the attention of Desmaretz, who appointed Clautrier as his secretary. As stated previously, Clautrier and his commis, Tuffereau, collected most of the documents preserved in the G^7 series in the Archives Nationales for the periods immediately before and during Desmaretz's ministry. As secretary, Clautrier's task was to assemble the papers that were to be put before Desmaretz for his signature. Clautrier thus did not have direct administrative responsibility for financial affairs. He was able to maintain his position as secretary in the contrôle général des finances after Desmaretz resigned in September 1715; in fact, he passed the job on to his son in 1749. Some of Clautrier's descendants were still working in the contrôle général des finances on the eve of the French Revolution. His long tenure in the ministry allowed him to continue preserving documents in the archives; however, he either did not have as much access after 1715, or his superiors did not support his efforts thereafter.[105]

The last important commis who worked for Desmaretz was Louis Le Cousturier, who came to Desmaretz's service after having served his predecessor, Rouillé du Coudray, as director of finances. Le Cousturier, like de la Garde, managed some extraordinary affairs. He was also involved in managing the farms. After Louis XIV's death, he would become the premier commis des finances, a position he would hold until his retirement in 1724. In 1730 he was in retirement when he responded to questions from Clautrier about organizations, such as the Grande and Petite Directions, that the new controller general, Philibert Orry, was thinking about reviving.[106]

As a relative of Colbert, Desmaretz had allies at court and in council to assist him in creating financial policy. The foreign minister, Jean-Baptiste Colbert de Torcy, was his cousin, and the head of the Royal Council of Finances, Paul de Saint-Aignan, duc de Beauvillier, was his cousin by marriage. Beauvillier had very little real influence over finances because his position was honorific. In fact, he pleaded ignorance of financial matters in 1685 when the king appointed him to his position. According to Saint-Simon, Beauvillier regarded Desmaretz as a financial wizard, but Saint-Simon claims that Beauvillier's opinion of Desmaretz changed as time went on. Beauvillier died in August 1714 and thus was not around to correct anything the duke said when Saint-Simon wrote his memoirs. In the Conseil d'en haut Beauvillier played a larger role as the chief spokesman for the peace or the *dévot* (pro-Catholic, in this case antiwar) faction.

In describing the court of Louis XIV in the year 1709, after Chamillard's replacement by Voysin, Saint-Simon[107] stated that there were three groups (*cabals*) in the court: the cabal of Meudon, centered around the Dauphin, who was called Monseigneur; the cabal of the Ministers, centered around the Duke of Burgundy; and the cabal of the Seigneurs (Lords), centered around Madame de Maintenon. He places Desmaretz and Torcy in the cabal of the Duke of Burgundy, along with Beauvillier and Chevreuse, while he states that the other ministers (Pontchartrain and Voysin) were part of Maintenon's group. In his habitual way of saying that he was above being involved in court affairs, Saint-Simon excludes himself from any of these cabals, although it is obvious that he was involved with the Burgundy circle more than any other. Among modern scholars, Le Roy Ladurie has renamed the Burgundy cabal the Colbertian-Burgundy cabal, thereby pointing to the problem with Saint-Simon's categorization.[108] Both Torcy and Desmaretz were not known to have any connection to the Duke of Burgundy's circle under the leadership of Fénelon. Their only ties were blood relationships to the wives of Beauvillier and Chevreuse, while their political stands often put them opposite Beauvillier, the leader of the peace party, on the Conseil d'en haut. The Colbertian Beauvillier was a pacifist and was often willing to accept any peace terms as he worked to find a way to bring an end to the War of the Spanish Succession. Meanwhile, the Colbertian Torcy and his cousin Desmaretz were less willing to accept just any terms, and wanted to hold out for better ones during 1709–10.

Beauvillier contributed to finances through his position as courtier, since he served as an intermediary between the council and the king's grandson, the Duke of Burgundy. Beauvillier had been Burgundy's governor when the latter was a child, and remained a close personal friend and advisor to the heir to the throne. Burgundy had been the titular commander during the disastrous campaign of 1708 that culminated with the defeat at Oudenarde and the fall of Lille. Gossip at court accused Burgundy of cowardice and hesitation in the face of the enemy, which had led to the defeat of France's army. The army had amassed large debts to its suppliers, who were promised payment on Burgundy's word alone. The leaders of these munitioners were the Paris brothers, Antoine and Claude, who brought their bills to court in January 1709 and presented them to Burgundy for payment. Burgundy sent Beauvillier to Desmaretz to settle accounts. The controller general did so, but not without informing the financiers through the intercession of another courtier and general, the maréchal-duc de Villeroy, that in the future they should appeal directly to the minister rather than embarrassing him in front of the king's grandson.[109]

Desmaretz came to rely on other members of his family as well to assist him in administering royal finances. His older brother Jean-Baptiste Desmaretz, seigneur de Vaubourg, had retired from government service in 1701 after having followed a traditional career for a son of a robe family. He had served briefly in the navy before becoming a counselor to the Paris Parlement in 1678, and later served as master of requests in 1681, before serving sixteen years as a provincial intendant in Pau (1685–87), Auvergne (1687–91), Lorraine (1691–98), Franche Comté (1698–1700), and Rouen (1700–1701). In 1682 he married Marie-Madeleine Voysin, the only sister of Daniel-François Voysin, the future war minister. Vaubourg's experience in provincial administration made him a valuable asset for his brother as finance minister. He emerged from retirement (he had surrendered his mastership of requests in 1699) to supervise grain commerce during the crisis of 1709 and to sit on the administrative committee that governed the General Farms when they went into régie that year. He was appointed a semester councilor of state in June 1709, served on various extraordinary committees of the King's Council, and joined the Council of Commerce in 1715.[110]

In 1664 Desmaretz's sister, Françoise-Nicole, married Michel-André Jubert de Bouville, scion of a family of Rouen parlementaires. Bouville had started his career in 1664 as avocat general to the Paris Cour des aides before becoming a master of requests in 1674, in which capacity he probably worked with Desmaretz, who joined that corps that same year. Bouville served for thirty-three years as a provincial intendant, at Limoges (1676–78), Moulins (1678–82), Alençon (1682–89), Limoges again (1689–94), and Orléans (1694–1709). He became a semester councilor of state in 1696 and succeeded to the position of ordinary councilor of state in 1709 on the death of Gabriel Nicolas de La Reynie, the former lieutenant general of police for Paris, while Vaubourg assumed his semester position. Bouville's seniority as councilor of state would be a valuable asset for Desmaretz when establishing new extraordinary commissions of the council because he could be made the chairman, as he was for the extraordinary commission that handled the affairs of the dixième in 1710.[111]

Desmaretz employed the abilities of another brother-in-law, his wife's brother, Louis Béchameil, marquis de Nointel. Like Desmaretz and Bouville, Nointel had become a master of requests in 1674. And like Vaubourg and Bouville, he had served for twenty-five years as a provincial intendant, in Tours (1680–89), Châlons (1689–91), and the troublesome Brittany (1691–1705). He became a semester councilor of state on September 20, 1700, and ordinary councilor of state on October 8, 1712. Desmaretz had

Nointel appointed to sit on the Council of Commerce in 1708, when he himself, as controller general, could no longer do so as a matter of etiquette.[112] Nointel would be a valuable ally in the struggle to keep the army in the field while avoiding bankruptcy. He would advise the minister on the mints, commerce, and military supplies. After the dismissal of Chamillard as war minister in June 1709, Nointel was named to chair a new extraordinary commission of the council governing military supplies and the awarding of supply contracts. Contemporaries referred to him as the director general of vivres and étapes.[113]

Vaubourg, Bouville, and Nointel sent many letters to government officials in Desmaretz's name after consulting with him. He trusted them to represent him to the business community, the tax farmers, the receivers general of finances, and the munitioners. Together with the intendants of finances and trusted commis like de la Garde and Le Cousturier, they handled the administrative detail that poured into the controller general's office.

These men were faithful underlings, official assistants, and relatives, but there were other officials who worked with Desmaretz who were none of these things. One such man was Henri Daguesseau, a councilor of state on the Royal Council of Finances since 1695. After having been a provincial intendant in Limoges (1666–69) and Bordeaux (1669–73), he was named intendant in Languedoc, where he served until 1685 and where his principal accomplishment was overseeing the completion of the Canal des Deux Mers that connected the Mediterranean to the Atlantic in 1681. He later served as a councilor of state on the commission that investigated conditions in the provinces in 1687. Under Controller General Pontchartrain, Daguesseau took over supervision of manufacturing and the grain supply during the famine of 1693–94. At the same time, he was given responsibility for overseeing the undistributed benefices, a responsibility that gave him direct access to the king. In 1699 he was charged with administering the pensions of the newly converted Catholics and the property of refugee Huguenots, a position that gave him greater access to the king, who took a personal interest in these affairs. Controller General Pontchartrain appointed Daguesseau to administer commerce and then to head the Council of Commerce when it was created in 1700. By the time Desmaretz became controller general, Daguesseau was seventy-three years old and in decline because of his age. Nonetheless, he and his son Henri-François, the *procureur général* (chief prosecutor) of the Paris Parlement, received the government's complete support in the desperate effort to keep Paris supplied with grain during the famine of 1709–10. Despite Daguesseau's importance, there is no evidence that he was consulted on financial matters that involved increasing the royal revenues; instead, he was consulted on commercial matters.[114]

The other councilor of state on the Royal Council of Finances was Michel Le Peletier de Souzy, the brother of former controller general Claude Le Peletier, who had taken his seat in October 1702 after surrendering his intendancy of finances to his son, Michel Robert Le Peletier des Forts, in December 1700. In addition to being director general of fortifications, in which capacity he met with Louis XIV once a week, he also chaired the bureaus of the council that administered the sale of the royal domain, certified titles of nobility, and, after Gabriel Nicolas de La Reynie's death in August 1709, governed the gabelles, the Five Great Farms, the taille, and other financial affairs. He was senior to Daguesseau as a councilor of state and sat on every bureau of the council of state that handled financial affairs. Despite his preeminence on the council and his role in administering the capitation during 1695–98, Souzy was not one of Desmaretz's close confederates. The extraordinary commission handling vivres and étapes that Nointel chaired actually pushed aside a similar commission that Souzy had chaired. Nointel's commission handled supply matters that went back to 1706, while Souzy's was restricted to supply problems before that date. His commission was referred to as the bureau of *anciens vivres et étapes.* His son, des Forts, was a prominent assistant to Desmaretz, but Souzy, like Daguesseau, did not play a significant role in financial affairs under Desmaretz.[115]

There was one other official upon whom Desmaretz relied for advice and assistance—Marc-René de Voyer de Paulmy d'Argenson, La Reynie's successor as lieutenant general of the police of Paris from 1697 to 1718. He was a severe man known to be fiercely anti-Jansenist. His son, the future foreign minister, said his father resembled Cardinal Richelieu more than any other man. The city of Paris was a major government headache because it was extremely large, the largest city in Europe at the time, and was thus subject to popular enthusiasms and shortages. There were frequent consultations and correspondence between Argenson and Desmaretz over the problems of commerce, the grain supply, and proposals to raise revenue. Argenson was given prominent appointments on various extraordinary commissions of the council that were created during Desmaretz's ministry, and Desmaretz sought his advice on a multitude of problems involving commerce and finances.[116]

When Desmaretz returned to court, he did so after an exile of twenty years. He was heavily dependent on his relatives and Chamillard, but by late 1708 or early 1709 there were rumors at court of a split between the two men.[117] Saint-Simon wrote that he detected a hint of glee in Desmaretz's eyes after Chamillard's dismissal as war minister. Chamillard's letters to Desmaretz after February 1708, when the latter became controller general, give a distinct impression of lecturing a subordinate on the way things had been done in the past. In a letter dated March 30, 1709, Desmaretz wrote to his cousin Torcy about his opposition to a scheme of Chamillard's to finance the extraordinary of war. The scheme, he said, was impossible to undertake because of the dismal failure of so many of Chamillard's previous attempts to do the same thing. After recounting each of those earlier fiascos, Desmaretz wrote, "All these facts and all these reasons are known perfectly to M. Chamillart [*sic*]. Why engage then, with the King, in explanations in which I will find myself forced to say things in a manner that I have avoided until the present with the greatest attention?"[118]

Chamillard and Desmaretz continued to clash during the winter and spring of 1709, and their conflict culminated in a meeting with the king in which all of Chamillard's complaints about Desmaretz's handling of military finances were actually shown to have been caused by decisions taken by the war ministry. In other words, Desmaretz provided money for one purpose that Chamillard or one of his commis spent on other purposes. After this rude clash, the two men ceased to pretend to be friends anymore, according to Saint-Simon.[119]

Chamillard's fall was caused by many reasons beside his conflict with Desmaretz. His clashes with Torcy over foreign affairs and the failure of the latter's mission to The Hague, from which he returned on June 2, 1709, created a negative attitude toward Chamillard among the Colbert faction at court. The royal family, especially the Duke of Burgundy and his wife, were anxious to blame Chamillard for the disastrous campaign of 1708. The complaints of France's generals over the supply situation during a war council on May 12, 1709, must also have weighed on the king's mind. In attendance were the Dauphin, the Duke of Burgundy, Chamillard, Desmaretz, the king, and three generals (Marshals Villars, Boufflers, and Harcourt). According to Saint-Simon, the generals complained of unpaid troops, a matter that would seem to have been Desmaretz's problem, but the generals showed themselves to be more ill disposed toward Chamillard.[120] In fact, several important nobles, including the marquis d'Huxelles and the duc d'Antin, began openly expressing their contempt for Chamillard. In d'Antin's case, he did so in the presence of Chamillard's son.[121]

While Chamillard's dismissal might have been caused by the reasons previously discussed, Torcy's return from the peace negotiations on June 2, 1709, probably tipped the balance against the war minister. Chamillard had been meddling in negotiations with France's enemies and, thus, complicating matters for Torcy. He was known to favor peace, and had declared that France's problems with financing the war would disappear if there were successful peace negotiations. Indeed, his practice as minister had become short-term, as if he based everything on the expectation of peace, of using expedients to get through the next problem, and of using money earmarked for one purpose to pay for something entirely different, without reporting the changes to his fellow ministers, particularly the controller general. When

Torcy arrived at Versailles, with a draft of a peace treaty deemed unacceptable because it demanded that French armies assist the Allies in expelling Louis XIV's grandson from Spain, Desmaretz was the only minister to join the Dauphin in voting against Beauvillier's plan to accept the peace terms before others at court lobbied the king to change his mind as well.[122] Quickly, however, the king modified his position in order to appease the Allies, while not quite giving up on his grandson: he recalled France's ambassador to Spain and sent orders recalling French troops from Spain. At the same time, the Council realized that another military campaign was unavoidable. Given all the criticism of Chamillard at court and his reputation as a man in favor of making peace with the Allies, his replacement was inevitable if the war was to continue.[123]

Chamillard was dismissed on June 9. His dismissal was a sign of the government's determination to resist the unreasonable peace terms offered by France's enemies. The appointment of Daniel-François Voysin[124] as secretary of state for war in Chamillard's place, and the creation of Nointel's commission to oversee military supplies were part of this hardline policy to fight for a better peace. Voysin had rejected an appointment to serve as a plenipotentiary to the peace talks in 1709. Immediately after Chamillard's dismissal, the king sent a royal letter to every provincial governor explaining why the peace had failed to materialize. He sent separate letters to every bishop in France to ask for prayers for the success of France's armies in the coming campaign, and to explain why the peace terms offered by the Allies were unacceptable.[125] When they heard the king's explanation, the people of France and the soldiers in the army responded with a surge of patriotic fervor to resist France's enemies and support the king.

Voysin was the son of a man who served as both master of requests and provincial intendant. He followed the typical career pattern of a master of requests himself: counselor in the Parlement of Paris (1674), master of requests (1684), intendant in Hainaut (1688–98), semester councilor of state (1694), and ordinary councilor of state (1708). Through his wife's social connections, he became a friend of Madame de Maintenon during the 1690s. Following the Peace of Ryswick in 1697, he was appointed to a commission established to negotiate the frontiers with the Spanish Netherlands. A hardworking administrator, he was not known to be well connected socially, and seemed to rely on the support of the king and Madame de Maintenon to maintain his power. He had no male children and, thus, did not have to provide for a successor. With Chamillard's and Maintenon's support, he took over the management of the affairs of the school at St. Cyr in 1701. He was considered and passed over for chancellor and controller general of finances in 1699. In February 1709 he was appointed to a commission that included Nointel and another councilor of state to examine the affairs of the Hogguer brothers, a pair of financiers who claimed that the crown owed them money for their efforts in supplying the army. Chamillard recommended Voysin to Desmaretz to examine the similar claims of Samuel Bernard. On June 9, 1709, Voysin was appointed to succeed Chamillard as secretary of state for war, and joined the Conseil d'en haut two days later. Voysin was a rude, tough administrator who, according to Saint-Simon, was not liked by the army or many people at court, despite his parties and gaiety. Nevertheless, he spent his first six months under the tutelage of Marshal Boufflers, one of the leaders of the military council that complained of Chamillard's mismanagement. Together with Nointel's new committee on military supplies, this new arrangement was a symptom of Louis XIV's continued oversight of military affairs that had begun with the death of Louvois in 1691.[126]

Voysin and Desmaretz began by cooperating with each other but Voysin's overzealous pursuit of what he perceived as the legal rights of the crown led to a clash between the two ministers. War financing was in catastrophic condition after the harsh winter of 1709. Voysin tried to use force to make the receivers general of finances pay the sums for which they had contracted at a time when no taxes were being paid. When Voysin lodged troops in the house of François Gallois, the receiver general of finances for Châlons,[127] Desmaretz sent a frantic letter to the war minister explaining that this act would destroy whatever credit Gallois had. Desmaretz believed that pressure should be applied more discreetly if the king's gens d'affaires were to be able to support his expenses. The hapless Gallois was eventually forced to sell his receivership and his furniture to pay his debts. Voysin, however, did learn to consult Desmaretz before adopting harsh measures that might topple the controller general's house of cards.[128]

The two ministers continued to clash over the quartering of troops during the winter of 1709–10 and the number of troops to be maintained in the 1710 campaign.[129] Desmaretz was convinced that the army had too many general officers and regiments that were understaffed but received money as if they were fully manned.[130]

The secretary of state for the Maison du Roi and the navy at the end of Louis XIV's reign from 1699 to 1715 was Jérôme de Phélypeaux de Pontchartrain, the chancellor's son.[131] Jérôme enjoyed the peculiar position of handling important administrative matters involving the navy, the colonies, the clergy, manufacturing, and the government of the city of Paris, without the prestige that came from sitting on the Conseil d'en haut. As he was only twenty-five years old when he became secretary of state in 1699, Louis XIV might have lacked confidence in his judgment. Jérôme must have felt slighted when Desmaretz rose quickly to that august body, especially since he himself had been in office longer.

Jérôme and Desmaretz had to cooperate on commercial matters in the Council of Commerce and in financing the navy. The naval minister's letters to Desmaretz are alarming to read because they are filled with gloomy descriptions of the sailors' conditions and dire warnings about the future, unless Desmaretz provided money immediately.[132] Jérôme's excesses earned him the patient understanding of those with calmer heads, like Desmaretz and d'Argenson, who learned to work around Pontchartrain during the grain shortage of 1709–10.[133]

In contrast to the exchanges with other ministers, there is no correspondence between Chancellor Pontchartrain and Desmaretz in the G^7 series in the Archives Nationales.[134] While there were exchanges between the commis of both men, it is impossible to assess fairly whether or not Desmaretz consulted with Pontchartrain, a former controller general, on finances. Pontchartrain's influence in the councils of government actually waned after he became chancellor. The remark in Chevreuse's letter to Fénelon about the chancellor's uselessness in the great affairs of state is but one measure of the respect in which he was regarded in 1709. His resignation as chancellor in July 1714 may have reflected fatigue after twenty-five years in the government following the death of his wife, and perhaps an acknowledgment of his lost influence. Or he may have been imitating the example set by former Controller General Le Peletier, who retired from the government following the Peace of Ryswick in 1697. Or Pontchartrain may have been unwilling to go along with the king's desire to alter the line of succession to the French throne by inserting his two illegitimate sons, the duc de Maine and the comte de Toulouse, into the list of successors to the crown.

The proliferation of local officials under the watchful eye of the controller general of finances and his constant correspondence with officials in every province of France made him the central figure in the royal government, the one closest to the pulse of France. Every official within the central government received information that they shared with their colleagues when necessary. Necessity forced every official to turn to the controller general for commercial and financial changes that would help the government overcome its difficulties. His sources of information extended through his provincial correspondence or his exchanges of information with his colleagues to include requests and proposals, from the court and beyond, to change France's financial establishment and raise more revenue.

Political unrest at the end of Louis XIV's reign never threatened the regime to the point that royal authority fell into disrespect. In fact, if we take the amount of appeals to the government to restructure the royal revenues as an example, royal authority garnered greater respect than ever. This flood of advice to the government must be seen as a recognition of the authority of the crown. The creation of institutions like the Royal Council of Finances and the Council of Commerce were efforts by the royal government to extend and manage its sources of information. Rather than regarding the larger amounts of bureaucratic debris available from the latter part of Louis XIV's reign as a symptom of opposition to the authority of the royal government, these documents may have resulted from the government's efforts to come to understand its people and the nature of France. In the course of this effort, government became a more pervasive presence on the local scene, and, in turn, made it seem reasonable for citizens to write letters appealing for change.[135]

Chapter 4

Handling Ideas for Reform

The Function of the Courtier

The court surrounding Louis XIV was the pinnacle of society of its day. The king, God's lieutenant on earth, was surrounded by his servants and the great families of France in much the same way that God was said to be surrounded by cherubim, seraphim, angels, and saints, in the religious doctrines of the time. The king controlled France just as God controlled the universe. Unlike the deity, however, Louis XIV had to rely on intermediaries to execute his will and report to him about the activities of his people. Louis relied on government officials as well as people at court to keep him informed and to act as liaisons with the people.

The court was more than a pretty ornament wherein foppish noblemen and high-fashioned noblewomen partied and socialized during the intervals between required attendance at the king's public appearances. The image of the court as a gilded cage cut off from French society and ignorant of the daily lives of France's people might satisfy some feelings of class antagonism but disguises the court's function. Courtiers used their proximity to the king and his government to provide services to people outside the court, including those residents of their provinces or seigneuries who wished to appeal to the king for favors, whether through courtiers' positions as governors or lieutenants general in the provinces, or simply as grace due from a great lord—noblesse oblige, so to speak.

Jacques Levron relates the tale of M. Grandet, mayor of Angers, whom the men of his city charged with journeying to court to petition the king for royal letters patent to establish a literary academy in Angers in 1685. The governor of Anjou would normally have assisted with this kind of appeal, except that the man who held this position at the time was Louis de Lorraine, comte d'Armagnac, who, as grand écuyer (squire) of France, was called Monsieur le Grand, and was known to be reluctant to make just any plea to the king. Fortunately for Grandet, he met a gentleman ordinary of the king named Chevais du Boullay, who originally came from Anjou. The latter agreed to place Grandet, an especially tall man, near the king's table during the royal supper so that the Sun King would see him easily. The king had met Grandet earlier in his reign during a dispute involving a Jansenist controversy at a seminary in Angers. Upon seeing him again near his table, Louis, who had a prodigious memory, asked Monsieur le Grand who this man was but the grand écuyer did not know. After discovering the reason for the mayor's journey to court, Monsieur le Grand arranged for Grandet to have an audience with the king the next day. The king agreed to grant the request to the good citizens of Angers.[1]

This story illustrates the role of both courtiers—Chevais du Boullay and Monsieur le Grand—as intermediaries between petitioners and the king. Except for the king's query to the governor of Anjou about Grandet's identity, there was no mention of the proper bureaucratic channel for handling this petition. Nor, apparently, did Grandet mention any bribes or graft involved in his pursuit of his goal. (Levron drew this story from Grandet's own memoirs.) This was simply a case of royal grace in the granting of royal letters to a loyal town in the provinces. It did not involve any personal favor for Grandet, such as property, employment, or privileges, which were the subject of most royal petitions.

A table at court was set aside to handle most petitions under the care of one of the secretaries of state, who served quarterly in this responsibility. The secretary of state who had this duty during a particular month would collect the *placets et requêtes,* as they were called, and either report them directly to the king or refer them to the proper official for doing so. Most of these petitions involved pleas for employment in the royal finances, exemptions from royal taxes, or the payment of pensions, gratifications, or gages. Although the controller general of finances did not administer the receipt of these petitions, he did receive many of these kinds of requests for employment directly or by referral.[2]

Desmaretz ordered his commis de la Garde to keep a list of employment requests that included the name of the petitioner, what was requested, and the name of the person who sponsored the petitioner. One such list, written by de la Garde on March 23, 1708, included among the sponsors the king, the Duchess of Burgundy, the Duke of Berry, the Duke of Orléans, the Duchess of Chevreuse, Chamillard and his son, Torcy, Desmaretz and one of his daughters, and a councilor of state. These were the intermediaries acting on behalf of the petitioners.[3]

There is no evidence of whether any money was involved in the transmission and awarding of these kinds of requests. Ideally, one would think that Louis XIV and his family—the Duchess of Burgundy and the Dukes of Berry and Orléans—were above accepting money for the granting of graces and boons, but how far down the social scale can these ideals be extended? Would the king's ministers and their families have been so gracious and incorruptible? Questions about graft- and bribe-taking are not just cynicism or rumor; certain courtiers had reputations for demanding money in return for the transmission of a successful petition.

In his story of Desmaretz's appointment as controller general of finances, Saint-Simon says that he spoke with Desmaretz on the afternoon that he became finance minister:

> I took the occasion to touch on a word about some considerable people on whom I found him to have a clear and present memory. I said to him at the same time that, since he had returned to affairs, he had to know the people who do business there and that I was very certain that he would not find Madame de Saint-Simon or me involved.

The Saint-Simons would not dirty their hands in *les affaires.* Desmaretz recognized the fact that the Saint-Simons had kept themselves out of such matters; then he "lashed out at prostitutions of this kind by people of the highest peerage, on the treasures that Mssrs. de Marsan and de Matignon, united together, had amassed without number or measure, and everything that Madame the Marshal de Noailles and her daughter the Duchess of Guiche did not cease to take, which, the four together among others, had hurt Chamillard so much."

Desmaretz named four important people at court who traded their influence for money, who prostituted themselves, in Saint-Simon's words. Saint-Simon defended Chamillard to the new controller general by relating that Madame de Saint-Simon had said that the king had ordered Chamillard, in regard to the maréchale de Noailles and her daughter, "to give them part, both of them, in all the affairs that were made or would be made, which surprised Desmaretz." Desmaretz was even more surprised to learn of the people who had enriched themselves by means of their contact with Armenonville, his counterpart as director of finances under Chamillard.[4]

The Noailles had been cultivating their connections at court for many years. They were closely attached to Madame de Maintenon and the Duchess of Burgundy. The marshal and his wife had a large number of daughters who had married prominent members of the households of the Burgundies and the Dauphin. These contacts were very important. It is possible that the people seeking employment whom the Duchess of Burgundy sponsored had used members of the Noailles family as their liaisons.[5]

The two brothers-in-law, Marsan and Matignon, bring us back to the family of Monsieur le Grand. Charles de Lorraine-Armagnac, comte de Marsan, was the youngest brother of Monsieur le Grand; his other brothers included the Chevalier de Lorraine, a close friend, and probably the homosexual lover, of the king's brother, the late Duke of Orléans. Marsan was a ladies' man who, according to Saint-Simon, plundered the fortunes of three widows: the maréchale d'Aumont, prevented from marrying Marsan by the king's orders; the marquise d'Albret, Marsan's first wife, who died in 1692; and the widow of Desmaretz's cousin Seignelay, Catherine-Thérèse de Matignon, who died in 1699. Marsan made a great fortune under Chamillard, much to the disgust of Monsieur le Grand, who must have had higher moral standards than Marsan, whom he called the Chevalier de la Proustière because of his constant courting of Chamillard's household manager, the abbé de la Proustière. Marsan was also close to prominent traitants like Jean Thévenin and Paul Poisson de Bourvalais.[6]

Jacques III Goyon, comte de Matignon-Thorigny, also had important contacts at court. He was one of six gentlemen who attended the Dauphin, Louis XIV's son. Surviving Marsan, who died in December 1708, Matignon would later trade on his relationship to his cousin Bercy, Desmaretz's son-in-law.[7]

A confusing set of influence-peddlers at court offered their services in return for fees or a share in profits. While it appears that many prominent families were involved, like the Noailles and the Lorraines, one must remember that living at court was expensive, especially if great families wanted to maintain appearances. The state depended on the ability of private individuals to borrow money and lend it to the crown. As the demands for money grew incessantly after 1688, the network of those willing to lend money to the state had to grow as well. The intermediaries at court were vital to the process of expanding the number of potential financiers, and they were motivated by the benefits they could reap by making these kinds of connections.[8] To be sure, there were courtiers like Saint-Simon who simply wanted to prove their importance by helping those who were less well connected. Both varieties of courtiers—those who sought to increase their income and those who obeyed the prerogatives of noblesse oblige—coexisted.

The method of attracting money thorough intermediaries becomes more complicated when one realizes that the intermediaries themselves had intermediaries. In other words, between the courtiers and petitioners were people of lesser social prominence who did not reside at court but had occasion to go there regularly. These people had become so numerous and demanding that, periodically, *lettres de cachet* permitted their arrest to remove them from court. Their endless demands for audiences and attention annoyed too many important people.

The *Dictionnaire de Trévoux* (1704) defined any member of this group as a *donneur d'avis*, meaning a giver of advice, someone who proposed a new method of augmenting royal revenues. This service was different from place-seeking. The state could increase its revenues in two ways, either by reducing the expenses deducted from the gross revenue by tax collectors, or by establishing new sources of revenue. The use of witnesses who reported excessive profit-taking dated back to the Middle Ages. The incredible increase in the reliance on extraordinary affairs of finances at the end of the seventeenth century only increased the importance of the latter functions of the donneur d'avis. If the king adopted a money-raising plan proposed by a donneur, he usually paid a gratification that the originator of the proposal and his intermediary would share.[9]

Madame Philippes Pochon de Rosemain was one such intermediary. The wife of a naval engineer, she spent fifteen years at court, from 1688 until her arrest in December 1702, employing her contacts in the department of the Maison du Roi and the navy to get certain programs adopted. When Argenson arrested her, the police discovered the names of every prominent member of the court in her papers. She confessed to having gotten thirty-three proposals adopted, including one for the right to sell a few lieutenancies in the army to a Breton gentleman, who resold them; one for the construction of a roofed grain and flour market at Fontainebleau; one for a tax on merchants who sold liqueurs and foodstuffs; one for the creation of offices of beer tasters and their controllers; and one for a traité to sell offices of subaltern judges which she successfully negotiated with the help of Armenonville. At the time of her arrest, she was working on proposals on behalf of some very important nobles, like the marquis de Saint-Héran, the Duchess of Villars, and the abbé d'Estrées. She confessed to knowing Chancellor Pontchartrain's valet, his nephew the abbé Bignon, and important people in the naval ministry. When questioned by Argenson about how she arranged the regulation of the pension owed to Madame de Rambouillet, she said: "To the first person who fell into my hands. Doesn't everyone know that there is no one at court who will refuse to earn 50 pistoles when the occasion falls to them, and who will not employ his best efforts to see it succeed?"[10]

Prominent financiers employed the services of lobbyists such as Madame de Rosemain to apply pressure to have their projects adopted. They also took other people's ideas and promised a handsome reward if the government used it. The all-consuming greed for money sometimes led to incidents of duplicity in which the benefits promised were never fulfilled. An excellent example of one such businessman was Paul Poisson de Bourvalais, who rose to prominence quickly after Pontchartrain became controller general in 1689.[11]

Bourvalais' rapid rise in importance stemmed from his resorting to certain cutthroat business practices. His business partner, a man named La Noue, had overextended his credit and sought to escape his creditors by turning his property over to friends like Bourvalais. The unfortunate La Noue put his trust in the wrong man. Bourvalais agreed to help La Noue by repaying his debts and thus becoming his principal creditor. He also agreed to help him hide out for a few years until the crisis passed. This fraudulent bankruptcy was discovered in 1701 and La Noue was sentenced to nine years in the galleys in 1703. He wrote a letter to Desmaretz in 1708, saying that, if his records could be returned to him, he could raise huge sums of money for the state. The Royal Council rejected his request.[12]

Bourvalais betrayed other donneurs d'avis, such as a certain Cordier, who came up with an idea to raise money for the government. He gave his idea to Bourvalais, who promised Cordier 20,000 livres if the project was adopted. When Bourvalais reneged on his word, giving the excuse that the project was not adopted in its original form, Cordier hired an officer in the dragoons to help him extort money from Bourvalais. They extracted two promissory notes from the financier by holding a gun to his head, but when they left his home Bourvalais shouted "Thief!" and the two malefactors were arrested. Cordier was executed, despite the fact that his wife claimed the protection of Louis XIV's sister-in-law, the Duchess of Orléans, for whom she worked. The execution was carried out in secret as a courtesy to Louis' brother, but Bourvalais, who was thereafter referred to as *valet du bourreau* (executioner's valet), never ventured outside except in a carriage with bodyguards.[13]

Despite Bourvalais' unsavory reputation, the state needed men who could borrow large sums of money more than it needed frustrated donneurs d'avis or bankrupts. Bourvalais' importance remained undiminished until the end of the reign as he continued to expand his property and social position. In 1710 he became the sole secretary and keeper of the past minutes of the council of finances. This office on the Royal Council was one of those which Desmaretz had pointed to in 1689 as necessary and requiring the presence of prominent financiers.[14]

The state required ever-increasing sums of money to pay for its defense and maintenance. The government used the profit motive to encourage people to lend money to the state. Profits were extended not only to lenders themselves but also to those who put the government in contact with potential lenders. The court became a vast network of place-seekers and influence-peddlers, with the great families of France marketing their positions to anyone who desired employment, monopoly, privilege, exemption, etc. The government may or may not have granted requests in return for bribes and kickbacks. At the same time, donneurs d'avis were not necessarily motivated by a desire for gain.

The court of Louis XIV had the all-too-human characteristic of mixing vice and virtue, to such a degree, in fact, that it is sometimes difficult to distinguish one from the other. Monsieur le Grand was the brother of one of the court's most notorious wheeler-dealers, yet he refused to pass on just any request.[15] Without evidence, we cannot assume that someone who passed along an idea was doing so for personal gain; nor can we eliminate that possibility. The court was awash with dealmakers and profit-seekers.

François de Neufville, maréchal-duc de Villeroy, was a close friend of Desmaretz's and succeeded Beauvillier as head of the Royal Council of Finances in September 1714. As governor of Lyon and the Lyonnais, he had ties to bankers with access to foreign money markets and was an important contact for them at court. He dined frequently with Marsan, Matignon, Monsieur le Grand, Prondre, and other prominent financiers and courtiers.[16] Given Desmaretz's reputation as someone who may have taken kickbacks in the past, we cannot say that he or his friend Villeroy were necessarily corrupt, even by the moral standards of the time, in these dealings, but we can say that they had regular contact with important financiers and influence-peddlers who supplied ideas for increasing royal revenue to the government. The control and management of such ideas, whether they came directly to the government from the provinces or through the intercession of courtiers, middlemen, or so-called *faiseurs d'affaires* (dealmakers), is indicative of how aware the government was of new ideas or criticism of its policies.

Ideas from Outside the Government

As the principal royal servant in charge of raising money and patronage in terms of employment and offices, the controller general of finances was the focal point of a large number of petitions. Some of these came by means of intermediaries at court, like Marsan or a host of others.[17] Some people sent petitions directly to the controller general in the hopes of avoiding any division of the spoils, or out of fear that, if a proposal was adopted, its originator might be attacked. M. de Lambertye from Toulouse wrote letters to Desmaretz in the fall of 1708, claiming to be speaking for a third party who had an undisclosed proposal that would raise 20 or 25 million livres but at some cost to the people. The third party wished to avoid revealing either his proposal or his identity out of fear of the locals' reaction. Lambertye hinted that an incident during Pontchartrain's tenure as controller general gave the inventor of this idea good reason to fear for his well-being.[18]

Other people were simply afraid that, if their ideas were written down, they would be stolen, either in the mail or at court. Sometimes these writers wanted the honor of an audience with the minister. One Baizé de Nerville from Huvillar wrote to Desmaretz, enclosing an account of the merchandise received at Bayonne. In addition, he said that he had a plan that would raise 20 million livres in the following year without resorting to partisans, but he would only reveal his project to Desmaretz, even though he claimed not to want any recompense for it. Desmaretz referred the matter to de la Garde, who apparently contacted Baizé de Nerville and was told in no uncertain terms that Baizé would only discuss the matter with the minister himself, whose protection he desired because he had a large family.[19]

While some ideas were kept secret, others were discussed discreetly. The kinds of opinions that the donneurs d'avis supplied were of two varieties, either information that would overcome abuses in the existing financial system, or ideas for new sources of revenue. One Sieur Gonthier, an employee in the aides at Avranches, said that he knew of people who were duping an officer at court by offering to exercise an office in the farms that belonged to this person, but were only promising to pay one-third of its real worth. Gonthier also wrote that he had other information that he would gladly explain to Desmaretz in person. Marginal notes indicate that the minister agreed to see Gonthier.[20]

M. L'herée, a royal *arpenteur* (land surveyor) in Lannion, in a letter of September 6, 1708, addressed to M. Colbert (*sic*), controller general of finances, wrote that he knew of incidents during the previous thirty years in which royal fiefs had been sold in Brittany but the full price had been hidden to prevent payment of the king's full share. Like most donneurs d'avis, the writer was unknown at court but he described himself as having worked in the Rennes Bureau of Finances and said that he knew Desmaretz's son-in-law Goësbriand's family.[21]

These reports or hints of fraud in the existing financial machinery, however helpful, were not as important to the state as the other type of advice concerning as-yet-untapped sources of revenue. Some of these proposals were really complaints about the operation of the existing system that those making the proposals saw as the cause of France's sad condition. Gilbert de Pontchateau from Angers complained that the officers who collected the taille and capitation were exempt from paying taxes, while they hounded taillables and collectors like himself—"these kind of wolves who eat others," he called them. Pontchateau claimed to earn only 200 livres per year, and to employ five workers whom he paid two sous a day. The real purpose of his letter was to request an exemption from the duty of being a collector, but he did suggest taxing the parish syndics, notaries, and sergeants by an amount that was at least as much as these officials paid for salt.[22]

Other systemic complaints contained a large dose of hatred directed at the traitants upon whom the government depended. Many proposals promised that the ideas they contained did not require the use of traitants and would not burden the people. One Rubentan in Paris hesitantly, almost fearfully, suggested that all taxes granted to traitants since the beginning of the war should be dropped, enabling the king to raise the capitation to 30 million livres per year, a sum that the writer claimed the grateful people would gladly pay. A second letter by Rubentan proposed that the gens d'affaires be forced to pay 500,000 livres each by threatening to increase the number of such people if they did not.[23] Rubentan was like many donneurs d'avis who wrote to the government in that he had little real knowledge of finances. For example, the capitation was already collecting 30 million livres. In order to increase the number of financiers, one would need to have on hand a number of wealthy people who were not already involved in the king's business.

Other writers suggested ideas that verged on class antagonism, such as taxing all carriages and mounted horses, or all houses bearing armorial insignias, or all rentes and moneys of account. Another familiar complaint concerned unfair exemptions from taxation, the arbitrary way in which the taille was apportioned, and the harshness of the archers and sergeants sent to enforce tax collection.[24]

The usual advice given, however, involved the creation of new offices, privileges, or rights that could be sold. The donneur d'avis who offered ideas of this kind usually asked to be given one of the newly created items, or to share in the profits from the traité.[25] An apparently selfish motive can be taken as evidence that the proponent of these sorts of ideas actually believed that his scheme was worthwhile. He believed either that the offices were worth as much as their prices, or that the traité would be profitable because the new items would sell.

Another kind of offer was made on behalf of people who wished to lend money to the crown. Such offers were made by middlemen, faiseurs d'affaires, like the abbé de Verneuil, who offered a million livres in cash,[26] or Père Fagon, who offered an unspecified loan, to be supplied quarterly either in coin or with some quantity of coin and royal paper, with repayment in coin only.[27] The financier Jean-Paul Bombarda offered 10 million livres for the 1708 campaign in Flanders, to be paid in equal monthly installments.[28] Whether or not Bombarda fulfilled his promise, by 1710 Samuel Bernard was lending the army in Flanders a million livres per month in return for repayments, including 16 percent interest.[29]

This flood of advice coming to the government had to pass through the Royal Council of Finances or at least be approved by Louis XIV before becoming law. To come before either king or council, a proposal had to be presented by the controller general of finances.[30] Desmaretz relied upon the assistance of his longtime aide de la Garde, who kept track of requests for employment and other privileges, along with proposals to increase revenue. Once Desmaretz felt that a proposal was worth considering, de la Garde's first duty was to make an abstract (*extrait*) of the letter or memorandum summarizing its main points. On many of the letters making such proposals Desmaretz wrote, "à M. de la Garde m'en parler" (to M. de la Garde to speak to me about it). De la Garde must have read the letters before the minister did, and was expected to provide background information on the identity of the writer and who could vouch for his character at court.

The marginalia of many of these letters reveal that Clautrier, Desmaretz's secretary, kept records of such correspondence and of which commis, intendant of finances, or other official the government had consulted on similar matters in the past.[31] The minister must have worked with both Clautrier and de la Garde in judging the proper way to handle various proposals. Many letters are simply marked *veu* (seen) or with an acknowledgment of when it was answered. For example, the Chevalier de Romainval in Dunkirk wrote to Desmaretz proposing that special advocates be created in all royal courts to speak for the ignorant or incompetent. He also believed that some sort of inspection should be undertaken to insure that those who had inherited positions in the judiciary be competent in order to weed out the incapable. Desmaretz dictated that either Clautrier or de la Garde tell the chevalier that this idea always met with opposition, and a response was sent on January 21, 1709.[32] The anonymous proposal to tax carriages and mounted horses referred to previously was simply marked *veu*, but a second letter was marked *veu* and *néant* (nothing), despite the writer's insistence that Colbert had approved of this idea.[33]

A letter from a Sieur Aubigny in Rethel asked permission to speak to the minister about an idea that would raise 500 million livres in three or four months, along with another plan to raise troops and horses without relying on partisans or burdening the people. Desmaretz wrote "M. de la Garde m'en parler" and the latter wrote simply "n" for "néant."[34] Evidently the two men considered Aubigny to be another donneur d'avis with little practical knowledge of the kingdom and its finances, a problem common to many of these writers.

Petitioners for places, exemptions, privileges, or audiences literally besieged the minister. Charles François Franchet de Ferrières, canon and archdeacon of Besançon and prior of Fontaines, went to court to present a placet for a position as well as a memorandum on a variety of money-raising ideas. His letter of October 24, 1708, begins: "I have been twice to Versailles to present my respects to Your Grandeur and to beg him to accord me his protection to His Majesty, but Y. G. was importuned by so many people that I dared not approach him."[35] This constant clamor outside the minister's offices must have made Desmaretz impatient when he did grant an audience, only to find that the petitioner's ideas were impractical or based on false information.

Once an idea passed the first reading by Desmaretz and his commis, the writer might be invited to an audience and told to bring his memoranda so that the minister could read them. Marginal notes in Desmaretz's correspondence reveal that he extended many such invitations, but there is no indication of the results of these audiences, or whether they actually took place. Given the lack of numbered addresses on streets, it was sometimes difficult to contact proposal writers, as in the case of a particularly persistent Sieur Cochard. He wrote four letters to the minister between December 6, 1708, and January 1, 1709, indicating that his address was rue des Petits Champs in Paris. De la Garde noted on one of the letters that two searches of the street failed to discover anyone who knew the man. Cochard must have been found because he was granted an audience on January 18, 1709.[36]

After an audience or the submission of memoranda, proposals were referred to the intendant of finances in charge of the department concerned, to a committee on the Council of State that governed such matters, to a commis like Le Cousturier, or to the provincial intendant if the proposal involved his province.[37] Other officials likely to be consulted were the provost of merchants in Paris or Lyon, the procureur general of the Paris Parlement, the lieutenant general of the Paris police, or the director of the Paris mint. Prominent financiers like Bourvalais, Prondre, Crozat, or Claude Miotte were also asked to advise the government on matters involving traités or fields of expertise like banking or tax collection.

After consultation with the proper officials or committees, the abstract of the proposal was amended to include the remarks of the consultees. The matter was then reported to the Royal Council of Finances, where Desmaretz himself recorded decisions. Many proposals were regarded as unworkable, bothersome to commerce, or distasteful. Once the Council approved a proposal, it worked out the terms of the edict or declaration. Afterwards, the terms of any necessary traité were negotiated, as well as the financiers to be included in the company of cautions. Either Desmaretz or de la Garde wrote the lists of proposals.[38] Most were never realized but were sometimes reworked by the government into marketable products.

The most radical proposals called for scrapping the entire fiscal system or a major part thereof and replacing it with some new structure that the donneur d'avis guaranteed would raise more money than the existing system. Many of these writers were influenced by the writings of Sebastien le Prestre de Vauban or Pierre le Pesant de Boisguilbert. For example, Sieur Riolor, the intendant of the maréchale de Duras, used Vauban's population estimates as the basis of his proposal to replace the aides, gabelles, taille, and capitation with something he called the Royal Tribute that the wealthiest 3 million people in France were to pay. He claimed that the Royal Tribute would be paid more willingly than the existing taxes because it would be easier for the clergy and nobility to collect their fees and tithes and, thus, pay their share of the tribute. The disappearance of the onerous taxes on commerce would allow for the free distribution of goods. All taxes created since 1670 should be suppressed. The gabelles would be reduced to their 1667 levels. Riolor divided the 3 million wealthiest taxpayers into fifteen groups according to their wealth, saying they would pay a total of 392 million livres, a sum Riolor claimed to be the amount taken by the existing system. The advantage of the Royal Tribute was that only 9.8 million livres would remain in the hands of the collectors, while the rest would flow to the Royal Treasury.[39] Riolor's system was a triumph of rationalism over realism, since it did not explain how it was going to overcome the ease with which the wealthy resisted paying taxes. Nor did Riolor explain how the king was to persuade the clergy to pay taxes, or how the collectors were going to collect money from the powerful.

The primary difficulties with the various schemes proposed by the donneurs d'avis were the problems involved in transitioning from the existing system to the new one, how the government was going to pay debts incurred under the existing system, and the inevitable time lag between dismantling one system and creating another. Nor did proposers take into account how their schemes would be implemented in the midst of a war with the enemy at the gates. Despite all of these problems, historians persist in praising the famous and politically connected reformers, such as Vauban, Boisguilbert, Fénelon, and John Law, who advanced radical ideas in the midst of war, ideas that promised to replace the complexities of the present system with a simpler one that would eliminate the corruption of the older system as well.

Reformers and Their Ideas

The problem of the apparent impoverishment of France during the latter part of the seventeenth century is a fact accepted by most historians.[40] Many writers cite La Bruyère's descriptions of the peasantry as "wild animals" living in dens—where they ate black bread, water, and roots in return for sparing other men the pain of agricultural labor—as written proof of the deteriorating situation in France's rural areas. Despite recent studies of the problems of a subsistence economy and its consequent demographic vulnerability,[41] contemporaries saw the problem as having other causes. Even the government was aware of the problem and struggled to ameliorate it. Desmaretz's advice to Le Peletier in 1687 contains the following:

> It is not a new thing to hear complaints of misery; most of the wisest people become, little by little, insensitive to speeches that are made on all sides, out of the habit of always hearing the same thing; but one can say that never has anyone spoken with as much truth of the misery of the people, and it suffices to see some provinces to be convinced of it.[42]

Other members of the government, like Desmaretz's predecessors, were not insensitive to the problem of declining farm prices and unemployment, but they, like Desmaretz, were suspicious of the panaceas or instant cures that some donneurs d'avis offered: "One cannot believe that it is possible to envisage at once certain means, neither to do a project that is so well concerted that, by following it exactly, one would result in reestablishing things in as good a condition as one would hope. It is a matter of application and follow-through that demands an exact knowledge of each province and of the trade that is done there."[43]

Many of Desmaretz's contemporaries saw the existing fiscal system as the cause of France's economic situation. Taxes fell mostly on the poor and were arbitrary, uncertain, and almost capricious. Impositions were determined by the needs of the state and not people's ability to pay. Perceptions artificially altered prices that were detrimental to commerce and, hence, harmed the very people whose livelihood was entirely dependent upon the ability to sell their goods in order to buy food. It is ironic that the major critiques of France's situation during the latter part of Louis XIV's reign blamed the fiscal system as the cause of this condition rather than the bad harvests and epidemics that occupy so much of the attention of modern historians. It is almost as if Vauban, Boisguilbert, and their emulators regarded such accidents of nature as the facts of life, the given of the human condition. If critics mentioned the famine of 1693–94 at all, they described it as worsened by the poverty that already existed because of the tax system. Perhaps these critics believed that the forces of nature were out of their hands, while human action could improve the economic system by removing certain artificial burdens on society.

Vauban is more famous as a military engineer who conducted many sieges and designed fortifications all over France, rather than as a demographer and social reformer. In the course of his professional life, Vauban had crisscrossed France as he directed the restoration of 118 fortifications or the construction of 33 new defense systems all over France. He earned the trust of Louis XIV, who encouraged him to write to him with any ideas he might have.[44] After the revocation of the Edict of Nantes in October 1685, Vauban became a critic of royal policy and an advocate for reform measures by 1689.

As he accumulated evidence of France's depopulation following the disastrous winter of 1693, Vauban took his findings as proof that the royal tax system had caused the calamity rather than natural causes.[45] He submitted a memorandum on the capitation to Pontchartrain in 1694, and read part of it to the king on April 6, 1695. He was later inspired to work on a project to develop a taille réelle, about which he wanted to speak to Louis XIV. Gradually, as he worked on these problems in collaboration with the abbé Vincent Ragot de Beaumont, he was persuaded to base his plan on the ecclesiastical tithe or *dîme*.[46] He claimed in a letter that he had read his new project over three evenings, for two-and-a-half hours at a time, wherein Louis XIV asked questions and applauded the results.[47] Controller General Chamillard attended some, if not all, of the sessions. Vauban had been circulating his ideas to government officials and friends, including the first president of the Paris Parlement, Achille III du Harlay, and Marshal Nicolas de Catinat, while Chamillard had sent a copy to the provincial intendant in Caen, Nicolas-Joseph Foucault. This royal attention must have sparked real interest at court and elsewhere into learning Vauban's ideas, thus guaranteeing that his book, when it was later published without permission, would be an underground best-seller of sorts, and his ideas, for example about France's population, would appear in so many projects submitted by the donneurs d'avis.

In his *Projet d'une Dixme Royale*, Vauban called for a major restructuring of finances that would establish the crown's revenues as a major proportion of the national revenue.[48] He called for the suppression of the taille, aides, provincial customs (*douanes* or traites), clerical *decimes* (taxes levied by the clergy on its property in order to pay the don gratuit to the king), and other duties. The only customs duty that would survive would be at the frontiers of France, so as to unify France by treating all royal subjects equally. Vauban divided sources of revenue into four categories: (1) the dîme of all fruits of the land, without exception; (2) the dîme of revenue of all houses in towns and *gros bourgs* of the realm, mills of all kinds, industry (including commerce, rentes, gages, pensions, appointments), and all other kinds of income not found in the first category; (3) the salt tax; and (4) fixed revenue, meaning the domain, casual revenues, feudal dues, and certain taxes on luxury goods.

Vauban wanted to replace the taille with a tax that would be proportionate to the wealth and income of individual taxpayers and could be payable in kind, unlike the taille, which had to be paid in money. Vauban's first fund was to be the revenue derived from 5 percent of a year's production from land in France. If the land was arable and sown, then the tax could be paid with a share of the harvest. If the land was woodland or prairie used for grazing livestock, the dîme could be paid in wood or livestock. He suggested leasing the right to collect the dîme to tax farmers who promised to pay the government a fixed fee annually, quarterly or otherwise. Their expenses would come out of their profits. Vauban estimated that the revenue from this fund would come to 60 million livres annually.[49]

The second category of revenue was payable in money because it was a product of an exchange of money. The same proportion of 5 percent was to be collected. The income from landed seigneurs that was derived from the product of their tenants or peasants was not to be included in this fund but in the first. Instead, the crown would take its 5 percent from the whole product of the land before the seigneur would receive his share of the 95 percent that remained. Vauban estimated that this second category would produce 15,422,500 livres.

Vauban wanted the gabelles of France to be unified into a single gabelle that was to be sold nationwide at the price of 18 livres per minot of salt. No one could be forced to buy a set quantity of salt, but the sale of salt was to remain a royal monopoly. Salt could be resold after it was purchased from the royal salt granaries. Vauban did allow that the price of salt could be adjusted during times of necessity to a maximum of 30 livres per minot.[50]

He calculated from his estimate of the French population and the amount of salt necessary to prepare fish, meat, and butter for export that the government would receive 23.4 million livres from the sale of salt.

The fourth fund was fixed and unchangeable. Vauban believed that the state could not or should not increase the prices involved in licensing, chartering, and notarizing fees. The revenue from royal land might fluctuate with the market price of its products, but the casual revenues would remain constant. Also included in this category were the tobacco monopoly, the post office, and taxes on luxuries, which, according to Vauban, included coffee, tea, brandy, and chocolate, among others. The total revenue from these fixed fees would be 18 million livres.

The total revenue derived from Vauban's dîme royale would be 118,822,500 livres. In case of necessity, he allowed the government to increase the proportion of the dîme by increments of ½ percent up to a total of ten increases, or a total tax of 10 percent. Salt prices could be raised by 24 sous per minot in each incremental increase. State revenue would increase by 9,822,500 livres per increment. Anything beyond three incremental increases would be "too strong" (*trop fort*), because Vauban did not believe that the realm could bear anything above 160 million livres, the highest level of taxation reached during the Nine Years' War from 1688–97.

Whether or not the king applauded Vauban's efforts, the reality of France's situation was that France had collected more than 160 million livres in taxes over several years during the Nine Years' War. The last year of the war alone had cost 218,971,172 livres, a figure higher than that given for the tenth incremental increase in the dîme of 215,645,000 livres. Vauban called for reducing revenues to 116,822,500 livres annually, a figure that would barely have paid for the government's expenses in 1700, the lowest amount since 1688. Government spending would never be so low again during the reign of Louis XIV.[51]

The real tragedy for Vauban was that, while he was lobbying for his ideas and having copies of his manuscript prepared for friends and interested parties, the threat of war returned with the death of Carlos II, the last Habsburg to sit on the Spanish throne, on November 1, 1700. His will left the Spanish crown and its empire to Louis XIV's grandson Philippe of Anjou. Louis XIV was faced with a conundrum. Either he could accept Carlos II's will and place his grandson on the Spanish throne in hopes that only Austria would contest the result, or he could try to enforce the treaty of partition he had negotiated with England and the Netherlands 1699 that divided the Spanish territories between Austria and France. If he decided to support the latter, France would have to conquer Spanish territory in Italy. Regardless of his choice, France was going to war. He decided that accepting the will would make Spain an ally in the fight with Austria rather than an enemy because the Spanish were unwilling to see their territories in Europe divided among other European powers. Vauban's project was lost in the scramble undertaken by Louis' government in a vain attempt to limit the war to a fight with Austria. By April 1702 a general war had begun that pitted France, Spain, and Bavaria against England, the United Provinces, Austria, large parts of Germany, Savoy, and eventually Portugal. French royal expenses in 1702 were about 172 million livres, and after 1704 would never be below 200 million until 1715.

Vauban, supported by Ragot de Beaumont, continued to lobby the government with his ideas.[52] He continued to be honored by Louis XIV, who made him a marshal in 1703 and admitted him as a chevalier or knight in France's highest order, the Order of the Holy Spirit, in 1705. Despairing of the chances for an early peace and in declining health, Vauban decided to publish his work on the dîme royale. He did request permission to publish a book entitled *Projet d'une Dixme Royale* on February 7, 1707, but the publication had already taken place. An arrêt of the Conseil privé dated February 14, 1707, condemned the book and ordered the arrest of its publishers and author.[53] The arrêt did not name the author but the government knew who it was. Vauban had only published a few hundred copies. He began recalling copies that he had given to friends. A renewed attack of bronchitis forced him to bed, where he died on March 30 of his seventy-fourth year.

Among the papers seized at Vauban's house was a manuscript entitled "Objections de M. le P. contre le projet de la dixme royale, et réponses de l'auteur dudit projet."[54] The identity of "M le P." is a mystery. Among the candidates who have been suggested for this honor are M. le Prince de Conti, who was known to be receptive to ideas about fiscal reform, M. "le" Pontchartrain (an unacceptable nominee owing to the orthographical problem), and M. le Peletier, the former controller general of finances who had retired from government in 1697. Another possible nominee is the former controller general's brother, M. le Peletier de Souzy, who, as director general of fortifications, was in regular contact with the military engineer Vauban. The manuscript in question, however, is not available to help.

There is, however, a manuscript in the Archives Nationales entitled "Réflexions sur la 'Traité de la dixme royale' de M. le Maréchal de Vauban," on the back of which Desmaretz has written "à M. Clautrier m'en parler."[55] The entire manuscript is in the handwriting of Jean le Pottier de la Hestroy (another M. le P.) who had been regularly corresponding with Clautrier, Desmaretz's secretary, since September 17, 1704, when he submitted memoranda on finances for Desmaretz to read.[56] De la Hestroy was a magistrate in Montreuil-sur-Mer who continued submitting memoranda to Desmaretz via Clautrier on commerce, money, and finances until the end of the reign.[57]

The first argument that de la Hestroy makes about the *Dixme Royale* is that Vauban was not the author but that Pierre le Pesant (another M. le P.), seigneur de Boisguilbert, actually wrote it. De la Hestroy considered that the *Dixme Royale* was too foolish to have been written by anyone as eminent as Vauban, while Boisguilbert was known to be a man with extravagant ideas. Both Vauban and Boisguilbert had met each other and discussed their ideas. In fact, the author of the *Dixme Royale* mentions a book called *Le Détail de la France*, a book written by Boisguilbert and published in 1695. De la Hestroy cites similarities between the two books.[58]

De la Hestroy makes his most serious criticisms of the *Dixme Royale*'s ideas by attacking the plan to replace the taille. If, as the *Dixme Royale* says, the taille was a good tax when it was first introduced under Charles VII, the problem was with the abuses that had appeared in its apportionment and collection, and not the tax itself. Those abuses were the work of inept, selfish, or vindictive collectors. Any new tax would be subject to the same problem. According to de la Hestroy, the taille was more efficiently collected than taxes associated with the royal tax farms, but the *Dixme Royale* called for farming the dîme, thereby leaving tax revenues to the mercy of tax farmers.

While de la Hestroy liked the idea of eliminating internal tariff barriers, he argued that such duties took the place of impositions in those provinces where the taille was significantly lower than in the pays d'élections. Unless those provinces were willing to raise the level of their impositions, he did not favor eliminating the tariff barriers between the Five Great Farms and the rest of France.

Ultimately, the acceptance of the dîme depended on the acquiescence of all France, something de la Hestroy did not foresee as possible. Any criticism of the state's resorting to extraordinary affairs overlooked the temporary necessity that caused the state to adopt such measures. Once the war ended, the extraordinary affairs would end. Without mentioning de la Hestroy's skepticism of the *Dixme Royale*'s estimates of France's wealth, size, and population, his arguments were likely to appeal to the pragmatic men in the government.[59]

De la Hestroy's ideas were circulated within the government. On September 25, 1707, he wrote to Clautrier acknowledging receipt of a mémoire on commerce from the secretary: "You spoke to me in passing about another for M. de Vauban. If you would like to send it to me, I will report it to you with great care."[60] De la Hestroy's reflections on the *Dixme Royale* begin with an acknowledgment of his having received a copy of the book from an unknown sender who was apparently impressed with the arguments in favor of the *Dixme Royale*. It seems likely that the person who sent the book to de la Hestroy was Clautrier.[61]

On November 13 of that same year, de la Hestroy wrote to Clautrier that he had not heard anything about a mémoire that he wrote for presentation to the Duke of Burgundy for approval. When de la Hestroy wrote on January 30, 1708, to congratulate Desmaretz for becoming controller general, he said that he was working on his mémoire on commerce, and then added: "Monsieur, my mémoire must not have been approved by Mgr. de Burgundy since M. Desmarais [*sic*] had not had any news and M. de Beauvillier had not wanted to say so." Clautrier responded on February 5 by denying the rumors about Desmaretz's new position and said: "Nothing can make me think that your big mémoire of the dixme royale has not been approved."[62]

The condemnation of the publication of Vauban's book did not mean that the royal government was not discussing his ideas, especially if the king himself had once applauded them. (Nor did it mean that Vauban died in disgrace, as many histories say.) The publication of books required royal permission. Vauban recognized this when he submitted a request for permission to publish his book. The government condemned the publication because it had not obtained royal permission to be published. In controlling who had access to ideas, the state was not condemning the ideas. When the king applauded Vauban's ideas, he created an environment where people at court and in Paris would want to know about Vauban's plans. The fact that Burgundy, Beauvillier, and Desmaretz were reading de la Hestroy's "Réflexions" indicates that they knew Vauban's ideas. And they were still considering those ideas one year after the book on the dîme royale had been condemned.

The Duke of Burgundy, as Louis XIV's eldest grandson and potentially the future king of France, was the center of a court faction, as was traditional in monarchies, that based its hopes on Burgundy's succeeding his grandfather as king. Beauvillier was one of the most important members of that faction, along with his brother-in-law, the Duke of Chevreuse. Both Beauvillier and Chevreuse corresponded regularly with François de Salignac de la Mothe-Fénelon, former preceptor to the royal grandchildren. Saint-Simon was also part of this aristocratic circle of reformers because he frequently exchanged memoranda on the causes and remedies for France's problems with both Beauvillier and Chevreuse. These reformers were more interested in changing the political organization of France to restore power to the aristocracy than in tax reform. Saint-Simon wrote favorably of Vauban's project, which was not adopted, he said, because it reduced the power of the controller general and an army of financiers.[63] The fiscal and financial ideas of Burgundy's faction are a bit more difficult to ascertain because these ideas were secondary to their political reforms. According to a biography of Burgundy published in 1782 by the abbé de Proyart, Burgundy accepted part of Vauban's ideas. He favored a single tax on agricultural goods that would be paid partially in kind by revenue farmers, who would in turn supply the army. He did not, however, favor a tax on commerce or industry.[64]

Fénelon, the intellectual leader of this coterie, had written a secret letter in late 1693 blaming France's problems on Louis XIV's absolutism and the government's subsequent policies. Fénelon saw Louis XIV's wars as the main cause of France's ills, especially the suffering of its people. The king eventually came to know of this letter, although he may not have known who wrote it. As a result of the controversy over Quietism and Madame Guyon, however, Louis ordered Fénelon to go to his archiepiscopacy at Cambrai on August 1, 1697, and stay there.[65]

As the Duke of Burgundy's teacher, Fénelon published in 1699 a fantasy book, *The Adventures of Telemachus,* by which he meant to establish the concept of an ideal kingdom in the mind of his student. While the book repeatedly recommends freedom of trade as the basis for establishing wealth and peace between nations, it also recommends the establishment of a society in which all the inhabitants produce their own food and make their own clothes. Indeed, the laws of this society prescribe regulations on clothing, food, furniture, ornamentation, and other matters, with the result that Fénelon's hypothetical ideal society actually has less liberty than anything Louis XIV attempted. In writing *Telemachus,* Fénelon reveals his ignorance about the basis of trade and how the economy works.[66]

In a mémoire discussing France's poor condition in the wake of the Great Winter of 1709, Fénelon admitted to having only the vaguest ideas about fiscal and financial policy. He also admitted to having no certain knowledge about France's financial condition.[67] In the celebrated "Table de Chaulnes" of November 1711 in which he and Chevreuse set down the fundamental principles of government for the Duke of Burgundy (who had become Dauphin after his father's death in April of that year), financial policy occupied only a brief paragraph in the section on internal administration:

> 3) Taxes. Cessation of the gabelle, Great Farms, capitation and dîme royale [i.e., the dixième, adopted in October 1710]. Sufficiency of sums that the Estates would raise to pay their share of the total of charges to the State.—Order of the Estates always more relieving than that of the king's farmers and traitants, without the inconvenience of eternalizing ruinous taxes, and of making them arbitrary. For example, taxes by the Estates on the country on salt, without gabelles. No more financiers.[68]

Fénelon and Chevreuse trusted that the Estates (provincial legislatures) that they wanted to establish would be altruistic about paying for government expenses. To reduce expenses, they planned to pare down the size of the royal court as well as the number of royal officials. They also believed that, by reducing taxation across the board, French agriculture, commerce, and industry would flourish. The only idea they seemed to share with Vauban was the suppression of internal tariff barriers.

Desmaretz probably knew of the ideas of the Burgundy circle. Beauvillier and Desmaretz were in regular contact as members of the three governing councils and the two directions of finances.[69] Burgundy and Desmaretz exchanged mémoires prior to the duke's becoming the Dauphin in April 1711.[70] During the next ten months, on the orders of Louis XIV, Burgundy and Desmaretz regularly worked together to instruct the prince on the kingdom's financial machinery.[71] We cannot know what impact these exchanges might have had on either man. It would be interesting to know the reaction of a practical man like Desmaretz to the fanciful daydreams of Fénelon and company. Unfortunately, Burgundy's death in February 1712 prevented him from becoming king and implementing his planned reforms.

Vauban's ideas provoked a different reaction from the always testy and explosive personality of Pierre le Pesant de Boisguilbert, another practical man of affairs, who had been lieutenant general of police since 1690 in Rouen, where he was in charge of enforcing laws about trade, including the book trade. He was also chief judge and president of the presidial court of the bailliage of Rouen. These two offices cost him 120,000 livres in 1690–91, and began his quarrels with other courts in Rouen over protocol and jurisdiction, as well as with various traitants over subsequent efforts to raise more money from officeholders.[72]

Boisguilbert's somewhat difficult personality frequently brought him into conflict with provincial courts or the municipal government of Rouen. One dispute involved the refusal of the merchant mercers of Rouen to supply him with the customary annual robe worth 75 livres. They claimed that he had enjoyed a share of the taxes that they were forced to pay to reunite the masters and guards of their craft to their guild.[73] Boisguilbert was a great critic of the extraordinary affairs that he claimed were destroying France, but it seems he was not above profiting from those same affairs.

In the course of these conflicts, the royal government took notice of Boisguilbert, and he began what was to become more than two decades of correspondence with the controllers general of finances. Saint-Simon says that Boisguilbert offered to enlighten Pontchartrain on his ideas about improving France's economic and financial condition in 1691. Pontchartrain granted him an audience but it ended abruptly when Boisguilbert warned the minister that a listener, on first hearing his ideas, might take him for a fool, but his ideas would begin to make sense after some thought. Pontchartrain was not normally a patient man and, like all controllers general, he was plagued with donneurs d'avis with grandiose schemes. He laughed and told Boisguilbert that he would prefer to keep the first impression, then turned away and refused to listen to his visitor's plans.[74]

Rouen was the center of an illicit book trade. Local printers were publishing books under the pretext of their being published outside France. Boisguilbert's duties as lieutenant general of police brought him into contact with these underground printers, whom he often had to fine or sentence to jail. In 1695, the year the capitation was established, a book was published in Rouen without royal permission entitled *Le Détail de la France, ou Traité de la cause de la diminution de ses biens et des moyens d'y remédier* (*The Detail of France, or Treatise on the cause for the reduction of its wealth and the means to remediate it*), written by "M. de S."[75] Boisguilbert later acknowledged authorship by asking people to read certain sections of his *Détail de la France*, which was reprinted several times before his death.[76]

The essence of Boisguilbert's criticism was that France's economic depression had begun after 1660, with the policies adopted by Colbert and his successors. The internal tariffs on foodstuffs artificially raised prices outside the area where the goods were produced, thus hampering trade. He called for an end to the aides and traites, claiming that French commerce would then increase. Its peasants and vintners would grow rich. Tax collection would thus be easier and less arbitrary, and could be set at a certain share of the product. He favored setting the capitation as a certain share of the wealth produced in France rather than basing it on social status. He opposed suppressing tax exemptions, except for those enjoyed by the tax farmers and financiers who had profited from Colbert's policies. Boisguilbert was clearly a precursor to the economic liberals of the eighteenth century who called for an end to trade barriers as well.

When Michel Chamillard became controller general of finances in September 1699, Boisguilbert's hopes to persuade the government to adopt his ideas rose. Prior to becoming intendant of finances in 1690, Chamillard had been the provincial intendant in Rouen during 1689–90. Boisguilbert's contacts with people inside the royal government multiplied because the tenure of the provincial intendants at Rouen was very short. Among Rouen's intendants were Jérôme Bignon, Pontchartrain's nephew, who was later provost of merchants of Paris (1708–16); Desmaretz's brother Vaubourg; and Urbain Guillaume Lamoignon de Courson, son of Lamoignon de Basville, the famous intendant of Languedoc. Bignon was in Rouen during 1693–94, Vaubourg during 1700–1701, and Courson during 1704–9.[77]

Vauban mentioned the *Détail de la France* in his *Projet d'une Dixme Royale.* Vauban and Boisguilbert had first met in December 1694 when Vauban was visiting Normandy to inspect its fortifications, as part of his duty as deputy commander of the forces prepared to repel an Allied landing in France. They met again in November–December 1699 while Vauban was working on his project. Both men agreed on the causes of France's economic woes—the abuses prevalent in the apportionment and collection of the taille, as well as the aides and traites. Vauban went even further than Boisguilbert in describing the capitation, exemptions from the taille, and the extraordinary affairs of finances as pernicious. The *Dixme Royale* has long sections that reiterate many of the arguments found in the *Détail de la France.* During the latter period of their acquaintance, Boisguilbert also came to know Vauban's assistant, the abbé Ragot de Beaumont. When he heard that Vauban had read his project to the king in June 1700, Boisguilbert sent a letter to Controller General Chamillard accusing Ragot de Beaumont of being the actual author of the proposal and listing twenty objections to the dîme royale.[78]

Boisguilbert's persistence in writing to Chamillard about his ideas for alleviating France's misery and simultaneously increasing royal revenues led to an audience with the controller general in the spring of 1702. Chamillard, who was at the time both controller general and secretary of state for war, referred many of Boisguilbert's letters to Chamlay, who kept a collection of Boisguilbert's papers during the next three or four years.[79] Chamillard's opinion of Boisguilbert's ides remained essentially unchanged throughout his many interviews with the Rouen magistrate. For example, in the margins of a letter from Boisguilbert dated July 18, 1703, the controller general wrote:

> I believe that three hours and three months [would be] well employed to work on a product such as the one that you propose to me; but I very much fear, by the knowledge I have acquired in affairs for a long time, that there is more concept in your project than reality. If you wish to send it to me, I promise you to read it; and if I find anything concrete, I assure you that I will profit from it.[80]

Marginal notes written by Chamillard on Boisguilbert's subsequent letters reveal that the controller general sincerely wanted to believe in Boisguilbert's optimistic predictions that his ideas would produce increased wealth for France and the crown, but he could not see any solid basis for the predictions themselves. At one point he wondered if Boisguilbert's long experience in government had somehow revealed something to him that no other experienced official could see. He then prayed for God to enlighten him (Chamillard) too. Later, exasperation led him to write that Boisguilbert never listened to any of the objections made to his ideas.[81]

A second audience with Chamillard in October 1703 brought Boisguilbert face to face with Desmaretz, who had just acquired the position of director of finances.[82] Boisguilbert's criticisms of Colbert, the new director's uncle, were hardly likely to endear him to Desmaretz. Poor Boisguilbert was an unvarnished optimist who believed that his reasoning was so sublime that his ideas, once heard, would silence all objections. He had first promised that his plan would increase royal revenues by 50 million livres, but by 1703 he had raised his projected increase to 80 million.[83] His attempt to demonstrate that France was less wealthy in 1703 than it had been in 1570, along with his promise that his plan would increase France's wealth by 400 million livres, led Desmaretz to accuse him of pure "speculation." Boisguilbert countered that Vaubourg liked his ideas and said that Colbert would have liked them as well.

Beginning in July 1704, Desmaretz and Boisguilbert corresponded regularly, but Desmaretz's remarks in the margins of Boisguilbert's letters show his skepticism.[84] For example, on a letter dated July 20, 1704, Desmaretz noted, "There is much more unintelligible nonsense (*galimatias*) than other things in this letter." In August, after an appeal from Boisguilbert, Marshal Vauban wrote to Chamillard that his friend promised "mountains and marvels" (*monts et merveilles*) and was "a little over stimulated in his thoughts," but these qualities did not prevent him from having good ideas. "Sometimes the most foolish give very good advice to the wisest," he wrote.[85]

Chamillard remained equally skeptical on two points. The first was Boisguilbert's claim that the less money there was in circulation, the more there was of it. The minister found this notion illogical because he doubted that France had 80 million livres in specie that the government could obtain simply by raising taxes. He also objected to the accusation that the protection that the government offered financiers deafened it to any proposal that would rid France of them. Chamillard simply denied this claim by saying that the financiers were a necessity until, and unless, a better way of raising money appeared.[86]

The network of people who read Boisguilbert's ideas broadened to include his counterpart in the Paris police, Argenson, and Michel Amelot de Gournay, the director of commerce.[87] These men were interested in the impact that Boisguilbert's program would have on commerce and the grain supply. Desmaretz's brother-in-law, Bouville, who was intendant of Orléans and owned lands in Normandy, was also intrigued by Boisguilbert's proposals. He promised to investigate in his generality to see whether the aides had harmed the wine trade, as Boisguilbert claimed.[88]

In the fall of 1705 the royal government planned to conduct an experiment with Boisguilbert's ideas in a select region of France, but the experiment did not take place. In addition to eliminating trade barriers, the experiment would have doubled everyone's capitation to equal a tenth (dixième) of their income, a fact that would have some bearing on later government decisions. Boisguilbert met with Armenonville (the other director of finances), Chamlay, and Bouville, who was to oversee the experiment in one or more elections in the generality of Orléans. The plan was to double the capitation while removing the aides, traites, and extraordinary affairs that Boisguilbert found so onerous to commerce. Boisguilbert believed that a grateful France would gladly pay higher impositions in return for the greater amount of wealth that increased trade would produced.[89]

The first sign of opposition to this experiment came from Nicolas le Camus, first president of the Cour des Aides, who protested that this kind of experiment would be contrary to the established laws, as well as prejudicial to the public and the legal jurisdictions, including the Cour des Aides. He asked to see a copy of the legal authorization that permitted the experiment so that he could make any comments to help avoid problems. Chamillard resisted this request, saying that such an experiment could not be undertaken lightly, and that he knew, from his own experience as the intendant in Rouen, of all the abuses in apportioning the taille. This experiment was the result of long study, not a whim.[90]

The project for the experiment was communicated to some, if not all, of the provincial intendants because Nicolas Lamoignon de Basville wrote to Chamillard in response to a request for his advice. Basville believed that any change to the tax system would be difficult to enforce on grounds that people pay their established duties out of habit. Any change would require years to put into operation, while the state needed prompt financial aid. In place of Boisguilbert's experiment, he recommended selling rentes on various sources of revenue, or even creating a voluntary subsidy that could be repaid in the form of rentes.[91]

Richard Bonney insists that the experiment was carried out in the election of Chartres in the generality of Orléans but he cannot produce any evidence to support this claim.[92] While it is difficult to prove a negative, the correspondence between Boisguilbert and the government never mentions the experiment again. No one discusses whether it proved or disproved Boisguilbert's belief that his ideas would increase wealth and thus make it easier to collect taxes. One possible reason why the government even considered the experiment is that it was also discussing, at the same time, a plan to divide the generality of Orléans to create a new generality centered on Chartres. Bouville, Desmaretz's brother-in-law, discussed this plan briefly with Desmaretz in a letter written on September 3 and 4, 1705. Desmaretz annotated the letter with a series of objections to the planned creation of a new generality, including the fact that it would be onerous to the king's affairs, would damage the credit of the receivers general, and would leave the generality of Orléans with only its winegrowing areas.[93] Perhaps the idea of experimenting with Boisguilbert's ideas was contingent on the creation of a new generality. The advantage of creating a new generality is that it would give the government a new set of receivers general to whom the crown did not owe any unpaid debts based on the existing tax system. The government might have thought that an experiment could be conducted by eliminating financiers' claims on the tax receipts of the new generality. In any case, the government either dropped the idea of creating a new generality, and thus killed the planned experiment, or abandoned the experiment itself, and therefore eliminated any reason to create a new generality, since neither action actually took place.[94]

Boisguilbert's prickly personality had aroused too many influential critics, including Argenson, Amelot de Gournay, Achille III de Harlay, and especially Chancellor Pontchartrain, who blamed him, as lieutenant general of police in Rouen, for the prevalence of illicit books from Rouen. Chamillard gave way before the opposition of Boisguilbert's critics and cancelled the planned experiment. Instead, he augmented the taille, aides, traites, and capitation by two sous per livre. In fact, Chamillard became so exasperated with Boisguilbert's impertinent demands for an audience that he rejected any appeals Boisguilbert made, either for moderations in the fees he had to pay for augmented gages, or for absorbing alternate offices of lieutenant general of police. Boisguilbert was left to the mercy of the traitants.[95]

Boisguilbert unleashed the bitterness he felt at his dashed hopes by preparing a book known as the *Factum de la France*,[96] which he published without obtaining royal permission after hearing that Vauban had published his *Projet d'une Dixme Royale* in 1707. Boisguilbert openly blamed the royal ministers for France's condition, and this time they struck back. The Conseil privé issued an arrêt on March 14, 1707, condemning the *Factum de la France*, and although it did not name the author of the work, the book's promise to increase royal revenue by 80 million livres left no doubt as to the identity of its author. Boisguilbert was exiled to Brive-la-Gaillarde in Auvergne for three months, thus depriving him of his principal source of income from his duties in Rouen.[97]

Desmaretz became controller general of finances shortly after Boisguilbert returned from exile. While Boisguilbert had audiences with Desmaretz, Vaubourg, and Chamlay during 1708–9, his ideas were never as well received as they had been in 1705. Desmaretz, however, did show mercy toward Boisguilbert in his struggles to pay the various traitants, especially Bourvalais, for the offices of alternate lieutenant general of police for Rouen. The traitants were demanding 44,000 livres, but Desmaretz, at Vaubourg's request, reduced the fees to 9,300 livres.[98]

Desmaretz's interventions on Boisguilbert's behalf raised new hopes in the always optimistic Boisguilbert that he might have a chance of seeing his ideas adopted after all. In the late summer of 1710 Boisguilbert presented a new proposal that he claimed would raise 100 million livres.[99] His last attempt to advocate his views to Desmaretz came in late 1712, but, after Desmaretz supported the reception of Boisguilbert's son as alternate lieutenant general of police for Rouen, the old man decided to stop importuning the minister on behalf of ideas he had spent a lifetime developing.[100] Boisguilbert died on October 10, 1714.

The Proposition to Establish a Royal Bank

The fundamental difficulty for the government with Boisguilbert's theories was not his attacks on the way the taille was levied. Chamillard and Desmaretz were perfectly aware of those problems. Nor was it that his ideas would impose taxes on those previously exempt from the taille, similar to Vauban's proposals. Boisguilbert actually favored maintaining exemptions founded on historical tradition, but not those that had been recently established. Desmaretz was also critical of newly created exemptions.

The greatest objection raised to Boisguilbert's ideas was that knowledgeable men in the government doubted that France had large, hidden sums of money, like Boisguilbert's much vaunted 80 million livres. They were convinced that large sums of gold and silver had been transported out of France to pay for French armies in Flanders, Germany, Italy, and Spain. They saw the declining volume of commerce within France as a symptom of this lost specie, as well as the result of internal taxes that were too high. The state depended on financiers, bankers, and traitants to raise money to pay for the armies and the government. Their entire credit system depended on inventing a variety of ways to raise money by persuading traitants to invest in these schemes. The merchandise created had to be so attractive to potential buyers that they would be willing to borrow money to purchase it. The growing difficulties that the traitants had in selling any new offices, rentes, or augmented gages convinced the government that there was no money to be had.

The government needed to expand the money supply within France by developing a new source of credit that would rid the French money market of the various kinds of paper and promissory notes that still went unpaid. None of the donneurs d'avis mentioned above addressed this problem. They all believed that their ideas would somehow produce enough coin to make them profitable. The problems caused by the dearth of coin or acceptable paper money were the main reasons for declining commerce and the unwillingness to invest in any new merchandise the government created. The government wanted to reanimate trade by increasing the money supply available for commercial transactions by eliminating the mint bills, promises on the Caisse des emprunts, bills of the various royal money handlers, assignations on future royal income, and promissory notes issued by traitants. To do so, it needed to encourage potential investors to provide a new source of credit so trustworthy that it would attract the necessary funds with very little delay. In short, France needed either new gold and silver mines or new paper to replace the old, untrusted paper. The new paper would have to be accepted in commerce as being as good as coin.

France did not have a royal bank that issued paper money. England, by contrast, had created this kind of institution in 1694. Several small European states, such as Genoa, Venice, and Amsterdam, had state banks that issued paper money that was accepted throughout Europe, but these institutions served as credit mechanisms for economies that were commercial. The profitability of the Dutch East India Company or the Genoese and Venetian trade in the Mediterranean provided the central element of confidence that supported the paper that the banks of Amsterdam, Venice, and Genoa issued. France, however, was primarily an agricultural country that traded predominantly in agricultural commodities.

The Bank of England was not a commercial institution like those of Amsterdam and Genoa. Because the English government had established it to help finance war in 1694, it was backed by government revenues and, thus, was a permanent method for funding the national debt. The English government immediately received a loan of 1.2 million pounds, while it set aside only 100,000 pounds annually to pay the 8 percent interest on the loan. By guaranteeing the loan in this manner and setting aside secured funds for the payment of interest, the Bank of England encouraged future investments or loans. In this way, the English government developed an institution to help manage its short-term finances. Eventually, it allowed holders of a million pounds' worth of government promissory notes to convert these notes to stock in the bank. Throughout the period from 1694 to the end of the War of the Spanish Succession, the Bank of England enabled the much smaller kingdom of England to lead the coalition of France's enemies.[101]

In order to attract investors willing to accept paper with the promise of future payments, France had to have a source of revenue that was sufficiently trusted to insure those loans. Since the dismantling of Colbert's Caisse des emprunts, the government had been relying on traditional sources of credit, like perpetual rentes, augmented gages, and the sale of offices to raise extra money. These traditional methods had overburdened the monarchy's financial machinery and caused a decline in the ordinary sources of income. Attempts to shore up these sources of revenue by reminting money or imposing a capitation had only produced modest increases in income. After the August 1704 defeat at Blenheim, which began a series of French defeats over the following years, the investing public began to lose confidence in France's ability to repay its loans. Declining trade produced a decline in income from the tax farms and made it difficult for the state to pay the interest on its debts.

Propositions to create a royal bank with the power to issue paper notes that were acceptable in trade had been coming to the royal government for years. The Chamlay papers in the Archives de Guerre contain proposals for creating a royal bank in 1694, the year that England created its bank. Some were nebulous schemes from people asking for a share of the profits or for a position as one of the principal backers of the bank, without having to contribute any real money.[102] John Law submitted an idea for a royal bank as early as 1707,[103] and Paul Harsin has speculated that Law might have been in touch with Chamillard as early as 1701, under the pseudonym Olivier du Mont.[104] Law's shadowy existence after his flight from England in 1695 until his participation in the debate over a land bank in Scotland in 1705 prevents ascertaining his whereabouts and activities during this period.[105] In 1713 he settled in Paris, where he began corresponding frequently with Desmaretz about his ideas for a royal bank. This correspondence led to several face-to-face meetings between the two men.[106] Edgar Faure theorizes that the discussions were sufficiently advanced for the Regent, in late 1715, to pick up where Desmaretz left off, but Faure cannot explain Desmaretz's opposition to Law's bank after 1718.[107]

One plan to create a royal bank was almost realized in 1709 during the ministry of Nicolas Desmaretz. The government needed a bank to help absorb debts that it had already contracted. It approached the problem from a position of weakness, however, because it did not have sufficient funds to guarantee any investment and needed wealthy outsiders to provide the initial capital to guarantee the bank's notes.

In the spring of 1708, after Desmaretz's appointment as controller general of finances, Samuel Bernard began pressuring the government to adopt his idea for establishing a royal bank.[108] As collateral for the many advances he had given the royal government to help fund its armies in foreign territory, Bernard and his business partner in Lyon, Jean Nicolas, had accepted large amounts of royal paper, which they were finding difficult to use to secure further loans. What they wanted was a new kind of paper that would guarantee their credit. On July 7, 1708, Bernard wrote to Desmaretz, after reading some of the schemes submitted recently for a bank that would absorb the mint bills with only a 5 percent discount on their face value. Bernard wrote that the new banknotes had to be redeemable in coin at the bank, and acceptable in commerce and at the Royal Treasury at face value. The denominations of these bills, the smallest of which was to be 100 livres, were so large that only the wealthy would ever have used this money. Thus, Bernard was asking for more than just a transfer from one kind of paper to another; he was calling for a tremendous increase in the money supply through inflation, an increase that would require a large financial investment to guarantee the necessary coin during the first ten months of operation until the new money was accepted.[109]

Bernard persisted during the summer of 1708 until Desmaretz referred the matter to Caumartin, the intendant of finances, who approved the idea. A group of government representatives, including Caumartin, Beauvillier, Le Peletier de Souzy, Daguesseau, and Chancellor Pontchartrain, met with Bernard to discuss the idea. On December 27, 1708, this group drew up a projected edict creating a royal bank. They all agreed that, in order for this bank to succeed, three major points were required.[110] The report of these meetings is in the Bibliothèque Mazarine but a shortened aide-mémoire of the report survives in the Archives Nationales in Desmaretz's handwriting, in which he copies the three major points necessary for the bank to succeed:

> The first [point is] that the loss on the mint bills increases or decreases according to events that determine opinion and their value; that this loss burdens those who endure it and is the occasion for unjust and immense gains for those who have specie; [and] that to stop a disorder that is so prejudicial to the state, it was necessary to fix the value of mint bills, which can only happen by repaying them, or in substituting bills that can produce specie when it is desired.
>
> The second point [is] that, in order to come by this establishment, the public must have confidence in the people who will be directors and backers of the bank:
>
> the Sieurs Bernard and Nicolas
> the Sieurs Fayard of Paris and Lyon
>
> And the third is that it was necessary to see actual and effective funds for the first months which cannot be less than four million per month, and that if the bank can be maintained during the first three months we can, with reason, hope that this establishment will produce very advantageous results.[111]

Rumors of the new institution leaked to the public, where they produced an increase in the negotiable value of mint bills from 72 to 85 percent of their face value. Financiers and speculators refused to accept them at such high prices, further slowing the pace of commercial transactions and the ability to contract loans. The new project had numerous opponents among those financial speculators who made great profits from buying mint bills during low periods and selling them when public confidence was higher. The extremely vulnerable position of Bernard and Nicolas because of their great indebtedness only increased the fears of many potential investors about the solidity of the new bank's backing. Bernard had been unable to meet all of his obligations during 1708, except by persuading his creditors to renew them for another year. People began to wonder why Bernard was involved in this bank project at all.[112]

In addition to the opposition of those with personal interests in the matter, there were patriotic reasons for opposing the establishment of a bank under a former Protestant (Bernard) and a Protestant refugee who was now a citizen of Geneva (Nicolas). The Council of Commerce objected that the creation of such a bank would only increase the shortage of real money in Paris and leave France at the mercy of foreigners (*étrangers*) to a greater degree than it already was, because any gold or silver would have to come from abroad on terms that foreigners demanded.[113]

The Royal Council of Finances continued to take steps toward creating the new bank. An extraordinary commission of the council was named on January 22, 1709, to govern the affairs of the bank under the chairmanship of Caumartin and including Chauvelin, Voysin, Harlay, Nointel, and Rouillé du Coudray. The bank would issue 72 million livres' worth of bills in denominations of 100 livres each. Caumartin was to keep a register of the mint bills received in exchange for the new bank bills.[114]

Everything seemed about to fall into place when the Fayards pulled out of the deal. They were to provide only 2 million of the original 12 million livres required to establish the bank. Nonetheless, Bernard could not find another investor to replace them and could not borrow the extra 2 million himself. By February 3, 1709, Dangeau recorded that the affair had failed. Caumartin blamed Bernard's obstinacy for alienating everyone, including the Fayards, in Lyon.[115]

The growing economic difficulties caused by the winter of 1709 threatened to upset the feeble international exchange organized around Lyon. The Lyon fair was maintained as a fiction through which international bankers made payments against loans contracted in Italy, the Swiss cantons, Germany, and Amsterdam. Four annual payments were made with interest in January, April, July, and October. The postponement of the January 1709 payment until April preceded the attempt to create a royal bank and heightened suspicions about Bernard's solvency. Rumors of the collapse of Bernard and Nicolas in February produced refusals by his creditors to accept anything but coin in return for the mint bills they had been given.[116]

Bernard and Nicolas continued to press for the creation of a royal bank during 1709, despite growing opposition in Lyon and Geneva to their project. Like a row of dominoes, banks in these two cities suspended payments on their debts, creating panics in both places. By April these matters were in the courts, but the royal government was soon involved as well.[117] Bernard and Nicolas tried to use this crisis as another reason to adopt their banking proposal, but Desmaretz remained hesitant. The arrival in French ports that spring of a large fleet of vessels from the Spanish New World loaded with over 30 million piastres worth of gold and silver eased the government's problems by allowing it to seize half of this specie and call for a massive reminting of money. The government was able to withdraw 43 million livres' worth of mint bills from circulation and stimulate commerce somewhat.[118] Desmaretz created a special extraordinary commission of the council to review the debts that Bernard claimed he was owed. Desmaretz also gave Bernard over 14 million livres' worth of rentes to negotiate with his creditors to settle his debts. Bernard finally went to Lyon to settle his problems, with the promise that the crown would pay him once the extraordinary commission settled his accounts.[119]

The bank fiasco turned Desmaretz away from these kinds of proposals because they would make him dependent on too many uncontrolled variables, such as the credit of someone like Bernard. The state lacked the resources to undertake any major ventures and faced growing difficulties as trade virtually ceased after the miserable harvest of 1709. Food prices reached unimagined heights, provoking riots in the cities and attempts by provincials to prevent food from being exported from their regions. Troops had to be stationed in Paris until the summer of 1710, as well as called out in the provinces from time to time. Disaster threatened at every turn as the payment of taxes ceased entirely. Desmaretz described the situation to the king in a mémoire dated August 26, 1709:

> The present situation of business is so bad that it causes those who are acquainted with it just anxieties about the unforgettable events that might be feared.
>
> For four months, all circulation of money has ceased. People are not paying the taille or the capitation at all.
>
> The excessively high price of grain forces them to reduce themselves to what is necessary to survive.
>
> They are not buying any salt at all. They are not drinking any wine. So the farms are falling and are reduced to less than two-thirds of their usual value.
>
> The extraordinary affairs that in the past have been the resource for supporting expenses instead of ordinary revenues can no longer be of any help, because we have exhausted the matter: creation of offices, alienation of the domain, constitution of rentes of all kinds, extraordinary impositions—all have been used.
>
> The clergy and nobility have paid taxes, and still pay them, which disturbs them and excites their complaints.
>
> The Parlements, the other superior companies, presidials, [and] the officers of ordinary justice and finances have paid immense sums; all these companies of officers owe as a body the value of their offices and are no longer in a state to furnish new finances to fill the new ways that the fertile imagination of the financiers can still produce.
>
> The credit of the farmers general, receivers general of finances, and the traitants has entirely fallen from the advances they have made; they amount, according to a verification that was made of them only six weeks ago, to more than 65 million livres. Very far from being in [a] condition to make new advances, all their creditors press them at the same time to pay, and, in order to force them, exert against them the fastest and most rigorous constraints.
>
> The condition of the bankers who have made payments for the king is known. The fall of the Sieurs Hogguer, Bernard and Nicolas, that of the Sieurs Tourton and Guiguer, and of others who practice banking with no more credit, have put the money markets of Lyon, Paris, and Geneva,

> and all the others into disorder. There are no resources to be expected from any banker.[120]

This was Desmaretz's jeremiad on the eve of the battle of Malplaquet, where French armies endured the worst bloodbath of the war and yet withdrew in good order, unlike their behavior after Blenheim, Ramillies, and Oudenarde, when their armies were eliminated as a fighting force. Yet, armies require money to be paid and supplied. Just where that money came from involves a discussion of what the government did do rather than what it did not do.

The government of Louis XIV was neither isolated from the suggestions of outsiders nor closed-minded about those suggestions. Impractical ideas like those of Aubigny de Rethel and politically impossible ones like that of the Chevalier de Romainval were rejected out of hand. Novel ideas like Vauban's and Boisguilbert's were given a hearing, sometimes many hearings. The impossible dreams of Fénelon would have to wait for a new king even to be considered. The government was aware of reform ideas, even though it struggled to prevent their publication. Within the government these ideas were discussed with an eye toward any possible success. The pressure of events demanded the adoption of new programs, however impractical they seemed. Even Desmaretz admitted that the financiers had wonderfully fertile imaginations for inventing venal offices or other kinds of merchandise they would support. The relentless torrent of war financing overwhelmed the government, pushing it along like a drowning man grasping at anything to stay afloat.

There was no time to replace the entire taxation system with a royal tithe or to await the increases in trade that Boisguilbert promised. Besides, the existing taxes were necessary to pay the debts undertaken against them. There was an immediate need for a new source of money. Any plan that offered a quick return to the government was more attractive than systems that required preparation and delay before the production of revenue. (A drowning man does not have time to build a new ship to replace the one that is sinking.) Historians have traditionally condemned the last quarter century of Louis XIV's reign as a time when the French government adopted expedients rather than undertaking major reforms. Any historical approach that emphasizes system and structure, however, overlooks the influence of events on men's minds. In the next chapter we shall discuss the expedients employed to help the government weather the crisis of 1708–11, with special attention to the year 1710, the year France did attempt to implement some changes.

Chapter 5

The Establishment of the Dixième

From Crisis to Crisis (1708–10)

When Nicolas Desmaretz became controller general of finances in February 1708, he found the royal finances in great disarray. Almost twenty years of expedients and war had dilapidated a credit system based on indirect taxation, the kind that most immediately suffered the repercussions of war. Like Pontchartrain in 1689, Desmaretz did not have time to prepare for new ways to finance France's war effort. He had to find funds to support the campaign of 1708 and to establish credit for future campaigns until peace was restored.

One of his first acts was to restore *liberté dans les conventions* (liberty to make agreements) among businessmen. An arrêt of October 29, 1707, which required that all payments be made with a mixture of paper and coin that included at least one quarter in mint bills, had restricted their freedom. This restriction was an effort to maintain the credit of royal paper that had upset commercial exchanges. An arrêt of February 25, 1708, allowed both buyers and sellers in large-scale business arrangements to set their own terms for payment.[1]

Desmaretz launched a series of complicated measures to attract the confidence of the business and investing community. He ordered that all money owed to the royal government be paid to the Royal Treasury rather than diverted to pay other expenses, a practice his predecessor had encouraged. When he centralized the collection of royal funds, a policy that had to be reinforced by other measures, Desmaretz was trying to give the controller general greater authority over the flow of revenue by enabling efforts to enforce the regularity with which comptables paid their debts to the Royal Treasury. Desmaretz wanted to end the unnecessary delays in repaying loans that the state's creditors had to endure, to establish priorities as to which payments should be made first, and to restore credit to the Royal Treasury by having large sums of money flow through it.[2]

Restoring credit was necessary in order to reduce the difference between the face value and negotiable value of royal paper. Desmaretz, whom many people in the business community apparently trusted (given the delight they expressed at his appointment),[3] used his contacts within the financial community to persuade those who held assignations against the revenue for the year 1708 to turn them in for assignations against future revenue. This action freed the receipts of 1708 for the payment of that year's expenses, instead of leaving them almost entirely exhausted. While surrendering a year's interest on debts by reassigning them, Desmaretz temporarily restored the government's ability to borrow for the 1708 campaign, in hopes that prompt repayment of these loans would attract more lenders.[4] One clever method Desmaretz used for attracting more loans was to flatter the financiers, something that Saint-Simon found disgusting. Desmaretz, in collusion with Louis XIV, invited Samuel Bernard to meet with him at Marly, where the king then "happened" upon them and invited Bernard on a tour of the wonders of Marly. Bernard emerged so flattered by the episode that he promised loans that he had previously been resisting.[5]

The government also launched a policy of monthly currency devaluations to encourage holders of assignations on 1708's revenue to convert their paper. If a holder of an assignation hoped to negotiate his paper for a profit, his chances of doing so were diminished because the legal value of hard currency was being reduced every month. The purpose of these devaluations was to reanimate commerce by forcing the exchange of coin that would soon lose its value, while also increasing the amount of coin in the various cashboxes of the tax farms that could be employed to pay debts or attract new loans.

The first year of Desmaretz's administration relied heavily on the kinds of measures that had been used in the past. Rentes were created at denier 16 (6.25 percent), for a total loan of 33.6 million livres. Desmaretz claimed that augmented gages on specific offices were also created to raise another 36 million livres,[6] but other sources suggest that as much as 46,227,824 livres, or even 52,958,850 livres, was actually raised.[7] The reason for the difference in estimates was that several traités signed in 1708 never produced the total amount that was expected. For example, a résultat of the council dated July 17, 1708, granted a company of traitants led by Bourvalais under the name of François Fontaine, the company's "straw man," the right to sell the offices of treasurers and receivers for various communities' funds. The members of these communities included officers of the ports, Halles, places, and markets of Paris collecting fees on merchandise and supplies entering the city. Out of the original forfait of 2.5 million livres, the company received a rebate of 416,666⅔ livres and was to pay the balance of 2,083,333⅓ livres in the following terms: 283,333⅓ livres as a down payment, and the rest in eight equal bimonthly payments of 225,000 livres beginning on October 1, 1708. If this traité had lived up to its original terms, the final payment would have been due on December 1, 1709, but the decline of commerce as a result of the winter of 1709 made these offices less attractive. The offices only paid 50,000 livres in gages, representing only 2 percent of the investment. The rest of the profits were to come from fees for handling the communities' funds. An arrêt of September 30, 1710, reduced the total forfait to only 1,118,076⅔ livres, to be paid, beginning on December 1, 1710, in eight quarterly payments, the first four of which were to equal 208,416⅔ livres, the last four being only 19,102 livres, 9 sous, 11 deniers each. The crown also acknowledged having already received 798,833⅓ livres which it owed Fontaine, along with 10 percent interest on these funds, totaling another 166,423 livres, 7 sous. The offices were not selling.[8]

A host of offices created in 1708 failed to sell, such as that of the *marqueurs de bas* (stocking markers), originally set at for 350,000 livres but suppressed on October 7, 1710;[9] certain offices in the waters and forests, originally priced at 1.2 million livres on March 10, 1708, but reduced to 768,078 livres by August 26, 1710;[10] or rights to be collected on the amortissements and francfiefs, set at 2.62 million livres by résultats of May 22 and July 31, 1708, but reduced to 1.38 million livres by September 16, 1710.[11] Some offices were ill fated, like those of the fifty *jurés* controllers of fruit in Paris created in June 1708. The Siberian freeze that settled on France from December 1708 until March 1709 killed many of the fruit and nut trees in France, and severely reduced the trade in fruits and nuts. This traité attracted not a single buyer and received official cancellation on February 7, 1713.[12] The government had to reimburse many of these kinds of traités later on because payment had been made to the government before any offices were sold.

Despite all these difficulties, the government did raise 229,059,467 livres in the last ten months of 1708, while it spent only 184 million in the same year.[13] The balance was to repay debts from previous years. While the government's credit might temporarily have been restored, the defeat at Oudenarde in July and the fall of Lille in December intensified the crisis by severely reducing tax receipts and producing the situation Desmaretz described to the king in August 1709.

Desmaretz had tried to restore confidence by promising to pay all the assignations against 1709's revenues in order to secure more loans in the aftermath of the failed bank experiment of January–February 1709.[14] The collapse of Bernard and Nicolas was, however, the latest in a series of bankruptcies that the government had been covering up since 1705. It could no longer call upon bankers to lend large quantities of money. France now descended further into financial difficulties, with a year of bread riots and public unrest, tarnishing the bright hopes that had accompanied Desmaretz's appointment to such an extent that, in a fit of pique, Desmaretz dared anyone else to do any better than he had done.[15] The government struggled to import grain from abroad in order to keep its price under control in the large cities of France, particularly Paris. The demand for more imports increased the demand for credit from abroad and raised expenses for 1709 to 221,110,547 livres, while ordinary revenue sank to 38,162,827 livres.[16]

In May 1709 the arrival in France of the Spanish treasure fleet that had fled from Allied raiders saved the government by providing the means to reduce the amount of mint bills in circulation by reminting money. The key provisions of the edict of May 1709 ordering the reform of coins called for the mints to accept one-sixth of the total amount of money brought to be reminted in mint bills. If a person brought 1,200 livres to be reminted, the total could include 200 livres in mint bills. The total would be repaid in coin with the new value of 5 livres for a silver écu and 20 livres for a gold louis. The previous value had been 4 livres, 8 sous, and 16 livres, 10 sous, respectively. The government was able to remove 43 million livres in mint bills from circulation.[17] The treasure fleet was an unexpected boon. In the past, individual ships had landed in France to deliver their gold and silver to France rather than Spain. Never before had an entire fleet landed in France, bringing 30 million livres' worth of metal that produced a profit of 11,370,773 livres for the government of Louis XIV. Desmaretz had hoped that this policy of currency reform would attract more gold and silver to France and thus restore monetary circulation. He claimed to have been successful and to have raised enough money to pay the troops for 1709.

The king wanted to expand the reminting effort by requiring all people to send their gold and silverware to the mint. A similar effort undertaken in 1689 had destroyed much of the gold and silver that had adorned Versailles since 1682, when it became the king's official residence. Chancellor Pontchartrain disagreed with the king's proposal, as he had done when he was controller general twenty years before, because he believed that the value of the artworks that would be lost in the reminting effort far exceeded that of the gold and silver that reminting would produce. He also felt that the profits of the scheme would be less than Louis expected, and that adopting the measure would embarrass France before the rest of Europe, which would see it as an act of desperation. Desmaretz agreed with the chancellor. In the end, Louis XIV carried the day in this argument, although Saint-Simon claimed that, while some people cooperated completely, most hid just as much gold and silverware as they sent to the mint. The memorialist admitted that he had been among those hiding their gold and silverware.[18]

Unfortunately, the high price of grain and its subsequent disappearance from commerce forced the government to resort to taxation in kind in order to supply the army and navy. This measure was "the most important affair and the one that brought the most pain," according to Desmaretz. To take the place of the taille and capitation for 1710 and 1711, the government imposed a tax on sacks of grain in all the provinces of France. The grain was to be valued at its market price and the cost of its shipment and storage was fixed but exorbitant. Desmaretz claimed that the government took a total of 557,900 sacks of grain in place of money. The price of each was between 30 and 40 livres, with a maximum estimated priced of 22,316,000 livres, but the total expenses for supplies in 1709 reached more than 45 million livres.[19] The crisis in military supplies led to the dismissal of Chamillard as war minister in June 1709, along with the appointment of Nointel, Desmaretz's brother-in-law, as inspector general of military supplies.

To avoid a major subsistence disaster throughout France, the government reduced or eliminated taxes on foodstuffs and livestock in 1709. It granted special privileges to those who lent either seed or money for the purchase of seed to ensure a good harvest in 1709 and 1710. Officials toured the countryside to determine the amounts of grain on hand and to seek out hoarders and speculators for punishment. France purchased as much grain as possible from the Mediterranean and the Baltic markets. The government made every effort to feed urban areas and prevent starvation, but, as Desmaretz himself said, "The miserable conditions of the realm during the year 1709 will not easily be erased from men's memories."[20]

As a result, the brevet of the taille for 1710 was reduced immediately by 6 million livres, and another 2 million shortly thereafter. To cover this loss of revenue, the government negotiated short-term loans with a variety of tax farmers and other gens d'affaires. It had not been able to lease the General Farms and, thus, administered them directly, with the help of the tax farmers. Shares of future revenue from the years 1710–17 were also consumed in advance, up to the amount of 52 million livres.[21] These attempts to cushion the burden on the people were insufficient. New extraordinary affairs were required to raise another 100 million livres or more.

The year 1708 had ended with an edict creating rentes for sale to people seeking exemption from the capitation. Anyone who could pay the equivalent of six years of his capitation could purchase rentes at denier 20 (5 percent) against the Hôtel de Ville of Paris, the provincial estates, or any source of royal revenue that the purchaser desired.[22] Money from this measure began flowing into the royal coffers in 1709. Additional rentes at denier 16 (6.25 percent) were created to keep the flow of money moving through the Royal Treasury. New offices were created but some of them were no more successful than the ones previously created in 1708.

The government had been working to cover up a series of bankruptcies that had been cascading through the corps of traitants since the fall of 1709. Many traités were proving to be unprofitable, but the financiers who backed them had borrowed large sums of money to meet their payment schedules with the government. In an effort to salvage the credit of its financiers, the government began reworking these arrangements. The first collapse began on October 2, 1708, with a résultat of the council for selling thirty-three offices of controllers of war for 792,000 livres minus one-sixth (132,000 livres) to the traitants.[23] An earlier résultat of June 26, 1708, had created thirty-three offices of commissaires des guerres for 1.2 million livres, with the same one-sixth rebate.[24] The government reworked both of these traités on October 19, 1709, and ultimately revoking the former. At the same time, it created thirty-two new offices under the terms of a simple *recouvrement* (collection), meaning that the Royal Treasury would receive any money collected, and the traitants would only keep one-tenth of the purchase price, as well as the usual two sous per livre (one-tenth) above the purchase price. The traité for the commissaires des guerres had only sold four of the offices, while it suppressed fourteen other offices in return for funds received. The traité for the controllers of war had only sold one office. The government worked out a new payment schedule with the traitants to repay them for the funds they had already paid. The total forfait for the thirty-two new offices was reduced from 1.26 million livres to 905,000 livres.[25]

The reworking of the traités in October 1709 was the beginning of a series of similar difficulties. The promissory notes issued by the various companies of traitants were clogging the money market, as was the paper of royal comptables. The government had already attempted to shore up the credit of this paper on July 13, 1709, when an arrêt ordered the traitants to set aside funds in specie to pay the interest on their notes at the rate of 10 percent annually. The intendant of finances who administered their traités was to check their accounts monthly. A repeat of this decision occurred on November 19, 1709, with an order that all promissory notes be renewed until repaid and that the interest be paid in specie, with the added requirement that, unless all the interested parties renewed the bills, those who refused to renew their own notes would be excluded from the traité. Legal protection from the seizure of property was extended to the traitants and their creditors as long as they paid the interest on these loans.[26]

In 1710 Desmaretz and his assistants were frantically renegotiating the terms of various unsuccessful traités by reducing the amounts of their forfaits, regulating the terms under which the cautions would repay their notes, or cancelling the traités altogether and arranging for the crown to repay its debts to the traitants from the profits of other extraordinary affairs created solely to repay these kinds of debts. Very few new traités arranged in 1710 were anything other than simple recoveries or collections. The traitants supported the collections as a means to continue earning money in order to pay off their debts. They were literally prisoners in their homes because they could not venture outdoors for fear of the crowd of process servers, huissiers, and sergeants seeking their arrest on warrants from a variety of courts.

On July 21, 1710, de la Garde reported in a mémoire to Desmaretz on the necessity of guaranteeing the promissory notes of the traitants. The mémoire criticized those traitants who claimed they were unable to honor their debts while busying themselves with purchasing land, houses, and offices. An examination of their accounts would reveal their profits and expose their true financial condition, de la Garde argued. He recommended that the interest on these people's promissory notes be set at 10 percent, payable in cash, and that royal huissiers be allowed to search their homes without permission, that a system for gradually retiring the principal and interest on these loans be adopted, and that the traitants not be allowed to enjoy any profits until these bills were retired. De la Garde's notes on this mémoire indicate that Desmaretz granted every recommendation except the unrestrained searches of traitants' homes by huissiers.[27]

Following the terrible winter of 1709, Louis XIV had attempted to negotiate a peace with the Allies, going so far as to send his foreign minister Torcy to conduct the negotiations personally in May 1709. The terms he brought back on June 2 were so onerous that the king rejected them, although he did make a gesture toward peace by withdrawing some French forces from Spain. The Allies had demanded that Philip V, Louis' grandson, abandon the Spanish throne, chased from it, if necessary, by French troops. In response, the king dismissed his friend Chamillard, the war minister, and issued an appeal to his people through his governors and the church. These actions provoked a patriotic response that preceded the bloodbath of Malplaquet in September. Thereafter, Tournai and Mons were besieged and fell to the Allies.

As France struggled to maintain its position in the war, the usual sources of money were drying up and the men in the contrôle général had to look elsewhere for funds if they hoped to endure another year of war. During the latter part of 1709, Desmaretz and Malet drew up a prospective revenue picture for 1710. According to their data, ordinary revenues were expected to reach just 54,767,120 livres; prospective extraordinary sources of revenue included 5.3 million livres in loans from the tax farmers and various financiers like Crozat, and 600,000 livres from Bourvalais for the office he would not purchase until February 1710. Another 1,966,666 livres was expected from four separate minor extraordinary affairs. The most hoped-for sources of revenue were the 24 million livres the clergy would pay in return for ending its annual subsidy of 4 million livres for the capitation, 14 million livres for alienating the farm of the control of notarial acts, and 17.2 million livres from the alienation of the paulette.[28]

The inclusion of the last two items establishes that Desmaretz and Malet drew up this document prior to December 1709, when these matters, particularly the alienation of the paulette, were decided. All officers outside the superior courts had to pay an annual fee to the treasury of the casual revenues if they wished to keep their offices as property in their estates. The edict of December 1709 decreed that this annual tax would be renewed every nine years and that the latest renewal was to expire at the end of 1710. The king was going to dispense all officers from paying this fee after December 31, 1709; instead, they would have to pay a sum equal to sixteen times the fee during the year 1710 in return for obtaining the right of *survivance* (heritability) for their offices. All officers, whether they held casual, inheritable, or domanial offices, would have to pay this new tax prior to December 31, 1710, or their offices would revert to the crown. By this measure, the crown alienated an annual revenue source in return for a one-time-only payment, just as it had done when it created rentes for those desiring exemption from the capitation.[29]

The farm of the control of notarial acts paid 1.48 million livres annually to the crown. This farm controlled the certification, at the local level, of documents that did not require the Great Seal of France but did require stamped paper or parchment in order to be recognized in a court of law. The government planned to sell this farm to the highest bidder on a province-by-province basis, either for ten years or permanently. Bidding began on May 6, 1710, and continued from province to province until February 26, 1711.[30]

The process of dismantling sources of royal revenue was not an original policy developed at the end of Louis XIV's reign; it had originated during the Fronde. There were limits to how much the king could sell because he had been alienating parts of his revenue since 1672 in the form of rentes, augmented gages, and new offices. The crown had tried to increase its revenue in 1695 with the creation of the capitation, but the new tax was suppressed at the end of the War of the League of Augsburg in 1698. The failure of the royal government to reorganize its finances after 1697 left it with little to sell when the War of the Spanish Succession began in 1701. The government entered this last and greatest war of Louis XIV's reign with little left to sell or alienate.

The capitation was recreated in 1701 but the revenues from this tax soon withered, until the government attached a 10 percent surtax in 1705. The surtax was extended to the taille and the General Farms before the end of the same year. These measures enabled France to survive the next two years, until Desmaretz came to power. He began manipulating government credit in such a way that he was able to get through 1708 with little difficulty. The fortuitous arrival of an entire fleet of Spanish ships loaded with gold and silver, reliance on taxation in kind, and the final dismantling of the royal revenue machinery supplied the necessary credit for 1709. From selling exemptions to the capitation, the government turned to auctioning off anything marketable—a lucrative tax farm, an annual subsidy of 4 million livres from the clergy, and the annual tax paid by royal officeholders.

A few minor sources of revenue—such as increased salt prices in Franche Comté or increased fees for shipping material on the Canal du Midi—were added to this officially sanctioned pillaging of the king's revenue.[31]

All of these frantic efforts were grinding away at an ever-decreasing amount of money. Desmaretz's prospectus for 1710 hoped to raise 126,769,486 livres, but it also predicted that expenses would reach at least 206 million livres. They actually exceeded 225 million livres.[32] The refusal of the General Farmers to renew their lease in August–September 1709 forced the government to allow the General Farmers to administer the farms directly and pay only as much as they received, minus a handling fee to pay their expenses. The loss of this credit mechanism in the wake of Bernard's earlier failure to establish a royal bank, and the loss of significant help from the traitants, left the government with only one group of solvent financiers—the receivers general of finances.

In December 1709 Desmaretz had secured the king's permission to create a deposit bank (*caisse*) called the Caisse Legendre after François Legendre le jeune, the man who signed its bills. The caisse was backed by the credit of twelve receivers general of finances, who would take in the revenue from the sale of exemptions from the capitation, the repurchase of the paulette, the clergy's payment to end its annual subsidy, and a small number of other extraordinary affairs. In return, this caisse issued paper that promised to pay the value of its receipts to the bearer with interest at a certain time in the future. Backed by the credit of these twelve receivers general and the income from a number of extraordinary affairs in finances, the Caisse Legendre enabled Desmaretz to organize the royal debt somewhat by abandoning all the unpaid royal paper to whatever value speculators would allow and concentrating the crown's most liquid assets to support the caisse and its bills. The Caisse Legendre sustained royal credit until the spring of 1715, when it foundered because of its inability to honor the large number of bills presented to pay the debts France owed to Bavaria and Cologne after the war.

There has been no research into the history of this credit bank, to my knowledge. The Archives Nationales has only one carton of material from the accounts of the caisse, and the only other descriptions of its activities appear in Desmaretz's *Compte rendu* and Malet's "Mémoires." It administered the collection of a number of extraordinary affairs without taking the customary rebates, and thus saved the crown one-sixth of the income from these measures. The receivers general only asked that the expenses of the caisse be paid along with the interest on any loans they made to the caisse. In the course of five years the caisse handled 400 million livres in funds and issued notes against this revenue.[33]

The French and Allies regarded the battle of Malplaquet differently. The French learned that they could lose a battle without collapsing as their armies had done after Blenheim in 1704 and Ramillies and Turin in 1706. The French suffered less than half the casualties of the Allies at Malplaquet. Marshal Villars told Louis XIV, "If God gives us the grace to lose another similar battle, your Majesty can count on his enemies being destroyed."[34] The Allies saw all of these activities by the French as signs of their increasing desperation. With the resumption of negotiations at Gertruydenberg in March 1710, the Allies made even stronger demands on the French, including that French forces drive Philip V from the Spanish throne without any Allied assistance. The French instead offered to pay 500,000 livres for allied troops to drive Philip from the throne. When the Allies rejected this proposal, the French royal government gave the text of France's concessions to Dutch newspapers to undercut the Allies' position of negotiation. The news of the collapse of the negotiations reached Versailles on July 16.[35]

Despite the aid that the Caisse Legendre provided in terms of credit, it did not increase the income of the crown. The government was forced to come up with a major source of revenue or accept whatever peace terms the enemies wished to offer. With the arrival of the news that negotiations had failed, Desmaretz called for new ideas from many people—financiers, intendants of finances, and others—because "it was necessary to assure an annual revenue to the king, like all of the other ways had done before."[36] The new revenue source was to be the dixième, a tax equal to one-tenth of the income produced by property ownership.

The Idea of Creating a Tax on Wealth

If the government was going to demonstrate its determination to continue the fight, France was going to have to alter its desperate financial condition radically. Consultations and discussions that took place in this environment would produce the dixième and a host of other measures in October 1710. Desmaretz's *Compte rendu* contains a defense of the measure[37] in which the minister describes all the resources the government had exhausted over the previous twenty-five years. He describes having to resort to asking diverse people, including intendants of finances, receivers general, and financiers, for ideas, which the government studied over a long period of time before adopting the new tax on wealth. Desmaretz says that a declaration (i.e., a temporary change in the law) ordered the imposition, not an edict (a permanent alteration of the law), on October 7.[38] While he confesses that the measure was a violent and extreme remedy, Desmaretz claims that its successful adoption helped to persuade France's enemies to make peace.

In subsequent paragraphs describing activities during 1711–12, Desmaretz alludes to other problems, such as the government's determination to liberate its revenues by converting assignations against 1711, 1712, and 1713 into rentes. The government had been unable to pay rentes because of the sharp decline in ordinary revenues following the winter of 1709. This delay in payments "gave reason to fear some angry reactions from the rentiers," but the government avoided the expected reactions by employing all the revenues of the General Farms to pay the rentes and by initiating legal pursuits against the commis of the farms to hasten the arrival of funds for that purpose. The gages of the superior courts were also in arrears because the product of the General Farms had fallen from the estimated 46 million livres (on average) to 31 million in 1709 and 40 million in 1710. In his discussion of the technical problems, the minister reveals that the activities of September–October 1710 involved more than just a new tax. They included efforts to absorb all royal paper in order to liberate revenues for 1711, 1712, and 1713, and to revive commerce through the circulation of hard currency.

Malet, who assisted Desmaretz in the writing of his *Compte rendu*, would write his own history of French finances describing the meeting at the minister's residence at La Marche in September 1710.[39] In attendance were two prominent officials in the contrôle général des finances, Le Rebours as the premier commis des finances and Bercy as the man responsible for all official accounting;[40] three councilors of state, Vaubourg, Nointel, and Bouville; and two receivers general, La Croix and Prondre. With Malet's help, Desmaretz described the government's problems and debts. Then he read a number of mémoires to the group discussing ways to solve the dilemma. Most of those assembled favored an idea submitted by Jean Orry for the establishment of a one-tenth (*dixième*) tax on the revenues from *biens fonds* (real estate, including land and the buildings on it); this idea would became the basis for the declaration in October. Desmaretz secured a loan of 18 million livres from the receivers general against the expected income from the dixième, while at the same time he reduced the interest rates on all rentes and augmented the gages created since 1689, as well as promises of the caisse des emprunts, to denier 20 (5 percent). New rentes were created to absorb the bills of the receivers general, farmers general, treasurers of the extraordinary of war, and assignations against revenues for the years 1711, 1712, and 1713.

The source most often cited for this period in French history is the duc de Saint-Simon,[41] who described the development of the dixième as a product of necessity inspired by the ideas of Vauban and Boisguilbert. He says that Desmaretz had never lost sight of their ideas, even though they had been persecuted for them. Because the king trusted him completely, Desmaretz was able to call together a committee of friends and relatives to study ways to increase royal revenues. This committee consisted of his brother Vaubourg, his brothers-in-law Nointel and Bouville, his son-in-law Bercy, Harlay de Cély (a master of requests who Saint-Simon says was totally devoted to Desmaretz),[42] and three master financiers. This group worked for less than a month on drawing up an edict for a tax that did not replace the taille and capitation but rather added to their number. According to Saint-Simon, Nointel and one of the financiers were so shocked by this development that they withdrew from the work of the committee in horror. Desmaretz, according to Saint-Simon, then presented the edict on September 30, 1710, to the Royal Council of Finances, whose members had not yet heard of it. Daguesseau asked to be given time to read it over before commenting on it, but the king said that, because the choice was either this new tax or letting the enemy occupy French soil, such a delay would be useless; the council would come to the same conclusion he had. Beauvillier, who in Saint-Simon's words was "seduced by his father-in-law Colbert's nephew, whom he believed to be an oracle in finances," spoke of the new measure as preferable to seeing the enemy ravage France. Thus, Saint-Simon says, the council approved Desmaretz's "edict."

Saint-Simon claimed that Chancellor Pontchartrain related the goings-on in the council to him the next day. The chancellor claimed to be outraged but Saint-Simon also said that Pontchartrain told him that no one on the Royal Council opposed the measure. Saint-Simon also says that the Dauphin and the Duke of Burgundy were supposed to have spoken against the measure at a private dinner party afterwards. For Saint-Simon, it was a great crime to expose every family's private fortune to the eyes of the financiers as the dixième required.

Saint-Simon adds a dramatic twist to the story when he says that Desmaretz enlisted the help of the king's confessor, Père Le Tellier, who in turn appealed to the good doctors of the Sorbonne to persuade the king that he had the power to adopt this kind of tax. Previously, Saint-Simon had told a similar tale about the adoption of the capitation in 1695; in this account, only the name of the king's confessor, Père de La Chaise, differs.[43] I do not believe that either story is true. Saint-Simon was just adding a dramatic detail to assist in his portrayal Louis XIV as being under the influence of the Jesuits. Louis had stated quite clearly in his memoirs of the year 1666 that kings have the authority to tax their subjects to pay for the needs of the state and its defense.[44]

The marquis de Dangeau tells a slightly different story in his journal entry of September 23, 1710. He refers to the tax as *une dîme royale,* which he claims had first been mentioned in the memoirs of the duc de Sully, Henri IV's great finance minister, before being worked on by Boisguilbert, who had spoken to Pontchartrain about it when the latter was controller general of finances. Dangeau also says that Marshal Vauban discussed the measure in great detail in a book. According to Dangeau, Desmaretz had each of these ideas examined by a committee consisting of Vaubourg,

Nointel, Bouville, Bercy, and three financiers, whom he names as La Croix, Prondre, and Orry. Dangeau says the Royal Council of Finances settled the whole matter on September 30, 1710. Accordingly, the king would receive a prodigious amount of money with which he could extinguish the mint bills and assure the regular payment of the rentes, all without the use of traitants. The edict had not yet appeared on September 30, so Dangeau did not know the exact manner in which the new imposition would operate. On October 6 he records that the king had enough cash on hand to increase the size of each company in the infantry by five men each at a cost of 20 to 30 francs per man. The edict decreeing what Dangeau continued to call the dîme royal was sealed by the chancellor on October 20, registered in the Paris Parlement, and made public on October 26.[45]

Another courtier, the marquis de Sourches, more properly describes the new tax as the "tenth denier on all the property in the realm" (*dixième denier sur tous les biens du royaume*). He mentions a rumor about this measure in the entry of September 21, 1710, in which he says that the new tax would provide 80 million livres. Sourches also mentions that the infantry would receive reinforcements of five men per company on October 2.[46]

Clearly, the accounts of the three courtiers, Saint-Simon, Dangeau, and Sourches, represent what they had found out at court, either through gossip or rumor. Their stories vary in some ways. Dangeau, for example, saw the idea for the new tax as originally appearing in the writings of Henri IV's finance minister and then reappearing in the writings of Boisguilbert and Vauban. Leaving Sully's ideas aside, the ideas of Boisguilbert and Vauban were not at all alike. Yet, both Saint-Simon and Dangeau believed they were related. It is not altogether improbable that neither man had read the writings of the two reformers. Saint-Simon confesses in several passages of his memoirs that he was totally ignorant of financial matters. In addition, Dangeau's list of the participants in the meetings that created the dixième does not include Harlay de Cély, but he does name the three financiers whom Saint-Simon did not identify. Dangeau does not retell Saint-Simon's dramatic story of the two men who withdrew from the initial committee in horror at the idea of such a tax.

Unlike the months of activity within the Royal Council of Finances during 1694–95 that led to the creation of the capitation, the minister carried the dixième into the council in its definitive form. There were, however, three council meetings between September 30 and October 20, when Chancellor Pontchartrain sealed the law. Usually Dangeau only mentioned that Desmaretz worked with the king after each Tuesday meeting of the Royal Council, but during this time he describes Desmaretz as working with Louis XIV after each meeting *assez longtemps* or *jusqu'à une heure et démie* as if there were something significant about this activity.[47]

A comparison of these five contemporary descriptions reveals some startling differences among the stories of what occurred at the council meeting that approved the dixième. There are three different lists of people who decided what policy to adopt. Desmaretz and Malet omit any reference to Vauban or Boisguilbert. They state that the new tax was imposed by a declaration (a temporary law), while Dangeau and Saint-Simon say it was an edict (a permanent measure). Although Dangeau was a conseiller d'état d'épée (one of three councilors of state drawn from the sword nobility) and Sourches was the grand provost (officer in charge of the court that enforced the law around the king), neither was close to the policymaking centers of government. Saint-Simon had close personal ties to Chancellor Pontchartrain, Beauvillier, and the Burgundy faction at court, but his description of the matter, written years afterward, is colored by his desire to see the whole affair as a conspiracy by the financiers to pry into the privacy of others. Only Desmaretz and Malet indicate that there were matters other than the creation of a new tax under discussion. Besides these published accounts of events surrounding the creation of the dixième, however, there are archival sources that can vouch for what really happened.

We have already seen that Boisguilbert submitted to Desmaretz a plan to raise 100 million livres during this time period. Boisguilbert mentioned to Argenson that it had been approved and referred to one of Desmaretz's premier commis.[48] Because no letters survive between Boisguilbert and Desmaretz or his commis between May 26, 1710, and March 14, 1711, in the Archives Nationales G^7 series of documents, we can only surmise that Desmaretz might have asked Boisguilbert to submit a mémoire on how to assure the king an annual revenue without reducing his other revenues. Desmaretz himself said, "In this extremity, we asked for mémoires from diverse people."[49]

De la Hestroy wrote to Clautrier on September 2, 1710:

> M. Tuffereau [Clautrier's commis] said to me that he had told you, Monsieur, that I had done a mémoire in relation to the present state of affairs containing the means to reestablish the king's credit and to easily find for him a fund of more than eighty million in revenue without touching that which he presently enjoys, easy and prompt to collect without being much of a burden on the people and without resorting to extraordinary affairs, which have in my opinion spoiled everything and lost the king's credit in the manner that the traitants have used them.

He asked for an invitation to explain his ideas in person. A later letter of October 17, 1710, indicates that Desmaretz responded with four half-pages or *demi-feuilles* of reflections on de la Hestroy's ideas.[50]

Using almost the same language as Desmaretz did to describe the requirements of the new source of revenue, de la Hestroy seems to confirm the idea that the government sought advice from many people, including the donneurs d'avis. The proximity in time between the submission of de la Hestroy's and Boisguilbert's ideas and the rumors about these kinds of measures indicates that the request for these mémoires preceded September. Many mémoires on new methods for raising money that bear dates from the summer of 1710 can be found in the Foreign Affairs Ministry archives and the Archives Nationales. A study of these mémoires will reveal the kind of advice the government was getting, and perhaps an idea of what it was thinking.

Many donneurs d'avis criticized the practices of the previous twenty-two years. The point of departure for their proposals was the capitation, criticized as being unfair because it taxed ephemeral qualities like social status while allowing wealth to escape taxation. Men with great wealth could purchase nobility or an office and thus remove themselves from the list of taillables, but might not pay enough under the capitation to compensate for the loss to the taille. Many writers called for transforming the capitation into a tax on wealth rather than social standing.

An anonymous mémoire dated July 15, 1710, contained three major ideas for increasing revenue. One was to lower the taxes in the General Farms that the writer claimed would increase revenues because the drop in prices would stimulate trade and make up for the loss in revenue through increased trade. A second proposal called for a more equitable distribution of the taille that would facilitate its collection by increasing the tax on those who were most able to pay. The last suggestion was to transform the capitation into a tax proportionate to wealth, the equivalent of either one-tenth, one-fifteenth, or one-twentieth of the revenues derived from offices, rentes, and personal income from wages. The author suggested that, to make this kind of tax more acceptable, the government should refrain from resorting to extraordinary affairs and try to control grain prices. Anyone who purchased rentes in exchange for a promise not to be taxed should have the interest rate on those rentes reduced. If this last idea was unacceptable to the government, the author recommended doubling the capitation on everyone who paid at least forty sous already.[51]

The person who submitted this new project on the capitation might possibly have been one M. de Malon, who wrote to Desmaretz after the adoption of the dixième, claiming that he had submitted an idea similar to the dixième to M. de Bercy, whose family name was Malon. M. de Malon claimed that he had served the king for twenty-seven years, and that he was presently acting as a commissaire des guerres. What he wanted was a gratification to help pay off his debts.[52] The registers of the contrôle général des finances mention that his mémoire was sent to des Forts, who administered the capitation.[53] It is possible that the anonymous mémoire dated July 15, 1710, was the same one that des Forts received.

On October 4, 1710, Charles Irenée Castel, abbé de Saint-Pierre,[54] sent a letter to Desmaretz from the Palais Royal, claiming, "I have worked for two years on a plan for a proportional capitation with the plan to offer it to you as soon as it was in condition to be shown." He went on to say that Desmaretz had devised a better plan that would save the state and help obtain an advantageous peace. Saint-Pierre did not, however, send his project.[55] Saint-Pierre was first almoner to the king's sister-in-law, the Duchess of Orléans, and a member of the Académie française. He spent his time at court as a sometime lobbyist and donneur d'avis for reforming the taille or a proportional capitation. In 1734 he did publish an essay in his *Ouvrages de politique* entitled "Pour perfectionner la capitation par le méthode des déclarations."[56]

Among other extant documents on the capitation is anonymous mémoire entitled "Nouveau projet première ébauche capitation proportionée" (New Project First Draft Proportional Capitation), dated August 6, 16, or 26, 1710. In it, the author criticizes the existing capitation as unfair to the poor, who, he says, pay more in proportion to their wealth than the rich. He calls instead for a graduated income tax that would not increase the taxes of the poor but would distinguish between the nobility and the bourgeoisie. For example, princes of the blood would pay one sous per livre (5 percent) of their revenue in taxes, while marshals and dukes would pay 10 percent, members of the superior courts 20 percent (except those whose fathers had been gens d'affaires, who would pay 30 percent), the gens d'affaires 35 percent, and merchants 40 percent. This proposed tax would require all people to make a declaration of their income, including debts that they owed or were owed. Anyone refusing to declare a debt would thereby cancel it. The crown could confiscate revenue that was undeclared by sharing it with collectors, who would search for tax evaders. Dependent children could be deducted at set rates for the total family income. Declarations of revenue would have to be submitted to a clerk by October 1 of every year, or pay 25 percent more for being late. Thus, the controller general would have an idea of the revenue to be expected by the first of every year. The total proceeds for this measure were supposed to increase the revenue from the capitation from 35 million livres to 140 million, a net increase of 105 million livres. The author of this proposal had some knowledge of the men who administered the capitation—Souzy and des Forts—and claimed to know how the Dutch paid their taxes.[57]

A later letter by the same author, dated simply 1710, responds to objections to his system and asks to have the *première ébauche* (first draft) returned because the author is working on a *séconde ébauche.* The following page, written in the same hand and also dated only 1710, requests consideration for the author's *Projet de paix perpetuelle de l'Europe.*[58] The abbé de Saint-Pierre would publish his *Projet pour rendre la paix perpetuelle en l'Europe* in 1712, but he had been circulating it to people like the Duke of Burgundy, who died in February of that year. The reference in this note in the Foreign Affairs Ministry archive could have been addressed to the foreign minister Torcy, who must have known the abbé because he would accompany the French plenipotentiaries to Utrecht in January 1712.[59]

The abbé de Saint-Pierre wrote to Clautrier, Desmaretz's secretary, on September 22, 1710, sending additions and responses to his original proposal, because he had heard rumors that Desmaretz was working on an edict relating to that proposal. He asked Clautrier to speak to the minister about it, if he found it to be a solid proposal, or even to read it to Desmaretz. The enclosed additions, numbered twenty to twenty-five, were in response to objections made to the original proposal. The author of the première ébauche made reference to a proposed edict on his proportional capitation, and Saint-Pierre's letter of September 22 contains new articles for just such an edict.[60]

Whatever influence the abbé de Saint-Pierre had on the formation of policy during September 1710 is difficult to determine, since he believed as late as September 22 that Desmaretz was ignorant of his ideas. He had been working on his plan since 1708 and had communicated it to Clautrier, who apparently sent him reactions in the form of objections to his ideas. His letters of September 22 and October 4 indicate his fear that France might falter unless something was done. He disliked his proposal but declared his willingness to support such harsh measures if the survival of the state depended on it. These were all attitudes that the men in the government shared.

Another donneur d'avis whose projects met with some consideration by the government was Adrien Cazier.[61] He claimed in his many letters that he had begun submitting mémoires to Colbert and Louvois in 1671, and that France's difficulties had begun after 1684 because of unspecified policies undertaken by the Dutch that had reduced the supply of money, and thus commerce, in France. After Louvois' death, Cazier claimed that Louis XIV himself had asked him to continue submitting his ideas to the government. Several of his mémoires and letters are addressed *au Roy*. Cazier served as director of the royal tapestry manufactory at Beauvais during 1708–9. Notes by Desmaretz and de la Garde in the margins of his letters or on extracts indicate that the king asked to read some of his mémoires and that Madame de Maintenon sponsored some of them as well. He came originally from Tournai and claimed extensive knowledge of Flanders, but he resided in Paris and had frequent audiences with Desmaretz, Armenonville, and Daguesseau, the latter of whom had asked him to read Boisguilbert's *Détail de la France.*[62]

It was not until the spring of 1710 that Cazier began expounding what he called his two systems, which he claimed Colbert would have adopted had he not died. Cazier addressed the original mémoire about these two systems to the king, but Chancellor Pontchartrain referred them to Desmaretz on the king's behalf on May 7, 1710. Desmaretz asked Cazier either to send his ideas in a more explicit form, or to work with de la Garde on his mémoires. Cazier had a tendency to be long-winded in his letters and was asked several times to restrain himself, to no avail.

Cazier's two systems[63] consisted of uniting all the extraordinary affairs to the General Farms, except those that should be suppressed because they were contrary to the good of the state and commerce. He also called for reducing the price of salt in order to reduce the amount of illegal salt trading. He also said that the capitation should be eliminated. These actions would increase the income of the king's subjects to such an extent that they would willingly accept the establishment of a tax on a share of the income from wealth (*biens-fonds*) at the rate of two- or even three-twentieths (10 or 15 percent). Cazier claimed that the Dutch and English used this system. To support his ideas, he enclosed excerpts from the speeches or writings of Henri IV, the duc de Sully, Cardinal Richelieu, and Chancellor Séguier, to show that they were opposed to expedients or that they believed that commerce should not be burdened by unnecessary taxes. Cazier proposed creating offices called *greffiers des insinuations* (clerks in charge of keeping track of property records) to keep track of everyone's wealth, and suggested that the taille receivers and the receivers general of finances collect the new tax.

Cazier's ideas in themselves are not very interesting. Desmaretz wrote in the margin of one of the man's many letters that, while he thought Cazier was capable of giving good advice, he had never found a mémoire that could be used because Cazier always stated his ideas in general terms, exaggerating the faults of the government and making magnificent promises without any practicable or solid proposals.[64]

What is interesting about the half-carton of letters from Cazier is that it contains three mémoires written by de la Garde, one of Desmaretz's closest collaborators, that reveal what de la Garde was thinking, and perhaps what the minister thought as well. A mémoire dated June 15, 1710, entitled "Réflexions sur les systemes de Sr. Cazier," rejected the first system as unworkable because, it said, the General Farmers were too busy with their own problems to take on anything like Cazier's proposal. All extraordinary affairs, however, could be turned over to "the twelve receivers general," meaning the Caisse Legendre. Moreover, certain unproductive extraordinary affairs should be suppressed, but the traitants should be made to account for their business so that the king could assume their debts and promise to repay them and their creditors at 5 percent interest. De la

Garde even spoke of suppressing all extraordinary affairs as a gesture of good will to the people. At the time he wrote this mémoire, the government was reworking or revoking many of these extraordinary affairs.

De la Garde's most important statement was his acceptance of the idea that taxes should be proportional to what each taxpayer could afford to pay. Those who had more should have to pay more than those who had less. He opposed the creation of *greffiers des insinuations* because it would delay the establishment of this tax. The provincial intendants and their subdelegates could demand declarations of income under threat of fines equal to quadruple the estimated tax. If a proportional income tax were adopted, de la Garde believed, the capitation and the extraordinary affairs could be suppressed. Those who paid for exemptions from the capitation would still be paid their rentes. If the council rejected this idea, the capitation would have to be doubled or tripled. Either way, de la Garde saw inconveniences. The closing lines make it plain that he wrote the mémoire to Desmaretz, who would have had to make any proposal to the Royal Council of Finances.[65]

Another mémoire, dated June 16, 1710, is a copy of one sent by Chancellor Pontchartrain's secretary, Millain.[66] Millain (or was he speaking for the chancellor?) believed that the existing fiscal system was onerous and was alienating the king's subjects, whose good will might be needed if the government was going to request any new tax. The crown, he said, should assume the debts of the traitants and promise to repay them with interest. It should also appeal to the royal courts and every corporate institution in the elections, down to the parish level, to meet and send deputies to an assembly of the elections to draw up cahiers with recommendations on what should be done after the traitants were eliminated. Millain expected that the people would gladly make a great voluntary effort.[67]

A letter from Fénelon to the duc de Chevreuse on August 4, 1710, echoed Millain's sentiments about calling on some kind of representative body. The archbishop wanted an assembly of notables to be called in order to decide France's future policies. He blamed Louis XIV's government for not informing the kingdom in the past about its war aims, and not calling upon the kingdom for ideas on how to finance the war effort. The failure of the peace negotiations in late July 1710 had provoked this desperate plea from Fénelon, who wanted peace, regardless of the price.[68]

At the same time, de la Garde and Desmaretz were conferring on other matters, particularly the ideas of Cazier. A document written by both Desmaretz and de la Garde reveals an interesting exchange between the two men. Enclosed in a cover sheet on which Desmaretz had written "À M. de la Garde qu'il me l'en parlé," and de la Garde wrote "Rapporté le P. 7bre 1710 à Marly" (reported the first of September 1710 at Marly), is a note by de la Garde, dated July 27, 1710, at Fontainebleau. The note contains a question from Desmaretz, asking about Cazier's mémoire of August 1710. In response, De la Garde wrote that he had sent this *grand mémoire* (big memorandum), dated to sometime in August 1710, to the minister, along with an abstract from an earlier mémoire by Cazier dated June 13. Then, he comments: "It appears that the principal of this is executed by the establishment of the *dixième des revenues* because the basis of its resource consists in the establishment of *vingtièmes*."[69] Desmaretz had resolved upon the dixième sometime prior to September 1, 1710. A letter from Cazier dated either August 12 or 13 reports rumors of a new tax of two sous per livre (a dixième) on revenues, which Cazier opposed unless the extraordinary affairs were suppressed. Cazier continued to claim that he was only obeying the king's orders by writing to Desmaretz because his long experience had taught him things that other people did not know. He asked the minister's pardon as he went on to say that Desmaretz should listen to him and even help him because his writings concerned the future of Desmaretz's ministry.[70]

There is a response to this letter, dated August 24, 1710, that Boislisle mistakenly published as being written by de la Garde to Boisguilbert. The response is merely a rough draft that a scribe was to put into proper form, but it does carry the minister's *bon*, even though de la Garde was the author. There is no indication to whom he addressed it, but it does acknowledge the receipt of a letter written on August 13, the probable date of Cazier's letter. The commis tried to explain why the ideas of the addressee had been rejected, despite his efforts to persuade the minister of their value. The minister had to take the whole problem of the realm's finances into consideration, and thus could judge better than anyone what was in the best interests of the kingdom as a whole, de la Garde wrote. Both the commis and the addressee should defer to the minister's judgment.[71]

Another letter of a similar type, dated simply August 9, is from an unknown commis (probably Clautrier) to an unknown addressee. In it, the commis promises to read the addressee's mémoire to Desmaretz when the minister is less occupied with business. The letter closes with an acknowledgment that no other time in history has been more painful or difficult for public officials, and that it was a great undertaking to wish to halt the torrent of usury, distrust, and bad faith in one blow (*tout d'un coup*). The commis wrote that it would require a single blow because such an operation could never succeed by degrees; moreover, unless it was perfected, it would fail.[72]

This letter expressed the opinion of the people around the minister that the government must take prompt and serious action if France was to survive the crisis at hand. A circular letter to the provincial intendants from Desmaretz, dated August 5, 1710, enhances this impression. In it, Desmaretz calls upon each intendant to conduct a general inspection of the condition of each parish, and to report on all financial and commercial matters, including unpaid taxes since 1700, abandoned lands, accounts of all tax collections, and preparations for winter quarters for the army. They should forward any recommendations on what should be done to revive commerce in the provinces, reestablish cultivation of the land, and better enable the king to support the war effort.[73] Desmaretz's letter is reminiscent of Pontchartrain's letter to the intendants in October 1694, on the eve of the debate on the capitation. Although Desmaretz made no mention of any new tax that might be adopted, he wanted the intendants to tour their provinces and provide the government with all kinds of information that it would need to decide future policy. The request for an investigation into all extraordinary affairs in the provinces was the key to helping the government decide what it should do about eliminating them when the time came.

Something was in the wind. The minister and his principal assistants had agreed to levy the dixième some time between July 27 and September 1, 1710. They had also decided that some great enterprise was needed to end the usury and bad credit in France's money markets. Yet, these kinds of decisions were too important to be made by the ministry alone. In September Desmaretz called together a group of trusted advisers to take some of the responsibility for this decision off his shoulders.

The Proceedings of September–October 1710

A letter from Le Rebours to Desmaretz on September 8, 1710, described some of this activity. He reported that M. de la Crois was drawing up accounts of what the new subsidy would produce in each generality. M. Prondre had spoken to Le Rebours about his ideas on the suppression of royal paper and on a mémoire by M. de la Ferrière. Desmaretz noted in the margin of this letter, which approved Delacroix's efforts, that he had returned Prondre's mémoire and that he and Le Rebours should examine the other matters at La Marche with Bouville on Thursday (three days later).[74]

An undated preliminary draft of the edict that created the dixième and called for its establishment on October 1 had a list of names in Desmaretz's handwriting: M. de bouville, M. de Nointel, M. Le Rebours (who had corrected this draft), M. de Vaubourg, M. de Bercy, M. Orry, M. de la Crois, and M. Prondre. This same group is named by Dangeau, with the addition of Le Rebours. This rough draft was to be circulated among the men listed, who were involved in all the discussions over the dixième.[75]

There is no evidence that Harlay de Cély was involved in any of the preliminaries, as Saint-Simon claimed. While there are letters from him to Desmaretz that indicate by their obsequious tone that he enjoyed the minister's protection,[76] Saint-Simon apparently connected him with the meetings that decided on the adoption of the dixième, simply because Harlay de Cély was named at a later date as a master of requests for the extraordinary commission of the council of state that would handle all appeals about the dixième.[77] Dangeau mentioned this connection in a later entry in his journal, but Saint-Simon may have confused this later reference to the original group.[78]

Elsewhere in his *Mémoires,* Saint-Simon blamed the intendant in Languedoc, Lamoignon de Basville, for the invention of both the capitation and the dixième.[79] There is no evidence at all to support this claim. In fact, letters from Basville to Desmaretz written after the establishment of the dixième show that he was opposed to the measure but acquiesced to the wishes of the King's Council.[80] Basville's opposition to experimenting with Boisguilbert's ideas in 1705, his denials to Desmaretz that he had spoken against the dixième in 1710, and his criticisms of any efforts to change the system of impositions in a letter to the duc de Noailles on December 26, 1715,[81] would seem to remove him from any list of fiscal innovators or reformers who favored anything beyond the traditional methods of reform, such as correcting abuses in the existing system.

The last three men on Desmaretz's list—Orry, de la Croix, and Prondre—were Saint-Simon's master financiers. Prondre was a receiver general of finances who was in the process of acquiring the presidency of the Paris Chambre des Comptes in 1711. This office would require him to give up his receiver generalship and withdraw from financial matters. Thus, he is a prime candidate for identification as the financier who Saint-Simon claimed withdrew from the dixième.

Claude François Delacroix had served as receiver general of finances in Moulins since 1677, making him one of the most experienced receivers general with whom the controller general would deal on matters concerning the entire corps of receivers general of finances. He had been close to Desmaretz since the latter's return to power in 1703, and he had a country home in Bercy that put him in contact with Desmaretz's son-in-law. He was also an ally of the Paris brothers, army suppliers who would soon emerge as major financiers throughout the early eighteenth century. Delacroix was also related to Mlle. Marie-Émilie Joly de Chouin, the secret wife of the king's son.[82] Once the new tax was decided, according to Le Rebours, Delacroix began estimating the revenue to be gained in the provinces. Malet said that he was responsible for securing a loan of 18 million livres from the receivers general, based upon the expected revenue from the dixième.

Malet claimed that Jean Orry was the man who originated the idea of the dixième, but he does not include Orry in his list of people who attended the meeting where the tax was approved. His name was, however, on Desmaretz's list of people to be included in the discussions. Orry began his career as a military supplier before working on the aqueduct at Maintenon and the port of Brouage. He later became a tax farmer. He was sent to Spain to help reestablish that country's finances to support the war effort, but his work led to conflicts and his forced expulsion from Spain. After returning from Spain in 1706, Orry acquired the office of president of the Metz Parlement. He advised Chamillard and submitted recommendations on financial affairs shortly after Desmaretz's appointment as controller general of finances. Some of these recommendations eventually became policy, such as alienating the farm of the control of notarial acts or alienating the paulette.[83]

Malet wrote that Desmaretz read mémoires to this group of advisers when they assembled at his estate at La Marche near Versailles in September. There are five mémoires in the Archives Nationales wrapped in a paper cover bearing the words "Memoires au sujet du dixième des biens et autres." One of them is dated July 27, 1710; another is titled "Extrait du Mémoire de M. de la F.," who could possibly be the M. de la Ferrière mentioned in Le Rebours' letter to Desmaretz.[84] Four of the mémoires deal with the problem of finding a new source of revenue, while the fifth calls for reducing the number of regiments and battalions in the army as a way to save money. The four discussing new revenue sources are between six and fourteen pages long, and only three of them call for some sort of income tax. None discusses any sort of taxation in kind, the equivalent of Marshal Vauban's premier fonds, although one does call for a tax on land.

The mémoire from M. de la F. discusses reducing the taille slightly and collecting part of the remainder in grain to help supply the army. It says that the king should have some way to predict his revenues and to be able to control his expenditures more efficiently. It theorizes that a new tax equal to one-twentieth of the value of all property would raise 50 million livres in addition to the taille and the capitation. Together with some kind of equalization of the gabelles across France, total ordinary revenues should equal 117 million livres. An investigation into the affairs of everyone doing business with the king should accompany this measure.

A mémoire that begins "La continuation de la guerre" speaks of the unproductive nature of extraordinary affairs during the preceding eighteen months, and the large amount of discredited paper in France. It compares the difficulties involved in establishing a dîme royale, which the city of Paris was demanding, to a tax on land, and concludes that, whatever the decision was, it must be based on three propositions: (1) the king needed 120 million livres more than his ordinary revenues; (2) royal paper must be suppressed; and (3) the new source of revenue must be practicable and certain.

A third mémoire discusses the intricacies involved in an income tax of a twentieth, a fifteenth, or a tenth. It discusses topics such as determining who should pay, exempting no one, defining income, and deciding what to do about the king's older taxes. It also examines the kind of information that would be needed to levy this new kind of tax fairly. The author recommends that the tax equal one-fifteenth or one-tenth because, he says, the rate could always be lowered, but it would be difficult to increase the rate once it was established.

Another mémoire in this carton that is not one of the five marked "Memoire au sujet du dixième des biens et autres" is dated August 21, 1710, and discusses reducing the interest rate on all rentes to denier 24 (4.16 percent) as a means of absorbing all royal paper and avoiding a rebellion, as the rentes had not been paid since 1709. The author of this mémoire reminds the reader that failure to pay the rentes had provoked the Fronde in 1648. He suggests accepting royal paper as a method for maintaining the level of the government's payments while increasing capital investment behind those payments. In other words, if the rentier received 1,000 livres presently at denier 16 or denier 20, he could continue to receive that amount by investing another 9,000 or 5,000 livres, respectively, in royal paper. Thus, the floating royal debt would be transferred to a permanent debt in rentes while eliminating royal paper from the money market.

Reading Saint-Simon's version of these events, one might conclude that the only thing to emerge from this climate of discussion was the new tax, the dixième, which the Royal Council of Finances adopted on September 30, 1710. Yet, the dixième did not appear in law until October 14. The delay resulted from the fact that the government was doing more than just declaring a new source of revenue; it wanted to end usury and bad faith *tout d'un coup*, as one of Desmaretz's commis wrote in August of that year. Dangeau described the dixième as more than just a new tax, but as a measure that would suppress the mint bills and ensure the regular payment of rentes. The government wanted an assured source of revenue and a way to restore credit to the various institutions that the monarchy depended on for money, such as the Caisse des emprunts, the farms, and the receivers general. The government had to remove bad money from circulation in order to restore good money.

An undated memorandum from within the controller general's office from the same time period lists all the laws the government had planned:[85]

Edicts, Declarations and arrêts rendered in the Month of October 1710 for the general arrangement of finances.

On October 7, 1710

Declaration for the reduction to denier 20 of the rentes and augmented gages created since 1689, and suppressing what remains unsold.

Arrêt excluding the dowager Queen of Poland from this reduction on the rentes constituted on the postes.[86]

Edict creating 500,000 livres in augmented gages at denier 20, to be collected from the officers instead of those suppressed by the above declaration.

Edict creating 1 million in rentes at denier 20, to be collected in five-year bills of the farmers and receivers general.

Edict creating 1,250,000 livres in augmented gages in favor of those who have invested in royal business, to be collected in bills of the treasurers of the extraordinary of war.

Arrêt ordering the receivers general and others who manage royal money to carry all the money they receive to the Royal Treasury and forbidding them from honoring any assignations against their receipts.

Declaration suppressing the mint bills and commerce in unreformed coin and fixing the price of such coin at the mints, which will accept one-fifth of any deposit in mint bills or assignations labeled to that effect.

Declaration regulating the doubling of the octrois and allowing towns to pay it all in mint bills, bills of the farmers general, or assignations to the Royal Treasury.

Arrêt ordering that the 6 million in bills of the farmers general be brought to Sr. Malet de Brunieres [This is not Desmaretz's commis Malet.] to be reformed, in order to be received at the mints or the octrois, while deducting the interest owed on them and liquidating those bills, for which he will give new bills to be received at the mints or octrois, and discharging the farmers general from these debts.

On October 14, 1710

Declaration reducing the interest to 5 percent and renewing the promises of the Caisse des emprunts.

Another of December 20 regulating the way in which the promises will be renewed and the interest paid.

Declaration levying the dixième on revenues des biens in the realm.

Another of December 27 regulating the manner in which this collection will be made by withholding the dixième from income from offices, augmented gages, rentes, pensions, gifts, and other similar revenues subject to the dixième.

A dossier of mémoires and preliminary drafts for the above edicts and declarations exists in the same carton. A preliminary list[87] written by Delacroix refers the various documents to several commis, including Malet, and to M. Orry, who wrote to Desmaretz on September 13, 1710, to say that he was working on the matters that the minister had asked Delacroix to tell him.[88] The month of September was thus filled with the finalization of the necessary legal documents required to execute all these measures.

The rush of activity surrounding the new tax might have made its first appearance before the Royal Council of Finances on September 30, as Dangeau and Saint-Simon claim, but the later council meetings and extended conferences between Louis XIV and Desmaretz must have discussed all these measures as well. The introduction of these measures before the Royal Council at the end of September might have caught the chancellor and Daguesseau completely by surprise, or perhaps it astonished them that the matters were introduced in completed form rather than as proposals for discussion, as the capitation had been in 1694. In any case, the preliminary drafts of the law establishing the dixième took the form of an edict, or a permanent law. The council must have discussed at least the disadvantages of an edict versus a declaration, because the law eventually appeared as a declaration, a temporary law.[89]

A preliminary draft of the declaration of the dixième was reworked by Le Rebours, then by Desmaretz himself, and finally by a commis or a scribe in the ministry. These three men all reworked the preamble that received most of the retouching in an effort to reduce the enormity of what the government was doing, and to explain why this sort of measure was necessary. The king, who is the speaker in any royal law, expressed his sincere wishes for peace and said that, despite his good intentions, the enemy had made his peace offers known in the courts of other princes so as to thwart any true peace negotiations. Since continued war was now inevitable and the crown had exhausted its resources, the king had consulted knowledgeable people about what France should do.[90] A royal council had examined their advice and had decided that there was no better method than to levy a tax equal to one-tenth of the income of France's subjects. While the enemy levied even greater taxes on their peoples than the dixième would extract, the king had to guarantee the payment of his paper, as well as assure himself of the necessary funds for war and the regular payment of the rentes, gages, and other charges against his revenue. He also promised to reduce the taille by one-fifth in 1711, to resort to no extraordinary affairs, and to end the dixième within three years of the end of the war.

In a letter to Le Rebours dated October 13, 1710, Desmaretz discussed the necessity of reorganizing the finances in order to be aware of receipts and expenses, but in a short paragraph he wrote: "I believe that there is no time to lose for the declaration of the dixième and for sending mémoires to the intendants to prepare for its establishment." He enclosed a mémoire about the method of collecting impositions in Holland using rebates and wondered if France could adopt a similar practice. If Le Rebours agreed, then the council could add another article to the declaration that established the dixième, or could issue an arrêt later. Desmaretz was skeptical that this kind of rebate could be offered in France, where the spirit of economy was less established and all the people devoted their efforts to escaping from contributing to necessary public expenses.[91]

The dixième declaration was not yet complete on October 13. Apparently the discussions within the ministry or the council had not yet been settled. Le Rebours still had the declaration and was to work on it with Desmaretz later. Desmaretz would have had to take it to the Royal Council for final approval on October 14, because the chancellor applied the seals on October 20. The council did not meet again until October 21.

The story of the adoption of the dixième and the other actions taken in October 1710 is a study in the history of events. Bankers (like Bernard), the General Farms, and the traitants had fallen by the wayside one after another in the course of 1708–9. The state turned to the receivers general and a policy of auctioning whatever would sell to enable the government to survive the campaign of 1710, which saw the fall of the cities of Douai, Saint-Venant, Béthune, and Aire, as well as the landing of Allied troops at Sète in August in a failed attempt to rekindle an uprising in the Cevennes. The failure to obtain peace and the rupture of negotiations in midsummer provoked a search for a way out of the morass of disorder into which the realm's finances had fallen. The policy of reforms in October 1710 was part of the government's determination to resist the enemy by showing its willingness to adopt extreme measures. The government also severed all trade with the Dutch on November 19, 1710, in order to underline its determination to fight.[92] In financial policy, this hardened attitude took the form of the many laws issued in October 1710.

The Laws of September–October 1710

The first law announcing the new policy was a declaration ordering that the interest rate on all rentes and augmented gages created since 1689 was to be reduced to denier 20 (5 percent). This measure included only perpetual rentes against the aides and gabelles, the postes, and the control of notarial acts. Lifetime rentes, rentes on the various *tontines*, or half-lifetime/half-perpetual rentes were excluded from this interest reduction. All unsold rentes and augmented gages were suppressed. The declaration promised that the government would start repaying these funds again in July 1711.[93] This interest rate reduction was unlike that undertaken by Pontchartrain in 1698–99 because, this time, the government created no new rentes at a lower interest rate to buy back the previous contracts. It simply reduced interest by law in order to reduce its own expenses.[94]

A second measure created 500,000 livres in augmented gages at denier 20 to be purchased by those officers whose gages the first measure had reduced.[95] The government wanted to raise 10 million livres by means of a forced loan from officeholders who had been able to raise money in earlier forced loans.

Another edict created 1 million livres in rentes at denier 20 against the aides and gabelles. Rather than raising more money, the government limited purchasers by requiring that these rentes could only be bought with bills that had been issued in 1705 and 1706 by the General Farmers and receivers general of finances with the promise of repayment in five years. The government had failed to remove these bills from circulation in 1708 and again in 1709, but the new edict promised that such bills would be null and void after July 1, 1711. The government instructed holders of these bills to bring them to the Royal Treasury to be cancelled and marked according to their value, along with the interest owed them. They could then take these bills to the Hôtel de Ville in Paris for the purchase of rentes equal to the principal and interest owed on the bills. The farmers general and receivers general were absolved from honoring these bills at any future date.[96]

Another 6 million livres' worth of these bills, along with the remainder of the mint bills and assignations in circulation, could be used to fulfill two other measures. In September 1710 the crown had doubled the price of the octrois, those perceptions levied by towns where such taxes did not exist as a substitute for either the capitation or the taille, or both. Towns that did not have octrois would be forced to levy them on goods that entered their borders. The newly added or doubled octrois were to be collected for the crown's profit.[97] A declaration of October 7, 1710, however, provided the towns with a way to avoid the new taxes if they would offer a *don gratuit* (free gift) that would only be accepted in mint bills, bills of the farmers general, or assignations against any future source of revenue for the crown. The towns were permitted to borrow money to pay this don gratuit by selling rentes with interest rates no higher than denier 20. The mayors and public officials were responsible for repaying these loans and reporting these matters to the local provincial intendant.[98] Several towns, provinces, and generalities made these kinds of arrangements with the crown.[99]

Another declaration allowed people to use mint bills or assignations as one-fifth of the total amount of money they were bringing to the mints for reminting. Apparently the reminting ordered in 1709 had not succeeded in completely reforming the money in circulation. This declaration established a value for unreformed money and ordered that mints to accept paper equal to one-fourth the amount of unreformed money, and to repay the total with new coins. The declaration did go on to say that, after February 1, 1711, neither the mint bills nor the unreformed coin would be valid for commerce.[100] To facilitate this policy, the mints were to accept mint bills and reduce their denominations to whatever amount the holders desired so that they would have the equivalent of one-fourth the sum of old coins they were depositing.[101]

A last measure designed to withdraw paper from circulation created 1.25 million livres in augmented gages at denier 20 to be purchased by the gens d'affaires, a catch-all term used to describe the farmers, subfarmers, traitants, subtraitants, suppliers, and others who did business with the crown, along with these people's employees, commis, and *caissiers* (treasurers). The augmented gages were to be purchased with funds consisting of one-fourth money and three-fourths bills—that is, mint bills, bills from the farmers general or receivers general, assignations, and, significantly, bills of the treasurers of the extraordinary of war. Those who did business with the war department would be the most likely to have this last kind of paper. This forced loan offered purchasers a permanent income in the form of inheritable gages, while it threatened to sever business relations with those who refused to buy the gages. Their names and the amounts they would be asked to pay were to be recorded on rolls drawn up in council. They were given the option of paying off the entire amount in bills against the treasurers of the extraordinary of war.[102]

All of the measures discussed thus far were designed to clean up the money market by removing discredited royal paper ("bad" money) from circulation in order to restore the circulation of "good" money that would revive the profitability of the tax farms and facilitate the collection of impositions. By invalidating the discredited paper money for any purpose other than those described above, and nullifying them after a certain date in the future, the government hoped that the removal of mint bills, bills against the various comptables and tax farmers, and assignations from previous or future years would restore business confidence and liberate revenues for the next three years to help attract new loans. All of these bills were issued in such large denominations that they only came into the hands of wealthy individuals, not everyday workers and peasants.

An arrêt of the Royal Council of Finances dated October 7, 1710, commanded all comptables and farmers to pay their funds directly to the Royal Treasury, as required by their leases or résultats, except in the case of those farmers who had to set aside money for the payment of rentes.[103] The tax collectors were no longer allowed to honor any assignations that the Royal Treasury would henceforth pay out; nor were they to issue assignations ever again. Instead, all bearers of assignations were to bring them to the Royal Treasury for renewal in whatever denominations they desired, so that these assignations could be taken to the mints or the Hôtel de Ville, or used as dons gratuits from the towns to exempt them from the doubled octrois. Interest on these assignations was to be 5 percent, payable from the date of issue until the time of conversion. Provincial intendants each received a letter with a copy of the arrêt ordering them not to command the disposition of any funds in the future.[104] Henceforth, the Royal Treasury would assign funds for the payment of expenses, on the orders of the controller general.

Through these measures, Desmaretz was centralizing the handling of royal funds and royal credit. In 1708 he had ordered funds to be paid to the Royal Treasury. Now he was withdrawing the power from anyone except the controller general to assign funds for the payment of expenses. His principal assistant in this matter was Le Rebours, whom the letter of October 13, 1710, charged with keeping monthly accounts of money received and money paid, so that Desmaretz could establish priorities in the payment of the government's bills. The two men had been exchanging ideas about how to centralize royal funds over the past several years. For Desmaretz, centralization was fundamental to any hope of reestablishing order in finances: "We will only escape this condition [of uncertainty] by re-establishing order. I am awaiting the discovery of great opposition: so many people profit from the derangement and have an interest in maintaining it, that one must be prepared to find continual obstacles. Meanwhile, I will not be discouraged at all, and if you agree, I expect that we will overcome them."[105]

The minister's grim determination to eliminate disorder in financial affairs refers to the efforts to centralize the distribution of funds and credit, and to seek out those who had profited from the existing disorder. The establishment of 1.25 million livres in augmented gages for the gens d'affaires was a pretext for investigating these peoples' affairs under the threat of legal constraints. Cazier had requested this kind of policy and de la Garde had agreed in June 1710. The government was ordering a crackdown by forcing traitants to make monthly accounts of their affairs to the intendants of finances. The rolls drawn up in council for purchasing augmented gages were based on lists of persons from the gens d'affaires who claimed they were unable to honor their agreements with the government or to repay their promissory notes. The government now demanded proof.

An extraordinary commission of the council was created on November 5, 1710, to hear all cases involving the dixième and the gens d'affaires. Bouville served as chair; other members included Bignon de Blanzy, des Forts, Desmaretz, Le Rebours, and Bercy.[106] Handpicked by Desmaretz, they divided their responsibilities as follows:[107]

M. de Bouville	financiers resident in Paris
M. Bignon de Blanzy	city of Paris houses communities under the jurisdiction of the provost of merchants dixième of merchants in the same jurisdiction

M. Desforts	pays d'estats and Flanders Metz country and the bishoprics with Alsace and Franche-Comté communities depending on the jurisdiction of the lieutenant general of police bankers and others who possess no wealth and *faire valoir* their money (i.e., make their money earn)
M. de Bercy	the nineteen generalities of the pays d'élections

This committee heard cases concerning the dixième, but Bouville and des Forts were in charge of the businessmen and potential speculators whom the government wanted to control. Des Forts, who sent Desmaretz the first list of "speculators, treasurers, and *gripe sous* [money holders]" on November 8, 1710,[108] was in charge of smalltime moneylenders who had discovered that they could make their fortunes by speculating in royal paper. Des Forts' connections, through the committee, with Argenson led the lieutenant general of police to conduct a series of searches, "raids" that resulted in the arrest or flight of many speculators.[109]

Bouville dealt with the major financiers. Another edict soon modified the one of October 1710 that had created 1.25 million livres in augmented gages. This new edict, issued in January 1711, created 600,000 livres in rentes, available to any gens d'affaires who wished to be exempt from the dixième.[110] By enforcing this measure, the government hoped to collect 12 million livres. A few letters from Bouville to Desmaretz or Clautrier indicate that he was negotiating with people like Bourvalais, Crozat, and others. Some sources say that the original list of November 1710 ordered Crozat to pay 600,000 livres.[111] One list of people taxed under this law is extant, but it bears no date and only totals 1,785,200 livres. It contains names of people like Bourvalais, whom the government called upon to pay 120,000 livres. The same carton contains an account in Bouville's handwriting, dated May 12, 1712, that shows that the government had received 6,573,256 livres out of an expected 11,111,200. Unfortunately, the account does not list names, only general categories, such as the subfarmers of the aides or the postes, although it does contain a generic category labeled "from individuals."[112]

The government had begun its efforts to tax wealth in the spring of 1710, when it created special rentes on the receivers general of finances for purchase by wealthy commoners who had not contributed their fair share to the war effort, either because they lived in towns that were exempt from the taille or the capitation, or because they had not bought any offices. These crackdowns or shakedowns did not endear the finance minister to the bourgeoisie. In fact, the only people who escaped this measure were the bourgeoisie of Paris, people whose children served in the army, or royal officeholders. This tax was referred to as the *taxes des aisez*, or the tax on the well off.[113]

These measures revealed the government's grim determination to milk every penny from the French economy. Idealistic reformers like Cazier, Boisguilbert, Vauban, and the abbé de Saint-Pierre had been willing to levy a tax based upon people's individual abilities to pay, but only if the government suppressed some of the existing taxes. The dixième added a new tax on top of those that already existed. The government, however, did grant some relief to taillables in the form of a reduction of the taille by more than 5.5 million livres for 1711 and a reduction in the price of salt by 3 livres per minot. In effect, Desmaretz was trying to make up for his failure to remove the other taxes by offering tax relief for those subject to those taxes.[114]

The declaration of October 14, 1710, that levied the dixième contains twelve articles.[115] The first five articles describe what was to be taxed: income from land, mills, and woods; rents on all houses; all charges, commissions, pensions, and offices that the royal government paid; all rentes on the Hôtel de Ville, the clergy, postes, tax farms, towns, provinces and provincial estates, augmented gages, and all payments of debts between individuals, including private rentes and the rights and privileges of government officials exercising their offices.

The dixième taxed property because the government was unable to tax the wages of workers or agricultural laborers. In other words, the dixième targeted income produced by property, including seigneurial dues, feudal dues, and any tithe (*dîme*) not paid to the church, along with wealth produced by the sale of agricultural products or manufactured goods. Thus, it was not an income tax per se. Even so, the dixième was a radical departure from traditional Old Regime tax policies because, by taxing all property equally, it did not recognize the difference between noble and common property. By not targeting the working class, the dixième aimed at wealth and wealth-producing property. The government of early modern France was unable to keep track of every royal subject (and every foreign resident) who earned income, but the creation of the control of notarial acts and its follow-up, the tax called the *centième denier*, enabled the government to track property ownership.

The rest of the declaration concerning the dixième described the acknowledgment of payments by the crown or its agents, the fabrication of rolls of the dixième (to be paid quarterly), and several other procedures. Among those discussed were the issues of withholding and payment (to the crown) of one-tenth of all rentes paid by individuals, as well as the requirement that all people file a declaration of their income, under penalty of fines for filing late or making false declarations. The declaration also stipulated that payments were to be made to the taille receivers in the pays d'élections, and to the receivers of the common deniers in the pays d'états. These officials were to follow the same procedures they had followed for payment of the capitation.

The dixième had very little to do with Vauban's dîme royale, although it was commonly called by that name at the time. There was no taxation in kind, and the dixième was not turned over to tax farmers, as Vauban had recommended. Nor did it suppress any of France's taxes on commerce, as Boisguilbert had advocated. It did not suppress the extraordinary affairs, as many people, including de la Garde, had suggested. In addition, it was not a tax reform in the sense that it replaced any of the existing taxes. The government had mortgaged most of the existing taxes to fund its war efforts prior to 1710. The men in government, along with the king, did not believe they could abolish these taxes without reimbursing the loans. The dixième grew out of the demands for more money that France's interminable wars caused at the end of Louis XIV's reign. In practice, it fulfilled the requirements laid down by Desmaretz: an assured revenue source that did not disturb the other revenues of the king. By setting these requirements, Desmaretz removed the possibility that any of the reformers would be satisfied.

Any attempt to ascribe the invention of this tax to Vauban, Boisguilbert, or Sully, as Dangeau and Saint-Simon did, is simply wrong. Many people were aware of Vauban's ideas for a dîme royale and equated the dixième to those ideas. The idea of a tax on wealth and the income it produced, however, preceded any of these men, and the payment of a tenth of one's income as a tithe (*dîme*) is mentioned in the Bible. The reformers wanted to replace the existing system, which they saw as unjust and inequitable. As long as the war continued, Desmaretz, if he wished to attract more loans, could not touch the existing system because so many debts were owed to it. He wanted to establish yet another source of revenue that would be easy to collect. While it is true that the finance ministry knew of the ideas of the various reformers, it cannot be said that the reformers were aware of the facts facing the ministry. The dixième was part of a policy designed to restore credit to the government; it was not a major overhaul of the system, as many reformers demanded.

The dixième was the capstone of a series of laws that were supposed to restore faith in the government on the eve of what was expected to be a showdown battle with France's enemies. Just because that showdown did not occur is no excuse for misunderstanding what the government saw as its goals. The fall of the Whigs in England in August 1710 led to an eventual change in England's war policies. The death of Emperor Joseph I of Austria in April 1711 left the Habsburgs with one claimant to the thrones in both Spain and Germany. The War of the Spanish Succession had begun as an effort to prevent France, the preeminent power in Europe, from having one of Louis XIV's family members on the throne of Spain, with all its possessions in Europe and abroad. Now, the war became a struggle between having a French candidate on the Spanish throne, or restoring the empire of Charles V, who had ruled both Spain and Austria in the sixteenth century. The English and the Dutch were less enthusiastic about both Spain and Austria under a single ruler.

The government of Louis XIV wanted to cut its expenses by mandating a cut in the interest rate due on a variety of loans, including perpetual rentes, augmented gages, and promises on the Caisse des emprunts. The government promised that the new interest rate would be paid regularly, beginning on July 1, 1711. In order to keep this promise, it had to clear the money markets of floating debt by providing some method for absorbing the various kinds of discredited paper that its agents had been issuing since 1701. Thus it created a variety of new long-term debts in the form of rentes and augmented gages to absorb this paper, in the hopes that the circulation of real money and the reanimation of commerce would result. The consequent revival of ordinary revenues would permit the payment of debts, both old and new. To enhance the new situation, the government concentrated the power to issue paper into the hands of the controller general of finances, while it also liberated its ordinary sources of revenue from any encumbrance for the next three years.

The dixième was the last measure that was supposed to provide the funds necessary to support the war effort. First, it created a new source of revenue by taxing income derived from property. Second, it cut the income of anyone who received money from the royal government by withholding 10 percent of that income. Government expenses thus received a second cut: the French government had already managed to reduce the interest on its debts to 5 percent, when the dixième further reduced that interest by another tenth, from 5 to 4.5 percent.

Desmaretz borrowed 18 million livres from the receivers general of finances immediately after the adoption of the new policy. He used this money to reinforce the army and prepare for the campaign of 1711. The government of Louis XIV had set its collective jaw for a battle that never came. After the death of Emperor Joseph I in April 1711, France began negotiations with the new British government. The new financial policies enabled France to withstand its minor losses of 1711 and rebound from them in 1712. These policies and the measures used to reinforce them were conducted in an atmosphere with considerably less tension. The period of crisis had passed, enabling France and its enemies to reach a peaceful conclusion to the War of the Spanish Succession.

Chapter 6

After the Dixième

The Dixième

The establishment of a new tax involved more than publishing a declaration. Now the French government either had to create a new bureaucracy to collect these funds, or had to give orders to the existing officials on how to handle the new revenues. In accord with previous practices, the clergy, the nobility, the various corporations of officers, and the pays d'états and their officers had to be pressured in some way to comply with the new tax. The problem of taxing the income earned by foreigners in France involved diplomatic issues as well. The pressures of war and the demand for money for the upcoming campaign season forced the government to make hasty decisions. Nonetheless, the government desperately wanted to avoid provoking rebellion by seeming to make arbitrary rulings on any of these matters.

The provincial intendants were pressed into service on all these decisions. Thus, the royal government took responsibility for the dixième at the very beginning rather than referring it to the Bureaus of Finances, the Treasurers of France, or the élus. Desmaretz asked that the provincial intendants draw up rolls listing the amount each taxpayer owed as soon as the declarations of income arrived rather than waiting for everyone to file declarations. The intendant was to send the government an estimate of the expected revenue from the dixième from his generality or province. He was also to send weekly accounts of receipts of the dixième along with reports on his activities to hasten the collection of this revenue.[1] Unlike previous impositions, such as the taille or the capitation, which were apportioned to each province, election, and parish, the dixième was levied on property owners and those individuals who received income in the form of rentes, gages, etc. The government had no idea how much revenue the new tax would produce. The intendants were to expedite matters locally in order to give the government an indication of the total amount of money it could expect. There was no precedent on which to base any estimate of revenue.

The government wanted to collect the payment for the last quarter of 1710 immediately. To expedite matters, officials did not have to record income declarations and tax rolls, or any other documents involved in determining and collecting the dixième, on stamped paper, or pay any duties for certification.[2] The police in various towns began circulating *avertissements* (announcements of the new tax) and posting them in public places.[3] In generalities where the intendants had recently changed, such as Limoges, where there was great disorder, the whole matter of tax collection was considerably delayed. Newly arrived intendant Charles Boucher d'Orsay wrote that officials had not collected taxes there for three years, that he had to redo part of the rolls of the capitation that interfered with the sale of franchises from it, and that he and his assistants were working from five in the morning until nightfall to prepare the capitation, the doubled octrois, and the dixième.[4] In La Rochelle, one Sieur Belluchau was working on the dixième rolls for the election of La Rochelle and Marennes, which had filed ten thousand income declarations, producing over 130 rolls. There were still twenty thousand income declarations at the office of the subdelegate's clerk.[5]

The money collected for the dixième was not to be mixed with funds collected from other taxes, but it was to follow the same channels as the revenue from the capitation, meaning that payments of taxes collected were to be made to the taille receivers in the pays d'élections and the receivers or treasurers of the estates in the pays d'états.[6] The officials in charge of paying the gages and appointments for the companies of officers were instructed to withhold one-tenth for the dixième.[7] The Royal Treasury would receive this money. Once the intendants had prepared and certified the rolls, they could begin collecting the tax.[8]

The earliest form of resistance to this measure took the form of delays in filing declarations of income. The declaration of the dixième of October 14, 1710, called for penalizing any persons who filed late declarations of income by requiring them to pay twice the amount they owed, quadruple for making a false declaration.[9] Originally, declarations were due within two weeks of the proclamation of the dixième, but this deadline was unrealistic because it took two weeks for some parts of France to learn of the new law. Instead of waiting for declarations of income to be filed, the government began threatening arbitrary measures, such as taxing homeowners in Paris on the basis of how much they paid to suppress the fees for street cleaning and lighting.[10] The government also put constraints on taxpayers by refusing to hear any cases involving the dixième unless the parties involved could prove that they had filed their income declarations or, after the dixième began to be collected, that they had paid at least one-third of the required amount on the dixième rolls.[11] Finally, on June 16, 1711, the government gave people two weeks from the date of notification in their parishes to file their income declarations, or risk being fined at twice the amount due from their estimated revenues based on an estimate of their property's income, or 5 percent of its value. Anyone who farmed someone else's property and kept one-third or more of its revenue had to declare the property's income or face a fine of 50 livres. Mayors and town officials were to provide the local intendant or subdelegate with an account of the houses and their owners within the town and its dependencies. Renters of these houses were to declare the amount of their rent payments and to whom they paid them. The same order was extended to parish syndics and two of the principal residents in rural areas for houses in the parish.[12]

There was no standardized text for a declaration, however. Each intendant had his own standards. The text for one declaration of the dixième can be found in the memoirs of Joseph François Ignace de Labat de Savignac, a counsellor in the Parlement of Bordeaux, concerning property owned by his mother. Anyone reading these memoirs, however, cannot but be aware that the declaration does not claim the true value of the property or the value of its product. This, alas, was a major problem in collecting and assessing the dixième. The government was too pressed for funds to insist on enforcing the dixième according to the letter of the law. In most cases, the government appeared to accept what a property owner declared, knowing that the declaration was untruthful.[13]

Once a provincial intendant had signed the dixième rolls, he was to send them to the taille receivers in the elections, who would immediately transmit copies to the mayors or syndics of the town or parish concerned. These local officials were to post the rolls on the door of the parish church after High Mass on the following Sunday. They were to send certificates verifying the date on which they received the rolls and the date they were posted to the taille receiver. Taxpayers had to make payments within two weeks of the date posted, and parish or town officials had to bring their receipts to the taille receiver within a week of that date. Along with this money, they had to report all unpaid sums and the names of those who did not pay or they would be responsible for the money themselves.[14]

Receipts from the dixième followed different channels from the other impositions. The amateur collector who handled funds from the taille and capitation was excluded from handling these funds. Instead, the responsibility for collection went to local venal officers. Unlike the collectors, who were required to pay their receipts by a fixed deadline, the mayors and syndics could account for what they did not receive and who did not pay. Tax delinquents would then be fined double the amount they owed according to the original dixième roll. The taille and the capitation were civil debts between the taxpayer and the parish. The dixième was a debt between the taxpayer and the state. The government could subject the taxpayer to a fine for failing to pay his tax or for falsely declaring his income.

Article VIII of the declaration of October 14, 1710, marked the gens d'affaires, people whose only property consisted of the capital they used for investment or speculation, for special surveillance. The general belief, as the government expressed through this measure, was that this group had escaped paying their fair share of the burden of taxation caused by the war. The provincial intendant had to draw up a special roll on which he was to list each of these speculators, with an estimate of their income and the reasons that led him to make these estimates. He was then to send this roll to the controller general of finances, who would inform the intendant of the king's intentions. Once the intendant was in possession of this information, he was to compose separate dixième rolls for the people the controller general had specified for each election, and send them to the proper taille receivers. All requests for moderation or discharge from the dixième from the gens d'affaires had to be transmitted to the controller general along with the intendant's advice for consideration by the council, meaning Bouville's committee.[15] Here again, the taxpayer owed a debt to the state rather than the parish, election, or generality. The central government made moderations and discharges as the court of last resort.

Two new officials appeared to supervise the activities of the older offices that handled the declarations of income, the compilation of the dixième rolls, and the revenue from the tax: the controller and director of the dixième. Each election had a controller of the dixième, to be nominated by the provincial intendant and approved by the controller general of finances. This official kept duplicates of every declaration of income and dixième roll. He reported any property that was omitted from either document to the controller general, who would see that he was rewarded for his diligence. The controller of the dixième kept a register of the dates on which the mayors and syndics received the dixième rolls and when these rolls were posted, the amount of the revenue on each roll, and the receipts (*quittances*) that he had issued for money received from taxpayers listed on these rolls. A separate register recorded the constraints employed by the taille receiver to force payment of taxes, as well as the expenses that these measures entailed. Every month the dixième controller sent the controller general an account from this second register. A third register recorded the amounts and names of all persons fined double for failure to pay their quarterly dixième on time, along with receipts of these fines and the quittances issued. As soon as possible, dixième controllers were to transmit a detailed account of the revenue to be expected from each town, bourg, and parish in their elections. In their monthly accounts to the controller general, they were to list in separate articles how much money had been received from the dixième rolls, from the fines, and from the financiers, speculators, and officers.[16]

Each provincial intendant also had an assistant called the director of the dixième who hastened the composition of the dixième rolls and their expedition to the proper taille receivers and local officials. He, like the controller, kept an eye out for undeclared wealth. Like the intendant, the director of the dixième toured individual generalities or provinces to check the registers of the taille receivers with those of the controller of the dixième and the receiver general. He reported monthly to the controller general on his activities and sent quarterly accounts of the expenses undertaken by all officials in the collection of the dixième. He also communicated any sign of corruption or negligence immediately to the controller general, although he acted under the direct orders of the provincial intendant, to whom he accounted for all of his activities.[17]

The government devised the machinery for handling the dixième from the mayors and parish officials up to Bouville's extraordinary commission on the King's Council. Working between this commission and Desmaretz was a commis named Antoine Barrangue.[18] He prepared instructions for the controllers and directors of the dixième and handled Desmaretz's correspondence from the provinces until Bouville's commission was established. Even then, Barrangue asked Desmaretz if he could continue to function as a liaison between the controller general and the commission, for the purpose of organizing the material for the finance minister.[19]

Bouville's commission had to address the problem of defining the kinds of income that would be subject to the dixième and how it was to be determined. The most difficult decisions involved revenue farming. Most noble and ecclesiastical lords employed estate managers or stewards to manage their estates through a lease. By the early eighteenth century, revenue farming was prevalent among bourgeois landowners and wealthy peasants. The government asked all such estate managers or farmers to file declarations of their income, of the lease payments they made, and to whom they made them. The farmers were to withhold the dixième from their payments and give the money to the taille receivers in the election where the property was located. Farms that extended across several parishes were to file declarations in the parish where the manor house was situated. Every proprietor was required to file one declaration in each parish where he had property.[20]

Loans between private individuals, also called rentes, were also subject to the dixième. Usually some property was put forward to pay the loan and any interest on it. The holder of the property was instructed to file a declaration listing to whom and how much he paid in rentes. The property owner was also to withhold one-tenth of the rentes and make payments to the official charged with receiving the dixième in his area.[21]

The administrative problem of who was to receive the money from each locality highlighted the difficulties inherent in privilege. Many kinds of income were privileged or went to privileged people. The government closed these avenues of escape by ordering the retention of the dixième from payments made by the officers of various corporate bodies for privileged institutions to the privileged people, for example the officers of the marc d'or, the Order of the Holy Spirit, commissaires in charge of seized property, and eventually to payments from all property of fugitive Huguenots, to list a few examples. In other words, the government was reducing its expenses by 10 percent by withholding that sum from payments made to privileged members of privileged organizations.[22]

Special collectors of the dixième were appointed for towns and provinces that were exempt from the taille and paid only extraordinary military subsidies. The tax receiver for Paris, Boucot, headed the administration for collecting the dixième in Paris under the instruction of the provost of merchants.[23] Residents of the town of Versailles presented their declarations to Sr. Fresson, bailiff of the city, and their payments to Sr. L'Evêque. Both men worked under the orders of Louis Blouin, one of Louis XIV's *valets de chambre* who was also the intendant of the palace and park of Versailles.[24] An inspector of the farms at Calais named Pierre de Chasteauneuf was named to collect the dixième in West Flanders, the Boullonais, and the land and towns of St. Omer, Montreuil, Calais, and Ardres. He could commission local receivers and worked under the intendants in both Amiens and West Flanders.[25]

Officers who were exempt from the taille and thus did not pay the local taille receiver posed another administrative headache. One of the secretaries on the Royal Council of Finances, Jean Goujon, was commissioned to collect the dixième from the officers who policed commerce in meat, wine, oils, and things of a similar nature. He was later charged with receiving the dixième from the officers of the superior courts in Paris, except for the Hôtel de Ville and the money from rentes and gages.[26] One Sieur Malet de Ternantes was commissioned to do the same for all employees of the General Farms and their subfarms, the farms and subfarms of the postes, all persons employed in supplying the army (vivres and étapes), the extraordinary and ordinary of war, and all the companies of traitants.[27]

Efforts to tax royal officials led to requests for exemption because the employees of the tax-collecting bodies were necessary for the continued supply of money to the state. The foreign minister Torcy, who had taken over responsibility for the post office when Le Peletier retired from the court, wrote to his cousin on March 21, 1711, asking that the masters of the postes be exempt from the dixième because of their heavy duties and constant travel. Desmaretz responded simply, "No, no one should be exempt from the dixième." This apparent hardline conceals the fact that the appointments of the commis of the aides had already been exempted. Torcy repeated his request, with the proviso that only commis of the postes, who earned less than 600 livres annually, receive exempt status. A mémoire from these officials states that the commis of other farms had already been exempted. The commis of the postes requested a ceiling of 700 livres per year. Desmaretz granted an exemption to those commis of the postes who made 500 livres or less annually. The higher-paid officials of all the farms remained subject to the dixième.[28]

This exemption was not the first, nor the most serious, from the standpoint of revenue. Foreign subjects who resided in France or made money in France presented the first major difficulty to the government. Foreign lenders were needed to keep the flow of credit open to France. On November 18, 1710, the government promised foreigners who purchased new rentes from the estates of Burgundy in order to exempt Burgundy from the capitation that their income from these rentes would not be taxed to pay the dixième.[29] It later extended this exemption to the citizens and lenders of Strasbourg in return for grain worth 410,973 livres, 10 sous, and to those of Alsace in return for 1,500,090 livres' worth of grain. Strasbourg and Alsace has already provided a large part of this grain for the 1710 campaign, but now, as effectively foreign provinces, they received a complete exemption from the dixième.[30] Foreign troops serving in the French army were also exempt from the dixième, as required by the treaties that recruited them. Other foreigners were not allowed to escape, however, except for the people of Savoy, which had its capitation increased by 200,000 livres annually instead of paying the dixième. Commis of the Savoy farms still had to pay the dixième.[31]

The French government granted the greatest exemption to the dixième to the clergy in return for a one-time payment of 8 million livres. In the summer of 1710 the clergy had given the crown 24 million livres in place of the capitation in order to cease the payment of 4 million livres they made annually as a subsidy. The clergy had borrowed more than 23 million livres to make the full payment of 24 million. An extraordinary assembly of the clergy met in June 1711 and voted to grant the king an additional 8 million livres in return for an exemption from the dixième. They had to borrow this money, and the rentes from this loan were also exempt from the dixième. The crown accepted the offer and exempted the income from all ecclesiastical property, benefices, pensions, rentes, gages, and other income that went to the clergy, secular or regular communities of either sex, foundations, confreries, or hospitals. The crown did not exempt the income from church property that was paid to laymen who were still subject to the dixième, except for the rentes that were paying the interest on the 8 million livres mentioned above. Goujon was commissioned to collect declarations of income from all the clergy so that the crown would be able to determine which income was exempt.[32]

The exemption of France's clergy did not include clergy defined as "foreign," meaning that their archdiocese was not recognized as French. The three bishoprics of Metz, Toul, and Verdun, whose archbishop was in the Holy Roman Empire, had to offer separate dons gratuits to gain exemption from the dixième. Verdun offered 23,000 livres, Toul offered 9,000, and

Metz offered 46,000. The rural clergy under French control in Longwy, Montmédy, Marville, Damvilliers, and the duchy of Carignan paid 2,800 livres for the same exemption. The Order of the Knights of Malta offered 60,000 livres to be exempted.[33]

The Sorbonne tried to claim an exemption from the dixième because of its relationship to the Church but the government denied it on the grounds that the Sorbonne did not contribute to the clergy's don gratuit. Desmaretz decided that all the income-producing property of the university was subject to the dixième except the residences of the faculty and the rooms used for lessons. The Sorbonne was well endowed, and a significant amount of property remained to be taxed. Just like a modern university, however, the Sorbonne was also well endowed with clever logicians and lawyers who constantly submitted new reasons why they should not pay. The commission of the dixième and the minister always rejected these reasons. Nonetheless, as of May 15, 1715, the Sorbonne had not paid anything toward the dixième.[34]

A policy of granting annual subscriptions (*abonnements*) to a host of provinces and towns in the pays conquis and the pays d'états further weakened the state's control over its subjects. This policy maintained a separation between those subjects under direct royal control and those who lived in a jurisdiction with some legal rights to bargain with the crown. It granted subscriptions to Maritime Flanders, Hainaut, Lille, Douai, Orchies, Ardres in Picardy, Cambrai and the Cambrésis, Bouchain, Calais, Saint Amand and its dependencies, Artois, Boulogne, Orange, Franche Comté (for 370,000 livres), Provence (for 500,000 livres), Marseille, Aigues Mortes, the county of Foix, Burgundy, Roussillon, Languedoc (for 780,000 livres), Bresse and Bugey, Gex, Lectoure, the Nebouzan, the pays de Marsan, Béarn, Bayonne, lower Navarre, Labour, Bigorre, Soule and the Four Valleys nearby, and the common marches of Brittany and Poitou.[35]

In granting exemptions and abonnements, the state surrendered any control that it might have claimed by establishing the dixième in these areas. Local officials could determine how this money was to be raised, but the royal government usually required that it be apportioned on the basis of the capitation, where possible. The royal government would still withhold one-tenth of its payments of all rentes, gages, pensions, and appointments paid out of royal monies to individuals in areas that had subscribed to avoid paying the dixième. The government was just excluding from the dixième any money derived from private sources, in return for the abonnements. Only the clergy, Alsace, and Strasbourg were completely exempt from the dixième.

The royal government was reduced to levying the dixième on the pays d'élections and a few other provinces, such as Brittany.[36] Its efforts to enforce the tax in these areas ran into problems from its own agents, the provincial intendants, who wished to base the new tax on the taille or the capitation in order to simplify its collection. Desmaretz rejected these proposals because he wanted the new imposition to pay for the war effort and not to be confused with other revenues that were needed to pay the royal government's debts.[37]

The crown naively hoped that local notables, particularly officeholders, would set an example for their neighbors by promptly obeying royal orders on the new tax. Instead, these local officials used their special ties to the government to transmit their complaints about the new tax, especially considering that they had not been paid their gages since 1709. To add to the confusion, the keepers of the Royal Treasury withheld the dixième from all payments for debts due before the creation of the dixième.[38] Difficulties enforcing the dixième usually resulted in the crown's extension of delays and moderations, because it desperately needed any money it could get. Sometimes, as in Brittany, pursuits against recalcitrant taxpayers, usually gentlemen, were suspended prior to and during the meeting of the provincial estates in order to avoid any problems with securing the province's don gratuit. Thereafter, pursuits resumed, and indeed were increased, by making public examples of the worst offenders in order to encourage less important people to pay what they owed. Some zealous royal agents, like François-Antoine Ferrand, intendant in Brittany, or Jérôme Bignon, provost of merchants of Paris, were willing to use force to obtain obedience, and possibly to put their zealotry on display for the crown.[39]

The imposition of the dixième did not avoid violent local protests. The number of rebellions caused by the dixième is difficult to establish because most of the revolts after 1710 were caused by a host of complaints involving all royal taxes, not just the dixième. Reports of local disturbances linked to the new tax came from Béarn, Périgord, La Rochelle, Picardy, Normandy, Limousin, Touraine, and the Montauban generality. Usually the local nobility provided the leadership for such protests, but the crown could also count on loyal local notables to assist in suppressing uprisings by calming the populace and setting a good example. To reinforce the impression the government wanted, the leaders of protests could be punished.[40] In any case, the severity of these revolts pales in comparison to the Fronde or even the Camisard revolt in the Cevennes during 1703–5. The government adopted a policy of moderation in enforcing the dixième, a policy that might share some responsibility for the success of its peaceful imposition.

Despite early expectations that the dixième would raise 60 million livres, the government's leniency in enforcing it, along with a willingness to grant exemptions and abonnements and accept whatever sum was easiest to collect resulted in a revenue increase of less than 29 million livres in the year 1711 (including the last quarter of 1710). Thereafter, the dixième produced a steady 22.5 million livres or so—less than the capitation had produced prior to the sale of exemptions in 1709.[41]

It is absurd to believe that 22.5 million livres represented one-tenth of the wealth produced in France, because the government was raising and spending more than ten times that amount to fund the war effort. The government was apparently unwilling to pursue the collection of the dixième with the rigor and ruthlessness of modern-day governments. In effect, Desmaretz and his colleagues were willing to translate the dixième into a de facto royal tribute, as some reformers had recommended, rather than to enforce the government's rights as stated in the law, in order to avoid provoking a major rebellion anywhere in France.

The history of the dixième as it existed during 1710–17 remains to be written. The lack of public records hinders this effort. Thus far, only one dixième roll has been uncovered, and it is not known whether others have survived.[42] Clearly, this new tax aroused opposition. The Duke of Saint-Simon, writing more than thirty years later, decried the intrusion into private family finances, particularly of those families who were supporting their reputations by borrowing money. The revelation of these kinds of secrets, by revealing the true foundations of a family's apparent wealth, could ruin families who had hitherto enjoyed places of honor. For Saint-Simon, who called Desmaretz a cyclops and his office at the contrôle général des finances a *bureau d'anthropophages* (a bureau of cannibals), this new tax was an affront to human decency and an abomination in the sight of God.[43] Yet, Saint-Simon wrote his memoirs after the re-creation of the dixième in the 1730s and 1740s. His rage indicates only what might have been the reaction of the propertied classes in a later period. This tax did not target the workers and propertyless for the first time. Thus, there is no historical record of what they thought about the new tax.

The government did not collect the dixième itself as the law demanded. Desmaretz himself believed the dixième was a temporary measure brought on by the war, and was therefore flexible about dixième declarations, moderations of the tax collected, and appeals for leniency. In a mémoire written for the king in February 1715, however, he stated that he believed that a great number of the declarations of the dixième made by individuals were false, and that it would be difficult to examine all the landholdings to determine the amount of income actually produced. He said that the calculations could be made, but that doing so would require rigor (*rigueur*). In other words, he was warning the king that a continuation of the dixième would require the government to be less lenient in seeking to collect the tax. John Law agreed that the government received less than half the dixième declarations called for by law, and stated that those it did receive undervalued the wealth produced by less than half of its true worth. He also criticized the king's ministers for being too reluctant to press matters. In any case, each intendant enforced the law as he saw fit. Lamoignon de Courson in Guyenne stated openly that he would only tax wealth at a rate of one-seventeenth or one-eighteenth of its value, rather than the tenth required by the law. His father, Lamoignon de Basville in Languedoc, while trying to compensate for his known opposition to new tax measures, pressed the property owners of his province for declarations of their property before he would consider any moderations or appeals.[44]

The hardship caused by all the measures of October 1710 cannot be underestimated. For example, Chancellor Pontchartrain as a local lord (*seigneur*) made efforts to alleviate poverty and suffering in the areas over which he had influence.[45] Among the wide variety of activities he and his wife undertook to assist the poor, one was the purchase of 16,000 livres in perpetual rentes in 1714 at denier 16 (6.25 percent) to produce an income of 1,000 livres to maintain twelve aged poor in Bordes. These rentes were lowered to denier 25 (4 percent) in 1716, thus reducing the income to 640 livres. This example can be used to illuminate the kinds of trouble endowed institutions faced when the French government forcibly reduced the interest rates on loans made before October 1710 to 5 percent. The government tried to soften this blow by exempting from the dixième all clerical revenues that would have effectively reduced all interest rates to 4.5 percent. Nonetheless, rentes were again reduced in December 1713 to denier 25 (4 percent).[46] Income invested at denier 16 that had produced 1,000 livres before 1710 would produce only 800 livres in 1711 (720 livres if the dixième was withheld), and only 640 livres after 1713 (576 livres with the dixième withheld). Unless the poor could find generous philanthropists, like the Pontchartrains, who were willing to donate money to make up for lost income, they could expect even greater hardships.

The dixième and its subsidiary measures did provide France with the necessary financial strength to endure three more campaigns until the war ended. Political changes in England led to the dismissal of Marlborough from all of his offices at the end of 1711. The new British commander was told to refrain from any combat operations during 1712, while negotiations took place. The campaign of 1712 produced a stunning French victory at Denain and the reconquest of some lost territory. Negotiations at Utrecht brought peace with Britain, the Dutch, Portugal, Prussia, and Savoy in April 1713. The Empire and Austria made peace at Rastadt-Baden in September 1714. While these negotiations brought some respite to the ministers of war and foreign affairs, Desmaretz's labors continued unabated. The expense of war did not end when the armies withdrew from the battlefield. The loans undertaken during the war had to be repaid. During the gradual cessation of hostilities after

1711, the controller general had to make plans to pay the state's everyday expenses and to restore self-sufficiency to royal finances.

Desmaretz's Postwar Policies

Reforming the royal finances, in the language of the early eighteenth century, meant suspending all wartime taxes and returning to the prewar status quo. At least, this was the kind of thinking that Nicolas Desmaretz advocated. His problem was maintaining royal credit while shifting from wartime to peacetime fiscal policies. The king had borrowed money that he had to repay if he was going to free his ordinary revenues and guarantee his income. In a variety of mémoires written after 1714,[47] Desmaretz wrote that the ideal condition for royal finances was that of the year 1683, the year of Colbert's death. He compared the situation at the beginning of 1715 to that which Colbert had faced in 1661, although, in the earlier period, the cause of France's financial condition had been criminal mismanagement and depredations of the royal revenues, while the situation in 1715 was the result of almost twenty-five years of war. Unlike his uncle, Desmaretz could not accuse his predecessors of criminal behavior because they had operated with Louis XIV's consent. He could not, therefore, propose the kinds of stringent legal proceedings that Colbert had employed in the 1660s to recover lost revenue.

One of Desmaretz's extant postwar mémoires is addressed to Louis XIV,[48] while the others are either for other members of the government or are discussion papers for Desmaretz's advisers. In the mémoire to the king, he describes the situations in 1661, 1683, and 1715, and provides brief accounts of the actions that Colbert and his successors took to ameliorate finances. He then goes into greater detail about the government's activities since 1708. Because it had taken Colbert more than twenty years to build the financial machinery that existed in 1683, Desmaretz states, it should not surprise Louis XIV if he were to learn that it would take another twenty years to rebuild it.

In 1661 royal taxes had extracted 84,222,096 livres, but only 31,845,041 livres reached the Royal Treasury. The rest went to pay for charges, including rentes, gages, and corruption. By a variety of harsh measures, Colbert built royal taxes up to 116,873,478 livres, minus only 23,375,274 livres for charges. By 1715, however, the Royal Treasury was only receiving 30,680,707 livres out of a total tax burden of 109,248,074 livres. While the difference between total revenue in 1683 and 1715 was only 7,625,497 livres, the Royal Treasury received 62,817,497 livres less in 1715 than it had in 1683 (see table 6.1). Desmaretz believed that returning royal income to 100 million livres should be the goal of his policy.[49] Thus, he had to reduce the charges on revenue by 62 million livres, while simultaneously increasing royal revenue by another 7 million. This income had been lost by alienating the domain, granting too many people exemptions from taxation,

Table 6.1. Ordinary revenues from 1683 and 1715.

Year	Taxes and Leases	Charges	Royal Treasury
1683	116,873,478	23,375,274	93,498,204
1715	109,248,074	84,567,367	30,680,707
Loss	7,625,404	62,817,497	
Increase	61,192,093		

Source: Boislisle, *Correspondance des contrôleurs généraux,* 3:623, and A.N. G^7 1903.

and creating loans in the form of offices, rentes, and augmented gages. All of these affairs were debts undertaken by the crown in times of distress. In addition, the crown had been amassing short-term debts in the form of mint bills, promissory notes, unpaid assignations, and the unpaid debts of the traitants.

In order to recover the lost revenue, Desmaretz faced three challenges. First, he had to guarantee the crown a revenue of 100 million livres annually, while also reducing expenditures to that level. Second, he had to find some way to repay or dismiss the loans and debts incurred because of the wars since 1688. And last, he had to determine the actual size of the debt in order to plan for repayment.

He tackled these problems in reverse order because no assured revenue could be found unless the debts were repaid. He had asked the provincial intendants in August 1710 for a report on the financial affairs in their provinces, including the operations of the farms, unpaid taxes, and extraordinary affairs of finances. He sent another copy of this letter on August 20, 1711, with additional instructions on these and other financial affairs. The product of the reports from 1710 is unavailable, but some of the research from 1711 is.[50]

When Desmaretz returned to public life under Chamillard in 1699–1700, one of his first tasks was to prepare an edict calling for research into the activities of the traitants since 1689. This ill-fated pursuit ended when war broke out in 1702. Nonetheless, one of the first actions taken by Desmaretz when he ascended to the official position of director of finances in October 1703 was to send letters to each of the provincial intendants asking for a report on the activities of the traitants.[51] Desmaretz would return again and again to supervising the traitants by requiring them to file reports on their activities. His letter of October 5, 1703, to the provincial intendants was followed by several more in 1704 and 1705. An arrêt of the council in 1705 ordered the traitants and their cautions to remit their résultats, accounts, and receipts to the council. After Desmaretz became controller general of finances in 1708, he sent a renewed request for information to Le Rebours and Poulletier, who would report to him.[52] Desmaretz used these reports to order the traitants to pay the funds called for in their traités. Sr. Barthelémy Rolland, commis and financier, was charged with collecting these debts.[53] Eventually, Desmaretz put Bercy, his son-in-law, in place of Le Rebours and Poulletier to receive all the information for any traité concluded before December 31, 1709. Any traitant, caution, or commis who withheld these accounts would be required to pay a fine equal to a sum that depended upon the total forfait of the traité.[54]

Desmaretz's letter of August 20, 1711, preceded an arrêt on August 29 of that year that ordered the traitants and their cautions and employees to turn in the accounts of their collections for any rights that they enjoyed.[55] The extraordinary commission of the council supervising this activity was the same as the commission supervising the dixième—headed by Bouville and including Bignon de Blanzy, des Forts, Desmaretz, Le Rebours, Bercy, Maupeou d'Ableiges, and Harlay de Cély. Rolland was to enforce the orders of this commission by using legal constraints on anyone who did not respond to a request for information within three days. In addition to the accounts of their companies' receipts, the traitants were also to hand over any register of the meetings of their companies after initialing each page.[56]

A letter from Ferrand, the intendant in Brittany, accompanies two *cahiers* (notebooks) in which tables describe all the extraordinary affairs of finances in his province, as well as the offices sold, their prices, their purchasers, a record of the payments made by the traitants, the profitability of these offices, and whether any unsold offices were salable.[57] Ferrand addressed his letters to Bercy, who referred them to Delacroix, who had been working on these kinds of matters with Desmaretz since as early as 1704.[58] André Chouraki, in *Les intendants des finances*, cites these documents as coming from the papers that Bercy turned over to the government when he left office in 1715. They actually belong, however, to Desmaretz's efforts to ascertain what debts the traitants owed to the crown, how much more money could be gained from officeholders, what the influence of these offices on the crown's revenues and commerce would be, and what it would cost to suppress them.

The French government collected some of the unpaid debts of these traités, with interest, after 1711. Desmaretz was, in effect, conducting a Chambre de justice, although he himself never applied that name to his dealings. He had expressed his distaste for this type of brutal measure in an early mémoire that he wrote on the role of the king's finance minister.[59] He would rather pressure the financiers to borrow a million livres for the crown than seize property that might only be worth 100,000 livres, he stated. By employing Bercy (his wealthy son-in-law), Delacroix (Bercy's neighbor), and Rolland (another financier), Desmaretz was using foxes to pursue foxes. The government charged Rolland with inspecting the accounts of a variety of comptables for double entries, mistakes, false entries, omissions, and other matters that might produce extra revenues for the crown.[60] This silent investigation avoided any shadow that the use of overt force might cast on the credit of these financiers. Desmaretz wanted to avoid the kind of purge that Le Peletier had used in the 1680s, because it might harm the crown's ability to borrow money. At the same time, he wanted to know what debts there were, exactly how many offices had been sold, and the prices and utility of these offices. He could then determine what money the government would need to repay the officeholders or financiers.[61]

The royal government could use this research into the history of its extraordinary affairs to squeeze more money from the more profitable offices. The government judged that the interest received in the form of gages and emoluments from some of these loans (offices) was too high. Thus, in October 1712, it asked the holders of any of thirty-three different kinds of offices created since January 1, 1688, to pay the equivalent of one-quarter more for their offices than they had originally paid. In other words, if an office cost 4,000 livres, the officeholder would have to pay another 1,000 livres for it. This measure was, in effect, a forced reduction of the interest earned on loans for offices. Unlike forced loans that offered augmented gages to officeholders, the government's new policy did not offer any increase in income to officeholders. Either an officeholder paid the additional fee, or he would lose his office and its profits. An edict of February 1713 added fourteen more offices to the original list, but eight offices were eventually removed from the second list, because the holders of these offices had lent more money to the crown since they purchased their offices.[62] The government was trying to get more money from officeholders rather than suppressing offices, an expense it could not afford.

Once the government had determined its total indebtedness, it had to devise some method of repayment. It had to find a way to raise money to absorb its short-term debts, suppress offices and reimburse their owners, reduce taxes without reducing income, and restore the crown's revenues to their prewar condition. To do so, the government turned to a credit mechanism developed by the French Church.

When the clergy paid the crown 24 million livres in 1710, they borrowed 23 million livres in the form of rentes and set aside a fixed amount of their income to pay the annual interest on those loans as well as reimburse the principal. They repeated this process in 1711 when they borrowed 8 million livres to exempt themselves from the dixième. They sold rentes at denier 12 (8.333 percent) and set aside 875,000 livres in revenue to pay interest of 666,666 livres, 13 sous, 4 deniers, while they used the rest to retire the principal.[63] In other words, unlike the royal government, which had no plan to repay perpetual rentes, the clergy set up a sinking fund to repay these rentes in order to recover lost revenue.

These reimbursable rentes, called *rentes tournantes,* did not permanently encumber the income of the borrower; nor did they require the lender to surrender his capital permanently. They were popular loans with the investing public because they were paid promptly and eventually repaid the capital on the original loans. The government had dabbled with medium-term credit mechanisms using the Caisse des emprunts, mint bills, and the five-year bills of the farmers and receivers general. Unfortunately, these experiments failed because the government could not guarantee the fixed revenue necessary to support the interest and repayment. When the farms became unprofitable after 1701, the promises of the Caisse des emprunts were worthless, despite increasing the interest rate to 10 percent in 1705. The government converted some of this paper in 1707 into five-year bills of the farmers or receivers general, but the winter of 1709 and the collapse of the credit of the General Farms turned these bills into more scraps of royal paper of dubious value. The Caisse Legendre appeared in 1710 but its credit was limited to providing for the state's most urgent expenses.

Another credit mechanism available to the state was the short-term loan made by the General Farmers or receivers general in the form of their bills, or by issuing assignations against future revenue from a particular source. The farms' collapse and problems collecting ordinary impositions made these kinds of short-term credit sources tenuous at best. The forced conversion in October 1710 of assignations on the revenue for 1711, 1712, and 1713 discredited this kind of paper.[64] When revenue failed to reach the predicted level, these loans would have to be reassigned to another source. When the farms went into régie in 1709, the government could no longer use the credit of the farmers general. The Caisse Legendre was absorbing all the credit of the receivers general of finances.

The only other credit mechanism available to the royal government was permanent loans in the form of perpetual rentes, offices, or augmented gages. There was never any plan to repay these loans. The government only had to set aside enough revenue to pay the interest as promised. Since 1709, however, there had been difficulty in meeting these obligations because revenue failed to reach expected levels. At any rate, Desmaretz saw the permanent encumbrance of the king's revenues as the cause of the crown's problems. He did not want to use one permanent encumbrance to replace another. He wanted to restore the 69 million livres in lost revenue by using some kind of reimbursable loan.

The government had already adopted the clergy's method for providing a sinking fund, of sorts, for retirement of the original loan. In July 1711 the men in the office of the contrôle général des finances began studying a project to create offices of inspectors of finances[65] who would tour one or more elections to check the accounts of the taille receivers and the parish collectors, as well as anyone else who handled royal money outside the tax farms. In January 1712 an edict created these offices and added an extra 3 deniers per livre (1.25 percent) to the taille in the pays d'élections in order to pay gages. When problems developed over the sale and jurisdiction of these offices, the government decided to suppress them in June 1712 and use the revenue from the 3 deniers per livre to support rentes at denier 12 (8.33 percent). The government was going to borrow 6 million livres and set aside 800,000 livres from the taille to pay the interest of 500,000 livres and reimburse the principal. These rentes proved to be so popular that three other issues were sold on the same terms in July and December 1713 and March 1714. Each of these loans would be repaid in thirteen years from the time they were contracted.[66] Desmaretz intended to employ a similar mechanism to help retire the total debt of the government.

The end of the war with part of France's enemies in April 1713 allowed the government to begin reducing taxes on commerce. The commercial treaty of Utrecht allowed the English and Dutch to export goods to France without paying the *droit de fret*, a tax of 50 sous per tun. The king ceased the alienation of his domain and began reducing taxes to their 1688 levels. Doubled rights on butcher shop inspectors at 3 livres per head were dropped. A tax of 20 sous per muid of wine was also eliminated. Doubled rights on all private tolls (*péages*) were abolished. Salt taxes were reduced in October 1713.[67]

The state reduced the interest on all perpetual rentes to denier 25 (4 percent) by an edict in December 1713. Unpaid interest would be added to the capital when the conversion was made. Any rentes acquired since April 1706, when the state had begun allowing royal paper to be used to purchase them, had their capital reduced to 60 percent of its face value, while adding any unpaid interest to the capital. Most rentes were two years behind in their payments. Lowering the interest rates on loans and reducing the value of the capital behind these loans was another sign of the government's hidden, partial bankruptcy. Desmaretz wrote that this process alone caused murmurs of discontent but saved the government 14 million livres annually.[68]

After the conclusion of the Peace of Rastadt-Baden in September 1714, Desmaretz had to plan for the retirement of all royal debts acquired since 1683. The state had gotten through the last years of the war almost entirely on the credit of the receivers general of finances and their Caisse Legendre. The king, however, had promised to suppress both the capitation and the dixième after the proclamation of peace. These two impositions together produced almost 44 million livres annually, a total that was more than the king's ordinary revenues produced after the deduction of these charges. Also, the dixième had the salutary effect of reducing expenses by retaining one-tenth of everyone's pensions, gages, appointments, and other government payments.

The research into the amount of royal paper that remained to be retired showed that on January 1, 1708, the government owed 526,766,398 livres, but that by the end of 1714 it had reduced that debt to 427,992,648 livres. During that time period, the crown had raised 1,564,585,188 livres (an average of 223,512,169 livres annually for seven years). In addition to the cost of its unretired paper, the crown had to raise 122,729,540 livres to cover expenses for 1715, as well as 26 million livres to pay the interest on the Caisse des emprunts and the missing funds of the General Farms. The total money needed just to retire these debts was 576,722,188 livres.[69]

Desmaretz recommended reducing expenses for 1715 by another 25 million livres, to less than 100 million livres.[70] If the government adopted his suggestion, the total debt would be reduced to 552 million livres. In addition, the crown expected the General Farms to show a deficit of 6 million livres, which funds from the Royal Treasury had to cover. The crown had to find a way to reduce the amount of charges against revenues that had increased by 61,192,903 livres since 1683. Desmaretz wanted the crown to be able to pay for its annual expenses of 100 million livres out of its ordinary revenues. He wanted a balanced budget. To achieve this goal, he would have to increase revenues coming to the Royal Treasury by approximately 70 million livres, either by increasing taxes or reducing the charges against revenue. These charges took the form of rentes, gages, and other loans with an interest rate between 5 and 10 percent, representing a total capital investment amounting to something between 700 million and 1.4 billion million livres. When he added the 552 million livres owed for past and present expenses, the total debt was between 1.25 and 1.95 billion livres. Desmaretz settled on an estimate of 1.5 billion livres.

Desmaretz wanted to borrow 1.5 billion livres to settle the debt by selling rentes tournantes like those of the clergy at denier 25 (4 percent). Because the state would only collect 110 million livres in ordinary revenue in 1715, he needed a source of revenue that did not exist in 1683. This new source would have to produce 60 million livres just to pay the interest, plus another 10 million livres or so to reimburse the principal. He received proposals for four different methods of doing so.

The first proposal suggested maintaining both the capitation and the dixième, despite the king's promise to suppress them. The capitation had only produced 21,680,680 livres after all the exemptions were granted during 1709–10, while the dixième had produced just 21,969,200 livres—in other words, the combined total of the two taxes was just 43,647,880 livres. Thus, these two taxes, as constituted in 1714, would not be adequate to the task Desmaretz envisioned.

A second proposal called for the suppression of the dixième, but a doubling of the capitation. The result, however, would produce even less revenue than the first proposal. It would also *increase* government expenses by removing the one-tenth withheld by the dixième.

A third proposal recommended suppressing both the dixième and the capitation as a gesture of good faith to the people. The crown should then create a new peace subsidy that would raise 70 million livres annually. While this proposal was, in the minister's mind, more appropriate than the previous two, it smacked of deception, because it first suppressed taxes and then created a new tax that would be an even greater burden than those suppressed. In addition, the new subsidy would also require entirely new tax rolls that would delay its establishment until they could be created.

Desmaretz favored a fourth proposal of having the provinces assume the debts of the state. In this scheme, the state would apportion the debt among the clergy and the provinces, and either give them certain revenue sources already in the crown's hands or create new sources of revenue for them. They would then sell rentes and administer their repayment.

Desmaretz had been exchanging thoughts on this kind of program with Michel de Barbarie de Saint-Contest, provincial intendant in Metz and plenipotentiary to the peace talks at Baden. Their first exchanges took place in 1713, but they did not begin serious discussions until after the proclamation of peace in the fall of 1714. Desmaretz requested further information on Saint-Contest's idea, which was very similar to his own. Saint-Contest called for each province to sell rentes at denier 25, to the equivalent of half their revenue from the combined dixième and capitation. All the revenue from these two taxes would then be employed to pay the principal and interest on the loan. Representatives from the three estates in each province (two clergy, two nobles, and two townsmen) would be in charge of administering these funds. The revenue would be collected and the rentes/reimbursements paid in each province.[71]

Desmaretz's plan was more far-reaching than Saint-Contest's in many ways. First, the minister knew that the dixième and the capitation, as they existed in 1714, did not produce the amount of money he needed. He recommended suppressing any exemptions to these two taxes, and requiring everyone to pay the capitation and dixième, without exception. He also believed that it was possible for the government to determine the wealth produced by property if it pursued a policy that granted no exemptions and investigated the truthfulness of all declarations. This kind of policy, however, could provoke opposition if not outright resistance, he warned the king. But, if the government adopted this policy, Desmaretz estimated, the capitation and dixième would produce about 57 million livres. He proposed adding another 2 sous per livre to the farms and the taille, thus raising another 15 million livres and providing the funding necessary for his daring plan without having to draw up new tax rolls.[72]

Desmaretz also called for a close inspection of all promissory notes and royal paper still in circulation, with the idea of refusing to honor those that were in suspect hands. He did not wish to recognize the claims of people who had not been issued the bills in the first place but had instead purchased them at a discount from someone who had lent money to the government. These speculators would only receive part of the face value of the royal paper. Now that the war was over, the crown could afford to be less than gentle with its financiers. Another symptom of this rigorous policy was the announcement of a shorter schedule for reporting all accounts of the comptables who had not done so since 1699.[73] Each comptable was to report his accounts on either a quarterly or semiannual basis until the accounts were brought up to date. Desmaretz also recommended the suspension of all uncollected extraordinary affairs of finances. These measures would meet with a certain amount of good will from the people being pursued by traitants and comptables for sums owed on these affairs. The suspension of the extraordinary affairs had first been recommended to the minister in 1710 but the crown was still dependent on any credit it could find at the time. Now that expenses were greatly reduced, Desmaretz wanted to pressure these groups for what they owed the crown, their excessive profits, and their false claims against the crown.

During the spring of 1715, the controller general tried to persuade the king to apply pressure to the clergy at their assembly that year, and to those provincial estates that were to meet in 1715. He believed that, if the crown could persuade these corporate bodies to obey, the rest of France would fall in line. In April 1715, while Desmaretz was still trying to persuade the king to adopt these policies, the Caisse Legendre foundered. The Electors of Bavaria and Cologne, who had been maintained in France since 1704, insisted that France pay them what it had promised in real money, a total of 5.7 million livres.[74] Desmaretz would spend the last months of Louis XIV's reign trying to salvage the credit of the Caisse. Its collapse weakened the government's hand in its attempt to face down the privileged orders that year.

The assembly of the clergy met in June and granted a don gratuit of 12 million livres. This assembly met every five years to discuss their problems and to offer the crown a free gift to take the place of taxes on the clergy. In 1710 they had paid 24 million livres to be exempted from the capitation, for which they had previously paid 4 million livres annually. In 1711 they met for an unusual session to vote on paying 8 million livres to be exempted from the dixième. Their offer in 1715 of 12 million livres equaled the combination of 4 and 8 million livres they had previously paid. The Royal Council of Finances accepted this gift in a meeting on July 9, 1715.[75] On that same day, the king declared that the capitation and the dixième would be maintained until the debts undertaken by the crown during the last two wars were repaid.

It is probably no coincidence that the clergy's offer of 12 million livres in 1715 was equal to the total amount they had paid to exempt themselves from the dixième and the capitation. The 1715 don gratuit was larger than any since 1690, when the clergy had offered the same amount. The gift in 1710 was an anomaly because the clergy was then paying the equivalent of six years' capitation to be considered exempt from any further payments. Their gifts in 1695 and 1705 were only 10 million livres, but those were war years. The year 1715 was a year of peace. The only other comparable year was 1700, another year of peace, when the clergy only offered 3.5 million livres.[76] The clergy was probably responding to pressure from the royal government by granting such a large don gratuit in 1715.

The declaration of July 9, 1715, that extended the dixième and the capitation began with an apologetic explanation of the reasons why the government had to adopt this kind of measure. In the document, the government tried to justify royal actions by recounting the taxes and offices that it had already suppressed. It promised to suspend the capitation and the dixième as soon as the king enjoyed all the revenues that had been alienated since 1689. All exemptions to the capitation save those granted to the clergy were abolished, raising the amount of revenue due from the capitation to its pre-1709 level. The declaration also suspended all activity of the traitants, all unsold offices created before 1713, and payment of any fees for the suppression of these kinds of offices.[77] Desmaretz explained to the procureur general of the Parlement of Paris, Henri-François Daguesseau, that the latter action was the object of the government's research into the activities of the traitants. He said that the government had revoked all traités and that the provincial intendants would receive orders when the information on each traité had been received and digested.[78]

To relieve the king's finances further, an edict in August 1715 suppressed all letters of nobility and the privileges they granted since January 1, 1689. It also revoked all exemptions from the taille and its collection that had been granted to any office created since that date with an original purchase price of less than 10,000 livres. In addition, it suppressed all the offices of subdelegates and their greffiers, as well as any office created in the elections since January 1, 1689.[79]

An arrêt of August 17, 1715, annulled all royal paper in the form of bills of the treasurers of the extraordinary of war and the artillery in order to hasten the return of good money and restore the commercial situation. The government had scheduled these bills for use in buying rentes created in July 1714, but it suppressed these rentes in August 1715.

The bills were thereafter to be converted into rentes tournantes at denier 25 (4 percent), with a total interest of 1 million livres. All bills that were not in the hands of their original recipients were to be reduced by one-half their face value. The revenues from the capitation of the city and generality of Paris were to pay these rentes. All unconverted bills would be void after January 1, 1716.[80]

Another arrêt of the same date called for converting all the promises of the Caisse des emprunts into 5 million livres in reimbursable rentes at denier 25. The revenue to pay these rentes was to come from the same tax increase of 2 sous per livre that had been added to support the reimbursement efforts planned for the revenue coming from the capitation and the dixième. Any bill or promise from the caisse des emprunts that was not in the hands of the original purchaser was to be reduced to half its face value for the purpose of purchasing rentes.[81]

Desmaretz was proposing similar measures to retire the promises of the Caisse Legendre, the bills of the receivers general, and the unpaid ordonnances of the royal government. Rentes were being created at denier 20 to be paid from the product of the capitation and dixième in the pays d'états, Provence, and the generality of Lyon, and the remaining revenues from Paris.[82] The finance minister ordered a check of all assignations and quittances comptables to find out how many were still in the hands of the persons who had originally received them. This act served as a prelude to an effort to remove these effects, as the government had already done with the bills of the treasurers of the extraordinary of war and the promises of the Caisse des emprunts.[83]

There was an undoubted parallel between the recommendations Desmaretz had made to Louis XIV at the beginning of 1715 and the activities of the government during that summer. The aging monarch apparently rejected any suggestions to create local committees to handle these funds. He did, however, renounce his promises to suppress the capitation and the dixième and reinforced those taxes by suspending any exemptions from them. He also ended the reign of the traitants in the provinces. Royal paper was inspected and reduced if it was found to be in the hands of people who had not helped the royal government during the war. The similarity between the minister's recommendations and the actions of the government reveal the amount of control the minister had over policy at the end of the reign.

Desmaretz estimated that the actions taken in August would liberate all the revenue from the Royal Treasury for 1715 and open a path for the major effort of recovering the revenues that had been alienated, in one form or another, since 1689. He would never begin that effort because time was running out. Louis XIV had been visibly declining for over a year. The king became ill in the middle of August and developed senile gangrene in both legs. He died on September 1, 1715.[84]

Desmaretz after Louis XIV's Death

In September 1683 Colbert's death had left Nicolas Desmaretz, Colbert's nephew, exposed and without protection. Almost exactly thirty-two years later, the death of Louis XIV left Desmaretz in a similar position, because the new king, Louis XV, was a child, aged five years and seven months. Louis XIV's nephew, Philippe, duc d'Orléans, thus declared a regency.

Traditionally, a regency meant a period of weakness for the monarchy. While this particular regency, referred to as The Regency in French history, would not endure the kinds of rebellions that shook the regencies of Catherine de Medicis in the 1560s, Marie de Medicis in the 1610s, or Anne of Austria in the 1640s and 1650s, Regent Philippe of Orléans would have to share power with those great nobles who had chafed under Louis XIV's ministerial despotism. The nobility wanted a voice in the councils of government and an end of the reign of the ministers. Louis XIV's will would have forced Philippe to share power with the duc de Maine (Louis' bastard son) and the maréchal-duc de Villeroy as governor of Louis XV. The dead king's will also created a regency council staffed by his ministers and generals. In order to get the Parlement of Paris to overturn the late king's will, Philippe had to agree to return the right of prior remonstrance, the right to present objections to any new laws before registering them. When the Parlement of Paris voted to overturn the will on September 2, 1715, each minister could begin counting the days he had left as a political force. The question was: Who would be the first to go?

The controller general of finances had the power to enforce the collection of taxes. Louis XIV's last controller general had created taxes that ignored the traditional privileges of the nobility to be exempt from direct taxation. He also governed a large amount of royal patronage that the new regent would want to control. Desmaretz's hardline on the comptables, traitants, and *aisés* did not win him any friends. He carefully hid the pressure he placed on these people, so as to avoid any serious harm to their ability to borrow money. This secretiveness left the public with the impression that he was their ally and protector. As the driving force behind a fiscal policy aimed at relieving the poor by taxing the rich, as an innovator whose tax policies resulted in lost income for royal pensioners, and as a constant reminder of the crown's intrusion into the life of the nobility, Desmaretz was a prime candidate for early dismissal. Although he had some powerful friends, like the marshals d'Huxelles and de Villeroy and the marquis d'Effiat, he was a relative newcomer to power. He would be the victim of another tradition of the monarchy—the vulnerability of the finance minister once the crown changed hands.

The proclamation of six councils of the Regency on September 15, 1715, spelled the end for Desmaretz. The new Regent excluded him from the regency council of finances and gave him his *congé* (leave).[85] Even so, the post of controller general of finances was not suppressed, just left vacant. The ministry offices were still referred to as the contrôle général des finances. Although Villeroy kept his position as head of the council of finances, Adrien-Maurice, duc de Noailles, was named president, and effective head, of this council. Desmaretz's commis, de la Garde, was too closely identified with the former finance minister to survive the transfer of power, and was dismissed along with Desmaretz. Clautrier became Noailles' secretary. Le Cousturier replaced Le Rebours as the premier commis des finances and became a confidant of the Regent in matters of finances.[86]

The intendants of finances, whom Saint-Simon called *les enfants du contrôleur général*, were soon dismissed. Their offices were suppressed in October 1715, and their papers turned over to the masters of requests attached to the regency council of finances. The fate of these men as individuals, however, depended on their standing at court. Caumartin and Le Peletier des Forts had been named councilors of state independent of their position as intendants of finances; their positions on the council were secure. Fagon and Poulletier remained masters of requests. Fagon was even promised the next vacancy as councilor of state. Poulletier would go on to be intendant at Lyon from 1717 until 1738, and would finish his career as a councilor of state and first president of the Grand Conseil, one of the sovereign courts. Both Le Peletier des Forts and Fagon would sit on the Regency council of finances.[87] Bercy was still a master of requests, but he was also Desmaretz's son-in-law. His continued ties to the business community irritated Noailles, who arranged for him to be exiled to his estates in Normandy and stripped of his office because of unsubstantiated accusations of corruption in his relations with the financiers.[88] Le Rebours and Guyet had neither offices nor strong family ties at court. They were simply Chamillard's relations and had enjoyed Desmaretz's protection. They were both dismissed, and their careers in government came to an end.[89]

Desmaretz was the first minister to be dismissed. Jérôme de Pontchartrain was forced to resign as secretary of state for the Maison du Roi and the navy in favor of his son, Maurepas, who was only fifteen years old. Voysin was forced to give up the war ministry but would remain chancellor until his death in 1717. Torcy obtained a position on the Regency council of foreign affairs and kept control over this post office for a few years. He was soon stripped of his position as secretary of state for foreign affairs, however. He was the last minister to be eased from power, possibly because he controlled less patronage than the others or because his personality and position made him acceptable as a technical adviser.[90] Desmaretz, however, was the only former minister who was denied a seat on any regency council.

Desmaretz defended his ministry by publishing his *Mémoire sur l'administration des finances depuis le 20 février 1708 jusqu'au 1er septembre 1715* in 1716.[91] His defense was simple: as controller general of finances, he had been the executor of Louis XIV's orders. The controller general, moreover, was a simple order-giver (*ordonnateur*) rather than a comptable, someone who actually handled royal funds. Jean Buvat's journal says that Desmaretz presented a copy of his mémoire to the Regent in August 1716.[92] While we do not know how widely read this document was, the abbé de Saint-Pierre reprinted it in his *Annales politiques* in 1757, and Sir James Steuart cited it in his *Inquiry into the principles of political oeconomy* in 1767.[93] Desmaretz's *Mémoire* was reprinted several times prior to 1789, on the eve of the Revolution. As such, it was a predecessor of Jacques Necker's more famous *Compte rendu*, which provoked demand for Necker's resignation in 1781 and led to many public debates in the decade leading up to the Revolution.

Desmaretz's later years were marred by scandal and sorrow as the Regency government resorted to traditional methods for escaping the royal debt. A Chambre de justice was called in March 1716. Desmaretz would testify before it on several occasions.[94] The Chambre offered attractive awards to anyone who reported criminal mismanagement leading to the recovery of lost revenue for the crown—that is, it paid donneurs d'avis. A woman named Lafontaine, widow of Madame Desmaretz's steward or estate manager, swore that she had worked for the minister by buying royal paper at low prices and bringing it to him. She also claimed that de la Garde had assisted her in this scheme. De la Garde was arrested and spent time in prison until this matter was cleared up. The woman's testimony was eventually burned in Desmaretz's presence, but not before he had suffered the indignity of having his property, and even the convent where one of his daughters was abbess, searched. De la Garde was released from prison and returned to Soissons, where his brother was a treasurer of France.[95] Madame Desmaretz contracted smallpox in late 1716 and lost her mind. She would spend the rest of her life in seclusion.[96]

Desmaretz was not dismissed or sent away from court in disgrace, as had happened in 1683. According to Saint-Simon, around the time of the investigation into the claims of Madame Lafontaine, Noailles tried to have Desmaretz exiled because he claimed that the former minister still had influence within the financial community. Saint-Simon claimed that he himself went to the Regent to appeal against exiling Desmaretz, after the marquis de Louville asked him to do so.[97] After the dismissal of Noailles in January 1718, there were rumors that Desmaretz would be recalled, but Argenson replaced Noailles.[98] Desmaretz still remained connected to the court, however. Several of his mémoires concern the reestablishment of royal finances in the period after 1715.[99]

Desmaretz continued to advocate the assumption of the state's debts by the provinces, while he rejected references to the Dutch or English systems as unsuitable for France. Interestingly, he supported the sale of reimbursable rentes at 2 to 4 percent interest against the revenues of the provinces, and the suggestion that a committee of three clergymen, three nobles, and three members of the Third Estate administer these rentes each province.[100] This type of proposal does not appear in any of the extant writings from Desmaretz to Louis XIV. Apparently he realized that the old king would reject a plan to give power to the provinces, but he may have believed that the Regent might be more open to it.

Desmaretz recommended the use of leases and résultats instead of double-entry bookkeeping for handling the accounts of the government's tax collections because he favored a system wherein the people who handled the king's money had a personal interest in doing so efficiently. The idea that double-entry bookkeeping would facilitate knowing the exact financial condition of the realm meant nothing to Desmaretz, who believed that a diligent minister always knew the situation. The efficiency of a system like centralized bookkeeping would deprive the crown of necessary credit during times of war. Desmaretz cited Colbert's activities in the 1660s and 1670s to prove his point.[101]

Desmaretz had been meeting with John Law frequently toward the end of Louis XIV's reign. The Scot had submitted mémoires on the advantages of a royal bank but, whatever Desmaretz's opinion was in 1715, his mémoires of February 29, March 8, and May 27, 1720, leave no doubt about his opinion of Law's bank.[102] Given his ties to the Paris brothers during the war[103] and Argenson's support for their "Anti-System" activities in 1718–19, Desmaretz probably supported their efforts to defeat Law's centralization of the entire machinery of royal finances under one bank after 1718. His mémoire on double-entry bookkeeping, though undated, was possibly part of his arguments in support of the "Anti-System" lobby.

Desmaretz's three mémoires from early 1720, when John Law was ascendant as controller general of finances, predicted the disaster of July 1720, when the Mississippi bubble burst. His first critique foresaw the collapse and feared that, unless the stockholders and debtors of the bank were forced to honor their debts, the king might find himself in debt for over a billion livres. The bank's paper had deprived the provinces of real money and was hurting commerce. Desmaretz called for reestablishing the receivers general of finances, the taille and capitation (the dixième had been suppressed in 1717), and the General Farms before disaster struck. He had doubts about the viability of the bank and its ties to overseas trade, "la Compagnie des Indes." He was still pleading for the creation of low-interest rentes to retire 800 million livres in royal debt, while he decried the export of gold from France as the cause of much misery and the excessive luxury of the *Mississippiens,* the investors in Law's overseas colonial enterprises.

These are the last public writings of Nicolas Desmaretz. He died on May 4, 1721, at his home on the rue de Richelieu after a brief illness.[104]

He survived Chamillard by eighteen days and preceded Argenson's death by four days. The former ministers of Louis XIV were dying off.

Desmaretz was an unpopular minister. At his death, Edmond-Jean-François Barbier, an avocat at the Parlement of Paris, remarked that Desmaretz had returned to power twenty years after his involvement, during Colbert's ministry, in some chicanery in the mints, for which he should have been hanged. Barbier asked who could have been a better choice for France's finance minister than a crook (*fripon*).[105] Another avocat, Mathieu Marais, however, called Desmaretz a clever man who had a plan that would have restored French finances within six years, had John Law not reversed these ideas to produce poverty where Desmaretz had wanted to create wealth.[106] A later controller general of finances called Desmaretz one of France's greatest finance ministers, considering the situation in which he found himself.[107] Voltaire agreed that Desmaretz was unpopular at the time of his dismissal, but remarked that the actions of several of his successors made people miss Desmaretz.[108]

The finance ministers of the eighteenth century would turn from one experiment to another, never showing that grim determination that had characterized Colbert and Desmaretz. Reform would come in brief spurts of activity until factions at court or among the sovereign courts forced either the inconstant Louis XV or the weak Louis XVI to change course. In this respect, Desmaretz was the last of the old breed and the first to suffer from the fickleness of French government in the eighteenth century. If France had sustained Desmaretz's method of retiring the debt after 1715, it might have avoided much of the turmoil that would come with the resumption of war in the 1740s.

Conclusion

This book has explored the political and economic thinking and actions of the government of Louis XIV during the latter part of the seventeenth century and the first decades of the eighteenth century, the so-called black hole of French historiography. The government at the end of Louis XIV's reign needs a definitive history. Until that history is explored and a definitive synthesis written, we will continue to see syntheses and popular history relying on sources such as the *Mémoires* of the Duke of Saint-Simon, a man who created myths about the events he was describing and indicted Louis XIV and his ministers for all sorts of crimes and misdeeds, rather than writing an impartial history of his times.[1]

Saint-Simon was undoubtedly a talented writer whose command of the French language[2] was so strong that he could make his readers believe that he had witnessed the events he described as they were taking place, even though Saint-Simon remained outside of *les affaires* until after the death of Louis XIV. Nonetheless, many modern histories continue to rely on his descriptions of people and events at the court of Louis XIV. This book has revealed many examples of Saint-Simon's unreliability as an eyewitness to the events of his time. While his animosity toward many people, including Desmaretz, colored his description of events that he did witness, he also described events that he could not possibly have witnessed, since he did not reside at court permanently until the late 1690s. He did not begin to write his memoirs until 1738, forty years after the earliest events he could have witnessed. When he completed his masterpiece in 1748, he was describing his last days at court in 1723, events that had happened twenty-five years previously. (Here historians should perhaps ask how good is anyone's memory of events that took place twenty-five or more years ago.) Saint-Simon was neither a witness to events at the beginning of the reign nor during the time of Colbert and Louvois, the so-called glory days of the reign.

Other than the king himself, Nicolas Desmaretz was the only person sitting on the Council of Ministers and the Royal Council of Finances at the end of the reign of Louis XIV who had sat on the highest councils of government during the glory days of the reign in the 1670s, when he was given the right to enter the Royal Council of Finances and to express an opinion. He had participated in Colbert's reforms of the tax farms and other aspects of the state's financial house of cards. While it is true that he had been absent from government for twenty years between 1683 and 1703, government officials consulted him and he still contributed to the debate about reforming the king's finances while increasing France's wealth during his time out of office. He was personally acquainted with the world of finance and government reform throughout the personal rule of Louis XIV.

The selection of Desmaretz as controller general of finances raises the question of how and why Louis XIV selected his ministers. The king inherited his first group of ministers from his mentor, Cardinal Mazarin. Thereafter, Louis himself was responsible for the selection of his ministers. In the case of the secretaries of state, he allowed a son to inherit his father's position. Thus, Louvois succeeded Le Tellier in 1677, Barbezieux succeeded Louvois in 1691, Seignelay succeeded Colbert in 1683, Torcy succeeded Croissy in 1696, and Jérôme de Pontchartrain succeeded his father, Louis, when the latter became chancellor in 1699. The king could only exercise his power to select a new secretary of state in two cases: when a secretary of state died without leaving a son capable of inheriting the office, or when Louis himself dismissed one man and appointed another. When Secretaries of State Hugues de Lionne and Barbezieux died without leaving heirs, in 1671 and 1701 respectively, Louis chose Pomponne to succeed Lionne and Chamillard to succeed Barbezieux. Louis would later dismiss both Pomponne (in 1679) and Chamillard (in 1709) and replace them with secretaries of his own choosing. In 1679 he selected Colbert's brother Croissy to succeed Pomponne, and in 1709 he picked Voysin to succeed Chamillard.[3]

The controller general's position was a commission rather than an office or charge that could be inherited, like a secretaryship of state. In other words, the controller general served at the king's pleasure. Nevertheless, Louis XIV never dismissed any of his controllers general. After having worked with Colbert, Mazarin's protégé, for twenty-two years, Louis XIV got the opportunity in September 1683 to select someone new for the position. He selected Le Peletier on the recommendation of Le Tellier, another of Mazarin's appointees, because the dying Colbert was too ill to advise him. Thereafter, each controller general recommended his own successor, and the king appears to have followed their advice: Le Peletier recommended Pontchartrain in 1689; Pontchartrain recommended Chamillard in 1699; and Chamillard recommended Desmaretz in 1708. The three men who served as controller general between Colbert and Desmaretz were anxious to quit the office and petitioned the king to relieve them of duty several times, something neither Colbert nor Desmaretz ever did.

Louis had dismissed Desmaretz from his positions as intendant of finances and senior aide in the controller general's office in 1683. Understandably, he was surprised even to hear Desmaretz's name mentioned in 1700. Yet, on the recommendation of his friend Chamillard, whose health had collapsed under the combined responsibility of the war ministry and finances, Louis appointed Desmaretz to be his finance minister (1708). Louis XIV had come to respect Desmaretz's competence by the time he appointed him finance minister. He was also responding to pressure from Chamillard to be allowed to resign, while at the same time the Colbert clan, Madame de Maintenon, the financiers, and the elite in Paris were pushing for Desmaretz to get the job. Certainly, by the end of the reign, Desmaretz appeared to have Louis XIV's ear, as his policy recommendations for settling France's debts were followed to the letter. The ascension of his son Maillebois seems to indicate that Desmaretz had royal favor.[4]

Sixteen months after Desmaretz succeeded Chamillard as finance minister, Louis XIV dismissed Chamillard as war minister because of military supply problems, disgruntled military leadership, quarrels among his ministers, and disrespect for the man in the royal court. The havoc caused by the terrible winter of 1709 probably played a role in his dismissal as well. Saint-Simon says that Louis XIV liked Chamillard the best of all the ministers. Although Pontchartrain had recommended Chamillard in 1699, the definitive selection of Chamillard raises the question of how he came to the king's attention in the first place, and whether his rise began simply because the king appreciated his abilities as a billiard player. The combined spectacle of the appointment of Desmaretz, a man the king had once called a crook, and the dismissal of Chamillard, a man the king called a friend, raises the legitimate question as to whether the aging Louis XIV was able to resist pressure from court and country.

This begs the question as to whether the aging Louis was still able to run his government in the same way that he had since coming to power in 1661. In his *Mémoires* the young Louis had said that he relied on Colbert to handle any details that he did not have time to process. In the 1690s he became more involved in government details, particularly military affairs. When he named Chamillard to be both war minister and finance minister, he promised to help him; he did so by creating the two offices of directors of finance and by assisting Chamillard with war ministry issues. Eventually, old age slowed the king down. He stopped attending evening events at court, such as operas, plays, or soirées. Instead, he retired to Maintenon's room to work every night with one of his ministers. He also became more impatient with the constant clamor of events and people seeking favors, offices, and changes of policy. An elderly king who was heavily involved in military and foreign policy was necessarily dependent on his ministers to handle other affairs. Their policies became his policies, for lack of an alternative. If they were capable men, then the king's dependence was wise, but if they were not capable, like Chamillard, then disaster would follow. For the most part, Louis XIV's later ministers, with the exception of Chamillard, were able men who performed well under difficult circumstances.

The decisions made by the government in the last thirty years of Louis XIV's reign reveal a lively group of men who had ideas and the will to execute them. This view contradicts the historically accepted image of these men as second-rate and in no way matching the capabilities of the great Colbert, Louvois, or the men Louis XIV had inherited from Mazarin. On the contrary, the ministers at the end of Louis' reign shared the ideas of their contemporaries and made significant changes in the existing system that led to the creation of the administrative monarchy and the French state. Indeed, in Desmaretz's case we find a man who kept track of reform ideas, met personally with advocates of reform, and discussed issues with other men in the government. During the time he was out of government service, Nicolas Desmaretz participated in the debate over how to create wealth and how to finance the state's wars by providing advice to his uncle Croissy and his cousins Seignelay and Beauvillier, who were still in the government. When the debate over political economy turned to how to raise more money to pay for France's war effort, Desmaretz agreed with people like Chamlay, Vauban, and Boisguilbert, who favored taxing wealth rather than adding to the burden of taxation that the poorer elements of French society were already paying. The measures that his ministry undertook, particularly the dixième, produced a strong reaction among his contemporaries, whether Saint-Simon, Barbier, Marais, or Voltaire. His significance in the history of French fisco-financial policy and state development is attested by their reaction to him as either a crook or one of the greatest finance ministers France had ever had.

In 1695 Controller General Pontchartrain decided against taxing wealth because he thought it was too dangerous and subject to abuses. He chose instead to create a new tax called the capitation that required everyone to pay, from the king's son, who was assessed 2,000 livres, down to the simple soldiers and day laborers, who were assessed 1 livre. The capitation was the first direct tax in the Old Regime to tax everyone. Despite alterations when it was reintroduced in 1701, it continued to tax the privileged orders along with the rest of French society. The capitation would remain in effect until the French Revolution.

The capitation altered the debate by revealing that social status did not necessarily equal wealth. The Duke of Saint-Simon thought of himself as belonging to the highest level of nobility after the royal family and the foreign princes, but he was not a wealthy man when compared to other dukes and peers, like the Noailles or the Rohans. Yet, the capitation put all dukes into the second class and taxed them each at 1,500 livres. The capitation also put the dukes on an equal footing with the intendants of finances, each of whom Saint-Simon described as rich. Nicolas Heudebert Dubuisson, for example, who had been intendant of finances from 1690 until 1714, left behind rentes with a total capital of more than 3 million livres. High-ranking noblemen, such as marquis, counts, viscounts, and barons were in the seventh class and taxed at 250 livres each, but Saint-Simon described Desmaretz's son-in-law the marquis de Goësbriand as very rich. The creation of the capitation apparently unleashed envy into the debate on taxation.

One reason for Pontchartrain's opposition to a tax on wealth might have been his awareness of how ignorant the government was about its subjects and their property. Vauban had invested his time trying to estimate the population of France because no one had any idea about how many French subjects there were. The government of Louis XIV had repeatedly sent out requests to the provincial intendants to discover the conditions within their provinces. The most famous of these requests went out in 1698, asking each provincial intendant to send in a report on his province for the education of the king's grandson and presumptive heir, the Duke of Burgundy, but each controller general from Colbert onwards had sought reports from the provincial intendants. Both Pontchartrain and Desmaretz sent out orders requesting reports on local conditions in preparation for levying either the capitation or the dixième. During this same time period, the government bureaucracy was growing and creating an archive of information that would allow it to keep track of property ownership. The establishment of the control of notarial acts in March 1693 made notarial records on property transfers available to the government. The establishment of the centième denier tax on the sale or transfer of property in December 1703 gave the government further data about property ownership. By the middle of the eighteenth century, the government would have the capability of measuring the honesty of tax declarations against its records.[5]

Pontchartrain also rejected a tax on wealth because he and other royal officials believed that the French people would not be willing to declare their wealth to the government or the financiers who collected royal taxes.[6] The government was afraid of provoking a rebellion in the midst of a war. Desmaretz himself feared the rise of an opposition to all of the measures undertaken in September–October 1710. Once the dixième was established, however, it presented the government with the opportunity to press the property owners more rigorously for more detail and thus more revenue for the state. Desmaretz's proposal for paying France's debts after the war did not seek to enforce the dixième and the capitation ruthlessly according to a strict interpretation of the law, but he did want to raise the combined revenue from these taxes from 43 million to 57 million livres by cancelling any exemptions and demanding more accuracy in the income declarations from property owners. More accuracy might have exposed the true wealth of the people who supported the financial system, the so-called Great Families whose wealth supported the whole financial apparatus of the monarchy, according to Daniel Dessert. These people prevented the Chambre de justice of 1716–17 from delving too deeply into where the financiers got their money. They would have resisted any attempt by Desmaretz to inquire into their true income as property owners or as investors in royal fundraising efforts.

The decision to adopt the dixième, a tax on wealth, was not just an assault on the privileges of those who were exempt from the taille and other direct taxes. The capitation had already demolished that privilege. The dixième taxed the income produced by property, and thus ignored the lowest elements of society who earned money from their labor. The dixième made no distinction as to whether the owner of a property was a peer or a peasant. If the property produced wealth, the royal government wanted one-tenth of that product. In effect, all property owners were equal and reduced to being taxpayers in the eyes of the government.

The dixième introduced another new element into the relationship between the government and the taxpayer. The taille had taxed parishes rather than individuals. Every taillable living in a parish was supposed to contribute to paying the parish's taille assessment. The taxpayer in the case of the taille owed money to his parish and not to the government. The debt was a civil debt between the parish and the taille receiver. The capitation as it existed between 1695 and 1697 altered that relationship slightly by requiring non-taillables to pay a direct tax. When the tax was reintroduced in 1701, however, the government returned to taxing institutions rather than individuals. When paying the taille and the post-1701 capitation, taxpayers negotiated with institutions that were intermediate between the people and the state, either the parish or corporate institutions to which the non-taillable belonged. The dixième, however, broke that barrier by requiring individual property owners to file declarations of their income with the provincial intendant who would be responsible for the collection of the tax. In effect, the property owner was asked to provide the evidence that would be used to determine his debt to the state. The dixième left the taxpayer at the mercy of the state, with no institutional group to speak for him. All appeals were to be made to the provincial intendant, with a final appeal to the King's Council. The French state was then in direct relationship with individuals rather than relating to them through intermediate institutions like the parish or the town government. At the time the step was almost unnoticed but it would produce resistance over the course of the eighteenth century whenever the government attempted to reintroduce the dixième or its successor, the vingtième.

When taken together with the other measures adopted in October 1710, the dixième attacked wealth in the form of property as well as rentes and money received from the government. The government reduced interest rates on rentes, affecting those who had already lent money to the government, the bondholders. The government then offered new loans to these same people as a kind of forced loan to make up for their lost income. The government created 600,000 livres in rentes specifically for the financiers and those involved in lending money to the crown, another forced loan. The crown also created several kinds of rentes that could only be bought with paper issued by various royal financial officers, such as the receivers general, Farmers General, or Treasurers of the Extraordinary of War, and removed this paper from the money market while only returning 5 percent on the capital. To cap all this activity, the royal government then ordered that it would reduce by one-tenth all payments from the royal government in the form of rentes, gages, pensions, etc. in order to pay the dixième owed on those royal payments. The victims of these measures were more likely to be wealthy people who could afford to lend money, politically connected people who had received pensions or some other form of largesse from the crown, and financiers and speculators on whom the government depended to finance itself.

Desmaretz and his commis Malet both claimed the dixième and other measures provided the funds necessary to continue the war and win a just peace for France. Desmaretz and his team did not adopt these measures out of some idea of promoting social justice by redistributing wealth. Like the famous American bank robber Willie Sutton who said he robbed banks because that was where the money was, Desmaretz was forced to tax the people with money, the people who had profited most from the government's policy of offering tax exemptions in return for rentes, offices, and other exemptions from taxation, because that was where the money was. If these people expected to continue to receive government payments, they would have to pay taxes.

Desmaretz planned to repay France's debts by using the reimbursable rentes (*rentes tournantes*). If he had been able to continue his plan after Louis XIV's death, France might have avoided some of the financial difficulties it encountered later in the eighteenth century. The Regency government instead first turned to creating a Chambre de justice to investigate the financiers, whom public opinion regarded as nothing short of criminals. The Regent then turned to John Law and his overly optimistic effort to expand the money supply to pay France's debts by introducing paper money backed by royal tax collections and speculation on the future profits of French colonial efforts in Louisiana and elsewhere. The whole experience resulted in a catastrophic collapse that left France with as much debt as it had had prior to the Law experiment. The government had suppressed the dixième in 1717 and, therefore, did not have the means to repay the debt according to Desmaretz's plan.

Desmaretz's ministry would cast a shadow over the rest of the eighteenth century because he had been able to impose a tax on wealth successfully, if only for a few years. Despite his unpopular public image in 1715, his reputation would improve during the course of the eighteenth century because he had successfully done what his successors would do with great difficulty. Although the dixième was suppressed in 1717, Old Regime governments continued to experiment with taxes on wealth for the rest of the eighteenth century. During the ministry of Controller General Philibert Orry, the dixième was recreated briefly during the War of the Polish Succession from 1733 until 1737, and then again during the War of the Austrian Succession from 1741 to 1749. Then, it was replaced with another tax on wealth called the vingtième (twentieth), which would remain in force until the French Revolution. The dixième and the other taxes on wealth devised in the eighteenth century undermined the very basis of the Old Regime because they ignored rank, family ties, and position by focusing solely on the income produced by property. On this issue alone, the dixième was a threat to the very foundations of the aristocratic society in which it appeared.

The seeds of the French Revolution were already at work, with a government seeking to tax everyone's wealth. All that remained was for the population to demand a voice in deciding who paid taxes and how the government spent the money. Along with his repayment plans, Desmaretz wanted to transfer the debts to the provinces and set up local committees to govern the repayment of the debts. These local committees would consist of members from the three estates: the clergy, the nobility, and the third estate. Even within the government of the most absolute of France's absolute monarchs, there were people like Desmaretz, Saint-Contest, and Millain, the chancellor's secretary, who believed that a representative group of some kind should decide some matters, in this case the repayment of loans. If the government had adopted this plan for settling the debts in some form, the politics of tax policy would have at least found a channel for discussion.

Jay Caplan, in his book *In the King's Wake*,[7] postulates that John Law's experiment undermined the foundations of French society by destroying the false hopes that the experiment had created. The foundations of the Old Regime had already been weakened before John Law began his experiment with tying the money supply to the stock market. The Law experiment came after an era of financial speculation brought on by the government's inability to pay its debts, as represented by the flood of royal paper in the money market. The entire debate over the role of taxation in supporting the war effort, and who should pay taxes and on what basis, had exposed the difference between social status and wealth, between privilege based on status and the ability to contribute materially to the state and its needs. The man who was most responsible for looking to wealth rather than privilege as the source of French financial strength was Nicolas Desmaretz.

Appendix 1

The Conseil d'en haut, or the Council of Ministers

On March 9, 1661, after the death of Cardinal Mazarin, Louis XIV called three men together to form what would become the Conseil d'en haut or Council of Ministers. These men, the ministers of state, would be his closest advisors. This council would discuss matters of important policy: diplomacy, war, peace, the Church, trade, and taxes.

For the rest of Louis XIV's reign, this council would meet two or three times a week, unless the king was traveling or ill. An oral invitation transmitted by one of the king's Swiss guards summoned people to join this council. Membership would fluctuate from a low of two men to a high of seven men. There were temporarily only two members of the Conseil d'en haut following the death of Hugues de Lionne on September 2, 1671, until his replacement could be recalled from Sweden; he arrived at court some time in January 1672. During the crisis years, from November 1708 to April 1711, the council had seven members. Usually, Louis expanded the membership when war was looming, and allowed the number of members to decline as peace returned.

During the years of Louis XIV's personal rule, from 1661 until his death on September 1, 1715, a total of nineteen men would be members of this council, including the king's son and two of his grandsons. Of the sixteen nonroyal members, three would be dismissed, but one of them would be recalled. Two others retired from the court voluntarily. Eight would die while they were members of the council, and four would still be sitting on the council at the king's death. His son and two grandsons all died while serving on it.

What follows is a list of the members of the Council of Ministers, with their dates of service, followed by a chronology of membership on the Council, with members listed according to seniority (i.e., with the most senior member first). Seniority was significant because the king usually asked for the opinion of the newest nonroyal members first.

List of Members of the Council of Ministers

1. Michel Le Tellier: March 9, 1661–October 30, 1685 (death)
2. Hugues de Lionne: March 9, 1661–September 2, 1671 (death)
3. Nicolas Foucquet: March 9, 1661–September 5, 1661 (arrest and dismissal)
4. Jean-Baptiste Colbert: September 6, 1661–September 6, 1683 (death)
5. Simon Arnauld de Pomponne: January 1672–November 18, 1679 (dismissal); July 21, 1691–September 27, 1699 (death)
6. François-Michel Le Tellier de Louvois: February 4, 1672–July 18, 1691 (death)
7. Charles Colbert de Croissy: November 18, 1679–July 28, 1696 (death)
8. Claude Le Peletier: September 6, 1683–September 18, 1697 (retirement)
9. Jean-Baptiste Colbert de Seignelay: October 4, 1689–November 6, 1690 (death)
10. Louis II de Phélypeaux de Pontchartrain: November 6, 1690–July 2, 1714 (retirement)
11. Louis de France, the Grand Dauphin: July 21, 1691–April 11, 1711 (death)
12. Paul de Saint-Aignan, duc de Beauvillier: July 21, 1691–August 31, 1714 (death)
13. Jean-Baptiste Colbert de Torcy: July 28, 1696–September 1, 1715 (end of the reign)
14. Michel Chamillard: November 23, 1700–June 9, 1709 (dismissal)
15. Louis de France, Duke of Burgundy: December 4, 1702–February 18, 1712 (death)
16. Nicolas Desmaretz: November 20, 1708–September 1, 1715 (end of the reign)
17. Daniel-François Voysin: June 9, 1709–September 1, 1715 (end of the reign)
18. Charles de France, duc de Berry: February 4, 1714–May 4, 1714 (death)
19. François de Neufville, maréchal-duc de Villeroy: September 2, 1714–September 1, 1715 (end of the reign)

Chronology of Members by Seniority

March 9, 1661	Le Tellier, Lionne, Foucquet
September 6, 1661	Le Tellier, Lionne, Colbert
September 2, 1671	Le Tellier, Colbert
January 1672	Le Tellier, Colbert, Pomponne
February 4, 1672	Le Tellier, Colbert, Pomponne, Louvois
November 18, 1679	Le Tellier, Colbert, Louvois, Croissy
September 6, 1683	Le Tellier, Louvois, Croissy, Le Peletier
October 31, 1685	Louvois, Croissy, Le Peletier
October 4, 1689	Louvois, Croissy, Le Peletier, Seignelay
November 6, 1690	Louvois, Croissy, Le Peletier, Pontchartrain
July 21, 1691	Croissy, Le Peletier, Pontchartrain, Dauphin, Pomponne, Beauvillier
July 28, 1696	Le Peletier, Pontchartrain, Dauphin, Pomponne, Beauvillier, Torcy
September 18, 1697	Pontchartrain, Dauphin, Pomponne, Beauvillier, Torcy
September 27, 1699	Pontchartrain, Dauphin, Beauvillier, Torcy
November 23, 1700	Pontchartrain, Dauphin, Beauvillier, Torcy, Chamillard
December 4, 1702	Pontchartrain, Dauphin, Beauvillier, Torcy, Chamillard, Burgundy
November 20, 1708	Pontchartrain, Dauphin, Beauvillier, Torcy, Chamillard, Burgundy, Desmaretz
June 9, 1709	Pontchartrain, Dauphin, Beauvillier, Torcy, Burgundy, Desmaretz, Voysin
April 11, 1711	Pontchartrain, Beauvillier, Torcy, Burgundy, Desmaretz, Voysin
February 12, 1712	Pontchartrain, Beauvillier, Torcy, Desmaretz, Voysin
February 4, 1714	Pontchartrain, Beauvillier, Torcy, Desmaretz, Voysin, Berry
May 4, 1714	Pontchartrain, Beauvillier, Torcy, Desmaretz, Voysin
July 2, 1714	Beauvillier, Torcy, Desmaretz, Voysin
September 2, 1714	Torcy, Desmaretz, Voysin, Villeroy

Appendix 2

Members of the Royal Council of Finances under Louis XIV

Chef du Conseil
Nicolas IV de Neufville, maréchal-duc de Villeroy (1661–85)
Paul de Saint-Aignan, duc de Beauvillier (1685–1714)
François de Neufville, maréchal-duc de Villeroy (1714–30)

Chancellor
Pierre Séguier (1633–72; may not have attended unless invited by the king)
Étienne III d'Aligre (1672–77; attended as keeper of the Seals until 1674, thereafter as chancellor)
Michel II Le Tellier (1677–85)
Louis Boucherat (1685–99)
Louis II Phélypeaux de Pontchartrain (1699–1714)
Daniel-François Voysin (1714–17)

Controller General of Finances
Jean-Baptiste Colbert (1661–83; intendant of finances until 1665)
Claude Le Peletier (1683–89; thereafter until he retired from the court in 1697)
Louis II Phélypeaux de Pontchartrain (1689–99)
Michel Chamillard (1699–1708)
Nicolas Desmaretz (1708–15)

Two Directors of Finances (1701–8)
1. Joseph-Jean-Baptiste Fleuriau d'Armenonville (1701–8)
2. Hilaire Rouillé du Coudray (1701–3)
   Nicolas Desmaretz (1703–8)

Two Councilors of State

1. Alexandre de Sève (1661–73)
   Pierre Poncet de la Rivière (1673–81)
   Louis Boucherat (1681–85)
   François d'Argouges de Ranes (1685–95)
   Henri Daguesseau (1695–1716)
2. Étienne III d'Aligre (1661–72)
   Henri Pussort (1672–97)
   Auguste-Robert de Pommereu (1697–1702)
   Michel Le Peletier de Souzy (1702–25)

Appendix 3

Controllers General, Directors, and Intendants of Finances

I

September 15, 1661–December 12, 1665

Controllers General of Finances
(offices suppressed December 12, 1665)
Barthelémy Hervart
Louis Le Tonnelier de Breteuil

Intendants of Finances
Jean-Baptiste Colbert
Denis Marin

II

December 12, 1665–September 6, 1683

Controller General of Finances
Jean-Baptiste Colbert (died September 6, 1683)

Intendants of Finances
Denis Marin (died June 25, 1678)
Vincent Hotman (died March 14, 1683)
Nicolas Desmaretz (appointed July 25, 1678)

III

September 7, 1683–September 20, 1689

Controller General of Finances
Claude Le Peletier (resigned September 20, 1689)

Intendants of Finances
Nicolas Desmaretz (resigned December 23, 1683)

Michel Le Peletier de Souzy (appointed January 7, 1684)
François Le Tonnelier de Breteuil (appointed January 7, 1684)
Louis II Phélypeaux de Pontchartrain (appointed April 25, 1687)

IV
September 20, 1689–September 2, 1699

Controller General of Finances
Louis II Phélypeaux de Pontchartrain (resigned September 2, 1699)

Intendants of Finances
Michel Le Peletier de Souzy
François Le Tonnelier de Breteuil
Nicolas Heudebert Dubuisson (appointed February 1690)
Louis-Urbain Lefèvre de Caumartin (appointed February 1690)
Michel Chamillard (appointed February 1690)
Joseph-Jean-Baptiste Fleuriau d'Armenonville (appointed February 1690)

V
September 2, 1699–February 20, 1708

Controller General of Finances
Michel Chamillard (resigned February 20, 1708)

Directors of Finances (created February 1701; suppressed February 1708)
Joseph-Jean-Baptiste Fleuriau d'Armenonville
Hilaire Rouillé du Coudray (resigned October 1703)
Nicolas Desmaretz (appointed October 22, 1703)

Intendants of Finances
Michel Le Peletier de Souzy (resigned December 23, 1700)
François Le Tonnelier de Breteuil (resigned June 1701)
Nicolas Heudebert Dubuisson
Louis-Urbain Lefèvre de Caumartin
Joseph-Jean-Baptiste Fleuriau d'Armenonville (resigned February 1701)
Armand-Roland Bignon de Blanzy (appointed September 21, 1699)
Michel-Robert Le Peletier des Forts (appointed December 27, 1700)
François Guyet (appointed August 31, 1704)
Alexandre Le Rebours (appointed August 31, 1704)

VI

February 20, 1708–September 15, 1715

Controller General of Finances
Nicolas Desmaretz (resigned September 15, 1715)

Intendants of Finances
Nicolas Heudebert Dubuisson (resigned July 16, 1714)
Louis-Urbain Lefèvre de Caumartin
Armand-Roland Bignon de Blanzy (resigned August 17, 1709)
Michel-Robert Le Peletier des Forts
François Guyet
Alexandre Le Rebours
Jacques Poulletier (appointed March 31, 1708; died April 2, 1711)
Charles Henri de Malon de Bercy (appointed August 17, 1709)
Pierre Poulletier de Nainville (appointed April 2, 1711)
Louis Fagon (appointed July 16, 1714)

Appendix 4

Glossary of Terms

Abonnement: Subscription. Some towns and provinces paid a fixed fee rather than having a tax such as the taille, capitation, or dixième administered by royal agents.

Aides: Excise or sales taxes.

Arrêt du conseil: A legal decision of the King's Council that was both sovereign and definitive on a point of law.

Arrêt en commandement: A decision made in the presence of the king.

Arrêt simple: A decision that did not require the king's physical presence.

Assignation: A payment assigned to a particular source of revenue; a promissory note issued by the government against future revenues.

Bailliage (or *sénéschaussée*): A royal court of the first instance, or a court of appeals for seigneurial courts. There were several hundred of these courts in France.

Billets des fermes (or *des receveurs généraux*): Promissory notes issued by tax farmers or receivers general as individuals.

Billets de monnaie: Promissory notes issued by the mints after 1701; mint bills.

Bourg: A small urban area lacking the walls necessary to make it a town, but recognized by the crown as larger than a village or parish.

Brevet de la taille: A royal letter indicating the amount of revenue expected from the impositions in a generality for the coming year.

Bureau des Finances: The court in each generality that heard cased involving the domain and the accounts of the local comptables.

Caisse: A fund managed independently by a comptable.

Caisse des emprunts: A special fund backed by certain revenues from the General Farms.

Capitation: A head tax established in 1695 and again in 1701 that taxed each person according to social status.

Chambre des comptes: A superior court that heard appeals from legal decisions of the Bureaus des Finances and judged the accounts of the crown's comptables.

Collecte: The duty to collect and be liable for the parish's imposition; every taillable was expected to perform this duty when his turn came.

Collecteur de la taille: The person in charge of collecting the impositions from a parish for payment to the taille receiver.

Commission de la taille: A royal letter fixing the expected revenue from the impositions in an election for the coming year.

Comptable: An officer charged with handling royal money.

Conseil d'en haut (also *Conseil des affaires*; *Conseil secret*; *Conseil des ministres*; sometimes called the *Conseil d'État*): An informal division of the King's Council consisting of his most trusted advisors on politics, foreign policy, and ecclesiastical affairs.

Conseil d'État privé (also *Conseil des parties* or *Conseil privé*; sometimes called *Conseil d'État*): A division of the King's Council that heard appeals of cases involving the crown's interests outside of finances.

Conseil d'État et des Finances (also *Conseil des finances ordinaires*): The division of the King's Council that heard appeals involving disputes over royal finances.

Conseil des Dépêches (Council of Dispatches): The division of the King's Council that handled interior administration of judicial, ecclesiastical, municipal, provincial affairs.

Conseil royal des finances (Royal Council of Finances): Division of the King's Council created in 1661 to administer royal finances, levy taxes, and decide on new financial policies.

Conseiller d'état: A member of the King's Council who had the right to sit on all councils except the Conseil d'en haut and the Conseil royal des finances. In 1673 the number of these officials was set at twenty-four ordinary and twelve semester (half-year) councilors.

Cour des Aides: A superior court that heard appeals on legal cases involving tax matters.

Cour des monnaies: A superior court that heard cases involving currency.

Debet des comptables: An unpaid debt owed by a comptable to the crown.

Declaration: A temporary law or an interpretation of an edict or an *ordonnance*.

Denier 20: An expression for the interest rate on a loan. In this case, the interest is equal to one-twentieth of the principal of the loan.

Dîme (*Dixme*): A tithe owed to the Church; a fixed share of the product of the land and livestock.

Dixième: A wealth tax established in 1710 on all income from property, regardless of the status of the person who owned the property.

Domaine royal: The king's property, including real property, seigneurial rights, and the law courts to administer them.

Don gratuit: A free gift to the crown given by the clergy and certain provinces in lieu of being taxed by royal agents.

Donneur d'avis: Someone proposing a method for increasing royal revenues.

Douane: See Traites.

Droit annuel (or simply *Annuel*): An annual tax paid to the crown by officeholders in order to maintain the right to pass their offices along to their heirs.

Écu: A royal coin, usually silver, with a value that varied with royal policy.

Edict: A permanent law on a single matter.

Élection: A district for financial administration within a generality with a court to judge tax matters and register the taille.

Élu: An officer in the court of an élection.

État au vray (*État au vrai*): The account of a comptable's receipts and expenses.

État de distribution: A list of ordonnances comptant of 1,000 livres or more that had to be signed by the controller general of finances and the king before presentation to the Royal Treasury, where the payments listed were to be made.

État du Roi: A legally binding table of receipts and expenses sent to a comptable.

Fermiers généraux (general farmers): Forty men who lent their credit to the crown in return for administering the General Farms and making payments on their lease.

Forfait: The total price of a traité or résultat before any rebates were granted.

Francfief: A fee owed by commoners who held noble land.

Gabelle: A tax on salt.

Gages: Salary paid to officeholders.

Generality: The administrative jurisdiction of a Bureau des Finances, administered by a provincial intendant.

Gens d'affaires: Tax farmers, traitants, financiers, and anyone involved in banking, commerce, and investment.

Grande Direction des Finances: Sometimes called the Conseil des finances, a subcommittee of the Conseil d'État et des Finances, in charge of administering finances until 1661, when it became a court of appeals for lesser cases not worthy of appearing before the whole Conseil.

Greffier: A clerk.

Homme de paille (straw man): The adjudicataire général of a tax farm or traité who was required to sign all documents in the name of the company but was usually not a major investor.

Impositions: Taxes imposed on people; often mistakenly called direct taxes.

Intendant: An all-purpose title given to officials with administrative responsibilities. There were household intendants, army or navy intendants, provincial intendants, and intendants of finances or commerce.

Livre: The monetary denomination used to fix the value of coins. Each livre had 20 sous (sol, in the singular), and each sol had 12 deniers.

Louis (*Louis d'or*): A coin, usually gold, with a value that varied with royal policy.

Maître des requêtes de l'hôtel du palais du Roi: "Masters of requests" charged with handling the requests or complaints received by the king.

Mandement de la taille: A royal letter fixing the revenue expected from the impositions from a parish for the coming year.

Octrois: Excise or sales taxes collected by a town or province.

Ordonnance: A permanent law on several matters.

Ordonnance comptant: An order for a treasurer to pay money to someone. It had to be listed on an état de distribution before it could be paid.

Ordonnance du petit comptant: An état de distribution of sorts that listed ordonnances comptants of less than 1,000 livres. It required only the signature of the controller general of finances.

Pain de munition: Daily rations for the troops.

Parish: The smallest administrative unit in the realm.

Parlement: A superior court of last resort for the king's justice, with administrative responsibilities as well.

Parties casuelles (*revenus casuels*): A special category of revenue with its own treasurer, who was in charge of selling venal offices when their holders died without paying the *droit annuel*, or died fewer than forty days after resigning. It also received the *droit annuel*.

Partisan: Another name for a traitant.

Paulette: A popular name for the *droit annuel*; from the originator of this tax, Paulet.

Pays conquis: The provinces most recently added to France: Flanders, Hainaut, Artois, and the three bishoprics of Alsace, Franche Comté, and Roussillon. Their rights were different from those of other French provinces.

Pays d'élections: The nineteen generalities where impositions were under the nominal control of the élections.

Pays d'états: The provinces where estates governed the levying and collection of impositions: Provence, Languedoc, Brittany, Burgundy, and Béarn.

Péages: Private seigneurial tolls, some of which were part of the royal domain.

Petite Direction des Finances: A subcommittee of the Royal Council of Finances created in 1661, excluding the chancellor but including the intendants of finances, and charged with administering the crown's ordinary revenues.

Plaçets (*et requêtes*): Pleas and appeals made to the king and received at court.

Ponts et chaussées: The royal administration of highways and bridges.

Postes: The post office, which was a tax farm in private hands.

Presidial: A special appeals court between the bailliage and Parlement.

Prévoté: A low-level court that heard civil cases.

Rapporteur: The member of the King's Council who presented business for discussion.

Receiver general of finances: A financier who held the office in charge of receiving the funds from a generality's impositions.

Régie: A government administrative body responsible to the Royal Council of Finances, not the *Chambre des comptes*.

Remise en dedans: A rebate (usually not more than one-sixth of the forfait) granted to a company of traitants and subtracted from the forfait.

Remise en dehors: A rebate granted to a company of traitants equal to one-tenth of the forfait collected from the purchaser of an office, etc. It was a surcharge on the price of the office, etc.

Rente: The interest payment on a loan in the form of an annuity.

Résultat du conseil: A traité or agreement, approved in council, that set forth the terms of a contract between the crown and a company of financiers.

Secrétaire du Conseil et Direction des finances (or *Secrétaire des finances*): One of four officers who served quarterly on the councils of finances and kept their records. These men were usually financiers who did business with the government.

Secrétaire du Roi: An office involving minor duties that ennobled the purchaser. Often referred to as "the soap for washing off commoners," holders of this office were automatically ennobled and, if they owned the office for at least twenty years, their nobility became permanent and they could sell the office. Thereafter, they and their descendants were ennobled.

Sol pour livre: A surtax on an existing tax, in this case a 5 percent increase.

Subdelegate: A subordinate of the provincial intendant; established locally to gather information and report on matters to the provincial intendant.

Syndic: The administrator who acted in the name of a community, such as a parish. These positions became venal in 1702.

Taillable: A person liable for the payment of the taille and other impositions, as well as its collection.

Taille: A direct tax levied on all unprivileged people based upon their estimated income in the *pays de taille personnelle* or the value of their nonnoble property in the *pays de taille réelle*.

Taille receiver (*receveur particulier de la taille*): A financier who owned the right to receive the revenues from an élection's impositions.

Taillon: A supplement to the taille for certain military units.

Taxe d'office: A special taille levied by the provincial intendant that was designed to prevent influential people from escaping payment of their share of the taille.

Traitant: A financier who signed a traité promising to pay certain sums to the crown in return for being given certain offices or other things to sell.

Traité: A résultat.

Traites: Tariff barriers between provinces or at the frontiers of the realm.

Trésorier de France: An officer in a Bureau des Finances.

Ustencile: Special payments to the troops during winter quarters that were levied in addition to the taille.

Vivres et étapes: Army supplies both during a campaign and at stages during the march to the front.

NOTES

Introduction

1. David D. Bien, "Officers, Corps, and a System of State Credit: The Uses of Privilege under the Ancien Régime," in *The French Revolution and the Creation of Modern Political Culture*, vol. 1, *The Political Culture of the Old Order*, ed. Keith Michael Baker (Oxford: Pergamon, 1987), 89–114; Gail Bossenga, *The Politics of Privilege: Old Regime and Revolution in Lille* (Cambridge: Cambridge University Press, 1991); and Michael Kwass, *Privilege and the Politics of Taxation in Eighteenth-Century France* (Cambridge: Cambridge University Press, 2000).

2. Daniel Dessert, *Argent, Pouvoir et Société au Grand Siècle* (Paris: Fayard, 1984); James B. Collins, *The Fiscal Limits of Absolutism: Direct Taxation in Early Seventeenth-Century France* (Berkeley: University of California Press, 1988), and *Classes, Estates, and Order in Early Modern Brittany* (Cambridge: Cambridge University Press, 1994); William Beik, *Absolutism and Society in Seventeenth-Century France: State Power and Provincial Aristocracy in Languedoc* (Cambridge: Cambridge University Press, 1995); Mark Potter, *Corps and Clienteles: Public Finances and Political Change in France, 1688–1715* (Aldershot, UK: Ashgate, 2003); and Darryl Dee, *Expansion and Crisis in Louis XIV's France: Franche-Comté and Absolute Monarchy, 1674–1715* (Rochester: University of Rochester Press, 2009).

3. Stanislas Mitard, *La crise financière en France à la fin du XVIIe siècle: La première capitation (1695–1698)* (Rennes: Imprimerie Oberthur, 1934); Alain Guéry, "État, classification sociale et compromis sous Louis XIV: La capitation de 1695," *Annales ESC* 41 (September–October 1986): 1041–60; François Bluche and Jean-François Solnon, *La véritable hiérarchie sociale de l'ancienne France: Le tarif de la première capitation (1695)* (Geneva: Droz, 1983); Michel Vergé-Franceschi, *La société française au XVIIe siècle* (Paris: Fayard, 2006).

4. William Beik, *A Social and Cultural History of Early Modern France* (Cambridge: Cambridge University Press, 2009), 20, cites Goubert on the Beauvaisis and Emmanuel Le Roy Ladurie on Languedoc, showing that more than 80 percent of the peasants in both locations did not own enough land to survive unless they worked for some other landowner. In 1675, 76 percent of the peasants in Coudray owned fewer than two hectares of land. In 1675 in Le Bosc, 66 percent of the peasants owned land worth less than 1.5 livres.

5. Marcel Lachiver, *Les Années de misère: La famine au temps du Grand Roi* (Paris: Fayard, 1991), discusses the evidence available for the seriousness of the weather problems and concludes that the winter of 1693–94 was worse than that of 1709. W. Gregory Monahan, *Year of Sorrows: The Great Famine of 1709 in Lyon* (Columbus: Ohio State University Press, 1993), relates the administrative, social, and fiscal problems caused by the famine in Lyon. Jean Nicolas, *La Rébellion française: Mouvements*

populaires et conscience sociale, 1661–1789 (Paris: Éditions du Seuil, 2002), 235, counted 193 riots or disturbances caused by the lack of food between February and September 1709.

6. Frank C. Spooner, *The International Economy and Monetary Movements in France, 1493–1725* (Cambridge, MA: Harvard University Press, 1972), 184 and 202. A marc of silver consisted of 288 grains or 250 grams of silver, according to the Système Usuel. See Ronald Edward Zupko, *French Weights and Measures before the Revolution: A Dictionary of Provincial and Local Units* (Bloomington: Indiana University Press, 1978), 103.

7. Herbert Lüthy, *La Banque Protestante en France, de la Révocation de l'Édit de Nantes à la Révolution* (Paris: SEVPEN, 1959), 1:96.

8. Pierre Goubert, *Beauvais et le Beauvaisis de 1600 à 1730: Contribution à l'histoire sociale de la France du XVIIe siècle* (Paris: SEVPEN, 1960), 1:76–77.

9. Philip T. Hoffman, Gilles Postel-Vinay, and Jean-Laurent Rosenthal, *Priceless Markets: The Political Economy of Credit in Paris, 1660–1870* (Chicago: University of Chicago Press, 2000).

10. John A. Lynn, "Recalculating French Army Growth during the *Grand Siècle*, 1610–1715," *French Historical Studies* 18 (1994): 881–906.

11. A fire destroyed the official records of the royal treasury in 1737. The general trend of revenue and expenses for the royal government can be found in some sources. See Jean-Roland Mallet (*sic*), *Comptes rendus de l'administration des finances du royaume de France* (Paris: Chez Buisson, 1789), 112–13. See also B.N. mss. fr. 7752, pp. 222–23. The latter is a manuscript copy of Malet's book, entitled *Mémoires sur l'histoire des finances . . .* , and François Véron Duverger de Forbonnais, *Récherches et considérations sur les finances de France depuis 1595 jusqu'en 1721* (Liège, 1758). A.N. KK 355 is an account book for the years 1661–98; according to notes, it was bound in 1712 by Pontchartrain, who appears to be the chancellor rather than his son, the secretary of state for the navy and the maison du roi. Alain Guéry, "Les finances de la monarchie française sous l'Ancien Régime," *Annales ESC* 33 (March–April 1978): 216–39, has estimates for the entire seventeenth and eighteenth centuries. In any case, Louis XIV's last controller general of finances, Nicolas Desmaretz, is the only source we have for royal income and expenses for the years of his ministry, 1708–15. Forbonnais uses his figures, while neither Malet nor KK 355 cover that period.

12. See the following works by John C. Rule: "Colbert de Torcy, an Emergent Bureaucracy, and the Formation of French Foreign Policy, 1698–1715," in *Louis XIV and Europe*, ed. Ragnhild Hatton (Columbus: Ohio State University Press, 1976), 261–88; "Gathering Intelligence in the Age of Louis XIV," *International History Review* 14 (November 1992): 732–52; "King and Minister: Louis XIV and Colbert de Torcy," in *William III and Louis XIV: Essays 1680–1720, by and for Mark A. Thomson*, ed. Ragnhild Hatton and J. S. Bromley (Toronto: Toronto University Press, 1968), 213–36; "The Administrative History of the Reign," in *The Reign of Louis XIV: Essays in Celebration of Andrew Lossky*, ed. Paul Sonnino (Atlantic Highlands, NJ: Humanities Press International, 1990), 95–110; and "Louis XIV, Roi-Bureaucrate," in *Louis XIV and the Craft of Kingship*, ed. John C. Rule (Columbus: Ohio State University Press, 1969), 3–102.

13. John C. Rule, "Royal Ministers and Government Reform during the Last Decades of Louis XIV's Reign," in *The Consortium of Revolutionary History*, ed. Claude C. Sturgill (Gainesville: University Presses of Florida, 1973), 1–35.

14. James B. Collins, *The State in Early Modern France* (Cambridge: Cambridge University Press, 2009), 191–238.

15. François R. Velde, "Government Equity and Money: John Law's System in 1720 France," May 14, 2004, http://www.heraldica.org/econ/law.pdf, argues, however, that Law's experiment did not reduce France's debt at all (pp. 8–10). In June 1717, before Law's experiment had really taken flight, France owed a total of 2,322 million livres, counting rentes, offices, royal IOUs, and interest, and in October 1724, after the Law experiment had ceased, France owed a total of 2,542 million livres.

16. For example, the preeminent English-language biography of Louis XIV, John B. Wolf's *Louis XIV* (New York: Norton, 1968), fails to mention either Louis XIV's last finance minister or any of the fiscal innovations during the last twenty-five years of the reign, even though the king played a role in the adoption of these measures as well as the selection of his ministers.

17. Pierre Goubert, *Louis XIV et vingt millions de Français* (1966; repr., Paris: Fayard, 1976), 348–49, can be found in *Louis XIV and Twenty Million Frenchmen*, trans. Anne Carter (New York: Pantheon, 1970), 300–301.

18. François Bluche, *Louis XIV* (Paris: Fayard, 1986), 777–78, can be found in the English translation *Louis XIV*, trans. Mark Greengrass (New York: Franklin Watts, 1990), 525–26.

19. A copy of Desmaretz's *Compte rendu de M. Desmaretz au Régent* can be found in *Correspondance des contrôleurs généraux des finances avec les intendants des provinces (1683–1715)*, ed. A.-M. de Boislisle and P. de Brotonne (Paris: Imprimerie Nationale, 1874–98), 3:673–82 (hereafter cited as Boislisle, *Correspondance des contrôleurs généraux*). Several manuscript versions are in A.N. G^7 1903. According to Jean Buvat, *Journal de la Régence (1715–23)*, ed. E. Compardom (Paris: Plon, 1865), 1:162, the presentation to the Regent was made in August 1716.

20. Printed copies of Desmaretz's *Mémoires de M. Desmaretz sur l'administration des finances depuis le 20 février de l'année 1708 jusqu'au 1er septembre 1715* can be found in the Bibliothèque Nationale and other European libraries, although it was reprinted in 1789. The B.N. copy bears a publication date of 1716. In addition, the B.N. carries a book entitled *Réponses et réflexions sur le compte que M. Desmaretz a présenté à S.A.R. Mgr. le Duc d'Orléans, Régent du Royaume*, published in 1717.

21. See Buvat, *Journal*, 1:95–96, 129–30, and 137, on accusations against Desmaretz and his appearance before the Chambre de justice.

22. Mallet [*sic*], *Comptes rendus*, 112–13. See also, B.N. mss. fr. 7752, *Mémoires sur l'histoire des finances*, 222–23. Malet's book has been reprinted with commentary: Margaret Bonney and Richard Bonney, *Jean-Roland Malet, premier historien des finances de la monarchie française* (Paris: Comité pour l'histoire économique et financière de la France, 1993), a major part of which was published in Richard Bonney's article "Jean-Roland Malet: Historian of the Finances of the French Monarchy," *French History* 5 (June 1991): 180–233.

23. The better-known examples of such works are Forbonnais, *Récherches et considérations*, 4:314ff., and 5:12ff.; and Antoine Jean-Baptiste Robert Auget de Montyon,

Particularités et observations sur les ministres des finances de France les plus célèbres, depuis 1661 jusqu'en 1791 (Paris: Le Normant, 1812), 80–85. Both works followed Malet's argument that the men who succeeded Colbert were lesser men, except Desmaretz, whom Malet considered his uncle's equal in managing finances.

24. Adolphe Vuitry, *Le désordre des finances et les excès de la spéculation à la fin du règne de Louis XIV et au début du règne de Louis XV* (Paris, 1885). I do not mean to slight the historical work of authors such as J.-J. Clamageran, *Histoire de l'impôt en France* (Paris: Librairie de Guillaumin, 1867–76), and Marcel Marion, *Histoire financière de France depuis 1715* (Paris: Rousseau, 1914–28), but they either relied extensively on published sources or, as in Marion's case, began their histories after the reign of Louis XIV.

25. René Dumas, *La politique financière de Nicolas Desmaretz, contrôleur général des finances (1708–1715)* (Issoudun: Imprimerie du Centre, 1927).

26. A. M. de Boislisle, "Avant-Propos," in *Correspondance des contrôleurs généraux*, 1:xvii–xxi. As an archivist, Boislisle was charged in the 1860s with transferring the documents in this series from the Bibliothèque Nationale, where they had resided since the Revolution, to the Archives Nationales.

27. Joël Félix, "Nicolas Desmaretz," in *Dictionnaire des surintendants et des contrôleurs généraux des finances du XVIe siècle à la Révolution française de 1789*, ed. Françoise Bayard, Joël Félix, and Philippe Hamon (Paris: Comité pour l'histoire économique et financière de la France, 2000), 108–12.

28. Thomas J. Schaeper, *The Economy of France in the Second Half of the Reign of Louis XIV* (Montreal: Interuniversity Center for European Studies, 1980), raises the question of how France was able to recover and prosper so quickly after the reign of Louis XIV, if it had been so impoverished.

29. See Mitard, *Première capitation*; Guéry, "Capitation de 1695"; and Bluche and Solnon, *Véritable hiérarchie sociale*.

30. See Thierry Sarmant and Mathieu Stoll, *Régner et gouverner: Louis XIV et ses ministres* (Paris: Perrin, 2010), especially 245–84. Luc-Normand Tellier, *Face aux Colbert: Les Le Tellier, Vauban, Turgot . . . et l'avènement de libéralisme* (Québec: Presses de l'Université de Québec, 1987), tries to argue that there were significant policy differences between the Le Tellier and Colbert clans.

31. Stéphane Guerre, "Nicolas Desmaretz et la prise de décision au conseil du roi," *Revue historique* 659 (September 2011): 596–97.

32. *Dictionnaire du Grand Siècle*, ed. François Bluche (Paris: Fayard, 1990), 857–58, article by Abel Poitrineau; *Mémoires de Saint-Simon*, ed. A.-M. de Boislisle, with the assistance of J. de Boislisle and J. Lecestre (Paris: Hachette, 1879–1928), 3:142n4 (hereafter cited as Boislisle, *Saint-Simon*). Further biographic information on Le Peletier can be found in Geneviève Mazel, *Claude Le Peletier (1631–1711): Le successeur de Colbert* (Paris: Éditions de la Marquise, 2003), and Françoise Bayard's short study of Le Peletier in *Dictionnaire des surintendants*, 95–98. I have not been able to consult Mathieu Stoll's thesis on Le Peletier, "Pouvoir et administration au Grand Siècle: Claude Le Peletier, ministre et contrôleur général des finances de Louis XIV" (defended in January 2008, École des Chartes), but I was able to read its *position de thèse* at http://www.books.google.com/books after searching for "Mathieu Stoll."

33. See Boislisle, *Saint-Simon*, 4:265n5.

34. *Dictionnaire du Grand Siècle,* 1223–25, article by Etienne Taillemite; Françoise Bayard's short study of Pontchartrain in *Dictionnaire des surintendants,* 98–101; Boislisle, *Saint-Simon,* 1:52, 6:268–92, and appendix 15, entitled "Pontchartrain d'après ses contemporains" (6:565–75); Jean-Luc A. Chartier, *De Colbert à l'Encyclopédie,* vol. 1, *Henri Daguesseau, conseiller d'état 1635–1716* (Montpellier: Presses du Languedoc, 1988), 284. The work and life of Louis de Pontchartrain remain to be evaluated in their entirety, since the task would involve law, the navy, culture, and finances. Two recent works focus on Pontchartrain's patron-client networks: Sara A. Chapman, *Private Ambition and Political Alliances: The Phélypeaux de Pontchartrain Family and Louis XIV's Government, 1650–1715* (Rochester: University of Rochester Press, 2004), and Charles Frostin, *Les Pontchartrain ministres de Louis XIV: Alliances et réseau d'influence sous l'Ancien Régime* (Rennes: Presses Universitaire de Rennes, 2006).

35. *Dictionnaire du Grand Siècle,* 293–94, article by Louis Trénard; Boislisle, *Saint-Simon,* 6:292–306. See *Mémoires du marquis de Sourches sur le règne de Louis XIV,* ed. Gabriel-Jules de Cosnac and Édouard Pontal (Paris: Hachette, 1882–93), 3:13n3 (for Chamillard's reluctance to leave court in 1689) and 11:26 (for Chamillard's statement to Desmaretz when the latter took over as controller general) (hereafter cited as *Sourches*). A short biography of Chamillard was written by Françoise Bayard in *Dictionnaire des surintendants,* 102–5; Emmanuel Pénicaut, *Faveur et pouvoir au tournant du Grand Siècle: Michel Chamillart, Ministre et secrétaire d'État de la guerre de Louis XIV* (Paris: École des Chartes, 2004), studies the war minister, not the finance minister, as does his biographical essay in *Les Ministres de la Guerre, 1570–1792,* ed. Thierry Sarmant (Paris: Belin, 2007), 297–307.

36. Thierry Sarmant, "Les pratiques gouvernementales de l'ancien au nouveau Régime: une enquête dans l'histoire de l'État," in Sarmant, *Ministres de la Guerre,* 29–42.

Chapter 1

1. The following discussion comes from George T. Matthews, *The Royal General Farms in Eighteenth-Century France* (New York: Columbia University Press, 1958), 4–19.

2. Ibid., 19–22.

3. Ibid., 34–53, 69–76.

4. There are several arrêts that relate the same information: A.N. $E790^B$, March 20, 1708, no. 2, fol. 5–7; E 810^B–11^A, December 3, 1709, no. 10, fol. 190–93; E 820^B, September 16, 1710, no. 50, fol. 159–60, and September 23, 1710, nos. 4–5, fol. 196–201.

5. Dessert, *Argent, pouvoir et société,* 59.

6. Matthews, *Royal General Farms,* 46–53.

7. Matthews, *Royal General Farms,* 51; and Le Peletier to Desmaretz, February 28, 1686, in Boislisle, *Correspondance des contrôleurs généraux,* 1:62, no. 242.

8. Matthews, *Royal General Farms,* 53–55.

9. A.N. R^4 825.

10. Matthews, *Royal General Farms*, 55–58.

11. A.N. O[1] 49, fol. 174[v] lists this declaration among those for the year. It was still in effect in 1712, when it was renewed for 1713 by arrêt in A.N. E 1965, fol. 415, September 6, 1712.

12. A.N. E 1948, fol. 203, August 8, 1709. The gabelles had produced 17,764,655 livres per year; the aides and traites 15,381,344 livres; and the domain 3.92 million livres.

13. A.N. E 1948, fol. 194–202, September 17, 1709. The régie was renewed annually: A.N. E 1953, fol. 194–95, August 19, 1710; A.N. E 1960, fol. 171–72, August 25, 1711; A.N. G[7] 1498 September 6, 1712; A.N. E 1971, fol. 331–32, August 29, 1713. Each arrêt extended the régie for the following year.

14. A.N. E 1976, fol. 35–43, September 15, 1714.

15. A.N. E 876[B], fol. 468–71, June 25, 1715.

16. A.N. G[7] 1142, a copy of the lease, October 5, 1715.

17. Matthews, *Royal General Farms*, 53.

18. Arsenal, mss. 4489, fol. 42–80.

19. Marcel Marion, *Les Impôts directs sous l'Ancien Régime, principalement au XVIIIe siècle* (Paris: Edouard Cornély, 1910), 3.

20. Collins, *State*, 203–4. See Dee, *Expansion and Crisis*, 167 on how the local elites in Franche-Comté borrowed money to pay military salaries that were in arrears in order to avoid violence by the local garrison.

21. Anette Smedley-Weill, *Les intendants de Louis XIV* (Paris: Fayard, 1995), 159–61.

22. The generalities of the pays d'*élections* at the end of Louis XIV's reign were: Paris, Amiens, Soissons, Châlons (Champagne), Orléans, Rouen, Alençon, Caen, Tours, Poitiers, La Rochelle, Bordeaux (Guyenne), Montauban, Moulins, Bourges, Riom, Limoges, Lyon, and Grenoble (Dauphiné). Montauban and Grenoble were part of the pays de taille réelle as well.

23. Marion, *Impôts directs sous l'Ancien Régime*, 4–5.

24. Ibid., and Georges Pagès, "Essai sur l'évolution des institutions administratives en France du commencement du XVIe siècle à la fin de XVIIe," *Revue d'histoire moderne* 7 (1932): 8–57, 113–17. Recent research has somewhat modified this position by citing the reliance of the intendant on local assistants called subdelegates who did have local ties. See Smedley-Weill, *Intendants de Louis XIV*, 157ff. In addition, the intendant was checked to some extent by the ties of clientage between local notables and court nobles or officials. See Sharon Kettering, *Patrons, Brokers, and Clients in Seventeenth-Century France* (New York: Oxford University Press, 1986).

25. Jean Villain, *Le recouvrement des impôts directs sous l'Ancien Régime* (Paris: Riviere, 1952), 8–14.

26. See various articles in *L'impôt des campagnes: Fragile fondement de l'État dit moderne (XVe–XVIIIe siècle)*, ed. Antoine Follain and Gilbert Larguier (Paris: Comité pour l'histoire économique et financière de la France, 2005), particularly the articles by Marie-Laure Legay on the *pays bas française*, Pierre Charbonnier on Auvergne, Françoise Bayard on the Lyonnais and Beaujolais, Francis Brumont on Armagnac, Alain Blanchard on the Soissonnais, and Brigitte Maillard on the pays d'élections.

27. Villain, *Recouvrement des impôts*, 159–61; Marion, *Impôts directs sous l'Ancien Régime*, 6–7.

28. Matthews, *Royal General Farms,* 27–30.

29. Dessert, *Argent, pouvoir et société,* 675, no. 452. Prondre began as a lawyer but became interested in the farms and army supply, and invested in seventy-nine traités between 1688 and 1704. He was receiver general of finances for Lyon from 1688 to 1711, when he became a judge on the Chambre des Comptes of Paris. He was one of the most heavily taxed financiers by the Chambre de justice of 1716–17, at 1.9 million livres.

30. Thierry Claeys, *Dictionnaire biographique des financiers en France an XVIIIe siècle* (Paris: SPM, 2009), 2:925–26. Rousseau served as a Secrétaire du Roi from 1695 to 1719, treasurer receiver general and payer of rentes from 1702 until 1736, and was one of the farmers of the *contrôle* of notarial acts from 1708 to 1711, as well as in the local farm of said acts in Lyon from 1710 to 1719. The Chambre de justice of 1716–17 taxed him, as an investor in royal finances, to pay 100,000 livres.

31. A.N. G^7 1498.

32. Matthews, *Royal General Farms,* 30–33.

33. The accounts in Boislisle, *Correspondance des contrôleurs généraux,* 2:583–604, for the years 1706 and 1707 record the receipts of this tax increase. The royal tax farms had a similar surtax added that same year. A declaration of August 19, 1705, increased everyone's capitation by the same 10 percent (A.N. O^1 49, fol. 179v). Marion reports the continuation of this tax in 1764 (*Impôts directs sous l'Ancien Régime,* 2–3n1, 52).

34. Armand Seligmann, *La première tentative d'émission fiduciaire en France: Étude sur les billets de monnaies de trésor royal à la fin du règne de Louis XIV (1701–1718)* (Paris: Presses Universitaires des France, 1925), 94.

35. Albert Cans, *La contribution du clergé de France à l'impôt pendant la seconde moitié du règne de Louis XIV (1689–1715)* (Paris: Picard, 1910), 96.

36. A.N. K 355.

37. A.N. KK 355. Mallet (*sic*), *Comptes rendus,* reports no records after 1695.

38. Spooner, *International Economy,* 199; A.N. R^4 825 shows the reforms of 1689, 1693, 1701, and 1704 producing less money in terms of 1715 currency. The amount coined declined from almost 1 billion livres to less than 200 million livres.

39. Seligmann, *Première tentative,* 69–86. Desmaretz, *Compte rendu,* in Boislisle, *Correspondance des contrôleurs généraux,* 3:673, reports the amount of paper money in trade.

40. Julian Dent, *Crisis in Finance: Crown, Financiers, and Society in Seventeenth-Century France* (New York: St. Martin's, 1973), 46–49.

41. A.N. O^1 38, fol. 318–20, edict of December 1694; O^1 39, fol. 88–90, edict of April 1695, and fol. 314–16, edict of October 1695; O^1 40, fol. 237–39, edict of June 1696; O^1 41, fol. 255, edict of May 1697. Lifetime rentes sold between denier 14 and denier 7 (7.1 percent and 14.2 percent). Rentes against the poste sold at denier 12 (8.3 percent) in March 1696 (A.N. O^1 40, fol. 126–29). Altogether, the government borrowed 93.2 million livres at either 7.1 percent or 8.3 percent. The legal limit was 5.5 percent. The rentes cost 6.8 million livres in annual dividends, to be subtracted from the revenues against which they were charged. Reducing them to the legal limit would only save the government 1.6 million livres annually.

42. A.N. O[1] 41, fol. 255ff., lists all edicts and declarations made in the year 1697. According to two edicts, rentes began selling at denier 18 in December, creating three million livres' worth. A.N. O[1] 42, fol. 332, edict of February 1698, created 2 million livres in rentes, but, according to fol. 332–33, two edicts in March–April 1698 created another 2 million livres in rentes at denier 20 (5.0 percent).

43. A.N. K 886, no. 5.

44. Martin Wolfe, *The Fiscal System of Renaissance France* (New Haven, CT: Yale University Press, 1972), 102.

45. Dent, *Crisis in Finance*, 54–58.

46. Examples of these kinds of machinations: A.N. E 789[B], no. 1, February 28, 1708, reunites the office of alternate lieutenant to the mayor of the town of Nemours to the already-existing office of lieutenant to the mayor in return for 1,500 livres plus two sous per livre; A.N. E 874[A], fol. 124–26, no. 2, April 6, 1715, suppresses the offices of commissaires of the reviews in the generality of Montauban in return for 20,000 livres to be paid by the taillables in 1716.

47. A.N. G[7] 1495 to 1498. These cartons contain copies of traités for the years 1685 to 1714. (Traités were legal agreements between crown and financiers, while traites were taxes collected by the General Farms at the boundaries of certain provinces.)

48. Dessert, *Argent, pouvoir et société*, 74–75.

49. Ibid., 63, defines the boundary as anywhere between 16.6 percent and 24.5 percent, but he is referring to the percentage of the total price of the goods to be sold. If the financiers only had to contribute five-sixths of the total prices of the goods created, then the one-sixth of the total they kept is equal to one-fifth (or 20 percent) of what they actually paid. In addition, the *remise en dehors* of two sous per livre (or one-tenth) is again a measure of the total price and not the actual payment by the traitants. This is potential profit rather than actual profit. The potential profit would only be realized if the offices sold quickly at little or no cost to the traitants, if the holders of other offices who might be affected by the new creations did not go to court to halt the sale of the new offices, and if the royal government did not make separate deals with the holders of affected offices, cutting the potential profit.

50. Desmaretz detested the necessity of doing this, as he related to Pontchartrain's son, the secretary of state of the navy and the maison du roi, in a letter dated November 10, 1708 (A.N. G[7] 13[B], fol. 134).

51. B.N. mss. fr. 7734, fol. 56.

52. Desmaretz, *Compte rendu*, in Boislisle, *Correspondance des contrôleurs généraux*, 3:676. A.N. E 856[B], fol. 104–5, no. 10, October 21, 1713, and A.N. E 1964, fol. 20, April 2, 1712, reduced the expenses that a purchaser of an office would pay in order to expedite sales. Preambles in both arrêts indicate that a large number of offices remained unsold in 1711, 1712, and 1713.

53. A.A.E., Mém. et Doc., France, 1023, fol. 80–85.

54. Mitard, *Crise financière*, 57–60.

55. Boislisle, *Correspondance des contrôleurs généraux*, 1:343–44, no. 1252. See Chapman, *Private Ambition*, 82–83.

56. Guéry, "Capitation de 1695," 1046.

57. Ibid., 1050.

58. The Duke of Saint-Simon accused the intendant of Languedoc, Nicolas Lamoignon de Basville, of inventing the capitation and later the dixième. Boislisle, *Saint-Simon,* 2:223, 6:287, 8:246–47, and 11:81. There is no documentary evidence to support this claim. Basville tended to oppose fiscal innovations.

59. Bluche, *Dictionnaire du Grand Siècle,* 294, article by Bluche; Mitard, *Crise financière,* 40–51.

60. Guerre, A[1] 2469, no. 53, undated, entitled "Réflexions sur la capitation."

61. Guerre, A[1] 2469, no. 2, entitled "Moyens de recouvrir promptement de l'argent."

62. Guerre, A[1] 2469, no. 54.

63. Guéry, "Capitation de 1695," 1041–60; Richard Bonney, "La concurrence étatique pour les ressources et l'innovation fiscale sous Louis XIV," in *État, Marine et Sociéte: Hommage à Jean Meyer,* ed. Martine Acerra, Jean-Pierre Poussou, Michel Vergé-Franceschi, and André Zysberg (Paris: Presses de l'Université de Paris-Sorbonne, 1995), 35–48. Vauban's "Projet de capitation" can be found in Boislisle, *Correspondance des contrôleurs généraux,* 1:561–65, or in *Les oisivetés de Monsieur de Vauban,* ed. Michèle Virol (Seyssel: Champ Vallon, 2007), 283–99, preceded by an essay by Michel Nassiet on the origin of Vauban's project (279–82).

64. Mitard, *Crise financière,* 61–62.

65. Guéry, "Capitation de 1695," 1046.

66. Mitard, *Crise financière,* 61–70; *Journal du marquis de Dangeau,* ed. Eud. Soulié and L. Dussieux (Paris: Firmin Didot, 1854–60), 6:105, 106, and 110 (November 13, 16, and 23, 1694, respectively) (hereafter cited as *Dangeau*).

67. *Dangeau,* 5:121, 134, and 136 (December 15, 1694, and January 11 and 15, 1695).

68. Marion, *Impôts directs sous l'Ancien Régime,* 50–51.

69. Mitard, *Crise financière,* 21–23, 74–78, 161–67. Mitard studied the capitation as a tax law. Bluche and Solnon, *Véritable hiérarchie sociale,* studied the capitation to see how society viewed itself, or at least how government officials saw their society.

70. The text of the declaration of the capitation can be found in Boislisle, *Correspondance des contrôleurs généraux,* 1:565–74.

71. The text of the declaration of March 12, 1701, can be found in ibid., 2:504–8. Unlike the declaration of 1695, the new declaration had twenty-eight articles describing how assessments and payments were to be made.

72. Kwass, *Privilege and Politics of Taxation,* 126n21.

73. Marion, *Impôts directs sous l'Ancien Régime,* 52.

74. Boislisle, *Correspondance des contrôleurs généraux,* 2:594, 599.

75. Ibid., 3:673–74.

76. See Bluche and Solnon, *Véritable hiérarchie sociale,* 99–114, for a list of all the professions and groups mentioned.

77. Dessert, *Argent, pouvoir et société,* 78–81.

78. A.A.E., Mém. et Doc., France, 137, fol. 34–41, can be found in Boislisle, *Correspondance des contrôleurs généraux,* 3:684–87. See J. F. Bosher, "'Chambre de justice' in the French Monarchy," in *French Government and Society, 1500–1850: Essays in Memory of Alfred Cobban,* ed. J. F. Bosher (London: Athlone, 1973), 19–40.

79. *Turcaret* was first performed in February 1709 in the midst of the Great Winter of that year. *Les Agioteurs* was written in 1710. See Arthur Tilley, *The Decline of the*

Age of Louis XIV; Or, French Literature, 1687–1715 (1929; repr., New York: Barnes & Noble, 1968), 101 and 110.

80. Dessert, *Argent, pouvoir et société,* 86–96.

81. See ibid., 403, 405, and 671–72, for his true biography. See ibid., 85, on how contemporaries believed that Bourvalais and his financial ally, Jean Thévenin the elder, had both begun life as lackeys. Contemporaries who wanted to cast aspersions on the background of someone would make disrespectful and untruthful references to that person's ancestors. A. M. de Boislisle, in his additions and corrections to *Mémoires de Saint-Simon,* repeats the claims that Bourvalais started life as a lackey and servant who attracted Pontchartrain while the latter was serving in Brittany (16:685). See also Christine Favre-Lejeune, *Les Secrétaires du Roi de la Chancellerie de France: Dictionnaire biographique et généalogique (1672–1789)* (Paris: SEDOPOLS, 1986), 2:1094–95; Jacques Saint-Germain, *Les financiers sous Louis XIV: Paul Poisson de Bourvalais* (Paris: Plon, 1950); Lüthy, *Banque Protestante,* 1:283 and 285–86; and Claeys, *Dictionnaire biographique des financiers,* 2:755–56.

Jean Thévenin the elder was the son of a prominent Protestant family from La Rochelle. His father, a soldier, had been ennobled for his loyalty to the crown during the Fronde. Thévenin entered royal finances during the War of the League of Augsburg, and continued until his death in 1709, by which time he had signed 107 traités, placing him third after Bourvalais and Miotte (who signed 112) in the list of traitants. He bought an office as Secrétaire du Roi in 1694, then became governor of Saint-Denis, and claimed the title marquis de Tanlay. Like Bourvalais, he was involved in managing property for Pontchartrain and other important families. Unmarried, he tried to leave his estate to Pontchartrain at his death but the latter refused it. His brother was Jean Thévenin the younger, who was involved in finances but much less so than Thévenin the elder, and usually as an ally. See Dessert, *Argent, pouvoir et société,* 80 and 695. Boislisle, *Saint-Simon,* 15:441n4, repeat the story that Thevenin was descended from a builder in Paris who became ennobled. See also Favre-Lejeune, *Secrétaires du Roi,* 2:1251–52.

82. Dessert, *Argent pouvoir et société,* 342–49; Françoise Bayard, *Le monde des financiers au XVIIe siècle* (Paris: Flammarion, 1988), 267–77.

83. Dessert, *Argent, pouvoir et société,* 124–32.

84. Ibid., 681. While Dessert claims that Renouard and his father had both been Secrétaires du Roi, Favre-Lejeune, *Secrétaires du Roi,* 2:1145, mentions only that a cousin, Jean-Baptiste, held such a position, indicating that Charles Renouard was simply involved in finances. Claeys, *Dictionnaire biographique des financiers,* 2:848–50; Boislisle, *Saint-Simon,* 8:302–5; *Sourches,* 7:73 (June 5, 1701); *Dangeau,* 8:117–18 (June 6, 1701). Guy Rowlands, *The Dynastic State and the Army under Louis XIV: Royal Service and Private Interest, 1661–1701* (Cambridge: Cambridge University Press, 2002), 129–32, sees the fall of Touanne and his business partner as proof that the financial system had reached its zenith and was no longer capable of supporting Louis XIV's policies.

85. Dessert, *Argent, pouvoir et société.* See also these other works by Daniel Dessert: "Finances et société au XVIIe siècle: À propos de la Chambre de justice de 1661," *Annales ESC* 29 (1974): 847–82; *Fouquet* (Paris: Fayard, 1987); "Pouvoirs et finances au XVIIe siècle: La fortune du Cardinal Mazarin," *Revue d'histoire moderne et contemporaine* 23 (1976): 161–81; and Daniel Dessert and Jean-Louis Journet, "Le lobby

Colbert: Un royaume ou une affaire de famille?" *Annales ESC* 30 (1975): 1303–36. Also see Julian Dent, "The Role of Clientèles in the Financial Elite of France under Cardinal Mazarin," in *French Government and Society, 1500–1850: Essays in Memory of Alfred Cobban,* ed. J. F. Bosher (London: Athlone, 1973), 41–49; Claude Dulong, *La Fortune de Mazarin* (Paris: Perrin, 1990); Joseph Bergin, *Cardinal Richelieu: Power and the Pursuit of Wealth* (New Haven, CT: Yale University Press, 1985); and Jean Villain, *La fortune de Colbert* (Paris: Comité pour l'histoire économique et financière de la France, 1994).

86. Lüthy, *Banque protestante,* 1:111–14.

87. Antoine Crozat, the son of a banker, became a taille receiver in 1682 before selling this office to his brother Pierre in 1686. Crozat held the office of receiver general of finances for Bordeaux from 1689 until 1707, became a Secrétaire du Roi in 1705, and treasurer of the king's orders in 1715. His wife, Marie Marguerite Legendre, was the daughter and sister of two receivers general of finances named François Legendre, of whom the brother would emerge as a major aide to Desmaretz. Crozat invested in twenty-nine traités between 1689 and 1704. He also invested in France's overseas trading companies. He was one of the most heavily taxed financiers by the Chambre de justice of 1716, which ordered him to pay 6.6 million livres. This sum was cut in half in 1718 and paid to support John Law's banking scheme. When he died in 1738, Crozat left an estate worth more than eight million livres. See Dessert, *Argent, pouvoir et société,* 565–66; Favre-Lejeune, *Secrétaires du Roi,* 1:404–5; Claeys, *Dictionnaire biographique des financiers,* 1:561–67; and Guy Chaussinand-Nogaret, *Les financiers de Languedoc au XVIIIe siècle* (Paris: SEVPEN, 1970), 85–123.

88. Lüthy, *Banque protestante,* 1:120–25; Bluche, *Dictionnaire du Grand Siècle,* 188, article by Françoise Bayard; Boislisle, *Saint-Simon,* 4:190; Favre-Lejeune, *Secrétaires du Roi,* 1:195–97. Bernard bought an office of Secrétaire du Roi in 1706 and kept it until his death in 1739. Claude Frédéric Lévy, *Capitalistes et pouvoir au Siècle des Lumières* (The Hague: Mouton, 1969–80), 1:49–75, devotes an entire chapter to the mystery of Bernard's wealth and his role in financing war and capitalist trade ventures in Europe. Dessert, *Argent, pouvoir et société,* 193–202 and 532–33; Claeys, *Dictionnaire biographique des financiers,* 1:208–12.

Chapter 2

1. *Lettres, instructions et mémoires de Colbert,* ed. Pierre Clément (Paris: Imprimerie Nationale, 1861–83), 7:164–83. A copy of this mémoire can be found in A.A.E., Mém. et Doc., France, 2015, fol. 60–85, entitled "Mémoire faire par Mr. Colbert en l'année 1659," copied in Desmaretz's own handwriting.

2. Louis XIV, *Mémoires for the Instruction of the Dauphin,* trans. Paul Sonnino (New York: Free Press, 1970), 34–35.

3. Michel Antoine, *Le Conseil du Roi sous le règne de Louis XV* (Geneva: Droz, 1970), 48.

4. A.N. E 1770, fol. 3–21, articles I to V, list who shall be a member of the Council of State. Almost simultaneous to the regulation of the Council of State,

Louis XIV also restricted the authority of the various sovereign courts in France to remonstrate against royal demands to alter the law. By the end of Louis XIV's reign there were fifteen regional *Parlements* or *Conseils supérieures* downgraded from sovereign courts, two *Cours de Monnaies*, nine *Chambres des Comptes*, four *Cours des Aides*, but only one *Grand Conseil*. Every official from the lowest to the highest courts had the title *conseiller du roi*, but they did not actually advise the king on policy matters. By a declaration of February 24, 1673, Louis XIV required that all of these courts register any laws that the King's Council demanded in advance of issuing any remonstrances or criticism of these laws. Thereafter, for the remainder of Louis XIV's reign, the superior courts as they were then called could not delay or halt the enforcement of any law passed by the King's Council. The king registered the February declaration in the last *lit de justice* of his reign on March 23, 1673. The *lit de justice* was a procedure by which the king took the courts into his council and used his personal authority to force the registration of any laws. While the king would consult the courts in advance of issuing any laws, Louis XIV himself made policy and law in council for the rest of his reign. See John J. Hurt, *Louis XIV and the Parlements: The Assertion of Royal Authority* (Manchester, UK: Manchester University Press, 2002), 38–66, and also Gauthier Aubert and Olivier Chaline (eds.), *Les Parlements de Louis XIV: Opposition, coopération, autonomisation?* (Rennes: Presses Universitaires de Rennes, 2010), for discussion of whether the courts opposed or cooperated with the royal government. As an example of consulting with the Parlement, see A.N. G^7 710, May 10, 1708: Desmaretz referred a proposal to create hereditary offices of clerks (*greffiers*) of the sentences and arrêts in all superior and ordinary courts to the procurer general of the Paris Parlement, Henri-François Daguesseau.

5. Antoine, *Conseil du Roi*, 46–48, 63–64.

6. Ibid., 67–68.

7. Georges Pagès, "Le Conseil du Roi sous Louis XIII," in *Études sur l'histoire administrative et sociale de l'Ancien Régime*, ed. Georges Pagès (Paris: Félix Alcan, 1938), 16–17; Roland Mousnier, "Le Conseil du Roi de Henri IV au gouvernement personnel de Louis XIV," in *La plume, la faucille et le marteau*, ed. Roland Mousnier (Paris: PUF, 1970), 158–60.

8. Louis XIV, *Mémoires*, 64. Mazarin, at his death, was supposedly the wealthiest private individual in France, if not Europe. He had amassed his wealth through successful government contracting, involving Foucquet as Surintendant des Finances and Colbert as steward of his household. After his death, Foucquet and Colbert both had evidence that could have resulted in either of their arrests, had they successfully convinced the king of the other's guilt. Colbert succeeded in winning the king's ear and bringing down his rival, who had better family ties. See Dessert's "Pouvoirs et finances" and *Fouquet*.

9. A.N. E 1713, fol. 173–75. Michel Antoine prints a copy of this regulation with a commentary written in 1767 at the end of his article "Les Conseils des Finances sous le règne de Louis XV," *Revue d'histoire moderne et contemporaine* 5 (1958): 187–97.

10. A.N. E 1726, fol. 389.

11. Antoine, *Conseil du Roi*, 59. John C. Rule, "Louis XIV at Work: Decoding the Council of Dispatches, 1690–1715," *Proceedings of the Western Society for French History: Selected Papers of the Annual Meeting* 23 (1996): 309–20. The Council of Dispatches was to survey internal political matters that did not involve taxes or royal finances.

12. A.N. E 1713, fol. 173–75, September 15, 1661.

13. A.N. E 1683^7, dossier for 1710. According to this document, on February 11, 1710, ten matters were reported before the Petite Direction. Nine were decided, but Controller General Desmaretz removed one from discussion.

14. See *Sourches*, 3:13–14 (January 11, 1689), on how Chancellor Boucherat was somewhat put out that the controller general had announced the appointment of several provincial intendants without consulting him. A note by Sourches says that when Colbert was controller general he did not consult with Séguier or d'Aligre but that he did consult with Le Tellier as chancellor. Sourches wondered whether Controller General Le Peletier had simply gotten tired of consulting with Boucherat. Louis XIV delayed the formal announcement until Boucherat could be told.

15. A.N. E 448^A, fol. 314–15, February 8, 1672; E 449, fol. 665–66, March 26, 1672; E 451, fol. 48, 80, 82, and 85, May 10, 1672, and fol. 357–58, May 24, 1672.

16. René Pillorget, "Henri Pussort, oncle de Colbert (1615–1697)," in *Le Conseil du Roi de Louis XII à la Révolution*, ed. Roland Mousnier (Paris: PUF, 1970), 265.

17. Boislisle, *Saint-Simon*, 2:78n2.

18. A.N. U 945^B, nos. 8–10.

19. A.N. E 661^A, fol. 84–85, no. 19, March 5, 1697.

20. Antoine, *Conseil du Roi*, 74–75.

21. Ibid., 155–56.

22. Ibid., 156–57. A.N. G^7 1903 has several mémoires on the bureaus and directions of finances.

23. Antoine, *Conseil du Roi*, 162–75.

24. Ibid., 156.

25. Ibid., 124; Rule, "Louis XIV at Work," 317.

26. Clément, *Lettres, instructions et mémoires de Colbert*, 2:ccii–iii.

27. *Mémoires du duc de Saint-Simon*, ed. Gonzague Truc (Paris: Gallimard, 1953), appendix 2, 3:1256–57, in an anonymous letter to Louis XIV written sometime between February 1712, when Louis' grandson, the Duke of Burgundy, died, and July 1714, when Louis XIV registered his will.

28. Antoine, *Conseil du Roi*, 339–41.

29. Ibid., 120, 348–49; Fr. Olivier-Martin, *Histoire du droit français des origines à la Révolution* (Paris: Éditions Domat Montchrestien, 1951), 444.

30. Louis XIV, *Mémoires*, 30–31; Antoine, *Conseil du Roi*, 379.

31. Antoine, *Conseil du Roi*, 349.

32. *Dangeau*, 1:88–89, lists the various groups of the King's Council for 1684. He does the same for 1686 on p. 272.

33. Antoine, *Conseil du Roi*, 68–71; Boislisle, *Saint-Simon*, appendix 1, 6:501–2.

34. Boislisle, *Saint-Simon*, 2:85n1; Jean-Pierre Labatut, "Le Chancelier Boucherat (1616–1699)," in *Le Conseil du Roi de Louis XII à la Révolution*, ed. Roland Mousnier (Paris: PUF, 1970), 94.

35. Antoine, *Conseil du Roi*, 68–70.

36. Michal Antoine, *Le coeur de l'État: Surintendance, contrôle général et intendances des finances, 1552–1791* (Paris: Fayard, 2003), 379, says that the Conseil d'État et des Finances ceased meeting sometime between 1685 and 1690, but this not indicated by looking at the number of arrêts reported by the masters of requests rather than the controller general.

37. Jean-Christian Petitfils, *Louis XIV* (Paris: Perrin, 1997), 514–25. See also Jean-Philippe Cénat, *Le roi stratège: Louis XIV et la direction de la guerre, 1661–1715* (Rennes: Presses Universitaires de Rennes, 2010), 178–95; Sarmant and Stoll, *Règner et gouverner*, 179ff.

38. A.N. K 2399, no. 16; P 2400, pp. 317–21; and O^1 45, fol. 228–30.

39. A.N. K 2410, no. 21.

40. A.N. E 3659.

41. Michel Antoine, *Le Conseil royal des finances au XVIIIe siècle* (Geneva: Droz, 1973), xlii.

42. Ibid., xlvii.

43. Truc, *Saint-Simon*, appendix 2, 3:1256–57.

44. A.N. R^4 825.

45. A.N. E 1683^{135-38}.

46. Mitard, *Crise financière*, 32.

47. *Dangeau*, 12:248–49. Dangeau first mentioned rumors of a dixième on September 23, 1710. He wrote that the tax was adopted at the same Royal Council meeting at which Desmaretz introduced it.

48. Boislisle, *Correspondance des contrôleurs généraux*, 2:476.

49. Antoine, *Conseil du Roi*, 25–31.

50. Ibid., 62; A.N. R^4 825, letter by Abbé de Saint-Pierre, July 3, 1702.

51. Mitard, *Crise financière*, 43.

52. Boislisle, *Saint-Simon*, 15:402–8.

53. Jean-Baptiste Colbert, marquis de Torcy, *Journal inédit de Jean-Baptiste Colbert, marquis de Torcy, ministre et secrétaire d'état des affaires étrangères, pendant les années 1709, 1710 et 1711*, ed. Frédéric Masson (Paris: Plon-Nourrit, 1854).

54. Ibid., 205–88 (June 21–22, 1710), 213–15 (June 28–29, 1710), and 222–26 (July 16, 1710).

55. Ibid., 230–31 (July 27, 1710) for Poland; 285 (October 8, 1710) for Scotland.

56. Ibid., 272–73 (September 23, 1710).

57. Ibid., 301–3 (November 9, 1710). See Thomas J. Schaeper, *The French Council of Commerce, 1700–1715: A Study of Mercantilism after Colbert* (Columbus: Ohio State University Press, 1983), 3–20, for a discussion of the origins of the Council of Commerce.

58. Louis XIV, *Mémoires*, 63 and 81.

59. A.N. E 1775, fol. 359–60, April 18, 1674.

60. These books are contained in B.N. mss. fr. 6763–82 for the years 1661–80. Each book is small but magnificently illuminated with gold lettering and color pictures. They are addressed to the king.

61. A.N. KK 1005^C, pp. 34–35, "Traitté des Administrations des Recettes et Dépenses du Royaume, 1735." As stated earlier, two books exist for 1710 and 1711. They are bound in Desmaretz's arms. B.N. mss. fr. 11151 is a very detailed project for 1711. A.N. MM 1007 is less detailed for 1710 but it contains more information about revenue sources.

62. A.N. E 838^A, fol. 181–90, April 12, 1712; A.N. E 1976, fol. 217–21, and E 870^B, fol. 2–11, December 18, 1714.

63. A.N. G^7 831, letter from Le Rebours to Desgranges, September 21, 1710.

64. A.N. G^7 716, October 29, 1709.

65. A.N. G^7 717.
66. A.N. G^7 719.
67. A.N. G^7 646.
68. A.N. G^7 723.
69. A.N. K 2410, no. 68, declaration of June 11, 1709.
70. A.N. G^7 1127.
71. A.N. K 2412, no. 24, declaration of April 29, 1709. A.N. E 1947, fol. 166, arrêt en commandement, dated April 23, 1709, granting preference in the repayment of loans to those lending money for replanting land, meaning that the lenders would be repaid before all other debts, including the taille.
72. Louis XIV, *Mémoires,* 65.
73. Stanis Perez, *La santé de Louis XIV: Une biohistoire du Roi-Soleil* (Seyssel: Champ Vallon, 2007).
74. Boislisle, *Saint-Simon,* 15:378–79.
75. A.N. G^7 1903 contains mémoires on the history of the controller general of finances. The best secondary work is still Henri de Jouvencel, *Le contrôleur général des finances sous l'Ancien Régime* (Paris: Librairie de le Société du Recueil Général des Lois et des Arrêts et du Journal du Palais, 1901), 23, 30–31. See Antoine, *Coeur de l'État,* for the shifting responsibilities and personnel in the finance ministry.
76. Jouvencel, *Contrôleur général des finances,* 35–46.
77. Ibid., 24–25.
78. Ibid., 47–51, 75–84.
79. Boislisle, *Saint-Simon,* appendix 1, 5:453–54.
80. Ibid., 11:347. The *gens de robe courte* were the royal servants, while the *gens de robe long* were judges in the royal courts.
81. A.N. KK 355, fol. 4.
82. A.N. KK 355, fol. 5–7. This list of provinces comes from *L'Almanach royal* (Paris: Laurent d'Houry, 1709), 45–46. On March 1, 1709, the war department and the foreign affairs department exchanged the Lyonnais and Dauphiné: see *Dangeau,* 12:89; Marie-Laure Legay, "The Beginnings of Public Management: Administrative Science and Political Choices in the Eighteenth Century in France, Austria, and the Austrian Netherlands," *Journal of Modern History* 81 (2009): 258–62.
83. A.N. KK 355, fol. 7–10.
84. A.N. KK 1005^C, "Traitté des Administrations des Récettes et Depenses du Royaume, 1733," pp. 45–46.
85. A.N. K 886, no. 7.
86. Jouvencel, *Contrôleur général des finances,* 181–82.
87. Ibid., 312–18.
88. Desmaretz, *Compte rendu,* in Boislisle, *Correspondance des contrôleurs généraux,* 3:673.
89. B.N. mss. fr. 7752, "Mémoires sur l'histoire des finances," by Malet, pp. 258–61. The information on the salary, forages, and supplies owed to each soldier is on pp. 287–300. See also Mallet, *Comptes rendus,* 101–4. The same figures can be found in A.N. MM 1007, fol. 18–23, in Desmaretz's projection for expenses in 1710.
90. See Guerre A^1 2263, Desmaretz to Voysin, October 11, 1710, in which Desmaretz reported that the mints had transferred 110,000 livres to the Treasury of the Extraordinary of War the week before. The Treasurer Duplessis had not checked

before reporting the contrary to Voysin: "I don't recall all the details here, but if we had a more active and capable treasurer, he would have spared you and me much time and many discussions."

91. See A.N. G^7 536, Voysin to Desmaretz, August 31, 1709, on the conditions he was able to get for supplying forages to the Army of Flanders. He asked Desmaretz to change the assignations into rescriptions, which would ease negotiations.

92. A.N. K 889, no. 41; anonymous letter to Louis XIV, in Truc, *Saint-Simon*, appendix 2, 3:1256–57.

93. A.N. K 889, no. 41.

94. A.N. G^7 694–748 contain proposals and projects to reform French finances and increase revenue during the years 1684–1720. Many officials often examined these proposals before they reached the Royal Council. For example, G^7 711 contains a proposal to create new offices in the Bordeaux *Cour des Aides*. Desmaretz sent the proposal to the intendant of Bordeaux on May 6, 1708. A councilor of state named Bignon (there were three Bignons on the Council of State) commented on the proposal on July 24, 1708. Desmaretz reported it to the Royal Council on July 26, 1708.

95. The controller general decided which intendant of finances would handle which extraordinary affair. See A.N. G^7 645, letter from the traitant Miotte, May 16, 1708, reveals this process. A.N. G^7 828–30 has a letter from one of the intendants of finances, Le Peletier des Forts, to Desmaretz, warning that Messrs. Miotte and Bourvalais would be coming to see him about exclusion from a company. Des Forts had refused to admit them to the company because Desmaretz was the "master" in those matters. There are numerous examples of this kind of jostling, as well as letters from the intendants of finances charged with administering a traité to the secretary of finances on duty that name the company of traitants upon whom Desmaretz had agreed.

96. A.N. G^7 1767.

97. Kettering, *Patrons, Brokers, and Clients*; Beik, *Absolutism and Society*; Bossenga, *Politics of Privilege*.

98. Alexis de Tocqueville, *The Old Regime and the French Revolution*, trans. Stuart Gilbert (1856; repr., Garden City, NY: Doubleday, 1955), 34–35.

99. Jouvencel, *Contrôleur général des finances*, 220–310 passim. Mathieu Stoll has argued in his thesis and in *Règner et gouverner* that the controller general was not as powerful as Tocqueville and others have said. Stoll's research focuses, however, on Le Peletier, an interim finance minister, rather than on an aggressive transformational figure such as Colbert, Pontchartrain, or Desmaretz.

100. B.N. mss. fr. 11151, fol. 101^v.

101. A.N. G^7 1903, "État des gratifications que les Pays d'États sont en usage de faire à chaque tenu d'États."

102. Antoine, *Conseil du Roi*, 214–15; Boislisle, *Saint-Simon*, 29:94–96.

103. *Dangeau*, 12:290–91 (December 19, 1708). Dangeau reported that Desmaretz had originally asked for only six or eight thousand livres, while the king had offered twelve. Boislisle, *Saint-Simon*, 16:435–37, appears to corroborate Dangeau's story. A.N. 0^1 52, fol. 169, has a copy of the letter granting the pension dated December 23, 1708.

104. Two works on the intendants of finances are: André Chouraki, "Les intendants des finances" (unpublished *thèse de droit*, Bibliothèque de la Faculté de Droit, Paris, 1959), and Françoise Mosser, *Les intendants des finances au XVIIIe siècle* (Geneva: Droz, 1978).

105. A.N. K 118^B, no. 88^3, *règlement* of May 13, 1657; no. 88^{10}, declaration of October 5, 1658; and no. 88^{13}, declaration of October 12, 1660.

106. An edict of February 1690 stated in its preamble that only two commissions of intendants of finances had existed since 1660, when four offices were suppressed (A.N. O^1 34, fol. 34–35).

107. Clément, *Lettres, instructions et mémoires de Colbert,* 1:477.

108. Chouraki, *Intendants des finances,* 59–66.

109. Clément, *Lettres, instructions et mémoires de Colbert,* 1:481.

110. A.N. K 118^B no. 88^2 lists the departments of the intendants of finances for the years 1658–59; no. 132 lists the departments of the controller general of finances and the intendants of finances for the year 1666. Colbert was responsible for commerce, the gabelles of France, the Great Farms, the convoy of Bordeaux, the *patente* of Languedoc, the streets and waterways of Paris, the *bois,* Burgundy, Brittany, Languedoc, the dikes along the Loire River, the *bâtiments* and royal households, the extraordinary of war, the artillery, the navy, the clergy, the mints, the *prévoté* of Nantes, the bridges and highways, and the domain. Marin was responsible for the nineteen generalities in the *pays d'*élections, the *rentes* on the Hôtel de Ville, the *octrois,* the Chambre des Comptes of Paris, and the Cours des Aides. Hotman was responsible for the aides; the *entrées*; the gabelles of Provence, Dauphiné, Valence, Languedoc, Lyon, and the three bishoprics; the *surtaux* and 40e of Lyon; the farm of Brouage; the 9 livres 18 sous of Picardy; the farm of Ingrande; fish, paper, and beer; ashes; the *marque de fer*, Provence, Navarre, Artois, the conquered provinces, and the three bishoprics; the Parlement of Paris; the Grand Conseil; and the Swiss Leagues.

111. Boislisle, *Saint-Simon,* 6:276n2.

112. A.N. O^1 28, fol. 1–2, commissions dated January 7, 1684.

113. Boislisle, *Saint-Simon,* 6:40n4 and 9:23–24 and notes. Breteuil was the same age as the king. He became a master of requests in 1671 and served as intendant in Picardy and Artois in 1674 and Flanders in 1683 before being named both intendant of finances and intendant in the army for the campaign of 1684. He became a semester councilor of state in 1685 and an ordinary councilor of state in 1697. He kept this position when his intendancy of finances was suppressed to make room for the offices of directors of finances. He died in 1705.

114. A.N. O^1 31, fol. 85–86, commission dated April 25, 1687.

115. Boislisle, *Saint-Simon,* 3:282n2; Bluche, *Dictionnaire du Grand Siècle,* 1466, in an article by Bluche; *Sourches,* 2:39–40 and note. Le Peletier created the third intendant of finances for Pontchartrain to the detriment of his brother. The entry dated September 13, 1689, repeats the claim that Le Peletier was known to have bad relations with his brother (*Sourches,* 3:154–55).

116. A.N. O^1 33, fol. 240–43, commission as controller general, September 20, 1689.

117. A.N. O^1 34, fol. 34–35, edict of February 1690.

118. Boislisle, *Saint-Simon*, 24:318n5; François Bluche, *Les magistrats du Grand Conseil au XVIIIe siècle* (Paris: Belles Lettres, 1966), 89; *Sourches*, 3:39 (February 13, 1689), and note.

119. Boislisle, *Saint-Simon*, 2:194n1, and 6:262–64 and notes. Claude Miotte, the son of a receiver in a salt granary, first invested in royal finances in 1696 but soon became one of the most important financiers in France, often partnering with Bourvalais. His name appears on 112 traités. He was a farmer general, an army supplier, a speculator in foreign trade, and, most important for his advancement, estate manager for several prominent people besides Caumartin, including the Dauphin's estate at Meudon. He became a secrétaire du roi in 1706, having been a secretary to the council of finances and later a clerk there. The Chambre de justice of 1716–17, however, fined him 1.5 million livres. Even though he had this fine reduced to 140,000 livres in 1718, he was never able to restore his finances. At his death in 1731, he left a vacant legacy. See Dessert, *Argent, pouvoir et société*, 649–50; Favre-Lejeune, *Secrétaires du Roi*, 2:970–71; and Claeys, *Dictionnaire biographique des financiers*, 2:454–55.

120. The paper generated by this dispute can be found in two places: B.N. fonds Morel de Thoisy, mss. 1282, fol. 176–225, and A.N. U 870. The Royal Council issued the regulation settling the dispute. A.N. E 1899, fol. 252, May 14, 1697.

121. Boislisle, *Saint-Simon*, 4:271–72, 9:17, 11:256, and 12:463. Saint-Simon claimed that he often had to use his influence with Chamillard as well as his friendships with both Desmaretz and Armenonville to referee disputes between the two men when they were both directors of finances. See Michel Antoine, *Le Gouvernement et l'administration sous Louis XV: Dictionnaire biographique* (Paris: CNRS, 1978), 103–4, with a picture of Armenonville facing p. 104.

122. Antoine, *Conseil du Roi*, 73–74.

123. A.N. O^1 43, fol. 274–76, commission dated September 5, 1699.

124. Boislisle, *Saint-Simon*, 6:274n2; Antoine, *Gouvernement*, 38–39. Bignon de Blanzy was one of three brothers who would all sit on the King's Council before the end of the reign. Descended from an illustrious family of intellectuals and lawyers, they each played a major role in assisting their uncle the chancellor in reforming royal institutions. Bignon de Blanzy would be the intendant for Paris from 1709 until his death in 1724. The abbé Jean-Paul Bignon played a major role in reviving both the Academy of Sciences and the Academy of Inscriptions, and eventually reclaimed the post of royal librarian that his father and grandfather had held. Already a councilor of state when his younger brother became intendant of finances, Jérôme Bignon became provost of merchants in Paris, where he played a major role in keeping the city fed during the terrible winter of 1709.

125. A.N. 0^1 44, fol. 468–70, edict of December 1700; fol. 623–24, provisions for the new office, December 20, 1700; and fol. 634–36, *survivance* to Michel Robert Le Peletier des Forts, December 27, 1700. Souzy resigned shortly thereafter. Des Forts was born April 24, 1675. He had become a master of requests on February 27, 1698, after working on the peace talks at Ryswick; see Boislisle, *Saint-Simon*, 6:266n4. He would marry the daughter of Nicolas de Lamoignon de Basville, intendant of Languedoc in 1706, and rise to be controller general of finances himself during 1726–30.

126. Boislisle, *Saint-Simon*, 9:24 and n7.

127. Ibid., 18n7; Antoine, *Gouvernement,* 222–23. He was given a supernumerary seat as a councilor of state when he gave up his directorship of finances in 1703, becoming a semester councilor of state before year's end, and an ordinary councilor of state in 1716. He served on the Regency councils of finances and commerce from 1716 to 1718.

128. Boislisle, *Saint-Simon,* 6:304–5.

129. Ibid., 15:386–7 and notes; A.N. O^1 52, fol. 467, provisions of office, March 31, 1708; Dessert, *Argent, pouvoir et société,* 673–74; Favre-Lejeune, *Secrétaires du Roi,* 2:1107–8. Six offices of intendants of commerce were also created in February 1708 at 200,000 livres each to help reimburse the two holders of the offices of directors of finances. These new officials helped to regularize the activities of the Council of Commerce by providing some form of administrative division of authority in the handling of affairs presented to that council. The intendants of commerce were masters of requests but not councilors of state by right. Desmaretz met with them or had others do so. In effect, he operated with the largest number of official assistants of any controller general: seven intendants of finance and six intendants of commerce. See Schaeper, *French Council of Commerce,* 23–24, 26, 31, and 35. The six intendants of commerce were Denis-Jean Amelot de Chaillou, Louis-François Lefèvre de Caumartin de Boissy (brother of the intendant of finances), Louis-Charles de Machault, Jean Rouillé de Fontaine, Charles Boucher d'Orsay (until 1711, when he sold his office to Noel Danycan de Landivisiau), and César-Charles Lescalopier. Biographies of each (except Rouillé de Fontaine) can be found in Antoine, *Gouvernement,* as they each went on to further careers in the next reign.

130. A.N. O^1 53, fol. 120–22, Blanzy's commission as intendant of Paris, August 17, 1709. A.N. G^7 545–50, for letters from Bercy to Desmaretz before he became intendant of finances. See also Boislisle, *Saint-Simon,* 13:124n7 and 18:116. Bercy was the son of a master of requests who had worked for Colbert. See Antoine, *Coeur de l'État,* 354, for the relationship between Bercy and Pontchartrain.

131. A.N. O^1 55, fol. 208–9, provisions of office for Pierre Poulletier de Nainville, April 2, 1711. *Dangeau,* 13:374, reports that the king promised his physician that his son would have the next vacancy. At Jacques Poulletier's death, seeing that his son was capable of filling the vacancy, the physician asked the king to give the office to Poulletier's son.

132. A.N. G^7 1841–48, no. 199, Dubuisson to Desmaretz, July 15, 1714, reported the successful settlement of a contract of sale for his office to Louis Fagon. He asked Desmaretz to request that the king give Dubuisson a councillorship of state in recognition of his long years of service. Dubuisson died in October 1715. Louis Fagon, like Poulletier *fils,* was born in 1680. He became a counselor to the Parlement of Paris in 1702 and a master of requests on January 2, 1709. His office of intendant of finances was suppressed in 1715 but he was given a seat on the Regency council of finances and named semester councilor of state in November 1715. He became intendant of finances again in 1722, when the positions were recreated. He died in office in 1744.

133. A.N. G^7 1903 and 1494.

134. For example, A.N. E 804^A, fol. 47–48 and 62–70, are an arrêt and résultat of May 7, 1709, granting Jean-Jacques Clément and his cautions the right to sell

offices of treasurers and their controllers in the navy and the *invalides*. Clément and thirteen cautions signed the contract on May 10, 1709. Fol. 69 is Caumartin's list of cautions that he sent to the secretary of finances du Jardin on May 30, 1709; this list was amended by fol. 67, which shows a name removed on June 1, 1709. All matters concerning this traité were referred to Caumartin.

135. A study of the original arrêts simples in finances acquaints one with the various scribes who wrote them. Many arrêts bear the initials or even the names of the intendant of finances whose office drew up the arrêt—i.e., M. Poull or M.L.R.

136. J. F. Bosher, *French Finances, 1770–1795: From Business to Bureaucracy* (Cambridge: Cambridge University Press, 1970), 34, 35, and 55.

137. Boislisle, *Saint-Simon*, 9:347–48.

138. Schaeper, *French Council of Commerce*, 35.

139. See A.N. G^7 13^B, fol. 226–27; E 1947, fol. 121–23; and E 1948, fol. 68 and 149, for examples of Caumartin's involvement in naval affairs.

140. A.N. G^7 1903, list of extraordinary affairs in the hands of the intendants of finances prior to 1708; G^7 1494, similar lists for the years 1708–13.

Chapter 3

1. Boislisle, *Saint-Simon*, 6:61–62n7. There is some confusion as to whether Desmaretz was the eldest child. His brother Jean-Baptiste died at age ninety-four in the year 1740, giving him a birth date in 1646 (17:452n9).

2. Ibid., 6:61–62n7 and 7:131n1. Boislisle says that Desmaretz began working for his uncle at age fourteen, but Desmaretz himself wrote that he began working in April 1664 (B.N. n.a.f., mss. 9505, fol. 6). Letters about him from his parents to Colbert are in B.N. Mélanges de Colbert, mss. 131 bis, fol 772, August 30, 1665, and in Clément, *Lettres, instructions et mémoires de Colbert*, 7:342 and 344–45.

3. Boislisle, *Saint-Simon*, 7:128–30 and notes. Saint-Simon repeats this story, insisting that the prior and other monks at Ourscamp told it to him (36:294–96). See B.N. mss. fr. 9692, fol. 114–15, for the Desmaretz (Desmarets) family's list of ancestors for Nicolas, with three secrétaires du roi prior to Nicolas's father, Jean. There is no evidence that Desmaretz was related to the Dauvet family, who were the counts des Marets as well as the grands fauconniers de France from 1650 to 1748. Nor was he related to the poet and dramatist Jean Desmarets de Saint-Sorlin (1595–1676), who was Cardinal Richelieu's protégé before he turned to religious writing after 1645.

4. Jean-Louis Bourgeon, *Les Colberts avant Colbert* (Paris: PUF, 1973), 223–24 and 227; Jean Bérenger, "Charles Colbert, marquis de Croissy," in *Le Conseil du Roi de Louis XII à la Révolution*, ed. Roland Mousnier (Paris: PUF, 1970), 156.

5. Boislisle, *Saint-Simon*, 7:127n3. Letters from Jean Desmaretz to Colbert on government matters can be found in B.N. Mélanges de Colbert, mss. 121 bis, fol. 1091–92; mss. 124, fol. 560; mss. 131 bis, fol. 772; mss. 134, fol. 185–86; and mss. 144, fol. 32.

6. B.N. n.a.f., mss. 9505, fol. 6.

7. Antoine, *Conseil du Roi*, 475–77; A.N. H^1 1450, no. 4, is a memorandum from the eighteenth century on the functions of this special section.

8. Assemblée Nationale, mss. 350, fol. 513, dispensation of age requirements to Nicolas Desmaretz, December 6, 1671.

9. Assemblée Nationale, mss. 353, fol 296, dispensation of age requirements to Desmaretz to become a master of requests, January 11 (or 28), 1674. B.N. Clairambault, mss. 648, fol. 390–91, dispensation from the regulation of January 3, 1673, which states that Desmaretz had been given the right to enter the council on April 27, 1672.

10. A.N. O^1 22, fol. 134–35, commission of intendant of finances to Nicolas Desmaretz.

11. A.N. E 542^B, fol. 457–58, February 27, 1683, and E 543^A, fol. 126–29, March 13, 1683.

12. B.N. n.a.f. mss. 9505, fol. 6–9.

13. Pierre Clément, *Histoire de Colbert et de son administration* (1874; repr., Geneva: Slatkine Reprints, 1980), 1:369–99.

14. Louis Béchameil (ca. 1630–1703) married Colbert's cousin in 1648 and was an active financial supporter of Mazarin's policy during 1655–60, when he participated in twenty-nine traités. From 1660 until 1687 he was secretary to the council, where he backed Colbert's policies and became surintendant of the household of Monsieur, Louis XIV's brother, the Duke of Orléans. Colbert protected Béchameil from the 1661–65 Chambre de justice investigation of the financiers and their practices during the Fronde; once his protector, Colbert, was dead, however, Le Peletier pursued him for debts owed to the crown, and he was forced to sell his office as secretary to the council. He was protected from complete disgrace by virtue of his family ties and his friendship with the king himself. See Dessert, *Argent, pouvoir et société,* 529.

Béchameil was well liked in society and admired for his taste in art, architecture, and landscaping, so much so that Louis XIV often consulted him on these matters. One of his daughters married Desmaretz in 1673 and another the duc de Brissac. His chateau and gardens at Nointel were much admired. He was popular at court and respected as an honest businessman, according to Boislisle, *Saint-Simon,* 11:94–97. Béchameil was a trusted financial adviser to Monsieur, who left a vast fortune for his family and created a massive estate at Saint-Cloud with Béchameil's advice. See Nancy Nichols Barker, *Brother to the Sun King: Philippe, Duke of Orleans* (Baltimore, MD: Johns Hopkins University Press, 1989), 169–70.

15. Andre Clautrier (or Claustrier) (d. 1703), besides being a gold thread manufacturer, was an investor in royal affairs. He was receiver general of finances in Lyon from 1679 to 1684. His involvement in the "Affair of the Four Sous Pieces" cost him this office and his fortune. See Dessert, *Argent, pouvoir et société,* 561.

Jean Solu was also an investor in royal affairs. He was receiver general of finances in Riom during 1674–81 after having been an investor in the General Farms of the gabelles during 1668–74. His involvement in the Affair of the Four Sous Pieces cost him his fortune, as it did his equally involved brother, Edmé (or Aimé). See Dessert, *Argent, pouvoir et société,* 691–92.

16. Christophe de La Live, seigneur de Bellegarde and Champ-Renaud, started his career as a commis to François Bellinzani, Colbert's principal assistant in commercial matters. La Live later became an investor in the farm of the mints. He was also a munitioner and an investor in the General Farms, and finished his life as a

secrétaire du roi. See Dessert, *Argent, pouvoir et société,* 616–17; Favre-Lejeune, *Secrétaires du Roi,* 2:768–70; and Claeys, *Dictionnaire biographique,* 2:58.

17. Arthur-Michel de Boislisle, "Desmaretz et l'affaire des pièces de quatre sols," in Boislisle, *Saint-Simon,* 7:529–34. A.N. K 903, no. 4, is a report written in Desmaretz's handwriting on a conference on minting held at Bellinzani's house on August 5, 1670. Desmaretz's notes on the four sous-piece affair are in A.N. G^7 1391, March 10, 1679; he describes the measures taken in two arrêts in A.N. E 1797, March 7 and 29, 1679.

18. According to Clément, *Lettres, instructions et mémoires de Colbert,* 2:225n1, Colbert was unable to work after August 17. Louis XIV mentioned the possibility of replacing Colbert in a letter to Seignelay on September 2, 1683 (2:cclvii, no. xxxv).

19. Montyon, *Particularités et observations,* 80–81, says that Louis considered Desmaretz, Le Peletier, and Jean-Herault de Gourville. Ezechiel Spanheim, *Relation de la Cour de France en 1690,* ed. Emile Bourgeois (1900; repr., Paris: Mercure de France, 1973), 176–77, lists the candidates as the Marshal de Bellefonds, Pussort, Gourville, and Le Peletier. They both say that Chancellor Le Tellier successfully maneuvered to have Le Peletier selected.

20. Boislisle, "Desmaretz et l'affaire," 538–39. The arrêt can be found in A.N. E 1819.

21. Boislisle, "Desmaretz et l'affaire," 539–46. Clautrier's testimony can be found in B.N. Clairambault, mss. 1073, fol. 116–20. See A.N. O^1 27, fol. 371 and 402, for Bellinzani's arrest. Desmaretz wrote that Seignelay told him to leave the court (B.N. n.a.f., mss. 9505, fol. 24). Saint-Simon, who was eight years old at the time and not an eyewitness to the event, made many questionable statements on this matter; see Boislisle, *Saint-Simon,* 7:132–36. The duke also stated that Seignelay, who died when the duke was fifteen years old, detested Desmaretz. Seignelay's letters to Desmaretz are solicitous and filled with concern for his cousin, whose fate was important to the Colbert clan.

22. Marie-Françoise Limon, *Traitants et fraudes dans le recouvrement de l' impôt: Affaires réglées par Claude Le Peletier, Contrôleur général des finances (1683–1689)* (Paris: LGDJ, 1995), explores some of these affairs.

23. Boislisle, "Desmaretz et l'affaire," 552–55; A.N. E 1840, fol. 26–28, January 28, 1687. Daniel Dessert and Jean-Louis Journet, "Le lobby Colbert: un royaume ou une affaire de famille?" in *Annales ESC* 30 (1975): 1303–36, traces the outlines of the network of financiers whom Colbert employed.

24. Boislisle, "Desmaretz et l'affaire," 534–38.

25. See B.N. n.a.f., mss. 9505, fol. 16–23 and 24–26, for Desmaretz's two essays on his fall in 1683.

26. See Hilton Root's "Institutions, Interest Groups and Authority in Ancien Regime France," *French History* 6 (December 1992): 414–15, and his *The Fountain of Privilege: Political Foundations of Markets in Old Regime France and England* (Berkeley: University of California Press, 1994), 40. The unattributed description is repeated in Richard Bonney, "'Le Secret de leurs Familles': The Fiscal and Social Limits of Louis XIV's *Dixième,*" *French History* 7 (December 1993): 385.

27. Dessert, *Argent, pouvoir et société,* says that the ultimate source of money for the financiers was the so-called Grands, the highest nobility and churchmen. Dessert has also been a leading critic of Colbert's management of the crown's finances,

assailing it for corruption and saying that Colbert's innovations were merely continuations of policies begun under Nicolas Foucquet, the unfortunate surintendant des finances who was arrested in 1661 because of Colbert's insinuations to Louis XIV. Colbert simply replaced Foucquet's financial supporters with supporters of his own. Dessert has repeated these criticisms of Colbert in subsequent writings, most recently in his *Le Royaume de Monsieur Colbert, 1661–1683* (Paris: Perrin, 2007), 169–284. See also his *Colbert ou le serpent venimeux* (Paris: Éditions Complexe, 2000).

28. Bergin, *Cardinal Richelieu,* 243–63; Dulong, *Fortune de Mazarin*; Claude Dulong, *Mazarin* (Paris: Perrin, 1999), 308–38, Claude Dulong, *Mazarin et l'Argent: Banquiers et prête-noms* (Paris: École des Chartes, 2002); Villain, *Fortune de Colbert,* 319–24; and André Corvisier, *Louvois* (Paris: Fayard, 1983), 502–3. Dessert, *Fouquet,* 348–52, says that Fouquet was worth 15 million livres when he was arrested in September 1661, but that he also may have had debts totaling at least 15 million livres. However, Jean-Christian Petitfils, *Fouquet* (Paris: Perrin, 1999), 535–46, says that Fouquet's wealth totaled 18 million livres, while his debts were more than 16 million livres.

29. Pénicaut, *Faveur et Pouvoir,* 405.

30. The information on Desmaretz's fortune comes from Mathieu Dusart's master's thesis, "La fortune de Nicolas Desmaretz (1648–1721) à partir de son inventaire après décès" (Paris: Université de Paris XII–Créteil, 2002–3). Madeleine Béchameil was allowed to keep 200,000 livres of her 300,000-livre dowry as her personal property rather than as part of the couple's community property, according to the marriage contract. Mazel, *Claude Le Peletier,* 90, says that Desmaretz sold a house in Saint-Germain-en-Laye to Le Peletier on July 7, 1684.

31. Sharon Kettering, "Gift-giving and Patronage in Early Modern France," *French History* 2, no. 2 (1988): 131–51.

32. B.N. n.a.f., mss. 9505, fol. 16–23 and 24–25, are two memoranda by Desmaretz about this period in his life. B.N. mss. fr. 10265, *Lettres historiques et anecdotiques* de P. Léonard, fol. 121 (March 30, 1686), announces Desmaretz's return to Paris. *Sourches,* 1:376, supports this story. Saint-Simon, however, wrote that Desmaretz was exiled to his estates for ten to twelve years (Boislisle, *Saint-Simon,* 7:136–37, 394–97).

33. A.N. O^{1} 51, fol. 59^{v}, March 16, 1707; O^{1} 52, fol. 35^{v}, March 14, 1708; O^{1} 53, fol. 132, September 11, 1709; O^{1} 54, fol. 87 and 89, June 4 and 10, 1710; O^{1} 57, fol. 142 and 181, August 15 and October 17, 1713; E 863^{B}, fol. 184–87, no. 1, May 26, 1714.

34. Boislisle, "Desmaretz et l'affaire," 535–36.

35. Ibid., 556–61; Boislisle, *Correspondance des contrôleurs généraux,* 1:62, no. 242, Le Peletier to Desmaretz, February 28, 1686.

36. B.N. n.a.f., mss. 9505, fol. 26.

37. A.N. M 614, no. 23, marriage of his sister-in-law Béchameil to the duc de Cossé-Brissac in April 1692; A.N. Y 267, fol. 139^{v}, May 13, 1696, marriage of his cousin Croissy to M. de Bouzols; A.N. Y 268, fol. 41^{v}, August 1, 1696, marriage of his cousin Torcy to Mlle. de Pomponne. He lived next door to Torcy in Paris on the Rue Vivienne, A.N. Q^{1}, 1099^{6}, fol. 150^{v} and 152. His mother inherited one-third of Pussort's estate, according to Pillorget, "Henri Pussort," 269. He settled the Pussort inheritance with his mother on September 28, 1697 (A.N. Y 270, fol. 98). He was on the governing council of Seignelay's minor children (A.N. E 1899, fol. 311–12).

38. A.A.E., Mém et Doc., France, 137, fol. 87^{v}; Boislisle, *Correspondance des contrôleurs généraux,* 2:472–73.

39. Boislisle, *Saint-Simon,* 7:127–37.

40. Beauvillier to the marquis de Louville, March 15 and May 2, 1701, in Georges Lizerand, *Le duc de Beauvillier (1648–1714)* (Paris: Belles Lettres, 1933), 456 and 459.

41. Boislisle, *Saint-Simon,* 7:128–38, and 394–97 from Saint-Simon's additions to Dangeau. These additions can also be found in *Dangeau,* 1:35 (added to July 8, 1684), 7:292–93 (added to April 13, 1700), 9:296–98 (added to September 19, 1703).

42. Boislisle, *Saint-Simon,* 11:252–57, says that the king was reluctant to acknowledge Desmaretz and received him coldly in comparison to his reception for other people who had been disgraced; *Sourches,* 8:181, simply says that, after dinner on September 19, 1703, Desmaretz entered the king's cabinet accompanied by Chamillard, and that the king's *valet de chambre,* François Quentin de La Vienne, was the only other person in the room. *Dangeau,* 9:296 (September 19, 1703), merely says that Chamillard brought Desmaretz to the king's cabinet. He goes on to say that Desmaretz and Louis XIV had not seen each other for twenty years. Both *Sourches,* 8:179 (September 18, 1703), and *Dangeau,* 9:292 (September 14, 1703), whose journals were written contemporaneously with events, had been predicting Desmaretz's return to finances.

43. Desmaretz's provisions of office as director of finances are dated October 22, 1703, in A.N. O^1 47, fol. 197. According to *Dangeau,* 9:328, and *Sourches,* 8:201, Desmaretz assumed his seat on the Royal Council of Finances on October 23, 1703. See A.N. G^7 1850 for the years 1704–8; B.N. mss. fr. 7939 is a register book of letters sent by Desmaretz in his own or Chamillard's name, beginning in October 1703; B.N. mss. fr. 7725 is a collection of documents about the farms that includes a discussion of the 1703 Templier lease of the General Farms in which the closing paragraph asks Monseigneur (meaning Chamillard) to refer these matters to Desmaretz because of his knowledge of the farms. Desmaretz's responsibilities for so many provinces (Alsace, Flanders, Franche Comté) under the administrative charge of the war minister probably brought him in regular contact with Chamillard, who relied on him to keep things in order.

44. A.N. G^7 1123 contains papers on the Huguetan bankruptcy. Jean Henri Huguetan and Étienne des Meuves were two Swiss bankers who promised to provide funds to the French armies in Italy and Spain. Their bankruptcy in 1705 led to Huguetan's flight from his creditors to Amsterdam, where he supplied the grand pensionary Anthonie Heinsius and the Allied powers with detailed information on the financial arrangements of the French. See Lüthy, *Banque protestant,* 1:149–68.

45. Pénicaut, *Faveur et pouvoir,* 93n198, quotes Chamillard as saying that Desmaretz wanted to eliminate Armenonville in order to have no equal.

46. *Dangeau,* 12:53–54 (January 9, 1709); Boislisle, *Saint-Simon,* 15:361–71. Charles Honoré d'Albert de Luynes, duc de Chevreuse, like Beauvillier, had married one of Colbert's daughters. He was a secret advisor to the king with access to government papers, although he did not sit on any council or hold any position beyond that of captain-lieutenant of the light horse.

47. *Dangeau,* 12:75 (February 9, 1709).

48. Ibid., 80–81 (February 20, 1709); A.N. O^1 52, fol. 22–24.

49. *Dangeau,* 12:64 (January 21, 1708).

50. A.N. G7 833, de la Hestroy to Clautrier, January 30, 1708, and Clautrier to de la Hestroy, February 5, 1708.

51. *Dangeau,* 14:349 (February 21–22, 1713). This sight must have impressed the future Louis XV, because he used the same idea of a chair with a removable back and arms when Controller General Orry was troubled by rheumatism. The ministers sat on backless, armless folding tabourets at council meetings. Only the king had a chair with a back and arms. See Antoine, *Conseil du Roi,* 121.

52. *Dangeau,* 15:388 (March 23, 1715), 390 (March 26, 1715), and 391 (March 30, 1715).

53. Boislisle, *Saint-Simon,* 17:190–95 and 38:178n3.

54. Ibid., 7:129 and 131.

55. Ibid., 38:178–79.

56. Ibid., 21:286.

57. Ibid., 21:289.

58. Ibid., 22:191.

59. Ibid., 25:77–79. The duke refers to Desmaretz as "such an ungrateful and gruff animal."

60. (François de Salignac de la Mothe-)Fénelon, *Oeuvres completes,* ed. M. Gosselin (1851–52; repr., Geneva: Slatkine Reprints, 1971), 7:288–90, letter of April 9, 1709.

61. Torcy, *Journal,* 13 passim.

62. B.N. mss. fr. 2875, fol. 87–89; A.N. G7 750–60, de la Garde to Desmaretz, June 19, 1709, concerning books that Desmaretz might want to purchase.

63. Dusart, "Fortune de Nicolas Desmaretz," 59–75. Although the library did have one book by Jansenius, Saint-Simon insists that he and Beauvillier had agreed that Desmaretz had no suspect religious beliefs. See Boislisle, *Saint-Simon,* 11:371.

64. *Sourches,* 13:24, 241, and 316; Boislisle, *Saint-Simon,* 19:215 and 24:237; *Dangeau,* 12:391 (April 18, 1709); Jacques Saint-Germain, *La vie quotidienne en France à la fin du Grand Siècle* (Paris: Hachette, 1965), 34.

65. B.N. n.a.f. 9692, fol. 112, lists Desmaretz's nine children, including Charlotte Thérèse, but Alexandre Dupilet, *La Régence absolue: Philippe d'Orléans et la Polysynodie (1715–1718)* (Seyssel: Champ Vallon, 2011), 302, cites a letter from Desmaretz saying that Charlotte Thérèse was his sister. Dusart, "Fortune de Desmaretz," lists eleven possible children, including two, rather than one, male children named Nicolas who died as infants.

66. Boislisle, *Saint-Simon,* 4:319; 15:212–17; 16:435; 19:412–15; 20:223, 235, 238, and 249; 23:2–3; 25:185; 29:29; and 41:89. Apparently, Goësbriand had a difficult relationship with his elderly father, whom he had shut away. Pontchartrain wrote to Desmaretz on March 21, 1695, and again on April 9, 1697, to explain the problem (A.N. O1 39, fol. 39; O1 42, fol. 60). The elder Goësbriand had been in and out of various royal prisons since 1679 (A.N. O1 23, order of July 1, 1679).

67. Boislisle, *Saint-Simon,* 13:124. See Charles Henri Malon de Bercy, *Lettres du château de Bercy (1712–1742)* (Paris: L'Harmattan, 2010), for a set of letters written by Bercy to a friend over the last years of his life, with some references to Desmaretz.

68. Boislisle, *Saint-Simon,* 16:435–37. See *Dangeau,* 12:240 (October 10, 1708), on Desmaretz's now having a permanent abode at Marly; 12:268 (November 21, 1708), on the king's telling Desmaretz he was minster of state; 12:290–91 (December 19,

1708), reporting on the discussion between the king and Desmaretz over the royal wedding gift; and 12:304 (January 9, 1709), for the marriage itself.

69. Boislisle, *Saint-Simon,* 11:257; 16:448 and 480; 20:351–53, with appendix 17, 23:2 and 266. *Sourches,* 13:326, reports on the way the sale of the charge of master of the king's wardrobe was handled on March 12, 1712. A.N. O[1] 56, fol. 82–85, contains provisions of charge of master of the king's wardrobe and the *brevet d'assurance* explaining how the heir of the office was to be paid the 500,000 livres. *Dangeau,* 7:292–93 (April 13, 1700), "Addition de Saint-Simon," has Saint-Simon writing to say that, after returning to be finance minister, Desmaretz became one of the king's favorites and was able to make his son's fortune, something no other minister had been able to do.

Maillebois would survive his father and become a maréchal de France in 1741 and have a less-than-stellar military career. His son Yves-Marie, comte de Maillebois, would be a member of the Royal Academy of Sciences and part of Madame de Pompadour's circle of friends. When Yves-Marie's sons died in the 1780s, he sold Maillebois to the FitzJames family before the Revolution. He was the last surviving male descendant of the Desmaretz clan.

70. Boislisle, *Saint-Simon,* 26:96n5. As Abbot of Saint-Bénigne, Pierre Desmaretz became a counselor in the Parlement of Dijon. He would become Abbé of Montebourg in the diocese of Coutances in April 1758. Saint-Simon died in a house on the rue de Grenelle in 1755 that he had been renting from Pierre Desmaretz since 1750. The Abbé Desmaretz died in 1771 at the age of eighty-four. Ibid., 26:417–25, appendix 1, contains letters about the Abbé Desmaretz, the defense of his thesis, and the benefices he received during his father's lifetime. A.N. G[7] 574 contains a mémoire recording that the king granted the abbey at Saint-Benigne to Desmaretz's son while at Marly on July 25, 1710.

B.N. n.a.f. 9692, fol. 112, lists nine children of Desmaretz's who reached adulthood. Besides the seven previously discussed, there were two military men: Louis Desmaretz, baron de Châteauneuf-en-Thymerais, and Henri Desmaretz, marquis de Marville. They apparently did not marry. The records about Louis are fairly meager. He rose to the rank of brigadier in 1719 and left the military in 1727. Henri was a captain in the cavalry in 1724, when he participated in the sale of his parents' home in Paris to the duc de Luxembourg. His share was one-sixth of the price, or 55,000 livres. See also *Dictionnaire de la Noblesse* (Paris: Veuve Duchesne, 1772), 5:566–67.

71. Joseph Bergin, *Crown, Church, and Episcopate under Louis XIV* (New Haven, CT: Yale University Press, 2004), 404–5. The agent general of the clergy represented the assembly of the clergy to the king. Since they were elected officials, the crown took a great interest in choosing reliable men and rewarded them with prominent bishoprics thereafter (130–32).

72. A.A.E., Mém. et Doc. France, 991, fol. 207–8, 212–13, and 214–22. The last is entitled "Mémoire concernant les finances depuis 1661 jusqu'en 1687." The title is written in Desmaretz's handwriting, and the text by a scribe. A copy of this memorandum can be found in A.N. G[7] 1903, written entirely in Desmaretz's handwriting. Boislisle published the latter, incorrectly dated 1686, in Boislisle, *Correspondance des contrôleurs généraux,* appendix 2, 3:543–47. Fragments of Desmaretz's criticisms of Le Peletier are in B.N. n.a.f., mss. 9505, fol. 3–5 and 10–16. A major piece of his

writing is in A.N. K 883, no. 3. One last piece from this period is A.A.E., Mém. et Doc., France, 1023, fol. 80–85. Boislisle, in "Desmaretz et l'affaire," wrote that it was possible that Desmaretz wrote the memorandum in A.A.E., Mem. et Doc., 991, fol. 228–31. If so, then Desmaretz was also the author of B.N. mss. frr. 1735 and 11149. His evidence for these claims is weak. There is no internal or external evidence to tie these last documents conclusively to Desmaretz.

73. Most of them are printed in Boislisle, *Correspondance des contrôleurs généraux,* 3:602–36. The originals of these documents can be found in A.A.E., Mém. et Doc., France, 137, fol. 76–87 and 122–26; A.A.E., Mém. et Doc., France, 237, fol. 44; A.N. G^7 1138–39 and 1903; B.N., mss. fr. 7765, fol. 1–22; and Forbonnais, *Récherches et considérations,* 4:65–85. Two documents not printed in Boislisle from this period are A.A.E., Mém. et Doc., France, 1209, fol. 388–90, and B.N., mss. fr. 7766, fol. 14–20.

74. A.A.E., Mém. et Doc., France, 137, fol. 3–5, 11–19, 21–32, 41–43, and 113–17; A.A.E., Mém. et Doc., France, 2015, fol. 183–84.

75. A.A.E., Mém. et Doc., France, 991, fol. 214–22; A.A.E., Mém. et Doc., France, 1209, fol. 388–90; Boislisle, *Correspondance des contrôleurs généraux,* 3:611–29.

76. B.N. n.a.f., mss. 9505, fol. 3–5 and 11–13.

77. B.N. n.a.f., mss. 9505, fol. 26. The mémoire can be found in A.N. K 883, no. 3.

78. B.N. n.a.f., mss. 9505, fol. 26.

79. Lévy, *Capitalistes et pouvoir,* discusses financiers and bankers from the late part of Louis XIV's reign until the end of the Regency.

80. A.A.E., Mém. et Doc., France, 991, fol. 214–22; A.N. G^7 1903 and Boislisle, *Correspondance des contrôleurs généraux,* appendix 2, 1:543–47.

81. Boislisle, *Correspondance des contrôleurs généraux,* appendix 2, 1:546. Desmaretz's imagery on the circulation of trade preceded the Physiocrats of the eighteenth century.

82. For example, Lionel Rothkrug, *Opposition to Louis XIV: The Political and Social Origins of the French Enlightenment* (Princeton, NJ: Princeton University Press, 1965), 87–110.

83. The traditional view of Colbert's policy is that it was protectionist and against free trade. Rothkrug develops his entire thesis on the political and social origins of the opposition to Louis XIV around the idea that it was Colbert's policies that sparked demands for free trade (ibid., 416–64, among others). Schaeper, *French Council of Commerce,* 59–65, has shown that the merchant members of the French Council of Commerce often cited Colbert on freedom of trade. The term *liberté de commerce* often appears in Desmaretz's administrative correspondence when referring to particular kinds of trade—for example, in wood, see Boislisle, *Correspondance des contrôleurs généraux,* 3:564, no. 1743, and note. Desmaretz was convinced that many of the measures taken by the government to pay its bills were actually noxious to trade and should be eliminated, if possible. As minister, he was constantly searching for some way to do so.

84. "Mémoire des commissaires du roi sur la misère du peuples et des moyens d'y remedier," in *Mémoire de la généralité de Paris,* ed. A. M. de Boislisle (Paris, 1881).

85. La Bruyère first published *Les caractères* in 1689.

86. Boislisle, *Correspondance des contrôleurs généraux,* appendix 2, 1:546–47.

87. Ibid., 3:606, mémoire to Torcy, May 12, 1710, and 3:634, memoire to the king, August 1715.

88. A.A.E., Mém. et Doc, France, 1023, fol. 80–85. The idea of asking private individuals to turn over their gold and silverware to the mints kept recurring in the Royal Council of Finances, despite the opposition of both Pontchartrain and Desmaretz as controllers general of finances. See Boislisle, *Saint-Simon*, 17:405–10; *Dangeau*, 12:432–23 (June 6, 1709).

89. For explanations of the developments, see http://www.archivesdelasarthe.com/DeclarationMutationDeces.asp and http://www.archivesdelasarthe.com/InstitutionControle%20.asp. The history of these acts is repeated in any number of departmental archives in France. Property in the Old Regime included seigneurial rights. The centième denier did not tax inheritances, property that was part of a dowry, or donations to religious institutions. An edict of October 1705 stated that, beginning on January 1, 1706, no exchange of property would be recognized by law until it was registered with the control of notarial acts. The centième denier still exists as a tax on property exchanges in France.

90. A.A.E., Mém. et Doc, France, 137, fol. 3–5.

91. Antoine, *Conseil du Roi*, 312–16.

92. Schaeper, *French Council of Commerce*, 23–24, 26, 31, and 34; Antoine, *Coeur de l'État*, 364–71.

93. Sarmant and Stoll, *Régner et gouverner*, 324–25. The figures for each ministry are only for headquarters staff and do not include any staff that might be in the provinces.

94. His most recent attempt can be found in Antoine, *Coeur de l'État*, 322–32.

95. Ibid., 323–24, 337, 354, and 361.

96. Ibid., 324, 335, and 354.

97. Ibid., 341–42.

98. Boislisle, in the introduction to Boislisle, *Correspondance des contrôleurs généraux*, 1:xvii–xxi.

99. A.N. G^7 1903 lists payments to commis for 1716 and 1718.

100. For biographical information on Malet, see: Boislisle, *Correspondance des contrôleurs généraux*, 1:xviii–xix; Favre-Lejeune, *Secrétaires du Roi*, 2:919; Bonney, "Jean-Roland Malet," 180–86; and Bonney and Bonney, *Jean-Roland Malet*, 9–14. Malet's poem can be found in B.N. Ye. 3486. Malet also wrote a poem praising Desmaretz that was printed in December 1713; it can be found in Arsenal, mss. 3128, fol. 206–7.

101. A.N. E 801^B, fol. 6–7, February 10, 1709, and E 816^A, fol. 261–63, May 13, 1710. On the back of the latter is a note indicating that the arrêt came from Le Rebours' office.

102. A.N. G^7 736 to 745 contain registers for the years 1708–16.

103. Bonney, "Jean-Roland Malet," 180–86; Bonney and Bonney, *Jean-Roland Malet*, 9–14.

104. Favre-Lejeune, *Secrétaires du Roi*, 1:341. Both Desmaretz's father and de la Garde's father had been treasurers of France in Soissons. De la Garde's correspondence is in A.N. G^7 867–81. A.N. G^7 750–60, de la Garde to Desmaretz, February 21, 1708, congratulates the minister on his appointment as controller general of finances and mentions thirty-two years of service. See A.N. G^7 1494 for lists of who was charged with extraordinary affairs between 1708 and 1713.

105. A.N. G^7 832–66 contain Clautrier's personal and business correspondence. He was addressed as Desmaretz's secretary up through September 1715. See A.N. G^7 832, Clautrier to abbé de la Proustière, October 21, 1703, in reply to an offer of

employment. For biographical sketches of Clautrier and his son, see Antoine, *Conseil royal des finances*, xxiv and nn19–22. For biographical information on Proustiere, see Boislisle, *Saint-Simon*, 6:306n1.

106. A.N. G^7 839 has thirty-five letters to Le Cousturier indicating his connection to Rouillé du Coudray before October 1703. A.N. O^1 47, fol. 93, contains two acquits patents for 3,000 livres each for Rouillé du Coudray and his commis Le Couturier (*sic*), June 10, 1703. The letters of Maintenon to Madame de Caylus, June 27 and July 17, 1716, in *Souvenirs de Madame de Maintenon*, ed. le comte de Haussonville and G. Hanotaux (Paris: Calmann-Lévy, n.d.), 3:116 and 124, mention Le Cousturier's visits. See also A.N. G^7 1903, Le Cousturier to Clautrier, October 27, 1730. Favre-Lejeune, *Secrétaires du Roi*, 2:822–23, indicates that Le Cousturier was the son of a financier who became secrétaire du roi during Colbert's lifetime. Le Cousturier had two brothers involved in the administration of the General Farms and a brother-in-law who was a general farmer.

107. Boislisle, *Saint-Simon*, 18:5–18.

108. Emmanuel Le Roy Ladurie (with collaboration of Janine Field-Récurat), "Système de la Cour (Versailles vers 1709)," *L'Arc* 65 (1976): 21–35, comments on this description of the court. (For a fuller version, translated into English, see Emmanuel Le Roy Ladurie, *The Mind and Method of the Historian*, trans. Siân Reynolds and Ben Reynolds [Chicago: University of Chicago Press, 1981], 149–73.) For an extended commentary on the same subject, see Emmanuel Le Roy Ladurie and Jean-François Fitou, *Saint-Simon, ou le système de la Cour* (Paris: Fayard, 1997), 181ff. (translated into English in *Saint-Simon and the Court of Louis XIV*, trans. Arthur Goldhammer [Chicago: University of Chicago Press, 2001], 121ff.).

109. A.N. KK 1005^D, "Discours de M. Paris de la Montagne à ses enfants pour les instruire de sa conduitte et celle de ses frères dans les principales matières du Gouvernement ou ils ont participié" (1729), 67–73. The four Paris brothers represented two pairs from different mothers. The elder two, Antoine (1668–1733) and Claude Paris de la Montagne (1670–1744), began their careers in finance during the 1690s and became munitioners or suppliers to the army. The younger two, Jean Paris de Montmartel (1690–1766) and Joseph Paris de Verney (1684–1770), began their careers in finance during the reign of Louis XIV but became more famous during the eighteenth century. See Dessert, *Argent, pouvoir et société*, 663–65. The latter three became secrétaires du roi, while the eldest was a treasurer general of the Extraordinary of War in 1704 and receiver general of finances for Grenoble during 1712–18 (Favre-Lejeune, *Secrétaires du Roi*, 2:1038–40).

110. Vaubourg's career was unaffected by his brother's fall in 1715. He became an ordinary counselor of state in 1719 and performed ceremonial duties at the coronation of Louis XV in 1722. See Boislisle, *Saint-Simon*, 17:452nn8–9. See also Antoine, *Gouvernement*, 84. Vaubourg as intendant wrote a report on Lorraine for the Duke of Burgundy in 1698; see *L'intendance de Lorraine et Barrois à la fin du XVIIe siècle*, ed. Marie-José Laperche-Fournel (Paris: CTHS, 2006).

111. Boislisle, *Saint-Simon*, 14:342n2; Antoine, *Gouvernement*, 133–34. Bouville as intendant wrote the report on Orléans for the Duke of Burgundy in 1698; see *L'intendance d'Orléans à la fin du XVIIe siècle* (Paris: CTHS, 1989). Bouville's son and Desmaretz's nephew, Louis Guillaume, also served as a provincial intendant—for Alençon (1708–13) and Orléans (1713–31)—during Desmaretz's ministry.

112. Since Desmaretz was not a secretary of state, he and Jérôme de Pontchartrain decided not to attend meetings of the Council of Commerce, to avoid difficulties over protocol. Instead, they sent representatives.

113. Boislisle, *Saint-Simon*, 6:61–62nn2 and 7; Antoine, *Gouvernement*, 25–26; A.A.E., Mém. et Doc., France, 224, fol. 9–20, has Nointel's comments on a mémoire on money; A.N. E 790^{A}, fol. 70–72, March 6, 1708, names Nointel to the bureaus of the farms of the postes and messageries and the gabelles and Five Great Farms; A.N. E 1943, fol. 295–96, June 5, 1708, lists Nointel as a member of the Council of Commerce. *Sourches*, 11:351 (June 9, 1709), reports that, on the same day that Chamillard was dismissed, Nointel was named director general of the vivres and étapes, replacing Poulletier. Chapman, *Private Ambition*, 80, reports that Nointel was a protégé of Chancellor Pontchartrain until Desmaretz emerged as controller general of finances. See also Boislisle, *Saint-Simon*, 20:165n2. A.N. G^{7} 1805, no. 417, is a list of papers turned over to Nointel by Poulletier. A.N. E 806^{A}, fol. 95–96, no. 34, July 2, 1709, names Nointel to the bureau of the domain and the aides in place of Voysin. The new extraordinary commission governing supplies is named in A.N. E 813^{A}, fol. 159–60, no. 36, February 4, 1710. It included Nointel, Rouillé du Coudray, des Forts, and Vaubourg, but eventually Argenson and Poulletier *fils* were added. Nointel's son and Desmaretz's nephew, Louis Claude, served as intendant in Auvergne during 1713–16.

114. Boislisle, *Saint-Simon*, 6:259n5; (Henri-François) Daguesseau, "Discours sur la vie et mort de M. Daguesseau, conseiller d'état, par M. Daguesseau, Chancelier de France, son fils," in *Oeuvres complètes du Chancelier Daguesseau*, ed. M. Pardessus (Paris: Fantin, 1819), 15:361; Isabelle Storez, *Le Chancelier Henri François D'Aguesseau (1668–1751): Monarchiste et libéral* (Paris: Publisud, 1996), 57–110; Chartier, *Daguesseau, conseiller d'etat*; Bluche, *Dictionnaire du Grand Siècle*, 52–53, s.v. "Aguesseau," article by Jean Pradel.

115. Boislisle, *Saint-Simon*, 3:282n2; Bluche, *Dictionnaire du Grand Siècle*, 1466, s.v. "Souzy," article by Bluche; A.N. E 799^{B}, fol. 109–10, describes the history of Souzy's commission.

116. Boislisle, *Saint-Simon*, 4:12n2; Bluche, *Dictionnaire du Grand Siècle*, 102–3, s.v. "Argenson," article by Frédéric d'Agay; Harold P. Anderson, "The Police of Paris Under Louis XIV: The Imposition of Order by Marc René de Voyer de Paulmy d'Argenson" (PhD diss., Ohio State University, 1978). D'Argenson rose to prominence because of his acquaintance with Lefèvre de Caumartin, whose sister he married. Subsequently, he rose through his ties to Pontchartrain to be a master of requests and a member of the council on captured vessels. He was named lieutenant general of the police of Paris on January 22, 1697. He would surrender this charge to become keeper of the seals in 1718 and president of the council of finances in 1719.

117. Boislisle, *Saint-Simon*, 17:186–95 and 446; *Dangeau*, 12:304 (January 9, 1709).

118. A.A.E., Mém. et Doc., France, 137, fol. 122–24.

119. Boislisle, *Saint-Simon*, 17:186–90.

120. *Dangeau*, 12:413; Boislisle, *Saint-Simon*, 17:391–94, and 179–94 on the quarrels between Chamillard and the other ministers.

121. Pénicaut, *Faveur et Pouvoir*, 151.

122. Lizerand, *Duc de Beauvillier*, 265–79.

123. Pénicaut, *Faveur et Pouvoir*, 151–59. Pénicaut sees this disgrace as the first sign of weakness from Louis XIV that the absolute monarch could be forced to do something because of outside pressure and, thus, an example of the kind of ministerial dismissals that came to characterize the governments of Louis XV and Louis XVI. See also Lizerand, *Beauvillier*, 264–67.

124. Boislisle, *Saint-Simon*, 6:264n3; Antoine, *Gouvernement*, 250–51; Bluche, *Dictionnaire du Grand Siècle*, 1621, s.v. "Voysin de la Noiraye," article by Abel Poitrineau; Jeanne Falque-Cador and Emmanuel Pénicaut, "Daniel-François Voysin de la Noiraye," in *Les ministres de la guerre, 1570–1792: Histoire et dictionnaire biographique*, ed. Thierry Sarmant (Paris: Belin, 2007), 307–17.

125. A.N. O^1 53, fol. 75–78, June 12, 1709.

126. Voysin was another of Saint-Simon's villains in his reconstruction of the court of Louis XIV. Voysin remained secretary of state for war when he became chancellor in July 1714, upon Pontchartrain's retirement. His principal impact as chancellor was to sign and support the registration of the edict of July 1714 that put the king's two bastard sons, the duc de Maine and the comte de Toulouse, in the line of possible successors to the throne. He also forced the registration of the Bull Unigenitus suppressing Jansenism and unleashing many of the political problems of the eighteenth century. Voysin knew when to change sides, and led the Regent's efforts to have the will of Louis XIV overturned. See Bluche, *Dictionnaire du Grand Siècle*, 1621, s.v. "Voysin de la Noiraye," article by Abel Poitrineau; Boislisle, *Saint-Simon*, 6:264n1, and appendix 2, 31:437–39; Antoine, *Gouvernement*, 250–51. On claims that Chamillard had ruined finances in the expectation of a quick peace treaty, see *Correspondance de Madame de Maintenon et de la princesse des Ursins, 1709: Une année tragique*, ed. Marcel Loyau (Paris: Mercure de France, 2002), 241, 243, and 347–48.

127. Dessert, *Argent, pouvoir et société*, 588, no. 198.

128. A.N. E 1956, fol. 25, January 27, 1710; G^7 536, Voysin to Desmaretz, March 18, 21, and 30, 1710; Guerre A^1 2262, nos. 163 and 184, Desmaretz to Voysin, March 13 and 29, 1710. A.N. E 832^A, fol. 353–54, September 5, 1711, and E 855^A, fol. 15–16, September 5, 1713, ordering Gallois to sell his furniture and books to pay the bills outstanding against him.

129. Letters from Voysin to Desmaretz in the fall of 1709 reveal that Voysin prepared material for Desmaretz's approval (B.N. mss. fr. 7752, pp. 261–62; A.N. G^7 536, passim). A.N. G^7 1806, nos. 31 and 115, are Desmaretz's figures for the 1709–10 winter quarters.

130. A.A.E., Mém. et Doc., France, 137, fol. 125, mémoire by Desmaretz, May 29, 1710; A.N. G^7 1138–39, "Mémoire sur l'état des affaires du Royaume," July 28, 1710, calling for a reduction in the number of regiments in order to reduce expenses.

131. Boislisle, *Saint-Simon*, 1:299n2 and 12:323–24, for his character according to Saint-Simon. See also Étienne Taillemite's biography of Jérôme in Bluche, *Dictionnaire du Grand Siècle*, 1225–26.

132. A.N. G^7 533–35, passim.

133. Anderson, *Police of Paris*, 257–64.

134. When Pontchartrain retired in July 1714, correspondence between his replacement, Voysin, who kept the war ministry, and Desmaretz for the years 1714–

15 is also not in the G[7] series. Correspondence with the chancellor must have been archived elsewhere.

135. See David Kammerling Smith, "Learning Politics: The Nîmes Hosiery Guild and the Statutes Controversy of 1706–1712," *French Historical Studies* 22 (1999): 493–534, and his "Structuring Politics in Early Eighteenth-Century France: The Political Innovations of the French Council of Commerce," *Journal of Modern History* 74 (2002): 493–537.

Chapter 4

1. Jacques Levron, *Les courtisans* (Paris: Éditions du Seuil, 1960), 105–8. A translation of this section of *Les courtisans* is in *Louis XIV and Absolutism,* ed. Ragnhild Hatton (Columbus: Ohio State University Press, 1976), 146–47.

2. A.N. G[7] 635–93 contain *placets et requêtes* for the years 1683–1740.

3. A.N. G[7] 645.

4. Boislisle, *Saint-Simon,* 15:379–82.

5. Levron, *Courtisans,* 101–2 (pp. 142–43 in Hatton, *Louis XIV and Absolutism*).

6. Boislisle, *Saint-Simon,* 3:14 and 16:394–401.

7. Ibid., 2:134n4, 7:70–76, and 9:35–45.

8. A.N. G[7] 562, Bonnier at Montpellier to Desmaretz, March 12, 1708, seeking Desmaretz's continued protection. Bonnier had sponsored a project that raised 600,000 livres and had received a 6,000-livre gratification. *Dangeau,* 12:318 (January 28, 1708), reports that Mlle. de Mailly received a pension of 2,000 écus and rentes with a total capital of 25,000 écus in return for advice from her mother that would raise two or three hundred thousand écus for the crown.

9. Levron, *Courtisans,* 99 (p. 141 in Hatton, *Louis XIV and Absolutism*). See also Françoise Bayard, *Monde des financiers,* chapter on *avis* and *donneurs d'avis,* 80–103.

10. Saint-Germain, *Financiers sous Louis XIV,* 182–87; Dessert, *Argent, pouvoir et société,* 671–72, no. 441.

11. Saint-Germain, *Financiers sous Louis XIV,* 1–20, 34, and 38.

12. Ibid., 39–40 and 46–56. A.N. G[7] 711, La Noue to Desmaretz, May 2, 1708, on which is written "*Rapporté*" (reported) and "*Néant*" (nothing).

13. Saint-Germain, *Financiers sous Louis XIV,* 44–46.

14. Ibid., 19–20; A.N. E 874[A], fol. 187–90, no. 3, April 16, 1715, indicates that Bourvalais had gotten his position in February 1710.

15. According to *Sourches,* 1:319 (October 1685), the king granted 10,000 livres to Monsieur le Grand in recompense for his *avis* on certain sums owed by Bauyn, master of the chambre de deniers.

16. Boislisle, *Saint-Simon,* 7:70–76 and 9:35–45. A.N. G[7] 837, Clapeyron (a banker from Lyon) to Clautrier, December 2, 1714, describes how Villeroy presented a group of Lyon merchants to the king at Marly. Clautrier's family was from Lyon.

17. Examples of the process include: A.N. G[7] 867–81, Desmaretz to de la Garde, May 1, 1705, on projects submitted by Marsan; A.N. G[7] 710, March 4, 1708, a memorandum submitted by the comtesse de Médavy on a project to raise 1 million livres.

18. A.N. G^7 712, letters of September 26 and October 13, 1708. There is no indication of the cause for alarm in this case.

19. A.N. G^7 712, letters of December 2 and 30, 1708.

20. A.N. G^7 712, letter of October 10, 1708.

21. Ibid. M. L'herée obviously knew of Desmaretz's relationship to Colbert and mistook the family name as being Colbert rather than Desmaretz.

22. A.N. G^7 711, letter of July 13, 1708.

23. A.N. G^7 712, letters of October 1 and 15, 1708.

24. A.N. G^7 712, anonymous letters of October 29 and November 5, 1708, on taxing carriages; A.N. G^7 710, Texendière to Desmaretz, February 6, 10, and 29, and March 24 and 31, 1708, on taxing armorials; A.N. G^7 712, Chevalier d'Ormesson in Narbonne to Desmaretz, September 3, 1708, on taxing capital; A.N. G^7 1130–31, Nassé, the royal procureur in Châteauneuf-en-Thymerais (where Desmaretz was baron) to Desmaretz, February 25, 1714; A.N. G^7 712, undated anonymous complaint about the taille.

25. A.N. G^7 710, Jagotz to Desmaretz, February 4, 1708, asking for a share in a traité which he claimed would raise 25 million livres in six months; A.N. G^7 645, Rollet (avocat in Bellay) to Desmaretz, March 24, 1708, claimed that Chamillard had given him graces for his ideas and hoped that Desmaretz would continue to do so.

26. A.N. G^7 712, letters of October 9 and November 3, 1708.

27. A.N. G^7 710, letter of February 29, 1708.

28. A.N. G^7 710, letter of April 4, 1708, with marginal note that it was reported to the Royal Council that accepted 7 million livres in total in return for 9 million livres in mint bills, earning 5 percent instead of the proposed 6 percent.

29. A.N. G^7 1121, Desmaretz to Voysin, April 10, 1710, describes Bernard's loan as an informal arrangement. Bernard submitted an account for 1711 that showed he had been giving 700,000 livres per month until April 1710, when he increased the loan to 1 million livres monthly, for which Bernard received 121,827 livres for the expense of exchanging the money into Flemish coin and 22,436 livres in interest. Any delay in the terms of repayment increased the interest to as much as 20 percent.

30. Most of the unadopted propositions for Desmaretz's ministry can be found in A.N. G^7 710–26.

31. Register books indicating to whom matters were referred can be found in A.N. G^7 736–45.

32. A.N. G^7 712, letter of December 13, 1708.

33. A.N. G^7 712, letters dated October 29 and November 5, 1708.

34. A.N. G^7 711, letter of May 6, 1708.

35. A.N. G^7 712.

36. A.N. G^7 712, letters of December 6, 14, and 18, 1708, and January 1, 1709.

37. A.N. G^7 711, letter of May 1, 1708, about uniting the bailliage and bureau in Mauriac that was referred to Le Peletier des Forts, as well as a list of proposals dated June 29, 1708, with a request that Le Cousturier examine the proposals and Desmaretz's remarks, then speak to the minister about them; A.N. G^7 717, March 17, 1710, a proposal requesting a nine-year monopoly for supplying the army, was examined by Nointel, Rouillé de Coudray, and Vaubourg before being rejected;

A.N. G^7 712, September 2, 1708, a proposal to create a sixth president in the Montauban Cour des Aides, was referred to the provincial intendant and a final decision was made on September 16, 1708.

38. A.N. G^7 712 has two such lists: one, dated December 27, 1708, is in Desmaretz's handwriting; the other, dated December 19, 1708, is in de la Garde's handwriting.

39. A.N. G^7 712, September 1708.

40. See Schaeper, *Economy of France*, for a survey of the literature and questions about whether France was faring as poorly as most historians have assumed.

41. Philip T. Hoffman, *Growth in a Traditional Society: The French Countryside, 1450–1815* (Princeton, NJ: Princeton University Press, 2000).

42. Boislisle, *Correspondance des contrôleurs généraux*, 1:545.

43. Ibid., 546.

44. See the letter dated June 13, 1693, in *Louis XIV*, ed. John C. Rule (Englewood Cliffs, NJ: Prentice-Hall, 1974), 52.

45. Michèle Virol, "Project de dîme royale: Sa genèse," in Virol, *Oisivetés de Monsieur de Vauban*, 696.

46. Seventeenth-century French spelled the term "dixme," though "dîme" will be used throughout, except when referencing original documents from the time.

47. Jacqueline Hecht, "Le vie de Pierre le Pesant, seigneur de Boisguilbert," in *Pierre de Boisguilbert ou la naissance de l'économie politique* (Paris: Institut Nationale d'Études Démographiques, 1966), 1:175–78; Jean Peter, *Le Journal de Vauban* (Paris: Economica, 2007), 318–24; Michèle Virol, *Vauban: De la gloire du roi au service de l'État* (Seyssel: Champ Vallon, 2003), 343–51; Michèle Virol, "Projet de dîme royale," in Virol, *Oisivetés de Monsieur de Vauban*, 695–705. Vauban described his sessions in a letter dated June 18, 1700, indicating that he had read his proposal to the king some time in May or early June.

48. Vauban's *Projet d'une Dixme Royale* can be found in Vauban, *La Dîme Royale*, ed. Emmanuel Le Roy Ladurie (Paris: Imprimérie Nationale, 1992), and in Virol, *Oisivetés de Monsieur Vauban*, 751–957.

49. Vauban's work has been of great interest to demographic historians because of his efforts, whether correct or incorrect, to estimate the total population of the kingdom of France.

50. See Roland Mousnier, *La dîme de Vauban* (Paris: Centre de Documentation Universitaires, 1968), 62ff. A minot equaled approximately 52.033 liters, according to Zupko, *French Weights and Measures*, 113. A minot of salt was enough salt to supply fourteen people annually. The price of a minot had been as high as 45 livres.

51. Vauban's tables for augmenting revenues can be found, for example, in Ladurie, *La Dîme Royale*, 148–51. Actual spending figures can be found in A.N. KK 355 for the years 1689–99, excluding 1696 and 1698. Tables from this source can be found in Boislisle, *Correspondance des contrôleurs généraux*, 1:598–99 and, for Desmaretz's figures for the year 1708–14, 3:673–82. Tables for the years 1700–7 can be found in Forbonnais, *Recheches et considérations*, 4:291 (facing) and 5:385 for 1715.

52. Ragot de Beaumont to Le Peletier de Souzy, September 19, 1704, in Virol, *Vauban*, 351.

53. Virol, "Project de dîme royale," 702.

54. Hecht, "La vie de Boisguilbert, 215n1.

55. A.N. G^7 1127. Another manuscript copy bound in d'Argenson's arms is in Arsenal mss. 4067.

56. A.N. G^7 833.

57. A.N. E 806^c–7^A, fol. 166–67, July 30, 1709, no. 59 names Jean le Pottier, chevalier seigneur de la Hestroy, as lieutenant général de l'épée in the bailliage of Amiens at Montreuil-sur-Mer. In B.N. mss. fr. 14294, fol. 158–265, written in 1704, de la Hestroy claims to be a lieutenant general in the admiralty at Dunkirk. Rothkrug, *Opposition to Louis XIV*, 435n130, and Schaeper, *French Council of Commerce*, 24, reveal that de la Hestroy was submitting ideas to the government as early as 1697.

58. A.N. G^7 1127, "Réflexions," 1–8; J.-B. Maurice Vignes, *Histoire des doctrines sur l'impôt en France: Les origines et les destinées de la Dîme Royale de Vauban* (1909; repr., Paris: Librairie Générale de Droit et de Jurisprudence, 1961), 9–13, points out the similarities between Vauban's work and Boisguilbert's *Le Détail de la France*.

59. A.N. G^7 1127, "Réflexions," 10ff.

60. A.N. G^7 833.

61. A.N. G^7 1127, "Réflexions," 1–2.

62. A.N. G^7 833.

63. Boislisle, *Saint-Simon*, 14:331–33. For his opinion of Boisguilbert, see 14:333–43.

64. Vignes, *Histoire des doctrines sur l'impôt*, 43–44. Burgundy wrote the memorandum in which he explained his ideas some time between 1709 and his death in February 1712.

65. Quietism emerged as a religious movement in Italy in the 1680s. Quietism is the belief that the spirit of God would visit a person in prayer and meditation, transcending any need to participate in mass or other church practices. The Church condemned some of the tenets of Quietism in 1687. Madame Guyon brought Quietism to France and attracted the support of Madame de Maintenon and Fénelon. When various senior clerics began criticizing the doctrine, Louis XIV took action to bring order to the Church of France. See Jacques Le Brun's article on Quietism in Bluche, *Dictionnaire du Grand Siècle*.

66. Gilbert Faccarello, *The Foundations of Laissez-faire: The Economics of Pierre de Boisguilbert* (London: Routledge, 1999), 61–63. Faccarello demonstrates that Fénelon's "liberal" attitude is the antithesis of anything advocated by Boisguilbert, who was a true liberal in the classic sense of the term.

67. Fénelon, *Oeuvres complètes*, ed. Gosselin, 7:159.

68. Ibid., 183.

69. Boislisle, *Saint-Simon*, 21:286–89 and 384. Beauvillier was dead when Saint-Simon wrote, so we have only his word on the subject.

70. Vignes, *Histoire des doctrines sur l'impôt*, 43n11.

71. According to Boislisle, *Saint-Simon*, 21:319–20, and *Dangeau*, 13:398 (April 28, 1711), the king ordered Desmaretz to work with Burgundy to instruct him on finances. Burgundy's faction did not survive Louis XIV. Chevreuse died in November 1712, Beauvillier in August 1714, and Fénelon in January 1715. Only Saint-Simon outlived the king, but by then he was hoping that his friend, the future Regent, would make the reforms he wanted.

72. Hecht, "Vie de Boisguilbert," 147ff. Hecht assembles an excellent collection of the correspondence from and about Boisguilbert on pp. 247–478, culled from the Archives Nationales, the Archives de Guerre, and departmental archives.

73. Ibid., 257–58, intendant of Rouen to Pontchartrain, November 24, 1692.
74. Boislisle, *Saint-Simon,* 14:326–27.
75. Hecht, "Vie de Boisguilbert," 157–59.
76. A.N. G^7 721, letters of October 27, 1703, and January 6 and September 21, 1704. This carton contains all of Boisguilbert's correspondence with the controllers general from 1691 to 1713. Of the three controller generals with whom Boisguilbert corresponded, only two letters to Pontchartrain survive, while sixty-eight to Chamillard survive, and seventeen to Desmaretz and his aides.
77. Smedley-Weill, *Intendants de Louis XIV,* 320 (chart).
78. A.N. G^7 721, letter of June 13, 1700, with attached "Traité sur la Dîme Royale."
79. Hecht, "Vie de Boisguilbert," 179. Guerre, A^1 2469, nos. 57 bis, 58–68, and 87–97, are either letters from Boisguilbert to Chamlay or copies of his mémoires.
80. A.N. G^7 721. His letter of December 31, 1701, insisted that three hours' reading of his latest book (*Factum de la France*) would reveal the truth behind his ideas.
81. A.N. G^7 721, notes on letters of November 23, 1704, and June 25, 1705.
82. A.N. G^7 721, letter of October 27, 1703.
83. A.N. G^7 721, letter of December 31, 1701, mentions 50 million livres, but by October 27, 1703, after meeting Desmaretz, he had raised the figure to 80 million.
84. A.N. G^7 721, six letters from July 1–22, 1704.
85. Boisguilbert to Vauban, August 22, 1704, and Vauban to Chamillard, August 26, 1704, in Hecht, "Correspondance de Boisguilbert avec Michel Chamillart," in *Pierre de Boisguilbert,* 1:325–27.
86. A.N. G^7 721, notes on letter of September 21, 1704.
87. A.N. G^7 721, letter of December 23, 1704.
88. Bouville to Desmaretz, November 22, 1704, in Boislisle, *Correspondance des contrôleurs généraux,* 2:207, no. 683.
89. A.N. G^7 721, letters from Boisguilbert dated August 27 and September 7, 10, 14, 17, and 24, 1705. Also, see Bouville to Chamillard (or Desmaretz), dated September 22 and 24, 1705.
90. A.N. G^7 721, Le Camus to Chamillard, dated simply September 1705, with marginal notes.
91. A.N. G^7 721, Basville to Chamillard, letter of October 11, 1705. The same letter can be found in Boislisle, *Correspondance des contrôleurs généraux,* 2:277–78, no. 891.
92. Bonney, "Secret de Leurs Familles," 387, and Bonney, "Concurrence étatique," 40–41. Simone Meysonnier, *La Balance et l'Horloge: Le Genèse de la pensée libérale en France au XVIIIe siècle* (Paris: Les Éditions de la Passion, 1989), 43, and Mireille Touzery, *L'Invention de l'impôt sur le revenue: La taille tarifiée, 1715–1789* (Paris: Comité pour l'histoire économique et financière de la France, 1994), 13, also state that the experiment took place.
93. Boislisle, *Correspondance des contrôleurs généraux,* 2:273, no. 875.
94. Touzery, *Taille tarifiée,* 37–54, discusses the experiments with the dixième in the election of Niort in the generality of La Rochelle during 1718–20 and its extension to the election of Pont-l'Évêque in the generality of Rouen. This happened at a time when John Law was experimenting with financial innovations in an effort to escape France's postwar debt problems. Boislisle, *Saint-Simon,* 14:342–43, speaks of

the proposed experiment and its failure because the marquis de Bullion demanded a reduction of the taille for his estates that was contrary to the principal of equal and proportional taxation that Boisguilbert was seeking to establish.

95. Hecht, "Vie de Boisguilbert," 189–91.

96. The whole title was *Factum de la France, ou Moyens très facile de faire recevoir au Roi quatre vingts millions par-dessus la capitation, practicables par deux heures travail de Messieurs les ministres, et un mois d'exécution de la part des peuples, sans congédier aucun fermier général ni particulier . . . et l'on montre en même temps l'impossibilité de sortir autrement de la conjoncture présente* (Factum of France, or a very easy means of obtaining for the king eighty million over and above the capitation, to be achieved in two hours' work for Messieurs les ministres and one month's application by the people, without dismissing any farmer general or individual . . . and the impossibility of escaping from the present conjuncture by any other means demonstrated simultaneously).

97. Hecht, "Vie de Boisguilbert," 197–201.

98. Ibid., 205.

99. A, N. G^7 1726, no. 313, d'Argenson to Desmaretz, September 6, 1710, in which d'Argenson wrote about an unknown project by Boisguilbert that was supposed to raise 100 million livres. The project does not survive. D'Argenson doubted its "certitude et solidité."

100. A.N. G^7 721, letter of January 29, 1713.

101. Bruce G. Carruthers, *City of Capital: Politics and Markets in the English Financial Revolution* (Princeton, NJ: Princeton University Press, 1996), 76–77.

102. Guerre A^1 2469 passim; A.N. G^7 716 and 718 contain bank proposals; Boislisle, *Correspondance des contrôleurs généraux,* 2:519–21 and 3:636–51, print some of these proposals, as well as others from A.A.E., Mém. et Doc. France, 137, fol. 57.

103. A.N. G^7 1629, Law to Chamillard, June 15 and July 18, 1707.

104. Paul Harsin, *Crédit public et Banque d'État en France du XVIe au XVIIIe siècle* (Paris: Droz, 1933), 15–36.

105. Antoin E. Murphy, *John Law: Economic Theorist and Policy Maker* (Oxford: Clarendon Press, 1997), 34–66.

106. Paul Harsin, preface to John Law, *Oeuvres complètes* (Paris: Librairie du Recueil Sirey, 1934), 1:xxxi–viii. In volume 2, Harsin reprinted part of the correspondence between Desmaretz and Law, along with two mémoires by Law. See also Murphy, *John Law,* 123–42.

107. Edgar Faure, *La banqueroute de Law: 17 juillet 1720* (Paris: Gallimard, 1977), 54–56. A.A.E., Mém. et Doc., France, 137, fol. 11–19 and 21–26, are Desmaretz's mémoires written during the Regency criticizing Law's bank.

108. Lévy, *Capitalistes et pouvoir,* 1:49–75; Jacques Saint-Germain, *Samuel Bernard: Banquier des Rois* (Paris: Hachette, 1960), 7–20; Dessert, *Argent, pouvoir et société,* 532–33, no. 37; Maya de Loen, *L'homme qui prêtait aux Rois* (Paris: Éditions de Fallois, 2003), 285–92; and Lüthy, *Banque protestante,* 1:71–77 and 121–25 on Bernard, and 188–226 on the crisis of 1709 and Bernard's role in it. Colonel Herlaut, "Projets de création d'une banque royale en France à la fin du règne de Louis XIV (1702–12)," *Revue d'histoire moderne* 8 (1933): 143–60, and André-E. Sayous, "La crise financière de 1709 à Lyon et à Genève," *Revue d'histoire économique et sociale* 24 (1938): 57–86 and 163–77, describe the story of the almost-bank of 1709 and the reasons for its failure.

109. A.N. G^7 1120, letters of July 7 and 26, and August 21, 1708.

110. Herlaut, "Projets de création d'une banque royale," 152–53.

111. A.N. G^7 716, "Proposition d'une banque."

112. Herlaut, "Projets de création d'une banque royale," 154–56; *Dangeau,* 12:297, first mentions the bank on December 31, 1708.

113. A.N. G^7 711, letter from the widow du Bois to Desmaretz, July 20, 1708, mentions the prejudice against Bernard and Nicolas in her attempt to have a different bank project adopted. A.A.E., Mém. et Doc., France, 137, fol. 130–32, and A.A.E., Mém. et Doc., France, 1182, fol. 290–93, are copies of the objections made by the Council of Commerce. A.N. G^7 1119, Desmaretz's remarks on a letter dated February 5, 1709, from one of Bernard's creditors, Lullin, reveal the minister's fears of an over-powerful Bernard, which he hoped to prevent by finding other people to join the backers of the bank.

114. A.N. E 800^B, fol. 16–19, two arrêts of January 22, 1709.

115. *Dangeau,* 12:323; A.N. G^7 1119, Caumartin to unknown (Desmaretz?), February 9, 1709.

116. Sayous, "Crise financière de 1709," 58–62 and 67–75.

117. Ibid., 75–84, and A.N. G^7 1121, Bernard or Nicolas to Desmaretz, August 17 and September 4, 1709, and January 4, 1710.

118. Desmaretz, *Compte rendu,* in Boislisle, *Correspondance des contrôleurs généraux,* 3:675; Lüthy, *Banque protestante,* 1:227.

119. Lüthy, *Banque protestante,* 1:211. A.N. G^7 1121 has a projected arrêt dated March 13, 1709, appointing Nointel, Voysin, and the accountant Le Bel to survey Bernard's accounts. A.N. E 857^B–58^A, fol. 189–92, December 2, 1713, acknowledged that the crown owed Bernard 1,705,332 livres for loans made during 1704–6.

120. A.A.E., Mém. et Doc, France, 137, fol. 85–87.

Chapter 5

1. Desmaretz, *Compte rendu,* in Boislisle, *Correspondance des contrôleurs généraux,* 3:674; A.N. E 789^B, February 25, 1708. Desmaretz mistakenly gave it the date of February 27.

2. Desmaretz, *Compte rendu,* in Boislisle, *Correspondance des contrôleurs généraux,* 3:674; A.N. G^7 1138–39, "Projet de régie du Trésor royale."

3. Boislisle, *Correspondance des contrôleurs généraux,* 3:1–2, no. 3, Trudaine (intendant at Lyon) to Desmaretz, February 25, 1708, and Bouville (intendant at Orléans) to Desmaretz, February 29, 1708.

4. Desmaretz, *Compte rendu,* in Boislisle, *Correspondance des contrôleurs généraux,* 3:674.

5. Boislisle, *Saint-Simon,* 16:34–37; *Dangeau,* 12:131 (May 6, 1708), but he does not name Bernard; *Sourches,* 11:75 (May 6, 1708), says that Bernard accompanied the king around Marly. Saint-Simon was scandalized at the fact that the king prostituted himself before someone like Bernard, as he had rarely shown anyone around Marly.

6. Desmaretz, *Compte rendu,* in Boislisle, *Correspondance des contrôleurs généraux,* 3:674.

7. See Forbonnais, *Récherches et considérations,* 4:314–27, for the first figure. B.N. mss fr. 7734 has the higher figure.

8. See A.N. G^7 1497 for a copy of the traité; A.N. E 820^B, fol. 517–19, September 30, 1710, for the new terms of the traité.

9. A.N. G^7 1497 and A.N. E 872^B, fol. 30–33, February 5, 1715, annul the traité because the offices were suppressed in 1710.

10. See A.N. G^7 1497 and A.N. E 790^A, fol. 260–62 for the commission of the traitants. See also A.N. E 819^B, fol. 468–77, August 26, 1710.

11. See A.N. G^7 1497 and A.N. E 792^B, fol. 259–69, for the résultats of May 22 and July 31, 1708. See also A.N. E 820^B, fol. 177–80, September 16, 1710.

12. A.N. G^7 1497 and E 793^B, fol. 99–107, June 12, 1708; A.N. E 847^B–48^A, fol. 388–89 February 7, 1713.

13. Desmaretz, *Compte rendu,* in Boislisle, *Correspondance des contrôleurs généraux,* 3:674.

14. A.N. E 801^B, fol. 6–9, February 19, 1709.

15. A.A.E., Mém. et Doc., France, vol. 137, fol. 83–84, July 26, 1709, in a letter to Madame de Maintenon.

16. Desmaretz, *Compte rendu,* in Boislisle, *Correspondance des contrôleurs généraux,* 3:675.

17. Ibid.

18. Boislisle, *Saint-Simon,* 17:405–10.

19. Desmaretz, *Compte rendu,* in Boislisle, *Correspondance des contrôleurs généraux,* 3:675.

20. See ibid. and A.N. E 1944, fol. 195–96, September 22, 1708; A.N. E 1947, fol. 75, March 5, 1709; A.N. E 804^A, fol. 3–4, May 7, 1709; A.N. E 807^B, fol. 151–52, August 27, 1709; A.N. E 1948, fol. 144–45, August 27, 1709, et. al., on loans and reducing or eliminating taxes on foodstuffs. On the year 1709 and its impact, see Monahan, *Years of Sorrow*; Lachiver, *Années de misère*; and Élie Berthet, *L'Année du Grand Hiver 1709* (Paris: Dentu, 1873).

21. Desmaretz, *Compte rendu,* in Boislisle, *Correspondance des contrôleurs généraux,* 3:675; A.N. E 809^B, fol. 266–67, October 29, 1709, reducing the taille for 1710 by a total of 8,132,605 livres in the pays d'élections.

22. A.N. G^7 1134, copies of the edicts of September 1708 and May 1709 creating 1 million livres in rentes for this purpose.

23. A.N. G^7 1497 and A.N. E 797^A, fol. 150–59.

24. A.N. G^7 1497 and A.N. E 793^B, fol. 359–71.

25. A.N. G^7 1497, June 26, 1708; A.N. G^7 1498, October 19, 1709; A.N. E 809^B, fol. 37–40, October 19, 1709, two arrêts concerning one of these résultats.

26. A.N. E 806^A, fol. 393–96, July 13, 1709; A.N. E 810^A, fol. 387–90, November 19, 1709; A.N. E 815^A, fol. 260–61, April 1, 1710.

27. A.N. G^7 717, mémoire of July 20, 1710, reported on July 21.

28. A.N. MM 1007, *Revenus du Roy, Année 1710,* fol. 9–10. The figures given are almost exactly the same as those found in B.N. mss., fr. 7752, Malet's "Mémoire sur l'histoire des finances," 246–47.

29. A.N. K 2412, no. 31.

30. B.N. mss., fr. 7734, for the years 1710 and 1711.

31. A.N. G^7 1498 and A.N. E 821^B, fol. 110–11, March 18 and October 21, 1710, on salt prices in Franche Comté; A.N. G^7 1498, résultat of May 6, 1710, on prices on the Canal du Midi.

32. A.N. MM 1007, fol. 10–13; Desmaretz, *Compte rendu,* in Boislisle, *Correspondance des contrôleurs généraux,* 3:677.

33. Desmaretz, *Compte rendu,* in Boislisle, *Correspondance des contrôleurs généraux,* 3:676; B.N. mss., fr. 7752, pp. 263 and 278; A.N. G^7 1102–7 contains accounts from the Caisse. Lüthy, *Banque protestante,* 1:225ff., has some descriptions amidst research into other topics.

34. John A. Lynn, *The Wars of Louis XIV, 1667–1714* (London: Longman, 1999), 334.

35. Torcy, *Journal,* 222–26 (July 16, 1710) and 230 (July 26, 1710). Louis XIV continued to play a double game over the next few months by sending the duc de Vendôme to Spain to take command of his troops there, while also sending the duc de Noailles to ask Philip V to leave the Spanish throne.

36. Desmaretz, *Compte rendu,* in Boislisle, *Correspondance des contrôleurs généraux,* 3:676.

37. Ibid. 3:676–77.

38. The declaration was actually dated October 14, 1710.

39. B.N. mss., fr. 7752, pp. 266–70; Malet, *Comptes rendus,* 146–47.

40. Both were also intendants of finances, but they attended this meeting because of their responsibilities within the controller general's office.

41. Boislisle, *Saint-Simon,* 20:159–81.

42. Louis-Auguste-Achille de Harlay-Bonneuil, comte de Cély, became a master of requests in 1707. He would become intendant at Pau in 1712, at Metz in 1715, at Strasbourg in 1724, and at Paris in 1728. He also became councilor of state in 1721. He died in 1739 as intendant of Paris. See Boislisle, *Saint-Simon,* 4:143n, and Antoine, *Gouvernement,* 127.

43. See Saint-Simon's addition to the journal entry of November 23, 1694, in *Dangeau,* 5:110–11.

44. Jean-Louis Thireau, *Les idées politiques de Louis XIV* (Paris: PUF, 1973), 72–73.

45. *Dangeau,* 13:248–49 (September 23, 1710), 254 (September 30, 1710), 257 (October 6, 1710), 265 (October 20, 1710), and 269 (October 26, 1710).

46. *Sourches,* 12:358 (September 21, 1710) and 372 (October 2, 1710).

47. *Dangeau,* 13:256 (October 4, 1710), 258 (October 7, 1710), and 261 (October 14, 1710). The king went to Marly October 8–18; therefore, the Royal Council did not meet on the Saturdays of October 11 and 18. Christophe Levantal, *Louis XIV: Chronographie d'un règne* (Gollion, Switzerland: Infolio, 2009), 2:805, relies on Dangeau to determine where the king was at this time.

48. A.N. G^7 1726, no. 313, D'Argenson to Desmaretz, September 6, 1710, marked "veu" by the minister. Bonney, "Secret de Leurs Familles," 387, insists that Boisguilbert was not consulted about the introduction of the dixième.

49. Desmaretz, *Compte rendu,* in Boislisle, *Correspondance des contrôleurs généraux,* 3:676.

50. See A.N. G^7 834 for both letters.

51. A.A.E., Mém. et Doc., France, 1173, fol. 107–12.

52. A.N. G^7 1138–39, letters of October 29 and December 15, 1710, and May 7, 1711.

53. A.N. G^7 739, register book entitled "Mémoires et placets renvoiées de 5 juillet 1710 à 3 mars 1711," entry dated August 6, 1710.

54. Bluche, *Dictionnaire du Grand Siècle,* 1396. Saint-Pierre, although a priest, was more attracted to the ideas of Descartes and rationalism than he was to any religious thought. He was named abbé of a wealthy monastery at Tirou in December 1702. He would later be secretary to the future Cardinal de Polignac, one of two plenipotentiaries to the negotiations for peace at Utrecht in 1712. He blamed Louis XIV for the wars at the end of the reign, and was critical of the way Louis XIV governed France, although his sentiments did not become known until the Regency, with the publication of his essay *Discours de la Polysynodie* in 1718. He was subsequently expelled from the Académie française, although his seat was not filled until after his death in 1743.

55. A.N. G^7 1135–37.

56. Paul Harsin, "L'Abbé de Saint-Pierre économiste d'après de nouveaux documents inédits," *Revue d'histoire économique et sociale* 20 (1932): 187n4.

57. A.A.E., Mém. et Doc., France, 1173, fol. 143–62.

58. A.A.E., Mém. et Doc., France, fol. 337–38.

59. See Merle L. Perkins, *The Moral and Political Philosophy of the Abbé de Saint-Pierre* (Geneva: Droz, 1959), 145, for the publication of his works; Édouard Goumy, *Étude sur la vie et les écrits de l'Abbé de Saint-Pierre* (Paris: Hachette, 1859), 29–30.

60. A.N. G^7 718.

61. A.N. G^7 722; half of this carton contains his correspondence with Desmaretz or de la Garde from 1703 to 1715. Favre-Lejeune, *Secrétaires du Roi,* 1:328. Cazier bought an office of Secrétaire du Roi in 1677 and sold it in 1699. He was a councilor in the Estates of Flanders and a counselor in the Parlement of Metz. According to Pierre Goubert, *Familles marchandes sous l'Ancien Régime: Les Danse et les Motte, de Beauvais* (Paris: SEVPEN, 1959), 121–22, Cazier was one of the creditors to the royal tapestry manufacture at Beauvais. He was put in place to administer the tapestry manufacture by the Council of Commerce but produced a financial mess that led the workers to revolt.

62. A.N. G^7 722, letter of May 1, 1705.

63. A.N. G^7 722, letters or abstracts dated June 9 and 13, and August 12 or 13, 1710.

64. A.N. G^7 722, on letter of December 17, 1710. Cazier would continue to submit mémoires of various subjects until the end of the reign.

65. A.N. G^7 722, June 15, 1710.

66. Jean-François-Louis Millain was the secretary to Chancellors Pontchartrain and Voysin before becoming secretary to the duc de Bourbon. He inherited his father's office of secrétaire du roi in 1695 and sold it in 1717. See Favre-Lejeune, *Secrétaires du Roi,* 2:968.

67. A.N. G^7 722, June 16, 1710.

68. Fénelon, *Oeuvres complètes,* 7:321–24. Fénelon seemed to be echoing Allied propaganda. The Allies, particularly the Anglo-Dutch, had been using publications in a propaganda war with France, calling for an Estates General to meet regularly in order to prevent the agressive and bellicose policies of Louis XIV from being repeated, on the theory that a representative assembly would be able to restrict the absolute monarch's aggressive tendencies. This propaganda war began in 1709 and continued until a peace treaty was signed. See Joseph Klaits, *Printed Propaganda*

Under Louis XIV: Absolute Monarchy and Public Opinion (Princeton, NJ: Princeton University Press, 1976), 211, 260–70.

69. A.N. G^7 722.

70. Ibid.

71. A.N. G^7 17; Boislisle, *Correspondance des contrôleurs généraux,* 3:310–11, no. 840.

72. A.N. G^7 17.

73. Boislisle, *Correspondance des contrôleurs généraux,* 3:695–97.

74. A.N. G^7 1138–39. I believe that Jean-Baptiste Louis Berryer de La Ferrière is the author of this mémoire. He had been a master of requests since 1678 and would die in 1743 as the grand dean of the masters of requests. See Antoine, *Gouvernement,* 29–30. His father, Louis Berryer, had been one of Mazarin's financial managers and later supported Colbert. He managed estates owned by the king's brother, was a secrétaire du conseil d'état as well as secrétaire du roi. The suspect financial activities that had made him very wealthy led to his downfall under Le Peletier. Nevertheless, members of his family would remain in positions of significance thereafter. See Limon, *Traitants et fraudes,* 23–24 and 72–75; Dessert, *Argent, pouvoir et société,* 534; and Favre-Lejeune, *Secrétaires du Roi,* 1:202.

75. A.N. G^7 1138–39.

76. A.N. G^7 575, an undated letter to the minister; A.N. G^7 1841–48, no. 198, letter of August 4, 1714.

77. A.N. E 828^B, fol. 59–60, May 12, 1711, commissioning Harlay de Cély and Maupeou to sit on this committee.

78. *Dangeau,* 13:445 (July 20, 1711). Saint-Simon used Dangeau's *Journal* to assist him in writing his *Mémoires.* His attitude was antipathetic to Harlay de Cély, in any case. See Boislisle, *Saint-Simon,* 38:140–41.

79. Boislisle, *Saint-Simon,* 2:223 and 6:287.

80. Boislisle, *Correspondance des contrôleurs généraux,* 3:320, no. 865, letter of November 17, 1710, and 3:331, no. 895, letter of November 21, 1710.

81. A.N. G^7 1127.

82. Boislisle, *Saint-Simon,* 14:396n4; A.N. G^7 1494, letter from Delacroix to Desmaretz, February 14, 1704; B.N. mss., fr. 7584, fol. 57, Delacroix's declaration of wealth to the Chambre de justice of 1716–17. See Bluche, *Dictionnaire du Grand Siècle,* 325, s.v. "Chouin" (article by Évelyne Legond); Claeys, *Dictionnaire biographique des financiers,* 1:626–27; Dessert, *Argent, pouvoir et société,* 613–14. Delacroix, son of a receiver general who was active in the early part of the reign, also participated in seventy traités between 1688 and 1708. He was also involved in supplying the army and navy.

The Dauphin emulated his father in secretly marrying a second wife whose nobility was considered beneath that of an heir to the throne. Like Maintenon, Chouin did not participate in official court ceremonies but she exerted influence over the Dauphin and his circle.

83. Favre-Lejeune, *Secrétaires du roi,* 2:1020–22. Jon Desmarest Rudd, "Philibert Orry and France's Contrôle Général (1730–45)" (PhD dissertation, Georgetown University, 1988), 18–71. Jean Orry was the son of a Paris merchant. He also was received as a member of the Order of St. Michel. His son would become controller general of finances under Louis XV. See A.N. G^7 1802, nos. 176 and 187–89, letters to Pontchartrain as controller general about army supplies during 1693; A.N.

G^7 645, two letters to de la Garde, April 11 and 15, 1708, about his position in the Metz Parlement; A.N. G^7 569, letter to Desmaretz, February 10, 1709, on the failure of the royal bank and his role during Chamillard's ministry; A.A.E., Mém. et Doc., France, 137, fol. 149–49, eighteen proposals by Orry made prior to April 10, 1710.

84. A.N. G^7 1138–39.

85. Ibid.

86. The dowager queen of Poland was the widow of Jan Sobieski, king of Poland from 1676 until 1696 and hero of the siege of Vienna in 1683. After his death, his queen, Marie Casimire Louise de la Grange d'Arquien, returned to her native France, where she died in 1716.

87. A.N. G^7 1138–39.

88. A.N. G^7 575.

89. A.N. G^7 1138–39. The difference between the form of an edict and a declaration appears in the salutation and the end of the preamble. Otherwise, the laws can look exactly the same. "Louis, par la grace de Dieu, Roi de France et de Navarre, à tous ceux présent et à venir" in an edict becomes "à tous ceux qui ces présentes lettres verront" in a declaration. Another minor word change takes place at the end of the preamble.

90. That is, rather than calling some sort of representative assembly, as Fénelon and Millain had recommended.

91. A.N. G^7 1138–39.

92. Schaeper, *French Council of Commerce*, 130.

93. See A.N. G^7 1138–39 for rough drafts and memoranda, and K 2413, no. 77, for a copy of the final declaration of October 7. A declaration of October 14 reduced the interest rates on promises of the caisse des emprunts from 10 to 5 percent; see A.N. G^7 1138–39 and K 2413, no. 79. This measure called for renewing the promises for four years but a declaration of December 20, 1710, called for renewing them annually until the war ended; see A.N. G^7 1138–39 and K 2413, no. 110.

94. The rentes against the postes held by the dowager queen of Poland were excluded from this interest rate reduction by arrêt; see A.N. E 821^A, fol. 212–13, October 7, 1710.

95. A.N. G^7 1138–39 and K 2413, no. 86, edict of October 1710.

96. A.N. G^7 1138–39 and K 2413, no. 83, edict of October 1710. Attempts to end the circulation of these bills had begun with a declaration of December 15, 1708; see K 2411, no. 55. Another million livres in rentes were created in June 1711 for the same purpose, extending the circulation of these bills until October 1, 1711; see K 2414, no. 34, edict of June 1711.

97. A.N. K 2413, no. 66, edict of September 1710.

98. A.N. G^7 1138–39 and K 2413, no. 76, declaration of October 7, 1710.

99. See A.N. E 837^A–76^A passim from March 8, 1712, for such deals with the generalities of Montauban, Alençon, Caen, Orléans, Bourges, La Rochelle, Tours, and Poitiers, the province of Béarn, a variety of towns in the Rouen generality, and the town of Bordeaux.

100. A.N. G^7 1138–39 and K 2413, nos. 75 and 78, declarations of October 7, 1710.

101. A.N. E 821^B, fol. 2–3, October 21, 1710. A declaration of July 6, 1709, had reduced mint bills to denominations as small as 200 livres to facilitate their receipt

at the mints; see K 2412, nos. 50–51. A similar measure permitted the farmers general to split their bills for the same reason; see E 821^{A}, fol. 156–59, October 7, 1710.

102. A.N. G^7 1138–39 and K 2413, no. 74, declaration of October 7, 1710. A declaration of December 4, 1708, had made an earlier attempt to convert bills of the treasurers of the extraordinary of war into rentes at denier 16 (6.25 percent); see K. 2411, no. 52.

103. A.N. E 821^{A}, fol. 119–22, October 7, 1710; A.N. G^7 1138–39, a mémoire of August 21, 1710, on why this should be done.

104. A.N. G^7 1138–39, letter of October 25, 1710.

105. A.N. G^7 1138–39.

106. A.N. E 1954, fol. 118–19.

107. A.N. G^7 1138–39, paper entitled "Project de département à faire entre messrs. les commissaires du Conseil pour le dixième des revenus des fons," written by Desmaretz.

108. A.N. G^7 828–30.

109. A.N. E 1958, fol. 11–12, January 12, 1711, commissioning d'Argenson and Harlay de Cély to search the homes of two speculators. A. M. de Boislisle, "L'impôt du dixième," in Boislisle, *Saint-Simon,* 20:469, mentions an entry in a Parisian diary describing the crackdown and imprisonments in the Bastille, For-L'Evêque, and the Châtelet. The term *agioteur* (speculator) was coined at this time. D'Argenson was in charge of the crackdown in Paris.

110. A.N. E 824^{B}–25^{A}, fol. 358–59, February 3, 1711, charges the gens d'affaires to pay funds to Sr. Bonny, a commis who was commissioned to enforce the edict of the previous month. Boislisle, "Impôt du dixième," 467, mentions that the edict of January 1711 replaced the one of October 1710.

111. A.N. G^7 545–50, letters from Bouville, January 5, 12, and 28, 1711; A.N. G^7 835, letter to Clautrier, January 13, 1711, mentions rolls of these taxes. See Boislisle, "Impôt du dixième," 469, for the figure about Crozat.

112. A.N. G^7 1594.

113. A.N. K 2413, no. 22, edict of March 1710, and K 2414, no. 48, declaration of October 3, 1711. A.N. G^7 739, book entitled "lettres renvoyées du 1er septembre à 22 novembre 1710," entries sent to Guyet on the "taxe des aisez."

114. A.N. K 2413, no. 85, declaration of October 21, 1710, reducing the price of salt; A.N. E 820^{A}–23^{C} passim for arrêts reducing the taille for 1711.

115. A.N. G^7 1138–39 and A.N. K 2413, no. 80, declaration of October 14, 1710. A declaration of December 27, 1710, instructed comptables in how to withhold the dixième from funds entrusted to their care; see A.N. G^7 1138–39 and A.N. K 2413, no. 111.

Chapter 6

1. A.N. G^7 1138–39, letter to provincial intendants, October 30–31, 1710.

2. A.N. E 822^{B}–23^{A}, fol. 119–20, no. 42, November 25, 1710.

3. See Bignon to Desmaretz, December 1, 1710, in Boislisle, *Correspondance des contrôleurs généraux,* 3:320–21, no. 865n; and Turgot de St. Clair to Desmaretz, March 9, 1711, in idem, 3:361, no. 1000.

4. Ibid., 3:377–78, no. 1066, letter of June 5, 1711.

5. Ibid., 3:388, no. 1095, letter of July 18, 1711.

6. A.N. E 823^{B}, fol. 62–63, no. 20, December 9, 1710.

7. A.N. E 823^{B}, fol. 64–65, no. 21, December 9, 1710; A.N. E 824^{B}–25^{A}, fol. 113–16, nos. 3–4, January 31, 1711.

8. A.N. E 824^{B}–25^{A}, fol. 109–10, no. 1, January 31, 1711.

9. A.N. K 2413, no. 80, Article XI.

10. A.N. E 824^{A}, fol. 330–32, no. 30, January 20, 1711.

11. A.N. E 823^{B}, fol. 292–93, no. 1, December 20, 1710; A.N. E 828^{B}, fol. 385–86, no. 15, May 26, 1711.

12. A.N. E 829^{B}, fol. 2–5, no. 1.

13. See Caroline Le Mao, *Chronique du Bordelais du Grand Siècle: le Mémorial de Savignac* (Bordeaux: Presses Universitaires de Bordeaux, 2004), 242–43, for the text of declarations of the dixième made by Joseph François Ignace de Labat de Savignac on his mother's behalf for property she owned in Savignac and elsewhere in the Bordeaux region in September 1711.

14. A.N. G^{7} 1138–39, mémoire accompanying letter to the provincial intendants of October 30–31, 1710.

15. Ibid.; A.N. E 829^{B}, fol. 245–46, no. 23, June 23, 1711, requiring that the gens d'affaires prove that they had paid half of their dixième before the crown would hear any appeal for a reduction or discharge.

16. A.N. G^{7} 1138–39, letter to the provincial intendants of October 30–31, 1710, and "Instructions pour les contrôleurs."

17. A.N. G^{7} 1138–39, "Instructions pour les directeurs."

18. The son of a prosecutor at the Châtelet, Barrangue purchased an office of avocat in the Parlement and in the councils as well as an office of secrétaire du roi in 1696. He was a major investor in extraordinary affairs, overseas trading companies, military and naval supplies, real estate development in Paris, and farming the revenues of the abbey of Saint-Germain-des-Prés. Despite his multiple financial investments, he died penniless. See Dessert, *Argent, pouvoir et société,* 526, no. 19, and Favre-Lejeune, *Secrétaires du Roi,* 1:164.

19. A.N. G^{7} 1138–39, letters to de la Garde or Desmaretz of November 29 and December 8, 1710; A.N. G^{7} 750–60, letter from de la Garde to Sr. Barrangue, "Con^{er} Sec du Roy"; B.N. mss. fr. 7587, fol. 24, identifies Antoine Barrangue as a "Sec du Roy," while his son is called a counselor to the Châtelet.

20. A.N. E 823^{B}, fol. 309–10, December 20, 1710.

21. A.N. E 824^{A}, fol. 96–97, no. 2, January 13, 1711; A.N. K 2414, no. 3, declaration of January 13, 1711.

22. A.N. E 1954, fol. 168, December 15, 1710, for the officers of the marc d'or; A.N. E 823^{B}, fol. 349–52, December 20, 1710, for seized property; B.N. Clairambault, mss. 1178, fol. 1581–83, letters patent of January 20, 1711, on officers of the Order of the Holy Spirit and marc d'or; Boislisle, *Correspondance des contrôleurs généraux,* 3:427, no. 1224, Roujault to Desmaretz, February 13, 1712, on the property of fugitive Huguenots.

23. A.N. E 822^{A}, fol. 417–18, no. 71, November 18, 1710; and A.N. E 823^{C}, fol. 97–98, no. 26, December 23, 1710.

24. A.N. E 1954, fol. 140–41, November 25, 1710.

25. A.N. E 822^{A}, fol. 419–20, no. 72, November 18, 1710; A.N. G^{7} 1138–39, Chasteauneuf to Desmaretz, October 9, 1710, offering to perform this service.

26. A.N. E 830^{B}, fol. 78–79, no. 26, July 7, 1711, and A.N. E 839^{C}–40^{A}, fol. 19–20, no. 4, May 28, 1712. Jean Goujon began as a taille receiver in Olonne, controller general of the rentes of the Chambre des Comptes in Paris in 1684, and as receiver general for Metz (1687–93). He bought an office of secrétaire du roi in 1689 and became a secretary on the Conseil d'État Direction et Finances in 1693, and kept both offices until his death in 1730. He was an investor in several extraordinary affairs. He was related by marriage to many important people at court. He was in constant contact with Desmaretz, socially and professionally. His daughter married Bouville's son and thus Desmaretz's nephew. See Dessert, *Argent, pouvoir et société*, 594, no. 214; Favre-Lejeune, *Secrétaire du Roi*, 1:643, Antoine, *Gouvernement*, 118; and Claeys, *Dictionnaire biographique des financiers*, 1:981–82. His brother Pierre was a receiver general of finances for the Three Bishoprics as well as an investor in royal finances.

27. A.N. E 840^{B}, fol. 176–77, no. 53, June 21, 1712. This is not Jean-Roland Malet, who was mentioned previously.

28. Boislisle, *Correspondance des contrôleurs généraux*, 3:363, no. 1009, and A.N. G^{7} 537–40, Torcy to Desmaretz, March 21, 1711, and January 16, 1712. Desmaretz's response of January 26, 1712, can be found in A.A.E., Mém. et Doc., France, 1186, fol. 56.

29. A.N. E 822^{A}, fol. 230–31, no. 4.

30. A.N. E 1956, fol. 297–303, two arrêts of January 13, 1711.

31. Boislisle, *Correspondance des contrôleurs généraux*, 3: 366–67, no. 1021 and notes, Desmaretz to the comte de Luc (ambassador to the Swiss), April 1, 1711.

32. A.N. E 1960, fol. 87–92, July 28, 1711, accepting the clergy's offer and permitting the loan. A.N. G^{7} 1138–39, a mémoire on how to carry out this exemption; A.N. E 836^{A}, fol. 207–8, no. 30, January 12, 1712, and A.N. E 836^{B}, fol. 149–50, January 19, 1712, commissioning Goujon.

33. A.N. E 844^{B}, fol. 16–17, no. 4, October 18, 1712, for Verdun; A.N. E 848^{B}, fol. 359–60, no. 9, February 21, 1713, for Toul; A.N. E 857^{B}–58^{A}, fol. 229–30, no. 24, December 2, 1713, for Metz; A.N. E 853^{B}, fol. 74–77, no. 24, July 18, 1713, for the clergy of Longwy, etc.; A.N. E 833^{B}–34^{A}, fol. 100–103, October 27, 1711, accepting 60,000 livres from the Order of the Knights of Malta.

34. Bignon de Blanzy to Desmaretz, May 15, 1715, in Boislisle, *Correspondance des contrôleurs généraux*, 3:588, no. 1828.

35. Hippolyte Maurice Houques-Fourcade, *Les impôts sur le revenu en France au XVIIIe siècle: Histoire du dixième and du cinquantième Leur application dans la Généralité de Guyenne* (Bordeaux: Eiret, 1889), 172–77. The arrêts ordering these subscriptions are in A.N. E 826^{A}–75^{B} passim.

36. Income declarations were difficult to get from nobles in Brittany, who expected that the province would make a subscription to escape the dixième; plus, the intendant was reluctant to use constraints during a meeting of the provincial estates. In any case, I have found no evidence that Brittany subscribed to escape the dixième. See Bonney, "Secret de Leurs Familles," 399.

37. See ibid., 255–77, for Desmaretz's debate with the intendant in Bordeaux. See also le Gendre (intendant at Montauban) to Desmaretz, March 31, 1711, in idem, 3:266, no. 1020.

38. Ferrand to Desmaretz, February 20, 1711, in ibid., 3:397, no. 984; and complaints of the Parlement of Dijon to Desmaretz, March 12, 1711, in idem, 3:339, no. 924 and note. See also A.N. G^7 1138–39, complaints of the marquis de Vibraye and the comte de Nogent of July 4 and 8, 1711, against actions of the Keepers of the Royal Treasury.

39. See Montaran (treasurer of the estates of Brittany) to Desmaretz, November 26, 1711, in Boislisle, *Correspondance des contrôleur généraux*, 3:414–15, no. 1181 and note; and Bignon to Desmaretz, October 7, 1711, in idem, 3:406, no. 1153.

40. For news of disturbances linked to the dixième, see ibid., 3:382, no. 1081; 3:388, no. 1096; 3:417–18, no. 1194; 3:520, no. 1572; and 3:544, no. 1675. The letter from Lamoignon de Courson at Bordeaux to Desmaretz, December 15, 1711 (no. 1194), explains how the government relied on loyal local men to set an example. Nicolas, *Rébellion française*, 143, describes one interesting rebellion in Normandy in 1713 wherein the rebels wanted the taille to be calculated in the same manner as the dixième, which would have transferred the tax burden, for the most part, from the taillables to the property owners.

41. See A.N. G^7 1138–39 for these figures. Desmaretz, *Compte rendu*, in Boislisle, *Correspondance des contrôleurs généraux*, 3:678, said the dixième never produced more than 24 million livres.

42. Bonney, "Secret de leurs familles," 394.

43. Boislisle, *Saint-Simon*, 20:166–78.

44. Boislisle, *Correspondance des contrôleurs généraux*, 3:626; Law, *Oeuvres complètes*, 3:55; Bonney, "Secret de Leurs Familles," 411–12.

45. Patrice Berger, "Rural Charity in Late Seventeenth-Century France: The Pontchartrain Case," *French Historical Studies* 10 (1978): 412–13.

46. A.N. K 2415, no. 101, edict of December 1713.

47. These are available in Boislisle, *Correspondance des contrôleurs généraux*, 3:613–36. The originals can be found in A.N. G^7 1903 and B.N. mss. fr. 7765, fol. 14–22. One mémoire that Boislisle omitted is in A.A.E., Mém. et Doc., France, 1209, fol. 388–90.

48. Boislisle, *Correspondance des contrôleurs généraux*, 3:614–19, and A.N. G^7 1903.

49. Boislisle, *Correspondance des contrôleurs généraux*, 3:618, and A.N. G^7 1903.

50. Boislisle, *Correspondance des contrôleurs généraux*, 3:695 and 698–97.

51. Ibid., 2:615, letter of October 5, 1703; B.N. mss. fr. 7939.

52. A.N. E 794^B, fol. 216, July 21, 1708.

53. A.N. E 794^B, fol. 204–7, July 21, 1708. Barthélemy Rolland de Pontferrière (1647–1718) was a secrétaire du roi, secretary and controller general of the extraordinary of war, and a banker. See Favre-Lejeune, *Secrétaires du Roi*, 2:1171–72.

54. A.N. E 802^B, fol. 331–36, no. 53, March 26, 1709, and A.N. E 829^A, fol. 350–51, no. 79, June 9, 1711.

55. A.N. E 1960, fol. 210.

56. A.N. E 836^B, fol. 218–21, no. 1, January 26, 1712, and A.N. E 836^C, fol. 148–51, no. 1, February 16, 1712.

57. See A.N. K 891, no. 31, for Ferrand's first letter (February 17, 1712), and nos. 30–31 for the *cahiers*. This entire carton, from nos. 1–95, is concerned with the provinces and generalities of Auvergne, Bordeaux, Brittany, La Rochelle, Lyon, Soissons, and Hainaut.

58. A.N. G[7] 1494, Delacroix to Desmaretz, February 19, 1704.

59. A.N. K 883, no. 3, May 29, 1689. He repeated his arguments in a mémoire dated January 28, 1717. A.A.E., Mém. et Doc., France, 137, fol. 34–41.

60. A.N. H[1] 1461, undated mémoire from after 1727 describing Rolland's activities.

61. Orders for the payment of the traitant's debts to the crown appear in A.N. E 867[B], fol. 22–31, nos. 7–8, September 15, 1714; A.N. E 868[A], fol. 236–51, nos. 19–22, October 6, 1714; and A.N. E 873[A], fol. 449–52, no. 23, March 16, 1715.

62. A.N. K 2415, nos. 47 and 62, edicts of October 1712 and February 1713; and A.N. K 2416, no. 66, edict of December 1714.

63. A.N. O[1] 55, fol. 96–107, and A.N. E 1960, fol. 87–92, July 28, 1711.

64. Desmaretz, *Compte rendu*, in Boislisle, *Correspondance des contrôleurs généraux*, 3:678.

65. See A.N. G[7] 1541 for the papers on these offices. A.N. E 836[B], fol. 333–36, no. 40, January 26, 1712, imposed a new tax of 3 deniers per livre.

66. Desmaretz, *Compte rendu*, in Boislisle, *Correspondance des contrôleurs généraux*, 3:678–80. The Abbé de Saint-Pierre, in his *Annales politiques* (London, 1758), 2:414–16, 423, and 434, praised these new rentes and linked their creation to the example set by the clergy and English business practices. A.N. K 2416, no. 17, edict of March 1714, said that another such loan was used to repay those people who had purchased the farm of the control of notarial acts. Rentes were sold at denier 16 (6.25 percent), with a total interest of 1.5 million livres. The farm was reconstituted with an annual lease price of 3 million livres, out of which 2.4 million livres went to pay the principal and interest on the rentes. The king thus kept 600,000 livres in revenue.

67. Desmaretz, *Compte rendu*, in Boislisle, *Correspondance des contrôleurs généraux*, 3:678. The laws suppressing these and other taxes along with fees paid to particular offices can be found in A.N. K 2415, nos. 92–93 and 109, and A.N. K 2416, nos. 9, 17, 48, 97, 100, and 104.

68. Desmaretz, *Compte rendu*, in Boislisle, *Correspondance des contrôleurs généraux*, 3:680, and A.N. K 2415, no. 101, edict of December 1713.

69. Boislisle, *Correspondance des contrôleurs généraux*, 3:619–22, and A.N. G[7] 1903.

70. B.N. mss. fr. 7766, fol. 14–20, is an incomplete mémoire written by Desmaretz that lists expected expenses for 1715 as more than 154 million livres. B.N. mss. fr. 7765, fol. 1–22 (Boislisle, *Correspondance des contrôleurs généraux*, 3:629–33), says that two earlier projections for expenses were made in October and November 1714. The mémoire in A.N. G[7] 1903 (Boislisle, *Correspondance des contrôleurs généraux*, 3:622–29) is dated February 1715 and includes detailed plans for reducing expenses from 122 to 97 million livres. The mémoire in B.N. mss. fr. 7766 must be one of the earlier projections.

71. B.N. mss. fr. 7767, fol. 151–59.

72. Boislisle, *Correspondance des contrôleurs généraux*, 3:622–29, and A.N. G[7] 1903. To justify extending the capitation and dixième to Louis XIV, Desmaretz cited England, Holland, and Germany, where he said the governments taxed all property and wealth to pay for the debts they had contracted during their wars.

73. See A.N. K 2415, no. 107, declaration of December 30, 1713, for the years since 1707; and A.N. K 2416, no. 19, letters dated April 5, 1714, for the years 1701–8.

74. Desmaretz, *Compte rendu*, in Boislisle, *Correspondance des contrôleurs généraux*, 3:681.

75. A.N. E 1980, fol. 97–120, July 9, 1715.

76. Cans, *Contribution de clergé de France*, 96.

77. A.N. K 2416, no. 95, declaration of July 9, 1715.

78. Daguesseau to Desmaretz, August 25, 1715, in Boislisle, *Correspondance des contrôleurs généraux*, 3:598, no. 1877.

79. A.N. G^7 1901 in a table listing the laws of 1715.

80. A.N. E 878^A, fol. 382–85, August 17, 1715.

81. A.N. E 878^A, fol. 378–81, August 17, 1715.

82. Boislisle, *Correspondance des contrôleurs généraux*, 3:635, and A.N. G^7 1903.

83. Boislisle, *Corrspondance des contrôleurs généraux*, 3:635, and A.N. G^7 1903; A.N. K 900, nos. 8–10 contain mémoires and a letter from a Sr. Carquet—who described himself, to Controller General Orry, as dean of the secrétaires du roi on January 30, 1737—on his activities in these matters under Desmaretz.

84. According to A.N. E 1683^{187}, the registers of the Royal Council of Finances for the quarter of July–September 1715, the council met and arrêts were issued on August 13, 17, 20, and 24. Desmaretz reported fifty-three arrêts on August 13, thirteen on August 17, forty-six on August 20, and fifty-seven on August 24. The meeting of August 20, however, might have included a meeting of the Petite Direction, because five masters of requests reported nine arrêts on August 20. The council on finances issued no arrêts thereafter until September 28, 1715.

85. *Dangeau*, 16:195 (September 20, 1715); Boislisle, *Saint-Simon*, 29:63–66.

86. A.N. G^7 1903, lists of payments to the members of the council of finances for 1716 and 1718, include Le Cousturier and Clautrier. On a visit by Le Cousturier, see Maintenon to Madame de Caylus, June 27, 1716, in Haussonville and Hanotaux, *Souvenirs de Madame de Maintenon*, 3:116. For Le Cousturier's career after Louis XIV, see Antoine, *Coeur de l'État*, 391 and 425.

87. Boislisle, *Saint-Simon*, 29:63–66 and 125–26, list des Forts and Fagon as sitting on the regency council of finances. They would both become intendants of finances again when the positions were revived in 1722. Des Forts would be controller general of finances from 1726 to 1730. See Antoine, *Gouvernement*, passim, for the later careers of Caumartin, Fagon, Le Peletier des Forts, and Poulletier.

88. See *Dangeau*, 16:231–32 (November 10, 1715), and Buvat, *Journal de la Régence*, 1:106–7. Dangeau wrote that Bercy was suspected of speculation in currency, while Buvat said that he was exiled because he had kept the Regent's chancellor waiting for two hours for an interview.

89. Guyet must have sold his office as master of requests. See Boislisle, *Saint-Simon*, 29:64.

90. Ibid., 29:91–92.

91. Nicolas Desmaretz, *Mémoire sur l'administration des finances depuis le 20 février 1708 jusqu'au 1er septembre 1715* (Paris, 1716). A copy is in the Bibliothèque Nationale. This mémoire is similar to the *Compte rendu de M. Desmaretz au Régent* that can be found in A.N. G^7 1903 and Boislisle, *Correspondance des contrôleurs généraux*, 3:673–82.

92. According to Buvat, *Journal de la Régence*, 1:162, the presentation was made in August 1716.

93. Bonney, *Jean-Roland Malet,* 3n5; and Joseph Michaud (ed.), *Dictionnaire universelle ancienne et moderne* (Paris: A. Thoisnier Desplaces, 1852) 10: 521.

94. Buvat, *Journal de la Régence,* 1:129–30.

95. Ibid., 1:137, reports de la Garde's arrest. Boislisle, *Saint-Simon,* 29:94–96, 314–19, 371, and 546–47. A note on p. 314 states that Mme. Lafontaine had been arrested as a speculator in March 1715 when Desmaretz was minister. Her testimony is in Boislisle, *Correspondance des contrôleurs généraux,* 3:682–84, from January 1717. *Dangeau,* 16:243 (November 23, 1715), reports the exoneration of both Desmaretz and his commis de la Garde; Ibid, 17:36 (March 3, 1717), reports that Mme. Lafontaine was the only woman condemned to the pillory by the Chambre de justice.

96. *Dangeau,* 16:498–500 (November 30, 1716).

97. Boislisle, *Saint-Simon,* 29:316–19. Saint-Simon made himself the hero of this story by claiming that he had stopped the Regent from exiling Desmaretz, a decision the Regent had already made. Saint-Simon said that Desmaretz personally thanked him for his intervention.

98. Maintenon to Caylus, January 31, 1718, in Haussonville and Hanotaux, *Souvenirs de Madame de Maintenon,* 3:263. *Dangeau,* 17:233 (January 22, 1718), reports that Desmaretz worked "assez longtemps" with the Regent. The marquis de Balleroy told his wife that Desmaretz was soon to return; see Dupilet, *Régence absolue,* 318.

99. A.A.E., Mém. et Doc., France, 137, fol. 3–5, 11–19, 21–26, 34–43, and 113–17 and A.A.E., Mém. et Doc., France, 2015, 183–84.

100. A.A.E., Mém. et Doc., France, 137, fol. 41–43.

101. A.A.E., Mém. et Doc., France, 137, fol. 3–5.

102. A.A.E., Mém. et Doc., France, 137, fol. 11–19 and 21–26.

103. A.N. KK 1005^{D}, "Discours de M. Paris de la Montagne à ses enfants pour les instuire de sa conduitte et de celle de ses frères dans les principles matières du Gouvernement ou ils sont participié" (1729), pp. 79–84.

104. Boislisle, *Saint-Simon,* 38:178–79. B.N. Clairambault, mss. 1096, fol. 186–89, a record of a trial over his son Maillebois's claims that Desmaretz's death was unexpected.

105. Edmond-Jean-François Barbier, *Chronique de la Régence et du règne de Louis XV (1718–1763), ou Journal de Barbier avocat au Parlement de Paris.* (Paris: Charpentier, 1857–58), 1:126 (May 6, 1721), found Desmaretz to be a crook, but Barbier was born in 1689. He was probably relating the stories he had heard, since he was not alive at the time.

106. Mathieu Marais, *Journal et Mémoires du Mathieu Marais avocat au Parlement de Paris sur le Régence et le règne de Louis XV (1715–1737)* (Paris: Firmin Didot, 1864), 2:126–27. Marais was born in 1665 and thus knew more of Desmaretz's history.

107. On Clément Charles Laverdy de Nizert, controller general of finances from 1763 until 1768, see Touzery, *Taille tarifiée,* 177.

108. Joseph Michaud, ed., *Dictionnaire universelle ancienne et moderne* (Paris: A. Thoisnier Desplaces, 1852), 10:521.

Conclusion

1. See Thierry Sarmant, ed., *Le Grand Siècle en Mémoires* (Paris: Perrin, 2011), 11 and 362. See also A. Chéruel, *Saint-Simon considéré comme historien de Louis XIV* (Paris: Hachette, 1865), for an extended critique of Saint-Simon's errors as an historian.

2. Ladurie and Fitou, *Saint-Simon ou le système de la Cour*, 512 (Ladurie and Fitou, *Saint-Simon and the Court of Louis XIV*, 346), compare Saint-Simon to Goethe and Shakespeare for his impact on his native language.

3. Thus, Pomponne was a man who was appointed in 1671, dismissed in 1679, and then brought back to the Conseil d'en haut in 1691.

4. Sarmant and Stoll, *Régner et Gouverner*, 131, state emphatically that Desmaretz did not have the ear of the king or of the princes.

5. By 1749, when the vingtième was created, the government had the records and data to enforce such a tax. See Bien, "Offices, Corps, and a System of Public Credit," 99.

6. Basville to the Controller General, October 11, 1705, in Boislisle, *Correspondance des contrôleurs généraux*, 2:277–78, no. 891; and Bonney, "Secret de leurs familles," 388–89.

7. Jay Caplan, *In the King's Wake: Post-Absolutist Culture in France* (Chicago: University of Chicago Press, 1999).

Bibliography

Primary Sources

Archives du Ministère de la Guerre. Paris.
Archives Nationales. Paris.
Collection Clairambault. Bibliothèque Nationale. Paris.
Collection Morel de Thoisy. Bibliothèque Nationale. Paris.
Collections Mélanges de Colbert. Bibliothèque Nationale. Paris.
Dossiers bleus. Bibliothèque Nationale. Paris.
Manuscrits français. Bibliothèque Nationale. Paris.
Manuscrits. Archives de l'Assemblée Nationale. Paris.
Manuscrits. Bibliothèque de l'Arsenal. Paris.
Mémoires et Documents, France. Archives du Ministère des Affaires Étrangères. Paris.
Nouvelles acquisitions françaises. Bibliothèque Nationale. Paris.

Printed Sources

L'Almanach royal, 1699–1716. Paris: Laurent d'Houry, 1699–1716.

Anonymous. *Réponses et réflexions sur le compte que M. Desmaretz a présenté à Monseigneur le duc d'Orléans, régent de France.* Paris: privately printed, 1717.

Barbier, Edmond-Jean-François. *Chronique de la Régence et du règne de Louis XV (1718–1763) ou Journal de Barbier avocat au Parlement de Paris.* 8 vols. Paris: Charpentier, 1857–58.

Bercy, Charles Henri Malon de. *Lettres du château de Bercy (1712–1742).* Edited by Jean-Claude Guiraud. Paris: Harmattan, 2010.

Boislisle, A.-M. de, and P. de Brotonne, eds. *Correspondance des contrôleurs généraux des finances avec les intendants des provinces (1683–1715).* 3 vols. Paris: Imprimerie Nationale, 1874–98.

Buvat, Jean. *Journal de la Régence (1715–1723).* Edited by E. Compardom. 2 vols. Paris: Plon, 1865.

Clément, Pierre, ed. *Lettres, instructions et mémoires de Colbert.* 7 vols. Paris: Imprimerie Nationale, 1861–83.

Daguesseau, (Henri-François). "Discours sur la vie et la mort de M. Daguesseau, conseiller d'état, par M. Daguesseau, chancelier de France, son fils." In *Oeuvres complètes du Chancelier Daguesseau,* edited by M. Pardessus (Paris: Fantin, 1819), 15:273–437.

Dangeau, Philippe de Courcillon, marquis de. *Journal du marquis de Dangeau.* Edited by Eud. Soulié and L. Dussieux. 19 vols. Paris: Firmin Didot, 1854–60.

Desmaretz, Nicolas. *Mémoire sur l'administration des finances depuis le 20 février 1708 jusqu'au 1er septembre 1715.* Paris, 1716.

Fénelon, (François de Salignac de la Mothe-). *Oeuvres complètes.* Edited by M. Gosselin. 10 vols. 1851–52. Reprint, Geneva: Slatkine Reprints, 1971.

Haussonville, le comte de, and G. Hanotaux, eds. *Souvenirs sur Madame de Maintenon.* 3 vols. Paris: Calmann-Lévy, n.d.

Institut National d'Études Démographiques, ed. *Pierre de Boisguilbert, ou la naissance de l'économie politique.* 2 vols. Paris: Institut National d'Études Démographiques, 1966.

Law, John. *Oeuvres completes.* Edited by Paul Harsin. 3 vols. Paris: Librairie du Recueil Sirey, 1934.

Le Mao, Catherine, ed. *Chronique du Bordelais au crépuscule du Grand Siècle: le Mémorial de Savignac.* Bordeaux: Presses Universitaires de Bordeaux, 2004.

Louis XIV. *Mémoires for the Instruction of the Dauphin.* Edited and translated by Paul Sonnino. New York: Free Press, 1970.

———. *Mémoires pour l'instruction du dauphin.* Paris: Imprimerie Nationale, 1992.

(Maintenon, Madame de, and la princesse des Ursins). *Correspondance de Madame de Maintenon et de la princesse des Ursins 1709: Une année tragique.* Edited by Marcel Loyau. Paris: Mercure de France, 2002.

Mallet (*sic*), Jean Roland. *Comptes rendus de l'administration des finances du royaume de France.* Paris: Chez Buisson, 1789.

———. "Discours prononcez dans l'Académie Française le samedy vingt-neuvième décembre, 1714, à la reception de . . . Monsieur Malet, Premier Commis de Monsieur Des Maretz, Contrôleur Général des Finances." *Académie Française* 58. Paris: Jean-Baptiste Coignard, 1715.

(Marais, Mathieu). *Journal et Mémoires de Mathieu Marais sur la régence et le règne de Louis XV (1715–1737).* Edited by M. de Lescure. 4 vols. Paris: Firmin Didot, 1863–68.

(Saint-Simon, Louis de Rouvroy, duc de). *Mémoires.* Edited by Gonzague Truc. 7 vols. Paris: Gallimard, 1953.

———. *Mémoires de Saint-Simon.* Edited by A.-M. de Boislisle, with the assistance of J. de Boislisle and J. Lecestre. 41 vols. Paris: Hachette, 1879–1928.

(Sourches, Louis François de Bouchet, marquis de). *Mémoires du marquis de Sourches sur le règne de Louis XIV.* Edited by Gabriel-Jules de Cosnac and Édouard Pontal. 13 vols. Paris: Hachette, 1882–93.

Spanheim, Ezechiel. *Relation de la Cour de France.* Edited by Émile Bourgeois. 1900. Reprint, Paris: Mercure de France, 1973.

Torcy, Jean-Baptiste Colbert, marquis de. *Journal inédit de Jean-Baptiste Colbert, marquis de Torcy, ministre et secrétaire d'état des affaires étrangères, pendant les années 1709, 1710 et 1711.* Edited by Frédéric Masson. Paris: Plon-Nourrit, 1854.

Vauban, (Sebastien le Prestre de). *Projet d'une dixme royale.* Edited by Émile Coornaert. Paris: Alcan, 1933.

———. *La dîme royale.* Edited by Emmanuel Le Roy Ladurie. Paris: Imprimerie Nationale, 1992.

———. *Les oisivetés de Monsieur de Vauban.* Edited by Michèle Virol. Seyssel: Champ Vallon, 2007.

Secondary Works

Alimento, Antonella. *Réformes fiscales et crises politiques dans la France de Louis XV: De la taille tarifiée au cadastre général.* Brussels: Peter Lang, 2008.

Anderson, Harold P. "The Police of Paris under Louis XIV: The Imposition of Order by Marc René de Voyer de Paulmy d'Argenson." PhD diss., Ohio State University, 1978.

Anonymous. *Dictionnaire de la Noblesse.* Paris: la Veuve Duchesne, 1772.

Antoine, Michel. *Le Conseil du Roi sous le règne de Louis* XV. Geneva: Droz, 1970.

———. *Le Conseil royal des finances au XVIIIe siècle.* Geneva: Droz, 1973.

———. "Les Conseils des Finances sous le règne de Louis XV." *Revue d'histoire moderne et contemporaine* 5 (1958): 187–97.

———. *Le coeur de l'État: Surintendance, contrôle général et intendances des finances, 1552–1791.* Paris: Fayard, 2003.

———. *Le gouvernement et l'administration sous Louis XV: Dictionnaire biographique.* Paris: CNRS, 1978.

Aubert, Gauthier, and Olivier Chaline, eds. *Les Parlements de Louis XIV: Opposition, coopération, autonomisation?* Rennes: Presses Universitaires de Rennes, 2010.

Barbiche, Bernard. "Ce que nous ne savons pas des mécanismes de l'administration financière." In Monnier, *Histoire institutionnelle,* 35–48.

Barker, Nancy Nichols. *Brother to the Sun King: Philippe, Duke of Orleans.* Baltimore: Johns Hopkins University Press, 1989.

Bayard, Françoise. *Le monde des financiers au XVIIe siècle.* Paris: Flammarion, 1988.

———. "Pour une autre histoire économique de la France de l'Ancien Régime." In Monnier, *Histoire institutionnelle,* 19–34.

Bayard, Françoise, Joël Félix, and Philippe Hamon, eds. *Dictionnaire des surintendants et des contrôleurs généraux des finances du XVIe siècle à la Révolution française de 1789.* Paris: Comité pour l'histoire économique et financière de la France, 2000.

Beik, William. *Absolutism and Society in Seventeenth Century France: State Power and Provincial Aristocracy in Languedoc.* Cambridge: Cambridge University Press, 1985.

———. *A Social and Cultural History of Early Modern France.* Cambridge: Cambridge University Press, 2009.

Berger, Patrice. "Rural Charity in Late Seventeenth Century France: The Pontchartrain Case." *French Historical Studies* 10 (1978): 393–415.

Bergin, Joseph. *Cardinal Richelieu: Power and the Pursuit of Wealth.* New Haven, CT: Yale University Press, 1985.

———. *Crown, Church, and Episcopate under Louis XIV.* New Haven, CT: Yale University Press, 2004.

Berthet, Élie. *L'Année du Grand Hiver 1709.* Paris: Dentu, 1873.

Bien, David D. "Offices, Corps, and a System of State Credit: The Uses of Privilege under the Ancien Régime." In *The French Revolution and the Creation of Modern Political Culture.* Vol. 1, *The Political Culture of the Old Regime,* edited by Keith Michael Baker, 89–114. Oxford: Pergamon, 1987.

Bluche, François, ed. *Dictionnaire du Grand Siècle.* 1990. Reprint, Paris: Fayard, 2005.

———. *Louis XIV.* Paris: Fayard, 1986.

———. *Louis XIV.* Translated by Mark Greengrass. New York: Franklin Watts, 1990.

———. *Les magistrats du Grand Conseil au XVIIIe siècle.* Paris: Les Belles Lettres, 1966.

Bluche, François, and Jean-François Solnon. *La véritable hiérarchie sociale de l'ancienne France: Le tarif de la première capitation (1695)*. 1983. Reprint, Geneva: Droz, 1995.

Bonney, Richard. "La concurrence étatique pour les ressources et l'innovation fiscale sous Louis XIV." In *État, Marine et Sociéte: Hommage à Jean Meyer*, edited by Martine Acerra, Jean-Pierre Poussou, Michel Vergé-Franceschi, and André Zysberg, 35–48. Paris: Presses de l'Université de Paris-Sorbonne, 1995.

———. "Jean-Roland Malet: Historian of the Finances of the French Monarchy." *French History* 5 (1991): 180–233.

———. *The King's Debts: Finance and Politics in France, 1589–1661*. Oxford: Clarendon Press, 1981.

———. "'Le Secret de Leur Familles': The Fiscal and Social Limits of Louis XIV's *Dixième*." *French History* 7 (1993): 383–416.

———. *Political Change in France under Richelieu and Mazarin, 1624–1661*. London: Oxford University Press, 1978.

———. "The State and Its Revenues in Ancien-Régime France." *Historical Research* 65 (1992): 150–76.

Bonney, Richard, and Margaret Bonney. *Jean-Roland Malet, premier historien des finances de la monarchie française*. Paris: Comité pour l'histoire économique et financière de la France, 1993.

Bosher, J. F. "'Chambre de justice' in the French Monarchy." In Bosher, *French Government and Society*, 19–40.

———. *French Finances 1770–1795: From Business to Bureaucracy*. Cambridge: Cambridge University Press, 1970.

———, ed. *French Government and Society, 1500–1850: Essays in Memory of Alfred Cobban*. London: Athlone, 1973.

Bossenga, Gail. *The Politics of Privilege: Old Regime and Revolution in Lille*. Cambridge: Cambridge University Press, 1991.

Bourgeon, Jean-Louis. *Les Colberts avant Colbert*. Paris: PUF, 1973.

Caillou, François. *Une administration royale d'Ancien Régime: le bureau des finances de Tours*. Tours: Presses Universitaires François Rabelais, 2005.

Cans, Albert. *La contribution du clergé de France à l'impôt pendant la seconde moitié du règne de Louis XIV (1689–1715)*. Paris: Picard, 1910.

Caplan, Jay. *In the King's Wake: Post-Absolutist Culture in France*. Chicago: University of Chicago Press, 1999.

Carruthers, Bruce G. *City of Capital: Politics and Markets in the English Financial Revolution*. Princeton, NJ: Princeton University Press, 1996.

Cénat, Jean-Philippe. *Le roi stratège: Louis XIV et la direction de la guerre, 1661–1715*. Rennes: Presses Universitaires de Rennes, 2010.

Chapman, Sara A. *Private Ambition and Political Alliances: The Phélypeaux de Pontchartrain Family and Louis XIV's Government, 1650–1715*. Rochester: University of Rochester Press, 2004.

Chartier, Jean-Luc A. *De Colbert à l'Encyclopédie*. Vol. 1, *Henri Daguesseau conseiller d'état, 1635–1716*. Montpellier: Presses du Languedoc, 1988.

Chaussinand-Nogaret, Guy. *Les financiers de Languedoc au XVIIIe siècle*. Paris: SEVPEN, 1970.

Chéruel, (Pierre) A(dolphe). *Saint-Simon considéré comme historien de Louis XIV*. Paris: Hachette, 1865.

Chouraki, André. *Les intendants des finances.* Unpublished *thèse de droit,* Bibliothèque de la Faculté de Droit, Paris, 1959.

Claeys, Thierry. *Dictionnaire biographique des financiers en France au XVIIIe siècle.* 2 vols. Paris: Éditions SPM, 2009.

Clamageran, J.-J. *Histoire de l'impôt en France.* 3 vols. Paris: Librairie de Guillaumin, 1867–76.

Clément, Pierre. *Histoire de Colbert et de son administration.* 1874. Reprint, Geneva: Slatkine Reprints, 1980.

Collins, James B. *Classes, Estates, and Order in Early Modern Brittany.* Cambridge: Cambridge University Press, 1994.

———. *Fiscal Limits of Absolutism: Direct Taxation in Early Seventeenth Century France.* Berkeley: University of California Press, 1988.

———. *The State in Early Modern France.* Cambridge: Cambridge University Press, 2009.

Corvisier, André. *Louvois.* Paris: Fayard, 1983.

Dee, Darryl. *Expansion and Crisis in Louis XIV's France: Franche-Comté and Absolute Monarchy, 1674–1715.* Rochester: University of Rochester Press, 2009.

———. "Wartime Government in Franche-Comté and the Demodernization of the French State, 1704–1715." *French Historical Studies* 30 (2007): 21–48.

Delaume, Geneviève. *Le Bureau des finances de la généralité de Paris.* Paris: Éditions Cujas, 1966.

Dent, Julian. *Crisis in Finance: Crown, Financiers, and Society in Seventeenth Century France.* New York: St. Martin's, 1973.

———. "The Role of Clientèles in the Financial Elite of France under Cardinal Mazarin." In Bosher, *French Government and Society,* 41–49.

Descimon, Robert. "La vénalité des offices comme dette publique sous l'Ancien Régime français. Le bien commun au pays des intérêts privés." In *La dette publique dans l'histoire,* edited by Jean Andreau, Gérard Béaur, and Jean-Yves Grenier, 177–242. Paris: Comité pour l'histoire économique et financière de la France, 2006.

Dessert, Daniel. *Argent, pouvoir et société au Grand Siècle.* Paris: Fayard, 1984.

———. *Colbert ou le serpent venimeux.* Paris: Éditions Complexe, 2000.

———. "Finances et société au XVIIe siècle: À propos de la Chambre de justice de 1661." *Annales ESC* 29 (1974): 847–82.

———. *Fouquet.* Paris: Fayard, 1987.

———. "Pouvoirs et finances au XVIIe siècle: La fortune du Cardinal Mazarin." *Revue d'histoire moderne et contemporaine* 23 (1976): 161–81.

———. *Le royaume de Monsieur Colbert.* Paris: Perrin, 2007.

Dessert, Daniel, and Jean-Louis Journet. "Le lobby Colbert: Un royaume ou une affaire de famille?" *Annales ESC* 30 (1975): 1303–36.

Dornic, François. *Louis Berryer, agent de Mazarin et de Colbert.* Caen: Université de Caen, 1968.

Dulong, Claude. *La Fortune de Mazarin.* Paris: Perrin, 1990.

———. *Mazarin.* Paris: Perrin, 1999.

———. *Mazarin et l'Argent: Banquiers et prête-noms.* Paris: École des Chartes, 2002.

Dumas, René. *La politique financière de Nicolas Desmaretz, contrôleur général des finances (1708–1715).* Issoudun: Imprimerie du Centre, 1927.

Dupilet, Alexandre. *La Régence absolue: Philippe d'Orléans et la Polysynodie (1715–1718).* Seyssel: Champ Vallon, 2011.

Durand, Yves. *Les fermiers généraux au XVIIIe siècle.* Paris: PUF, 1976.

———. *Finance et Mécenat: Les fermiers généraux au XVIIIe siècle.* Paris: Hachette, 1976.

Dusart, Mathieu. *La fortune de Nicolas Desmaretz (1648–1721) à partir de son inventaire après décès.* Unpublished *thèse de maitrise,* Université de Paris XII (Créteil), 2003.

Faccarello, Gilbert. *The Foundation of Laissez-faire: The Economics of Pierre de Boisguilbert.* London: Routledge, 1999.

Faure, Edgar. *La banqueroute de Law: 17 juillet 1720.* Paris: Gallimard, 1977.

Favre-Lejeune, Christine. *Les Secrétaires du Roi de la Chancellerie de France: Dictionnaire biographique et généalogique (1672–1789).* 2 vols. Paris: SEDOPOLS, 1986.

Follain, Antoine, and Gilbert Larguier, eds. *L'impôt des campagnes: Fragile fondement de l'État dit moderne (XVe–XVIIIe siècle).* Paris: Comité pour l'histoire économique et financière de la France, 2005.

Ford, Franklin L. *Robe and Sword: The Regrouping of the French Aristocracy After Louis XIV.* 1953. Reprint, New York: Harper & Row, 1965.

Formel-Le Vavasseur, François. *Le Duc de Saint-Simon, comte de la Ferté-Vidame, mémorialiste et épistolier: rétrospective documentaire.* Paris: Books on Demand, 2009.

Frostin, Charles. *Les Pontchartrain ministres de Louis XIV: Alliances et réseau d'influence sous l'Ancien Régime.* Rennes: Presses Universitaires de Rennes, 2006.

Goubert, Pierre. *Beauvais et le Beauvaisis de 1600 à 1730: Contribution à l'histoire sociale de la France du XVIIe siècle.* 2 vols. Paris: SEVPEN, 1960.

———. *Familles marchandes sous l'Ancien Régime: Les Danse et les Motte, de Beauvais.* Paris: SEVPEN, 1959.

———. *Louis XIV and Twenty Million Frenchmen.* Translated by Anne Carter. New York: Pantheon, 1970.

———. *Louis XIV et vingt millions de Français.* 1966. Reprint, Paris: Fayard, 1976.

Goumy, Édouard. *Étude sur la vie et les écrits de l'Abbé de Saint-Pierre.* Paris: Hachette, 1859.

Gruder, Vivian R. *The Royal Provincial Intendants: A Governing Elite in Eighteenth-Century France.* Ithaca, NY: Cornell University Press, 1968.

Guerre, Stéphane. "Nicolas Desmaretz et la prise de décision au conseil du roi." *Revue historique* 659 (2011): 589–610.

Guéry, Alain. "État, classification sociale et compromis sous Louis XIV: La capitation de 1695." *Annales ESC* 41 (1986): 1041–60.

———. "Les finances de la monarchie française sous l'Ancien Régime." *Annales ESC* 33 (1978): 216–39.

Harsin, Paul. "L'Abbé de Saint-Pierre économiste d'après de nouveaux documents inédits." *Revue d'histoire économique et sociale* 20 (1932): 186–218.

———. *Crédit public et Banque d'État en France du XVIe au XVIIIe siècle.* Paris: Droz, 1933.

Hecht, Jacqueline. "Le vie de Pierre le Pesant, seigneur de Boisguilbert." In *Pierre de Boisguilbert, ou la naissance de l'économie politique,* 1:121–244. Paris: Institut Nationale d'Études Démographiques, 1966.

Herlaut, Colonel. "Projets de création d'une banque royale en France à la fin du règne de Louis XIV (1702–12)." *Revue d'histoire moderne* 8 (1933): 143–60.

Hoffman, Philip T. *Growth in a Traditional Society: The French Countryside, 1450–1815.* Princeton, NJ: Princeton University Press, 2000.

Hoffman, Philip T., Gilles Postel-Vinay, and Jean-Laurent Rosenthal. *Priceless Markets: The Political Economy of Credit in Paris, 1660–1870.* Chicago: University of Chicago Press, 2000.

Houques-Fourcade, Hippolyte Maurice. *Les impôts sur le revenu en France au XVIIIe siècle: Histoire du dixième and du cinquantième Leur application dans la Généralité de Guyenne.* Bordeaux: Eiret, 1889.

Hurt, John J. *Louis XIV and the Parlements: The Assertion of Royal Authority.* Manchester, UK: Manchester University Press, 2002.

Jouvencel, Henri de. *Le contrôleur général des finances sous l'Ancien Régime.* Paris: Librairie de le Société du Recueil Général des Lois et des Arrêts et du Journal du Palais, 1901.

Kettering, Sharon. "Gift-Giving and Patronage in Early Modern France." *French History* 2 (1988): 131–51.

———. *Patrons, Brokers, and Clients in Seventeenth-Century France.* New York: Oxford University Press, 1986.

Klaits, Joseph. *Printed Propaganda Under Louis XIV: Absolute Monarchy and Public Opinion.* Princeton, NJ: Princeton University Press, 1976.

Kwass, Michael. "A Kingdom of Taxpayers: State Formation, Privilege, and Political Culture in Eighteenth-Century France." *Journal of Modern History* 70 (1998): 295–339.

———. *Privilege and the Politics of Taxation in Eighteenth-Century France.* Cambridge: Cambridge University Press, 2000.

Labatut, Jean-Pierre. "Le chancelier Boucherat (1616–1699)." In *Le Conseil du Roi de Louis XII à la Révolution*, edited by Roland Mousnier, 87–101. Paris: PUF, 1970.

Lachiver, Marcel. *Les Années de misère: La famine au temps du Grand Roi.* Paris: Fayard, 1991.

Legay, Marie-Laure. "The Beginnings of Public Management: Administrative Science and Political Choices in the Eighteenth Century in France, Austria, and the Austrian Netherlands." *Journal of Modern History* 81 (2009): 253–93.

Le Roy Ladurie, Emmanuel. "Versailles Observed." In *The Mind and Method of the Historian*, 149–73. Translated by Siàn Reynolds and Ben Reynolds. Chicago: University of Chicago Press, 1981.

———. "Système de la Cour (Versailles vers 1709)." In collaboration with Janine Field-Récurat. *L'Arc* 65 (1976): 21–35.

Le Roy Ladurie, Emmanuel, and Jean-François Fitou. *Saint-Simon ou le système de la Cour.* Paris: Fayard, 1997.

———. *Saint-Simon and the Court of Louis XIV.* Translated by Arthur Goldhammer. Chicago: University of Chicago Press, 2001.

Levantal, Christophe. *Louis XIV: Chronographie d'un règne.* 2 vols. Gollion, Switzerland: Infolio, 2009.

Levron, Jacques. *Les courtisans.* Paris: Éditions du Seuil, 1960.

Lévy, Claude-Frédéric. *Capitalistes et pouvoir au Siècle des Lumières.* 3 vols. The Hague: Mouton, 1969–80.

Limon, Marie-Françoise. *Traitants et fraudes dans le recouvrement de l' impôt: Affaires réglées par Claude Le Peletier, contrôleur général des finances (1683–1689).* Paris: LGDJ, 1995.

Lizerand, Georges. *Le duc de Beauvillier (1648–1714).* Paris: Belles Lettres, 1933.

Loen, Maya de. *L'homme qui prêtait aux Rois.* Paris: Éditions de Fallois, 2003.

Lüthy, Herbert. *La banque protestante en France, de la révocation de l'édit de Nantes à la Révolution.* 2 vols. Paris: SEVPEN, 1959–61.

Lynn, John A. "Recalculating French Army Growth during the *Grand Siècle,* 1610–1715." *French Historical Studies* 18 (1994): 881–906.

———. *The Wars of Louis XIV 1667–1714.* London: Longman, 1999.

Marion, Marcel. *Histoire financière de France depuis 1715.* 7 vols. Paris: Rousseau, 1914–28.

———. *Les Impôts directs sous l'Ancien Régime, principalement au XVIIIe siècle.* Paris: Édouard Cornély, 1910.

Matthews, George T. *The Royal General Farms in Eighteenth-Century France.* New York: Columbia University Press, 1958.

Mazel, Geneviève. *Claude Le Peletier (1631–1711): Le successeur de Colbert.* Paris: Éditions de la Marquise, 2003.

Meuvret, Jean. *Études d'histoire économique.* Paris: Armand Colin, 1971.

Meysonnier, Simone. *La Balance et l'Horloge: La Genèse de la pensée libérale en France au XVIIIe siècle.* Paris: Les Éditions de la Passion, 1989.

Michaud, Claude. *L'Église et l'Argent sous l'Ancien Régime: Les receveurs généraux du clergé de France aux XVIe–XVIIe siècles.* Paris: Fayard, 1991.

Michaud, Joseph, ed. *Dictionnaire universelle ancienne et moderne.* 45 vols. Paris: A. Thoisnier Desplaces, 1852.

Mitard, Stanislas. *La crise financière en France à la fin du XVIIe siècle: La première capitation (1695–1698).* Rennes: Imprimerie Oberthur, 1934.

Monahan, W. Gregory. "Lyon in the Crisis of 1709: Royal Absolutism, Administrative Innovation, and Regional Politics." *French Historical Studies* 16 (1990): 833–48.

———. *Year of Sorrows: The Great Famine of 1709 in Lyon.* Columbus: Ohio State University Press, 1993.

Montyon, Antoine Jean-Baptiste Robert Auget de. *Particularités et observations sur les ministres des finances de France les plus célèbres, depuis 1661 jusqu'en 1791.* Paris: Le Normant, 1812.

Monnier, François, ed. *Histoire institutionnelle, économique et financière: questions de méthode (XVIIe–XVIIIe siècles).* Paris: Comité pour l'histoire économique et financière de la France, 2004.

Morineau, Michel. "Budgets de l'État et gestion des finances royales en France au dix-huitième siècle." *Revue historique* 536 (1980): 289–336.

Mosser, Françoise. *Les intendants des finances au XVIIIe siècle.* Geneva: Droz, 1978.

Mousnier, Roland. "Le Conseil du Roi de Henri IV au gouvernement personnel de Louis XIV." In *La plume, la faucille et le marteau,* edited by Roland Mousnier, 141–78. Paris: PUF, 1970.

———. *La dîme de Vauban.* Paris: Centre de Documentation Universitaire, 1968.

Murphy, Antoin E. *John Law: Economic Theorist and Policy Maker.* Oxford: Clarendon Press, 1997.

———. "John Law et la gestion de la dette publique." In *La dette publique dans l'histoire*, edited by Jean Andreau, Gérard Béaur, and Jean-Yves Grenier, 269–96. Paris: Comité pour l'histoire économique et financière de la France, 2006.

Nicolas, Jean. *La Rébellion française: Mouvements populaires et conscience sociale, 1661–1789.* Paris: Éditions du Seuil, 2002.

Olivier-Martin, Fr. *Histoire du droit français des origines à la Révolution.* Paris: Éditions Domat Montchrestien, 1951.

Pagès, Georges. "Essai sur l'évolution des institutions administratives en France du commencement du XVIe *siècle* à la fin de XVIIe." *Revue d'histoire moderne* 7 (1932): 8–57, 113–17.

———. "Le Conseil du Roi sous Louis XIII." In *Études sur l'histoire administrative et sociale de l'Ancien Régime*, edited by Georges Pagès, 7–38. Paris: Félix Alcan, 1938.

Pénicaut, Emmanuel. *Faveur et pouvoir au tournant du Grand Siècle: Michel Chamillart, Ministre et secrétaire d'État de la guerre de Louis XIV.* Paris: École des Chartes, 2004.

Perez, Stanis. *La santé de Louis XIV: Une biohistoire du Roi-Soleil.* Seyssel: Champ Vallon, 2007.

Perkins, Merle L. *The Moral and Political Philosophy of the Abbé de Saint-Pierre.* Geneva: Droz, 1959.

Peter, Jean. *Le Journal de Vauban.* Paris: Economica, 2007.

Petitfils, Jean-Christian. *Fouquet.* Paris: Perrin, 1999.

———. *Louis XIV.* Paris: Perrin, 1997.

Pillorget, René. "Henri Pussort, oncle de Colbert (1615–1697)." In *Le Conseil du Roi de Louis XII à la Révolution*, edited by Roland Mousnier, 255–74. Paris: PUF, 1970.

Potter, Mark. "Coalitions and Local Politics in Seventeenth-Century France." *French Historical Studies* 31 (2008): 29–50.

———. *Corps and Clienteles: Public Finance and Political Change in France, 1688–1715.* Aldershot, UK: Ashgate, 2003.

Poujol, Robert. *Basville: roi solitaire du Languedoc, intendant à Montpellier de 1685 à 1718.* Montpellier: Presses du Languedoc, 1992.

Root, Hilton. *The Fountain of Privilege: Political Foundations of Markets in Old Regime France and England.* Berkeley: University of California Press, 1994.

———. "Institutions, Interest Groups, and Authority in Ancien Regime France." *French History* 6 (1992): 411–34.

Rothkrug, Lionel. *Opposition to Louis XIV: The Political and Social Origins of the French Enlightenment.* Princeton, NJ: Princeton University Press, 1965.

Rowlands, Guy. *The Dynastic State and the Army under Louis XIV: Royal Service and Private Interest, 1661–1701.* Cambridge: Cambridge University Press, 2002.

Rudd, Jon Desmarest. "Philibert Orry and France's Contrôle Général (1730–45)." PhD diss., Georgetown University, 1988.

Rule, John C. "A Career in the Making: The Education of Jean-Baptiste Colbert, Marquis de Torcy." *French Historical Studies* 19 (1996): 967–96.

———. "The Administrative History of the Reign." In *The Reign of Louis XIV: Essays in Celebration of Andrew Lossky*, edited by Paul Sonnino, 95–110. Atlantic Highlands, NJ: Humanities Press International, 1990.

———. "Colbert de Torcy, an Emergent Bureaucracy, and the Formation of French Foreign Policy, 1698–1715." In *Louis XIV and Europe*, edited by Ragnhild Hatton, 261–88. Columbus: Ohio State University Press, 1976.

———. "Gathering Intelligence in the Age of Louis XIV." *International History Review* 14 (1992): 732–52.

———. "King and Minister: Louis XIV and Colbert de Torcy." In *William III and Louis XIV: Essays 1680–1720, by and for Mark A. Thomson,* edited by Ragnhild Hatton and J. S. Bromley, 213–36. Toronto: Toronto University Press, 1968.

———. "The King in his Council: Louis XIV and the '*Conseil d'en haut.*'" In *Royal and Republican Sovereignty in Early Modern Europe: Essays in Memory of Ragnhild Hatton,* edited by Robert Oresko, G. C. Gibbs, and H. M. Scott, 216–41. Cambridge: Cambridge University Press, 1997.

———. "Louis XIV at Work: Decoding the Council of Dispatches, 1690–1715." *Proceedings of the Western Society for French History: Selected Papers of the Annual Meeting* 23 (1996): 309–20.

———. "Louis XIV, Roi-Bureaucrate." In *Louis XIV and the Craft of Kingship,* edited by John C. Rule, 3–102. Columbus: Ohio State University Press, 1969.

———. "Royal Ministers and Government Reform during the Last Decades of Louis XIV's Reign." In *The Consortium of Revolutionary History,* edited by Claude C. Sturgill, 1–35. Gainesville: University Presses of Florida, 1973.

———, ed. *Louis XIV.* Englewood Cliffs, NJ: Prentice-Hall, 1974.

Saint-Germain, Jacques. *Les financiers sous Louis XIV: Paul Poisson de Bourvalais.* Paris: Plon, 1950.

———. *La vie quotidienne en France à la fin du Grand Siècle.* Paris: Hachette, 1965.

———. *Samuel Bernard: Banquier des Rois.* Paris: Hachette, 1960.

Sarmant, Thierry, ed. *Le Grand Siècle en Mémoires.* Paris: Perrin, 2011.

———, ed. *Les Ministres de la Guerre, 1570–1792.* Paris: Belin, 2007.

Sarmant, Thierry, and Mathieu Stoll. *Régner et gouverner: Louis XIV et ses ministres.* Paris: Perrin, 2010.

Sayous, André-E. "La crise financière de 1709 à Lyon et à Genève." *Revue d'histoire économique et sociale* 24 (1938): 57–86, 163–77.

Schaeper, Thomas J. *The French Council of Commerce, 1700–1715: A Study of Mercantilism after Colbert.* Columbus: Ohio State University Press, 1983.

———. *The Economy of France in the Second Half of the Reign of Louis XIV.* Montreal: Interuniversity Center for European Studies, 1980.

Seligmann, Armand. *La première tentative d'émission fiduciaire en France: Étude sur les billets de monnaies de trésor royal à la fin du règne de Louis XIV (1701–1718).* Paris: PUF, 1925.

Smedley-Weill, Anette. *Les intendants de Louis XIV.* Paris: Fayard, 1995.

Smith, David Kammerling. "Learning Politics: The Nîmes Hosiery Guild and the Statutes Controversy of 1706–1712." *French Historical Studies* 22 (1999): 493–534.

———. "Structuring Politics in Early Eighteenth-Century France: The Political Innovations of the French Council of Commerce." *Journal of Modern History* 74 (2002): 490–537.

Smith, Jay M. "No More Language Games: Words, Beliefs, and the Political Culture of Early Modern France." *American Historical Review* 102 (1997): 1413–40.

Spooner, Frank C. *The International Economy and Monetary Movements in France, 1493–1725.* Cambridge, MA: Harvard University Press, 1972.

Storez, Isabelle. *Le Chancelier Henri François D'Aguesseau (1668–1751): Monarchiste et libéral.* Paris: Publisud, 1996.

Tellier, Luc-Normand. *Face aux Colbert: Les Le Tellier, Vauban, Turgot . . . et l'avènement de libéralisme.* Québec: Presses de l'Université de Québec, 1987.

Tilley, Arthur. *The Decline of the Age of Louis XIV: Or, French Literature, 1687–1715.* 1929. Reprint, New York: Barnes & Noble, 1968.

Tocqueville, Alexis de. *The Old Regime and the French Revolution.* 1856. Translated by Stuart Gilbert. Garden City, NY: Doubleday, 1955.

Touzery, Mireille. *L'invention de l'impôt sur le revenu: La taille tarifiée 1715–1789.* Paris: Comité pour l'histoire économique et financière de la France, 1994.

Velde, François R. "Government Equity and Money: John Law's System in 1720 France." May 14, 2004. http://www.heraldica.org/econ/law.pdf.

Vergé-Franceschi, Michel. *La société française au XVIIe siècle.* Paris: Fayard, 2006.

Vignes, J.-B. Maurice. *Histoire des doctrines sur l'impôt en France: Les origines et les destinées de la Dixme Royale de Vauban.* 1909. Reprint, Paris: Librairie Générale de Droit et de Jurisprudence, 1961.

Villain, Jean. *La Fortune de Colbert.* Paris: Comité pour l'histoire économique et financière de la France, 1994.

———. *Le recouvrement des impôts directs sous l'Ancien Régime.* Paris: Riviere, 1952.

Virol, Michèle. *Vauban: De la gloire du roi au service de l'État.* Seyssel: Champ Vallon, 2003.

———, ed. *Les oisevetés de Monsieur de Vauban.* Seyssel: Champ Vallon, 2007.

Vuitry, Adolphe. *Le désordre des finances et les excès de la spéculation à la fin du règne de Louis XIV et au début du règne de Louis XV.* Paris, Calmann-Lévy, 1885.

Wolf, John B. *Louis XIV.* New York: Norton, 1968.

Wolfe, Martin. *The Fiscal System of Renaissance France.* New Haven, CT: Yale University Press, 1972.

Zupko, Ronald Edward. *French Weights and Measures before the Revolution.* Bloomington: Indiana University Press, 1978.

INDEX